I WOULD'VE SWORN THEY'D YANK THE SERIES AFTER 10 WEEKS...
QUIT WHINING AND KEEP WORKING!!
SLURRRP

和月伸宏

NOBUHIRO WATSUKI

## A YEAR ALREADY... WHO'D HAVE THUNK IT?!

ALREADY IT'S BEEN A YEAR SINCE "RUROKEN" STARTED INITIAL PUBLICATION IN JAPAN. JUST LIKE THE SCENE TO THE LEFT ILLUSTRATES, TO ME THAT'S A REAL SHOCKER! IT'S A TOUGH THING, HAVING A DREAM REALIZED...BUT KEEPING THAT DREAM GOING AFTER IT *HAS* BEEN, IS EVEN TOUGHER—AND THAT'S WHAT THIS YEAR'S TAUGHT ME. IT'S BEEN A CASE OF DEALING WITH CHRONIC FATIGUE AND A LACK OF MAN-POWER, BUT I'M GONNA HANG IN THERE AND DO WHAT I CAN.

***Rurouni Kenshin***, which has found fans not only in Japan but around the world, first made its appearance in 1992, as an original short story in ***Weekly Shonen Jump Special***. Later rewritten and published as a regular, continuing ***Jump*** series in 1994, ***RUROUNI KENSHIN*** ended serialization in 1999 but continued in popularity, as evidenced by the 2000 publication of **Yahiko no Sakabatô** ("Yahiko's Reversed-Edge Sword") in **Weekly Shonen Jump**. His most current work, ***Busô Renkin*** ("Armored Alchemist"), began publication this June, also in ***Jump***.

**RUROUNI KENSHIN**
VOL. 5: THE STATE OF MEIJI SWORDSMANSHIP
The CHONEN JUMP Manga Edition

STORY AND ART BY
**NOBUHIRO WATSUKI**

English Adaptation/Gerard Jones
Translation/Kenichiro Yagi
Touch-Up Art & Lettering/Steve Dutro
Cover, Graphics & Layout/Sean Lee
Editor/Avery Gotoh

Editor in Chief, Books/Alvin Lu
Editor in Chief, Magazines/Marc Weidenbaum
VP, Publishing Licensing/Rika Inouye
VP, Sales & Product Marketing/Gonzalo Ferreyra
VP, Creative/Linda Espinosa
Publisher/Hyoe Narita

The rights of the author(s) of the work(s) in this publication to be so identified
have been asserted in accordance with the Copyright, Designs and Patents Act
1988. A CIP catalogue record for this book is available from the British Library.

Printed in the U.S.A.

Published by VIZ Media, LLC
P.O. Box 77010 • San Francisco, CA 94107

SHONEN JUMP Manga Edition
10 9 8 7 6 5 4
First printing, May 2004
Fourth printing, September 2008

THE WORLD'S
MOST POPULAR MANGA
www.shonenjump.com

SHONEN JUMP MANGA

# Rurouni Kenshin

## MEIJI SWORDSMAN ROMANTIC STORY

## VOL. 5: THE STATE OF MEIJI SWORDSMANSHIP

STORY AND ART BY
NOBUHIRO
WATSUKI

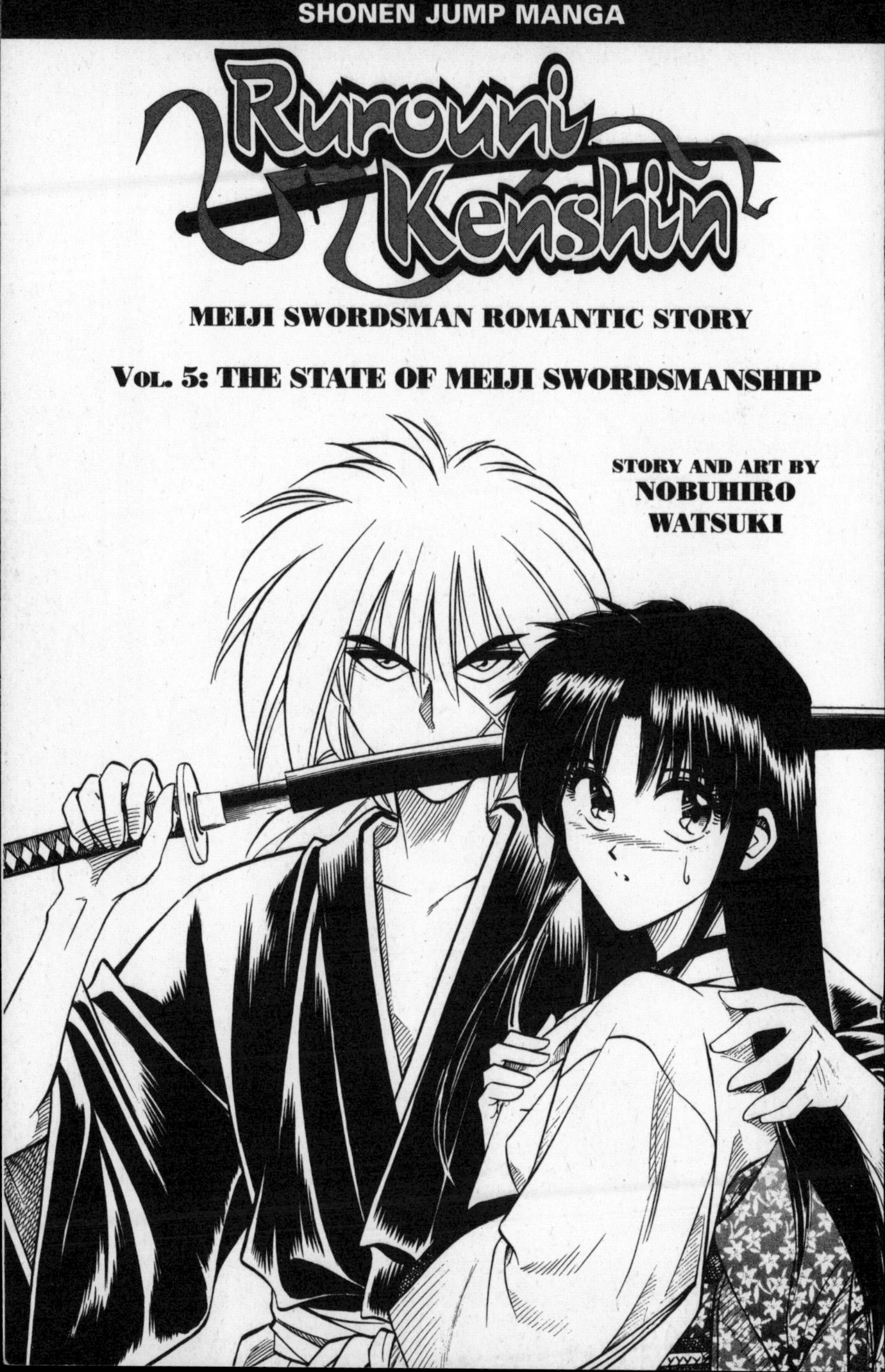

# CAST

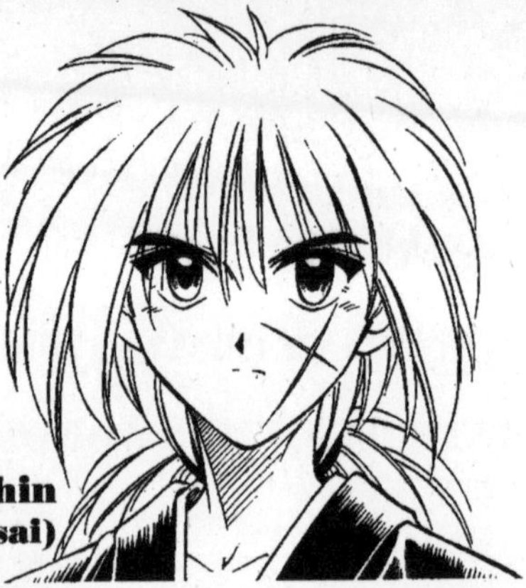

緋村剣心（人斬り抜刀斎）

**Himura Kenshin (Hitokiri Battōsai)**

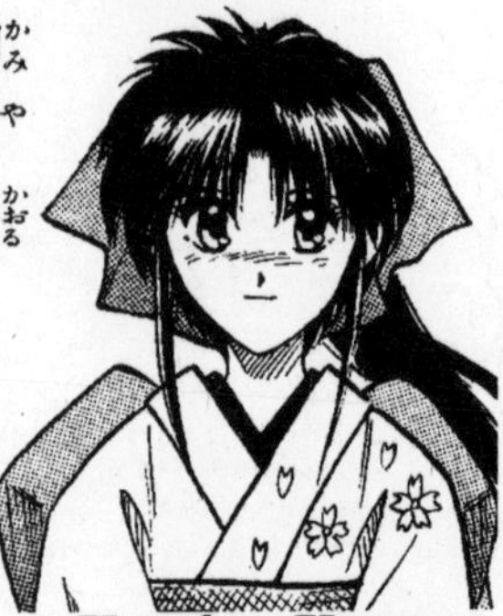

神谷薫

**Kamiya Kaoru**

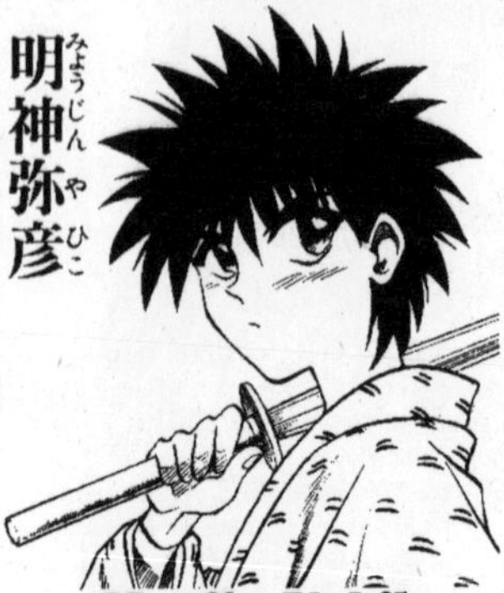

明神弥彦

**Myōjin Yahiko**

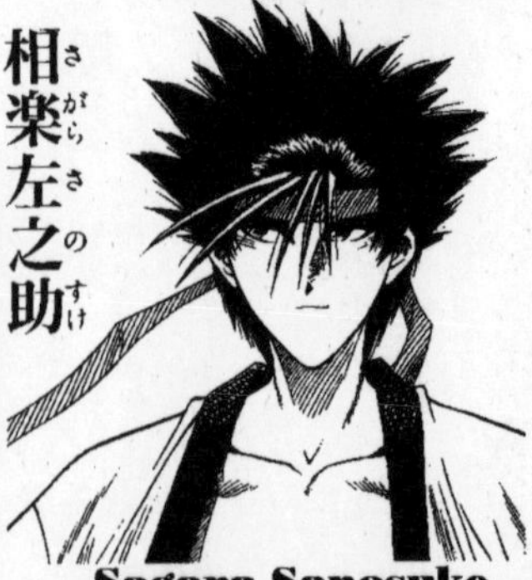

相楽左之助

**Sagara Sanosuke**

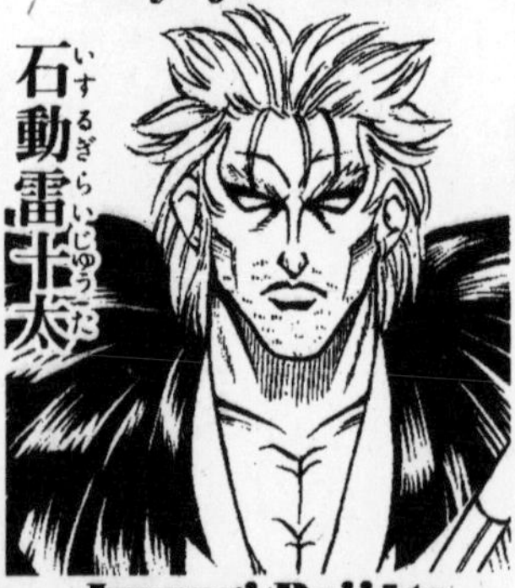

石動雷十太

**Isurugi Raijūta**

# るろうに剣心

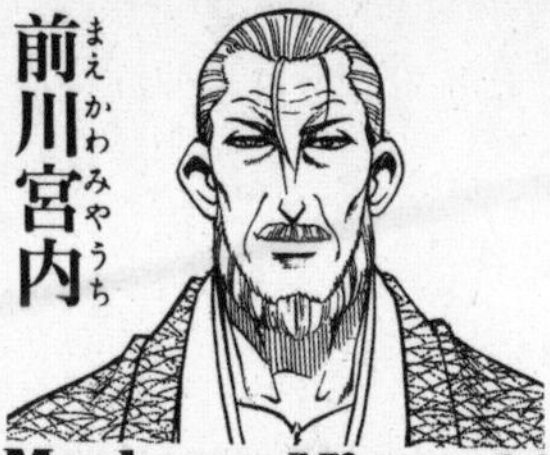

前川宮内（まえかわみやうち）

Maekawa Miyauchi

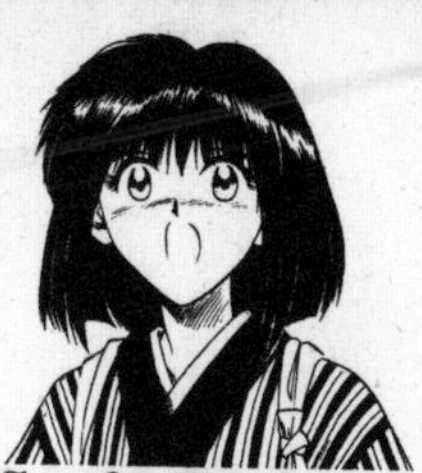

三条燕（さんじょうつばめ）

Sanjō Tsubame

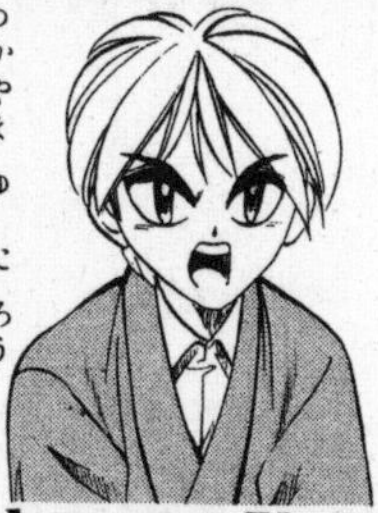

塚山由太郎（つかやまゆたろう）

Tsukayama Yutarō

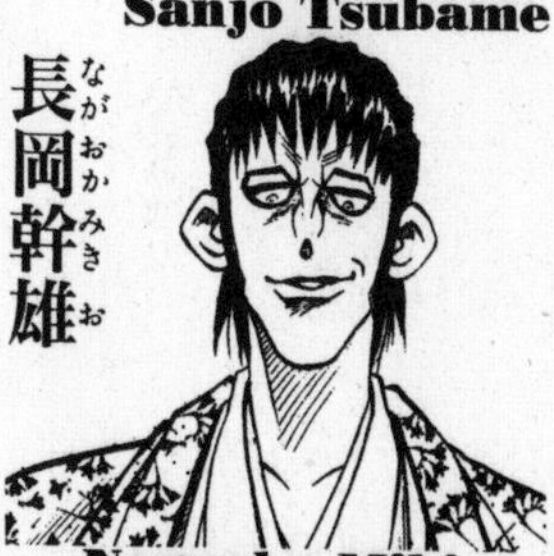

長岡幹雄（ながおかみきお）

Nagaoka Mikio

## THUS FAR

**Himura Kenshin—the man who carries a *sakabatō* to prohibit himself from killing people. Once he was known as *hitokiri*—the assassin Himura Battōsai, a legend of incomparable awe among the pro-Imperialist *Ishin Shishi* patriots who fought for the new era—but since the end of the civil war, he has been *rurouni*. After solving the case of the "fake Battōsai," he's remained at the Kamiya dojo, where Kamiya Kaoru is acting instructor. Soon after, Myōjin Yahiko—a young man Kenshin saved from the yakuza—joined the dojo, which had lost all its students. Sagara Sanosuke, who gave up being a "fight merchant" after meeting Kenshin, goes in and out of the dojo frequently, making it a far more lively place than when Kaoru used to live there alone.**

**Changing the assassin's blade into a weapon that cannot kill, *rurouni* Kenshin freely continues to defend the people. His next adventure is....**

# CONTENTS

**RUROUNI KENSHIN**

Meiji Swordsman Romantic Story

BOOK FIVE: THE STATE OF MEIJI SWORDSMANSHIP

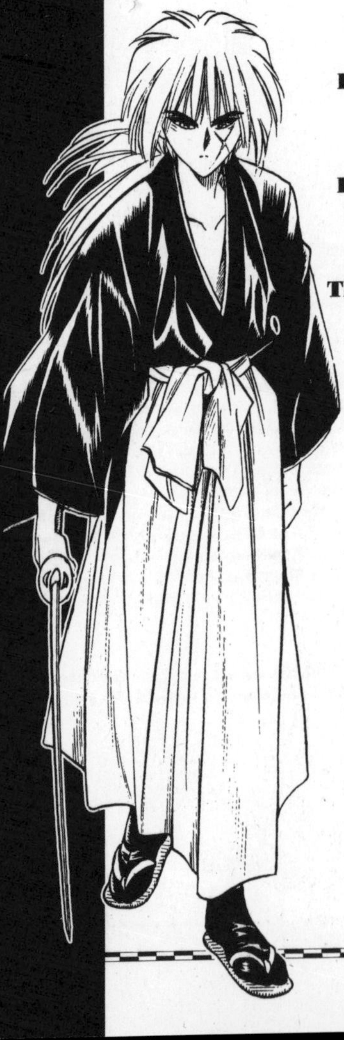

READ THIS WAY

# Act 31
# Bonus Story: Yahiko's Battle (1)

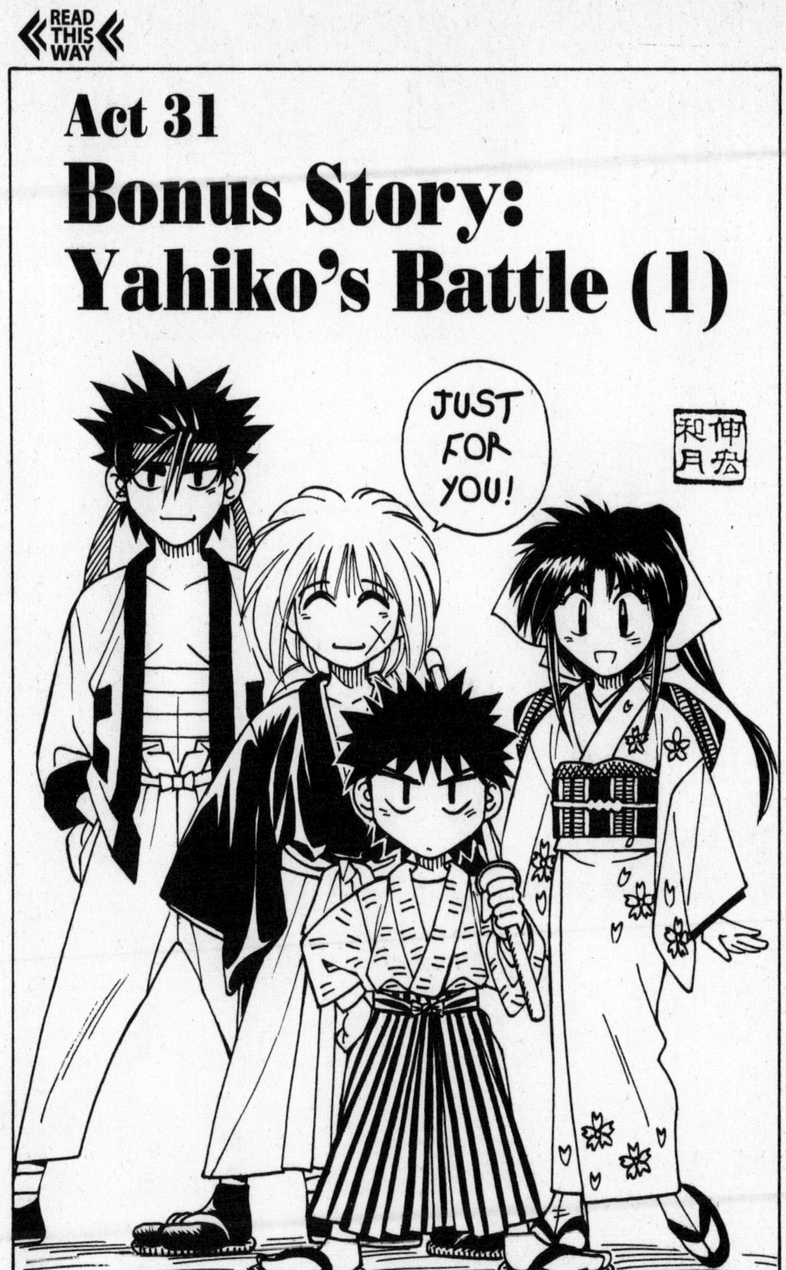
JUST FOR YOU!
伸宏
和月

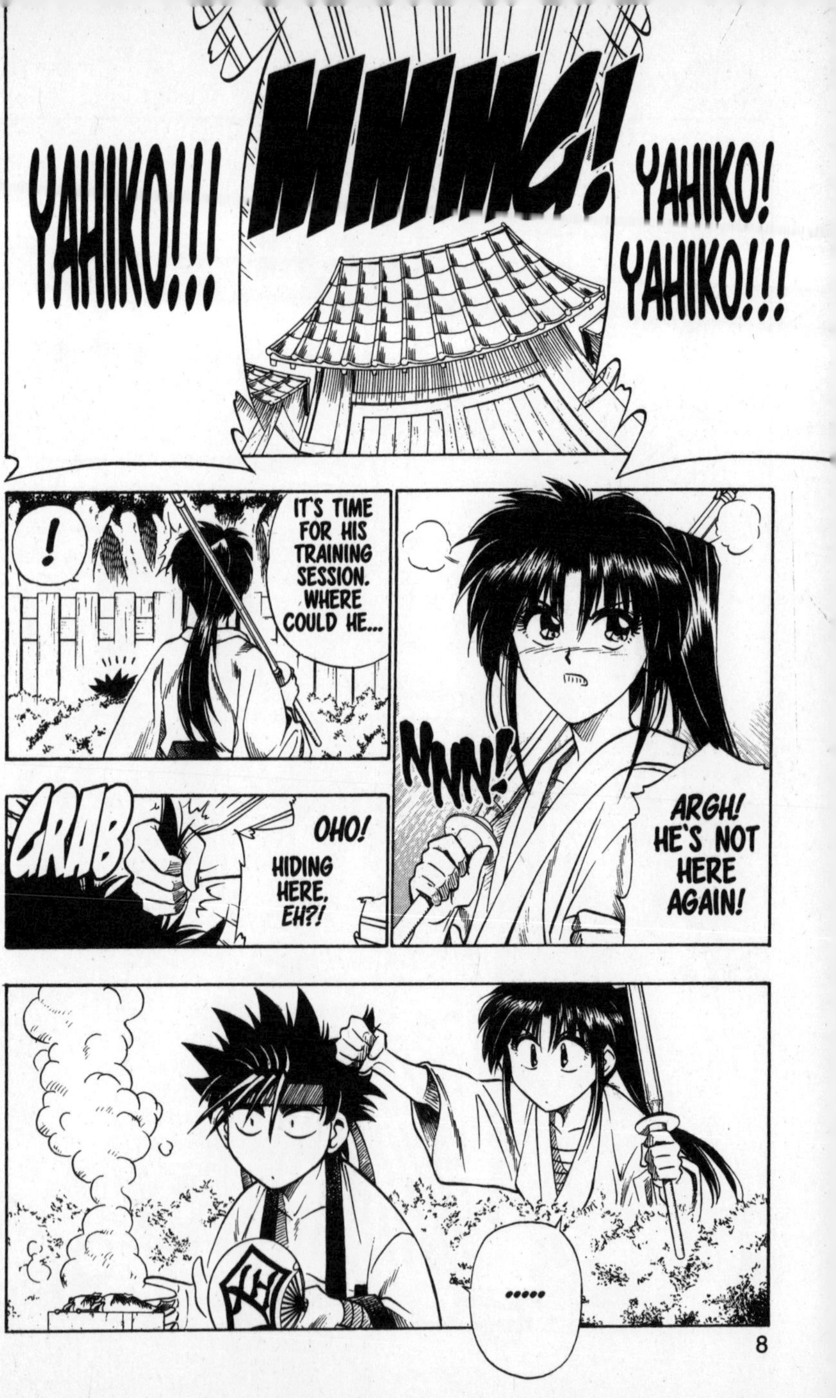
YAHIKO! YAHIKO!!!
MMMG!
YAHIKO!!!
NNN!
ARGH! HE'S NOT HERE AGAIN!
IT'S TIME FOR HIS TRAINING SESSION. WHERE COULD HE...
!
OHO!
HIDING HERE, EH?!
GRAB
.....

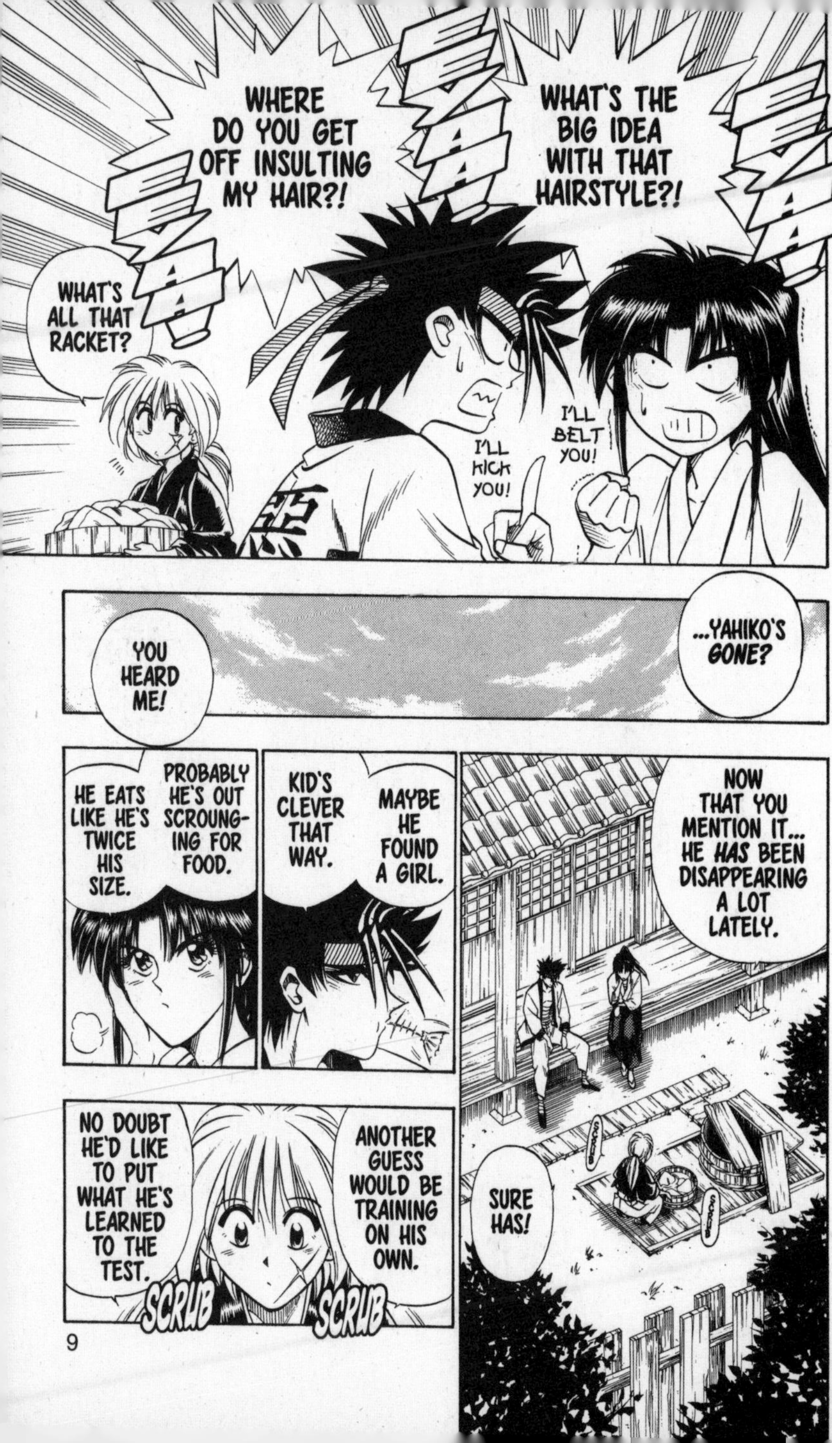
WHAT'S THE BIG IDEA WITH THAT HAIRSTYLE?!
WHERE DO YOU GET OFF INSULTING MY HAIR?!
I'LL BELT YOU!
I'LL KICK YOU!
WHAT'S ALL THAT RACKET?
...YAHIKO'S GONE?
YOU HEARD ME!
NOW THAT YOU MENTION IT... HE HAS BEEN DISAPPEARING A LOT LATELY.
SURE HAS!
MAYBE HE FOUND A GIRL.
KID'S CLEVER THAT WAY.
PROBABLY HE'S OUT SCROUNGING FOR FOOD.
HE EATS LIKE HE'S TWICE HIS SIZE.
ANOTHER GUESS WOULD BE TRAINING ON HIS OWN.
NO DOUBT HE'D LIKE TO PUT WHAT HE'S LEARNED TO THE TEST.
SCRUB
SCRUB

READ THIS WAY

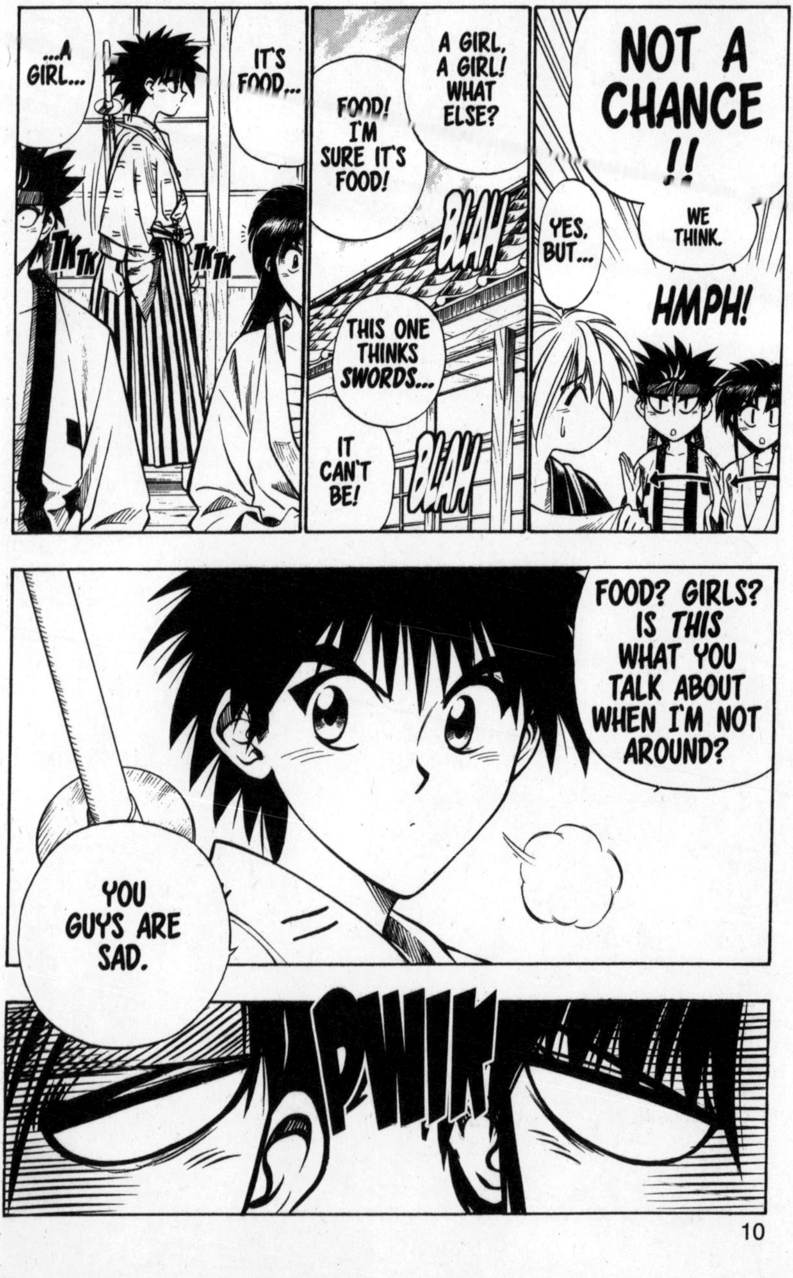

NOT A CHANCE!!
WE THINK.
YES, BUT...
HMPH!
A GIRL, A GIRL! WHAT ELSE?
FOOD! I'M SURE IT'S FOOD!
BLAH
THIS ONE THINKS SWORDS...
IT CAN'T BE!
BLAH
IT'S FOOD...
...A GIRL...
TK TK
TK TK
FOOD? GIRLS? IS THIS WHAT YOU TALK ABOUT WHEN I'M NOT AROUND?
YOU GUYS ARE SAD.
PWIK

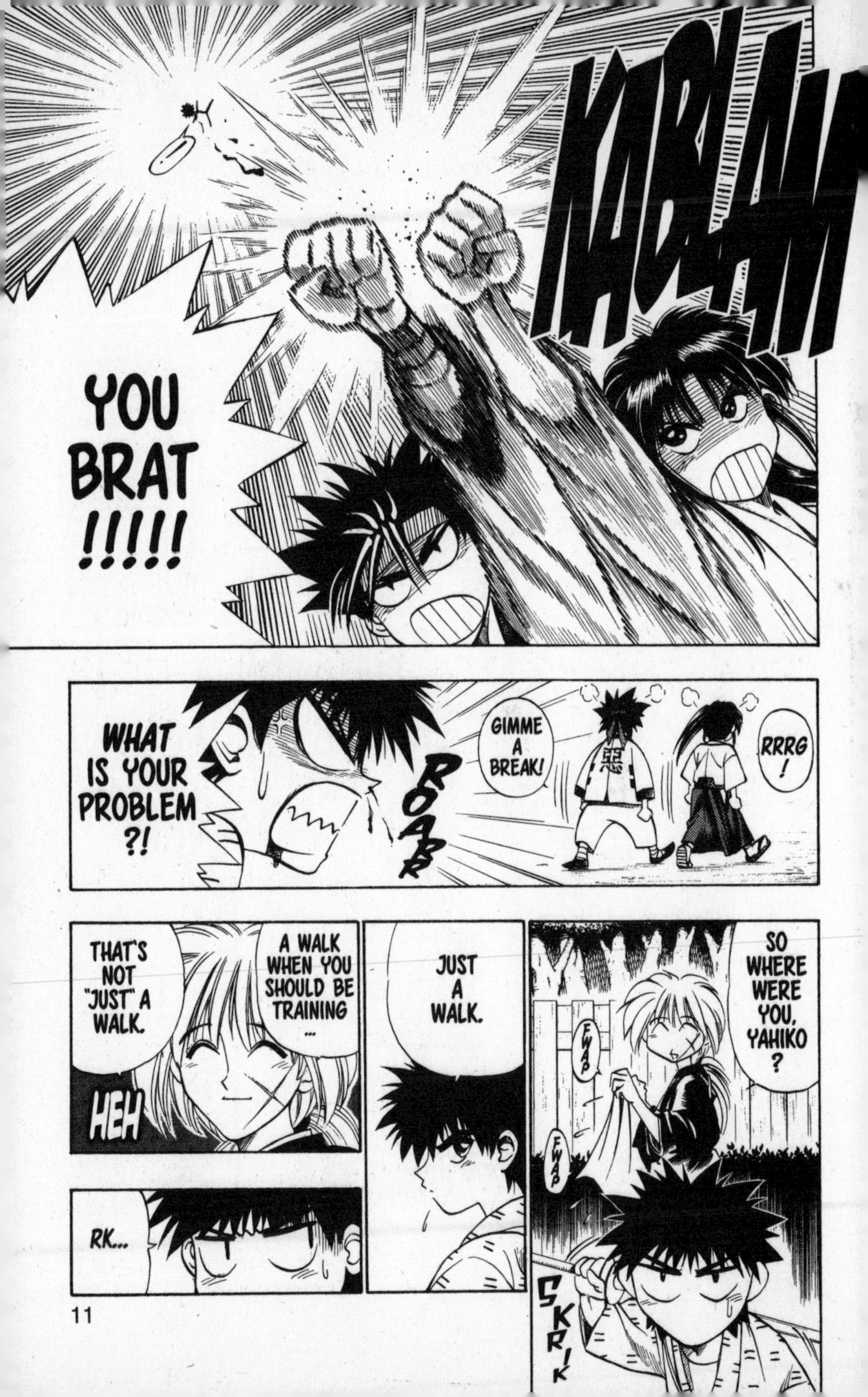
KABLAM
YOU BRAT!!!!!
RRRG!
GIMME A BREAK!
ROAR
WHAT IS YOUR PROBLEM?!
SO WHERE WERE YOU, YAHIKO?
FWAP
FWAP
SKRIK
JUST A WALK.
A WALK WHEN YOU SHOULD BE TRAINING...
THAT'S NOT "JUST" A WALK.
HEH
RK...

READ THIS WAY

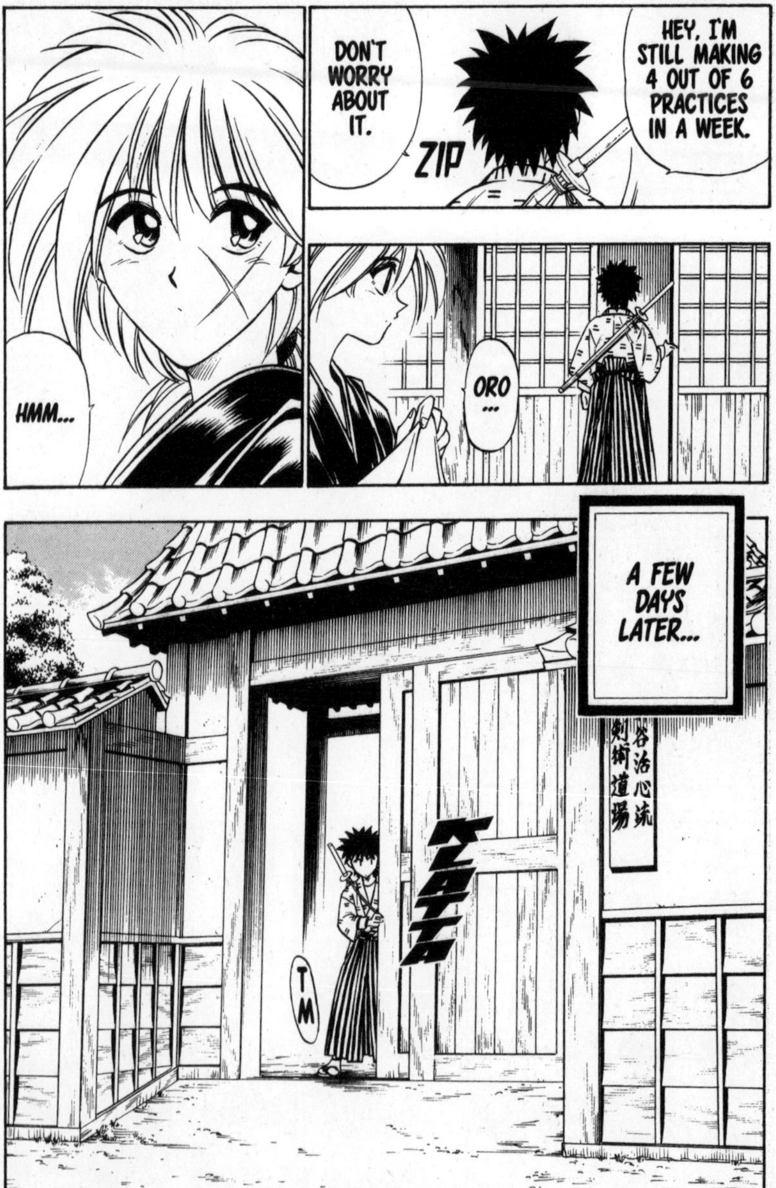
HEY, I'M STILL MAKING 4 OUT OF 6 PRACTICES IN A WEEK.
DON'T WORRY ABOUT IT.
ZIP
ORO...
HMM...
A FEW DAYS LATER...
谷活心流
剣術道場
KLATTA
TM

READ THIS WAY

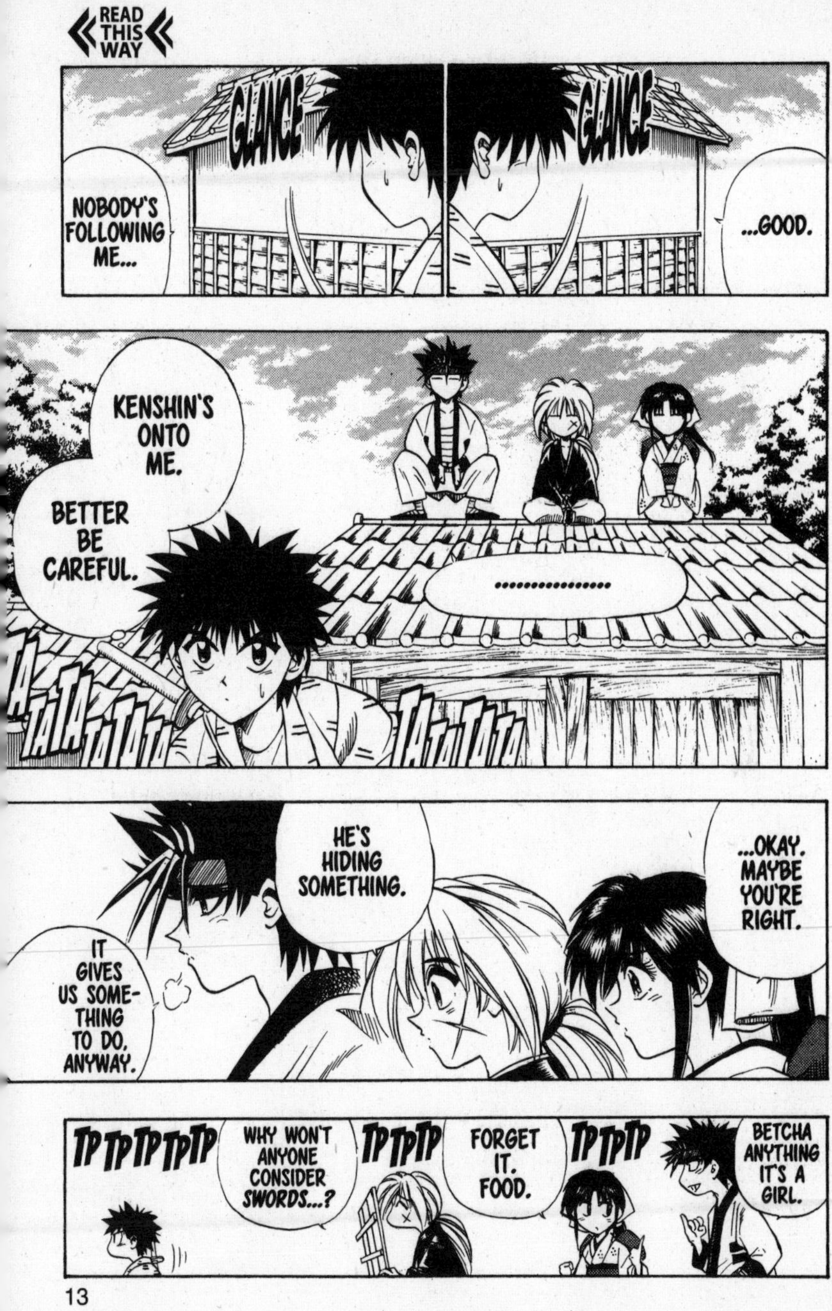

GLANCE
...GOOD.
GLANCE
NOBODY'S FOLLOWING ME...
.................
KENSHIN'S ONTO ME.
BETTER BE CAREFUL.
TATATATA
TATATATATA
...OKAY. MAYBE YOU'RE RIGHT.
HE'S HIDING SOMETHING.
IT GIVES US SOME-THING TO DO, ANYWAY.
BETCHA ANYTHING IT'S A GIRL.
TP TP TP
FORGET IT. FOOD.
TP TP TP
WHY WON'T ANYONE CONSIDER SWORDS...?
TP TP TP TP TP

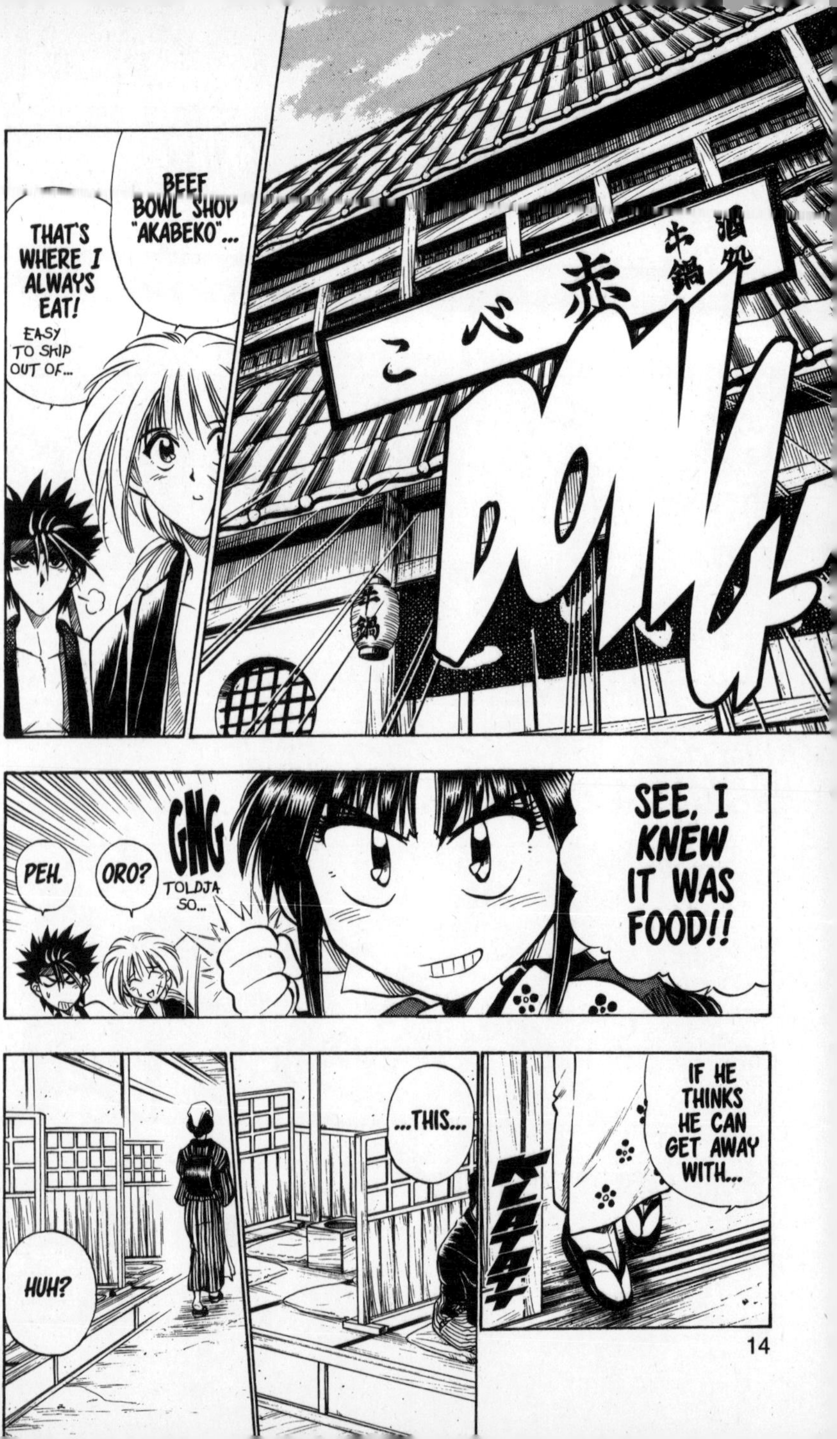
赤べこ
DON
BEEF BOWL SHOP "AKABEKO"...
THAT'S WHERE I ALWAYS EAT!
EASY TO SKIP OUT OF...
SEE, I KNEW IT WAS FOOD!!
GNG
TOLDJA SO...
ORO?
PEH.
IF HE THINKS HE CAN GET AWAY WITH...
...THIS...
HUH?

READ THIS WAY

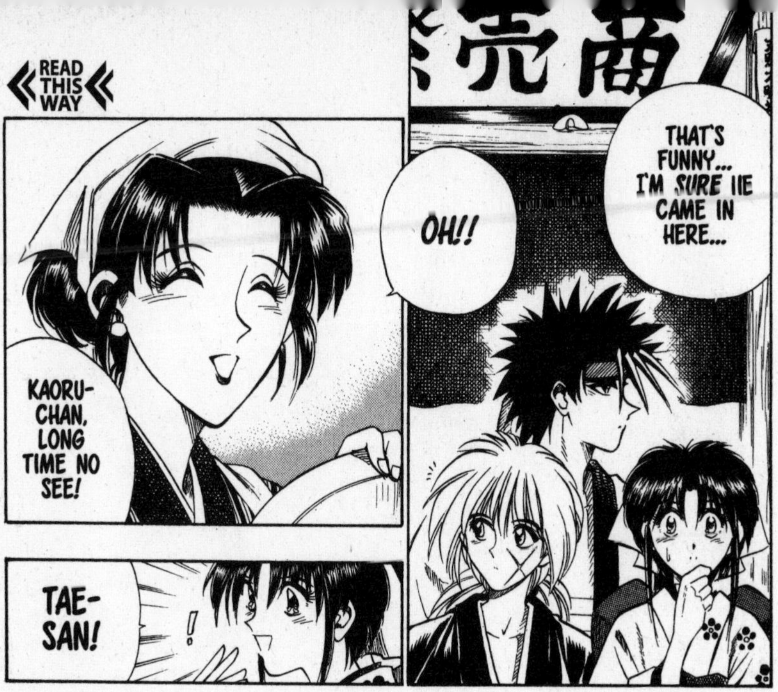
THAT'S FUNNY... I'M SURE HE CAME IN HERE...
OH!!
KAORU-CHAN, LONG TIME NO SEE!
TAE-SAN!

Long time no see, indeed. Watsuki here. The 3rd volume of the CD books has been decided on: the "Jin-e" episodes. At the time I'm writing this, it's just been decided, so I have no information about the script or the voice-actors. The script probably will be based pretty closely on the original story, with a little massaging to increase the appearances of Sanosuke and Yahiko. For the voice-actor, I'd like someone with a mature but cool voice. In my mind, Jin-e is a mad hero, so I'd like to avoid an actor with a high voice–basically, though, I'm leaving it to Jump Media Mix and Fukui-san. I didn't expect it to get so far–and it's all because of you readers. Recently, I've been given a really tough schedule, and honestly speaking, I've had some times when I've wanted to quit writing. But it's too early to "give up" on manga. As long as there are people who read, support, and anticipate, I will have to write, and will want to write. I'm going to keep working on "Ruroken," keeping my original goals in mind.

Watsuki

和月伸宏

READ THIS WAY

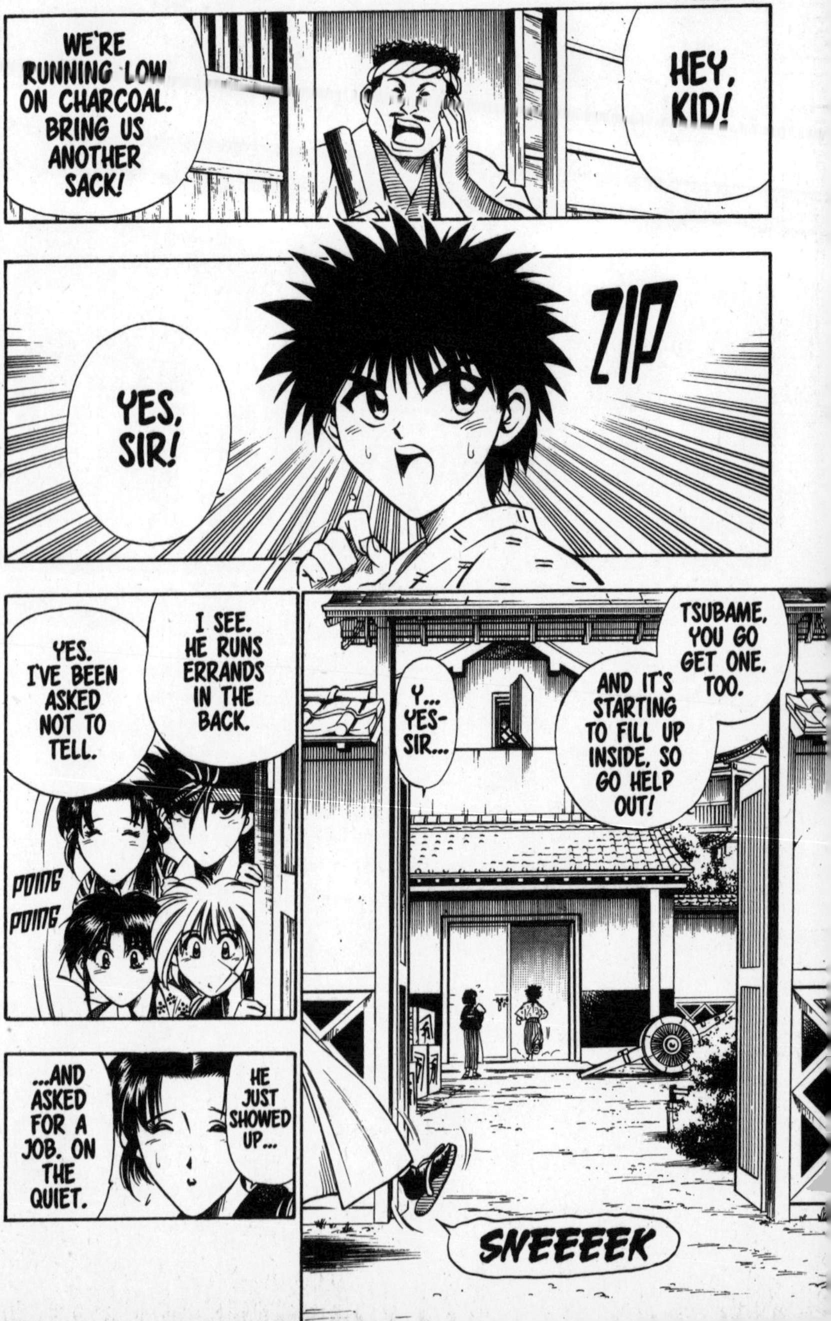
HEY, KID!
WE'RE RUNNING LOW ON CHARCOAL. BRING US ANOTHER SACK!
ZIP
YES, SIR!
TSUBAME, YOU GO GET ONE, TOO.
AND IT'S STARTING TO FILL UP INSIDE, SO GO HELP OUT!
Y... YES-SIR...
SNEEEEK
I SEE. HE RUNS ERRANDS IN THE BACK.
YES. I'VE BEEN ASKED NOT TO TELL.
POING
POING
HE JUST SHOWED UP...
...AND ASKED FOR A JOB. ON THE QUIET.

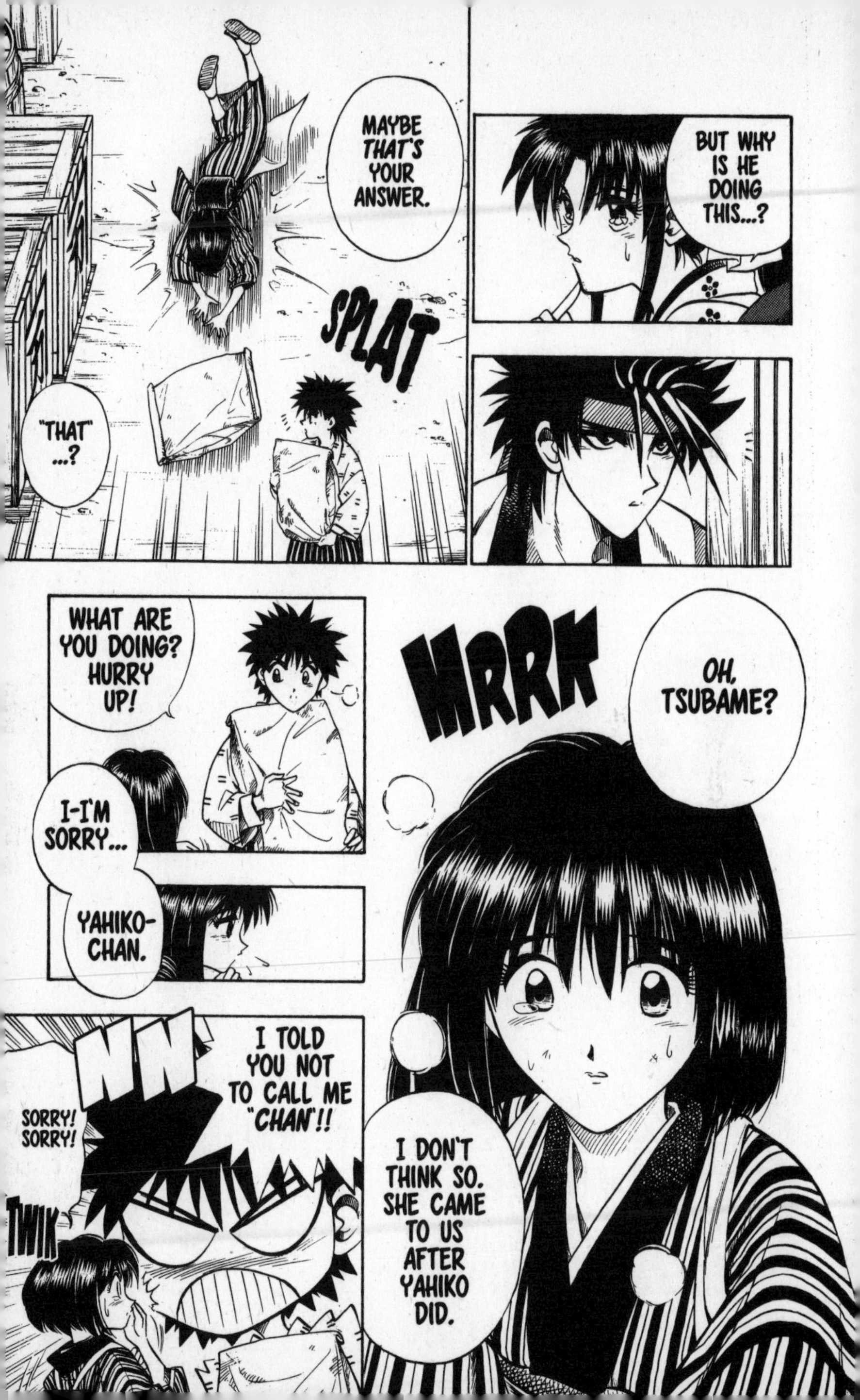
BUT WHY IS HE DOING THIS...?
MAYBE THAT'S YOUR ANSWER.
SPLAT
"THAT" ...?
MRRK
OH, TSUBAME?
I DON'T THINK SO. SHE CAME TO US AFTER YAHIKO DID.
WHAT ARE YOU DOING? HURRY UP!
I-I'M SORRY...
YAHIKO-CHAN.
NN
I TOLD YOU NOT TO CALL ME "CHAN"!!
SORRY! SORRY!
TWIK

READ THIS WAY

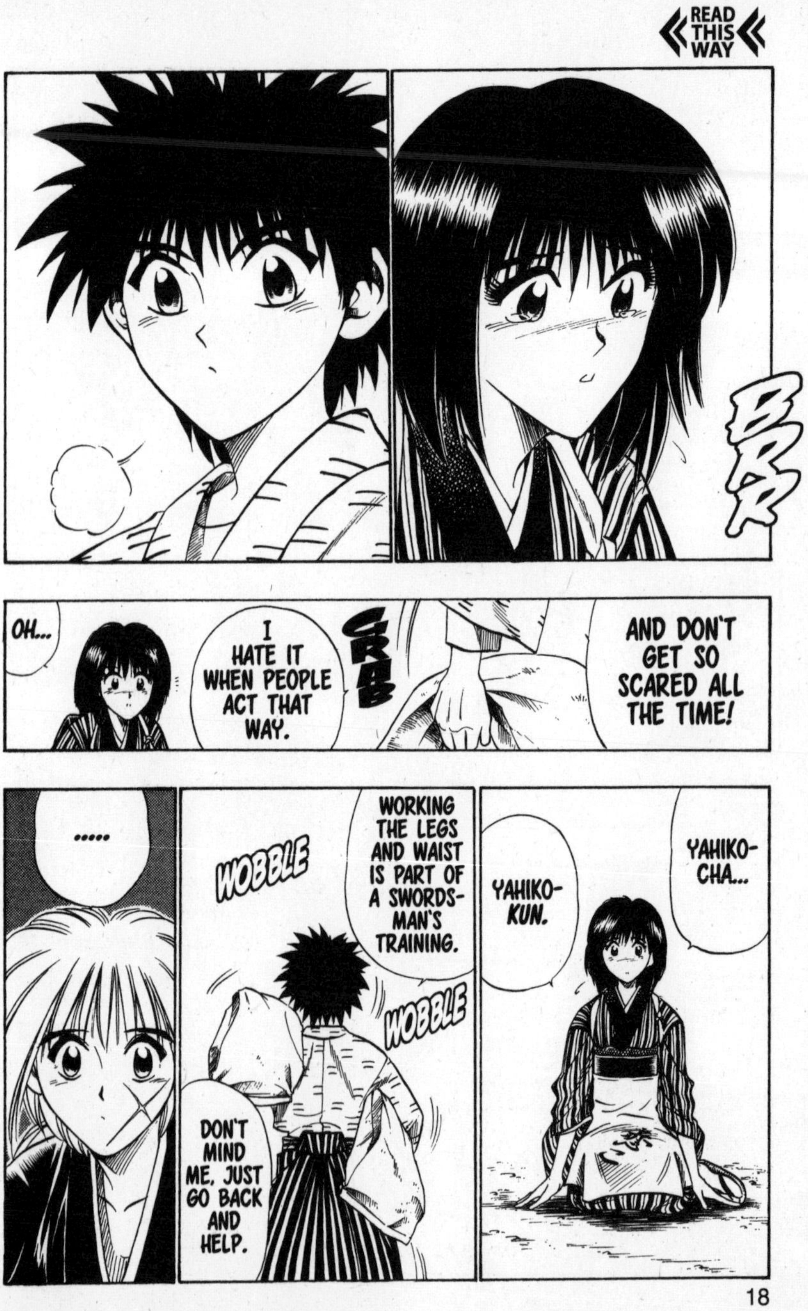

AND DON'T GET SO SCARED ALL THE TIME!
GRAB
I HATE IT WHEN PEOPLE ACT THAT WAY.
OH...
YAHIKO-CHA...
YAHIKO-KUN.
WORKING THE LEGS AND WAIST IS PART OF A SWORDS-MAN'S TRAINING.
WOBBLE
WOBBLE
DON'T MIND ME, JUST GO BACK AND HELP.
.....

READ THIS WAY

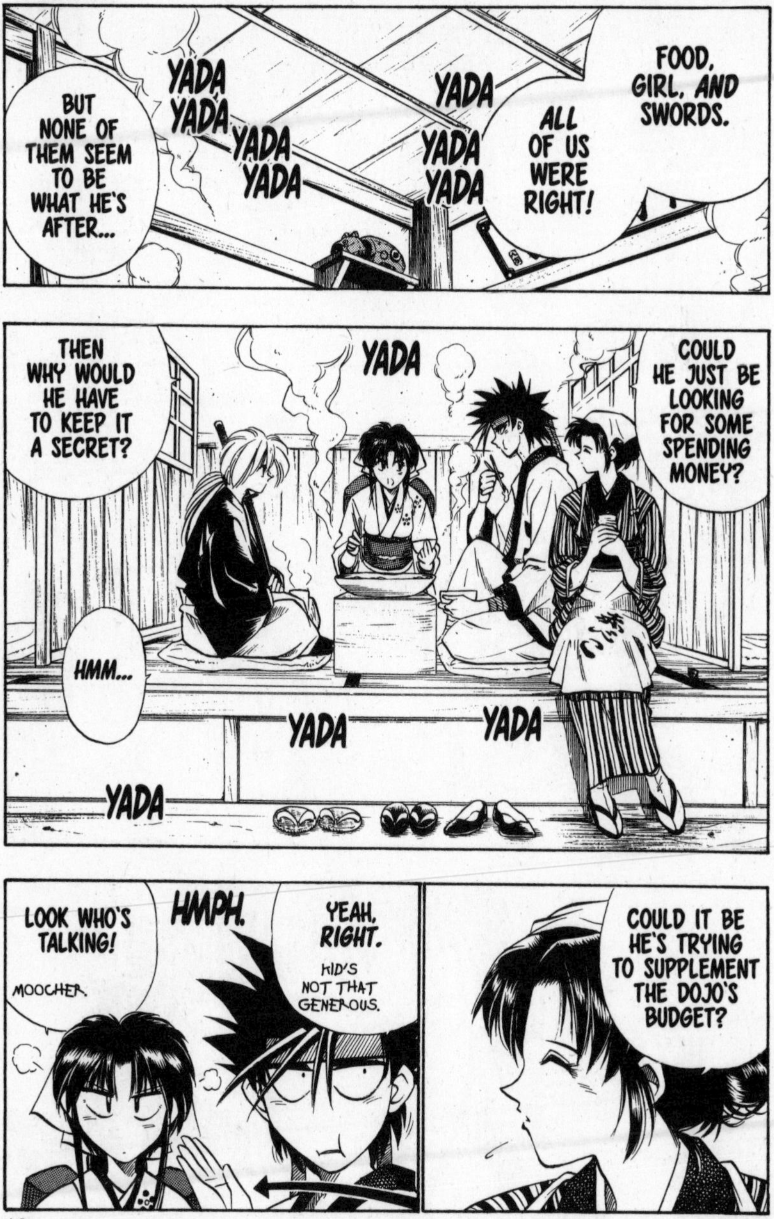

FOOD, GIRL, AND SWORDS.
ALL OF US WERE RIGHT!
YADA YADA YADA
YADA YADA
YADA YADA
BUT NONE OF THEM SEEM TO BE WHAT HE'S AFTER...
COULD HE JUST BE LOOKING FOR SOME SPENDING MONEY?
YADA
THEN WHY WOULD HE HAVE TO KEEP IT A SECRET?
HMM...
YADA
YADA
YADA
COULD IT BE HE'S TRYING TO SUPPLEMENT THE DOJO'S BUDGET?
YEAH, RIGHT.
KID'S NOT THAT GENEROUS.
HMPH.
LOOK WHO'S TALKING!
MOOCHER.

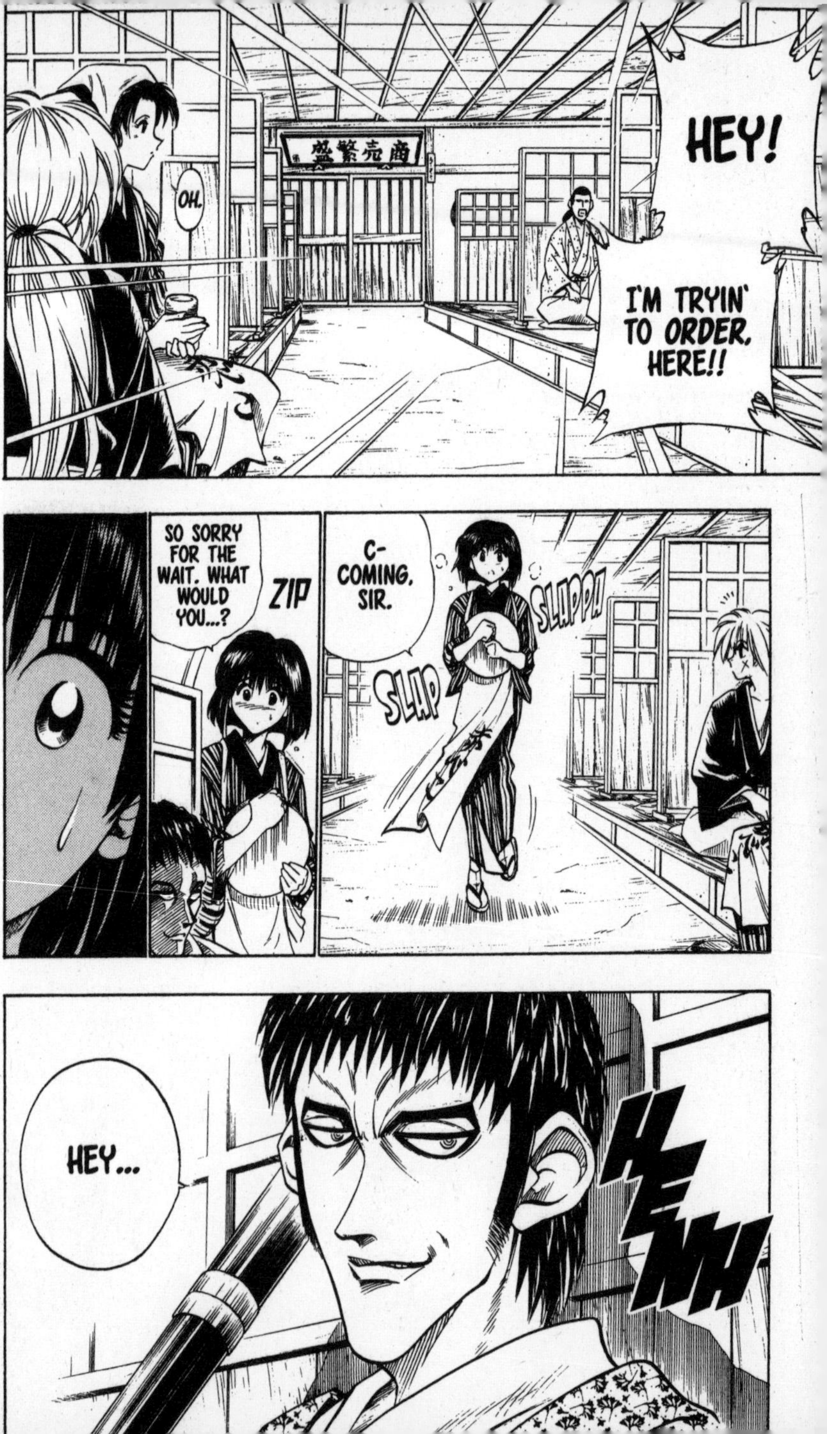
HEY!
I'M TRYIN' TO ORDER, HERE!!
OH.
C-COMING, SIR.
SLAPPA
SLAP
SO SORRY FOR THE WAIT. WHAT WOULD YOU...?
ZIP
HEY...

READ THIS WAY

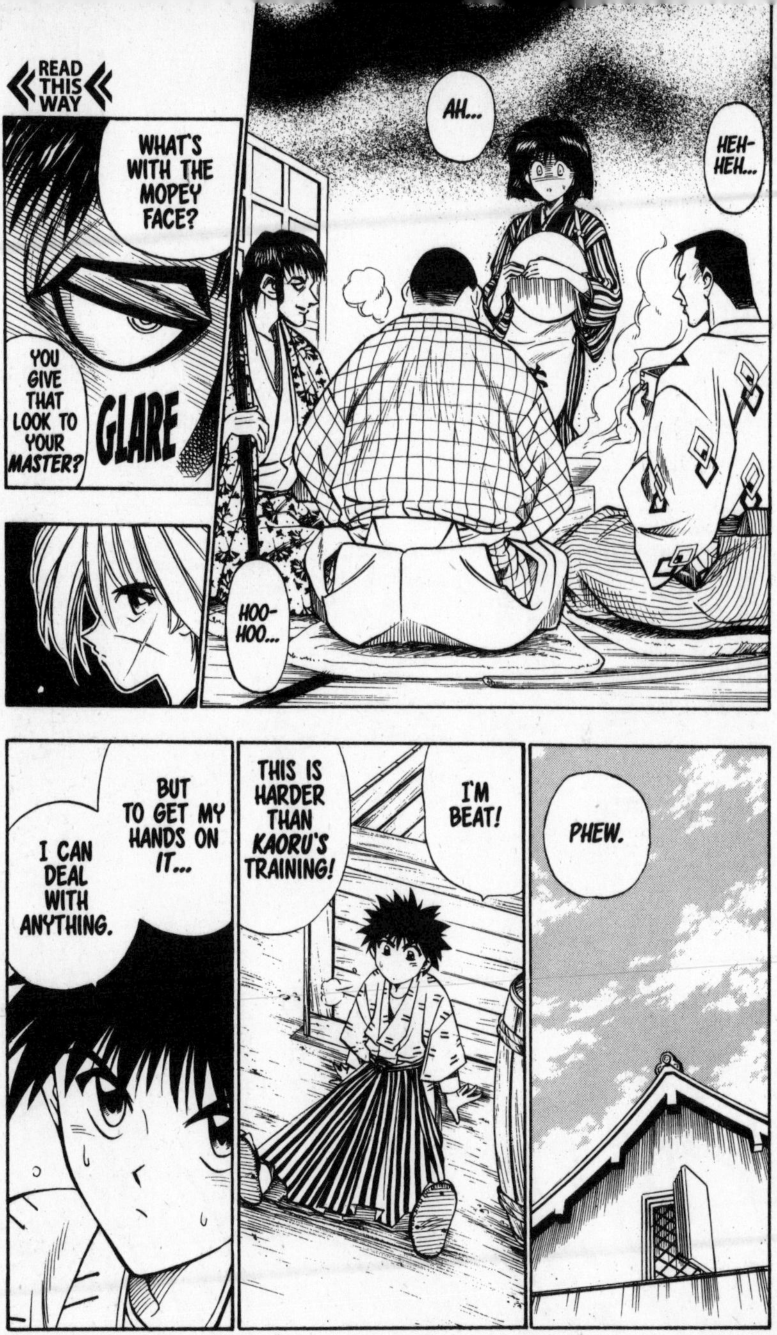
HEH-HEH...
AH...
HOO-HOO...
WHAT'S WITH THE MOPEY FACE?
YOU GIVE THAT LOOK TO YOUR *MASTER?*
GLARE
PHEW.
I'M BEAT!
THIS IS HARDER THAN *KAORU'S* TRAINING!
BUT TO GET MY HANDS ON IT...
I CAN DEAL WITH ANYTHING.

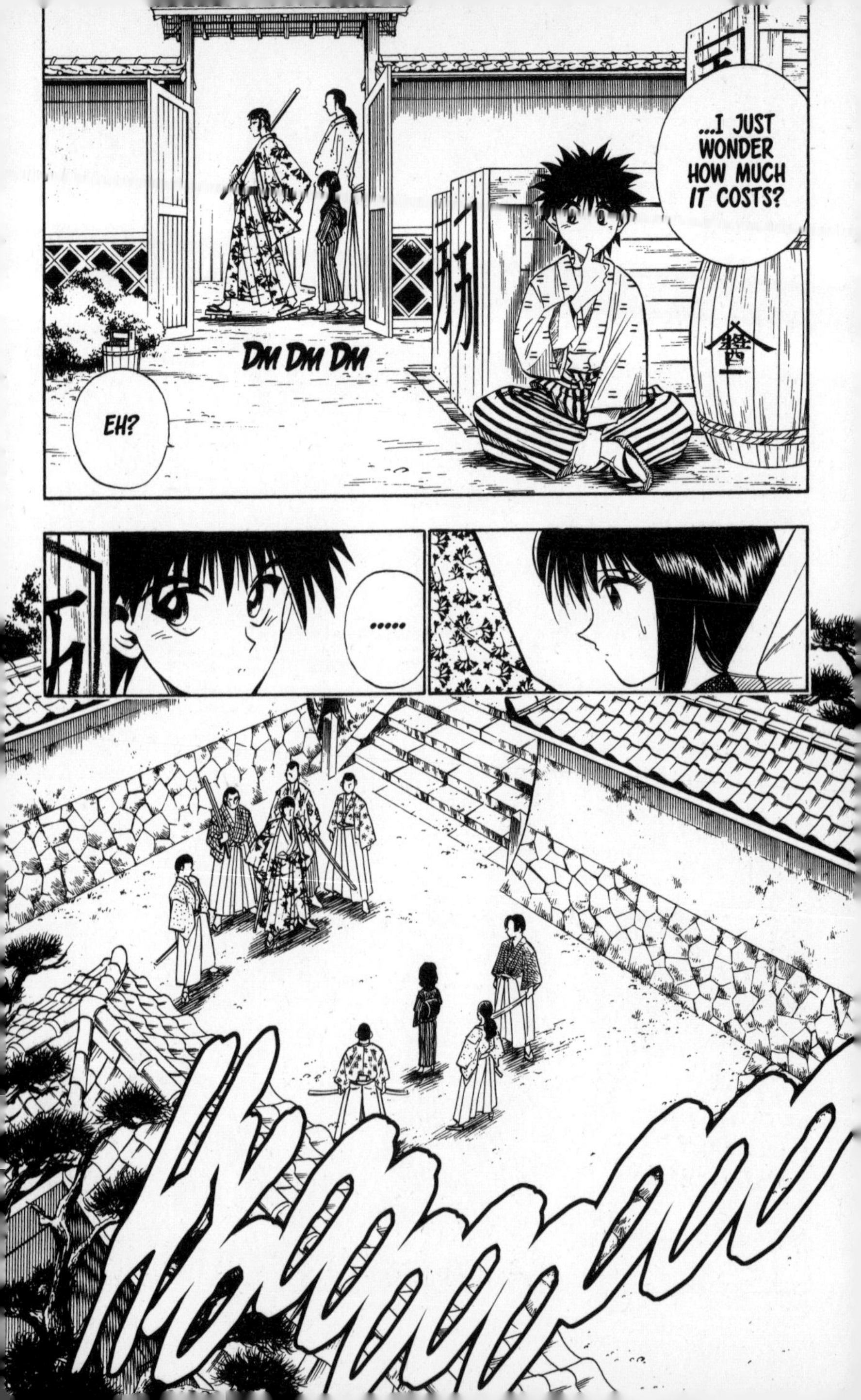
...I JUST WONDER HOW MUCH IT COSTS?
DM DM DM
EH?
......

READ THIS WAY

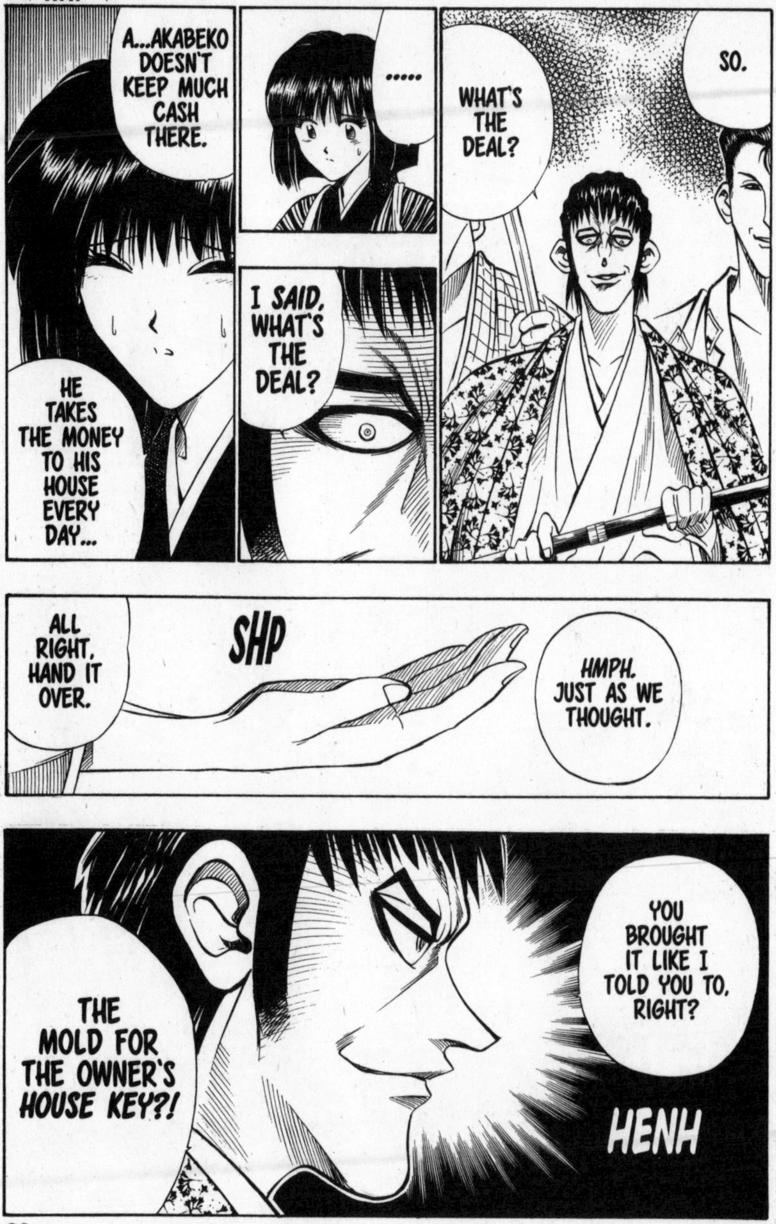
SO.
WHAT'S THE DEAL?
.....
I SAID, WHAT'S THE DEAL?
A...AKABEKO DOESN'T KEEP MUCH CASH THERE.
HE TAKES THE MONEY TO HIS HOUSE EVERY DAY...
HMPH. JUST AS WE THOUGHT.
SHP
ALL RIGHT, HAND IT OVER.
YOU BROUGHT IT LIKE I TOLD YOU TO, RIGHT?
HENH
THE MOLD FOR THE OWNER'S HOUSE KEY?!

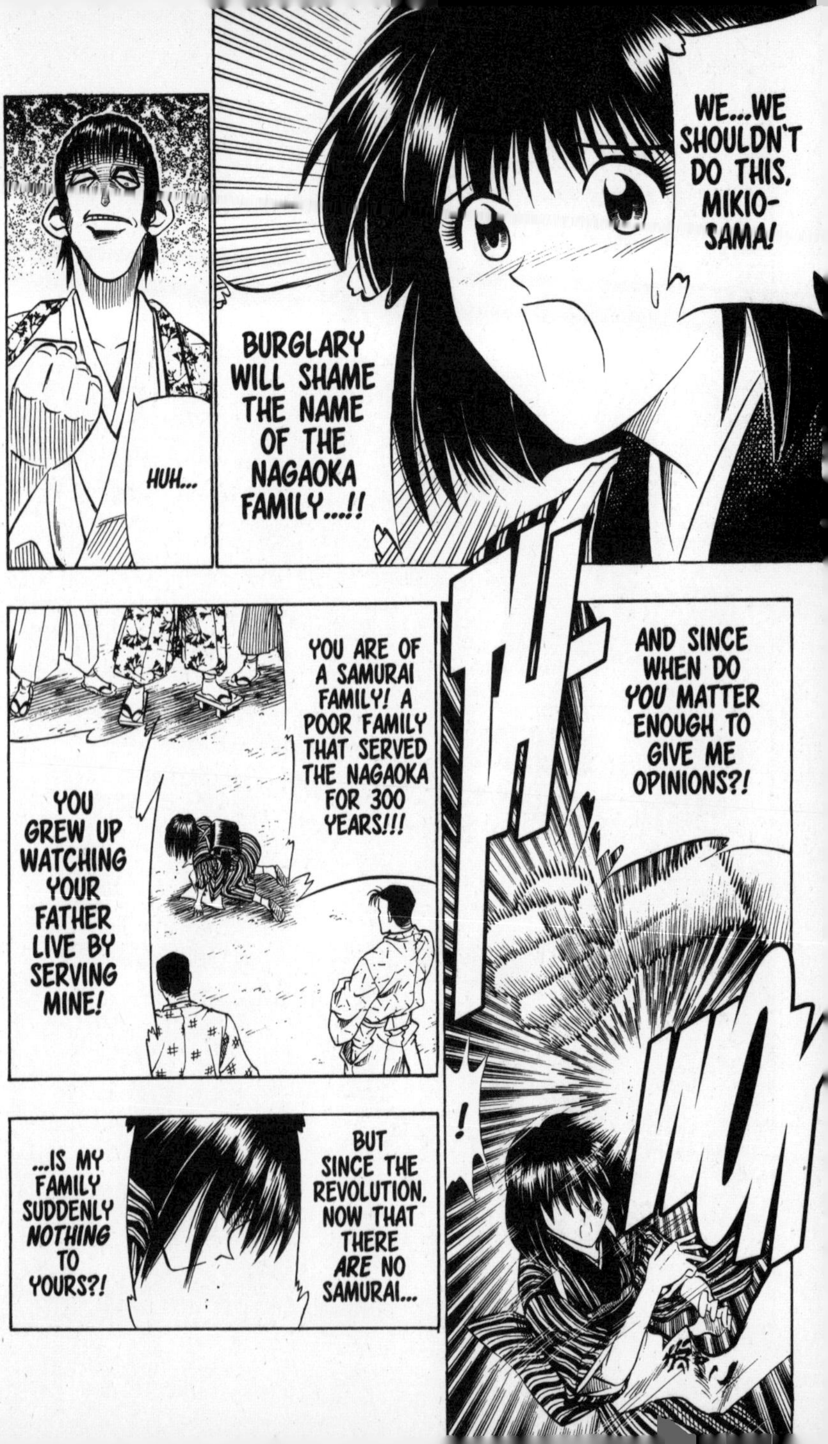
WE...WE SHOULDN'T DO THIS, MIKIO-SAMA!
BURGLARY WILL SHAME THE NAME OF THE NAGAOKA FAMILY...!!
HUH...
AND SINCE WHEN DO *YOU* MATTER ENOUGH TO GIVE ME OPINIONS?!
!
YOU ARE OF A SAMURAI FAMILY! A POOR FAMILY THAT SERVED THE NAGAOKA FOR 300 YEARS!!!
YOU GREW UP WATCHING YOUR FATHER LIVE BY SERVING MINE!
BUT SINCE THE REVOLUTION, NOW THAT THERE *ARE* NO SAMURAI...
...IS MY FAMILY SUDDENLY *NOTHING* TO YOURS?!

READ THIS WAY

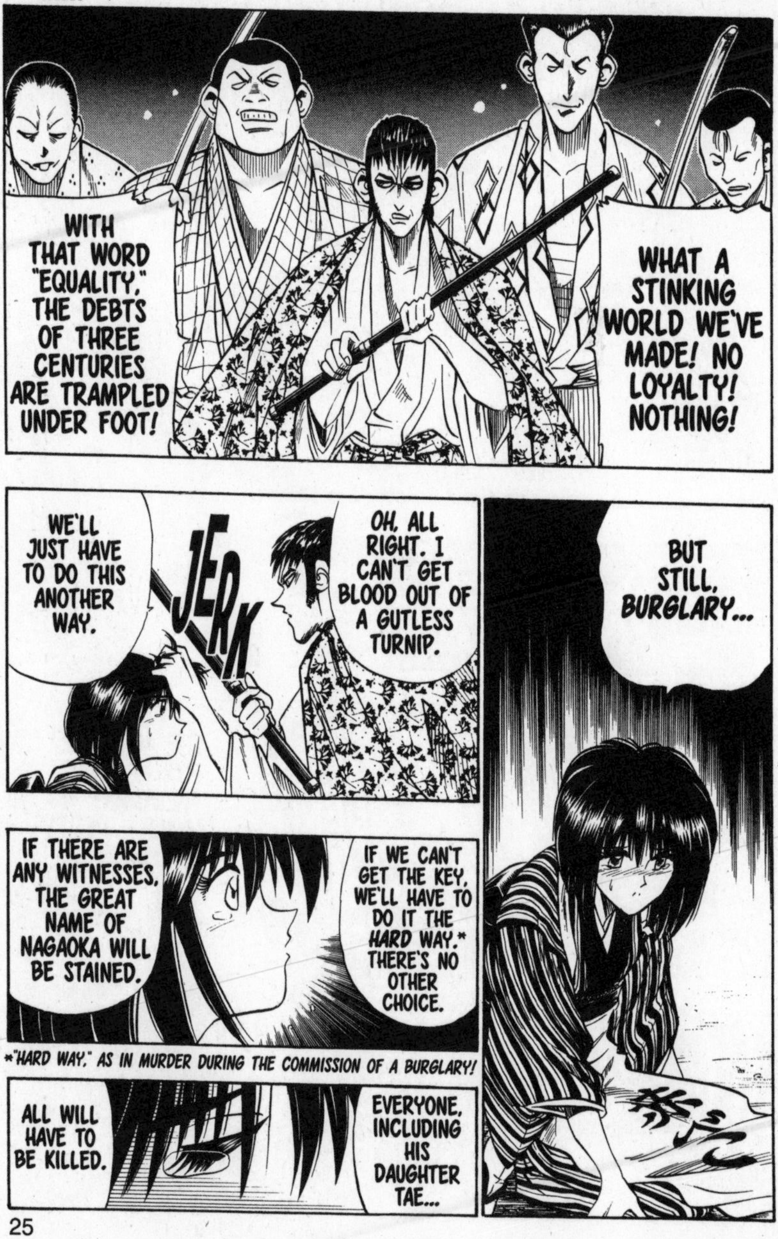

WHAT A STINKING WORLD WE'VE MADE! NO LOYALTY! NOTHING!
WITH THAT WORD "EQUALITY," THE DEBTS OF THREE CENTURIES ARE TRAMPLED UNDER FOOT!
BUT STILL, BURGLARY...
OH, ALL RIGHT. I CAN'T GET BLOOD OUT OF A GUTLESS TURNIP.
JERK
WE'LL JUST HAVE TO DO THIS ANOTHER WAY.
IF WE CAN'T GET THE KEY, WE'LL HAVE TO DO IT THE HARD WAY.* THERE'S NO OTHER CHOICE.
IF THERE ARE ANY WITNESSES, THE GREAT NAME OF NAGAOKA WILL BE STAINED.
*"HARD WAY," AS IN MURDER DURING THE COMMISSION OF A BURGLARY!
EVERYONE, INCLUDING HIS DAUGHTER TAE...
ALL WILL HAVE TO BE KILLED.

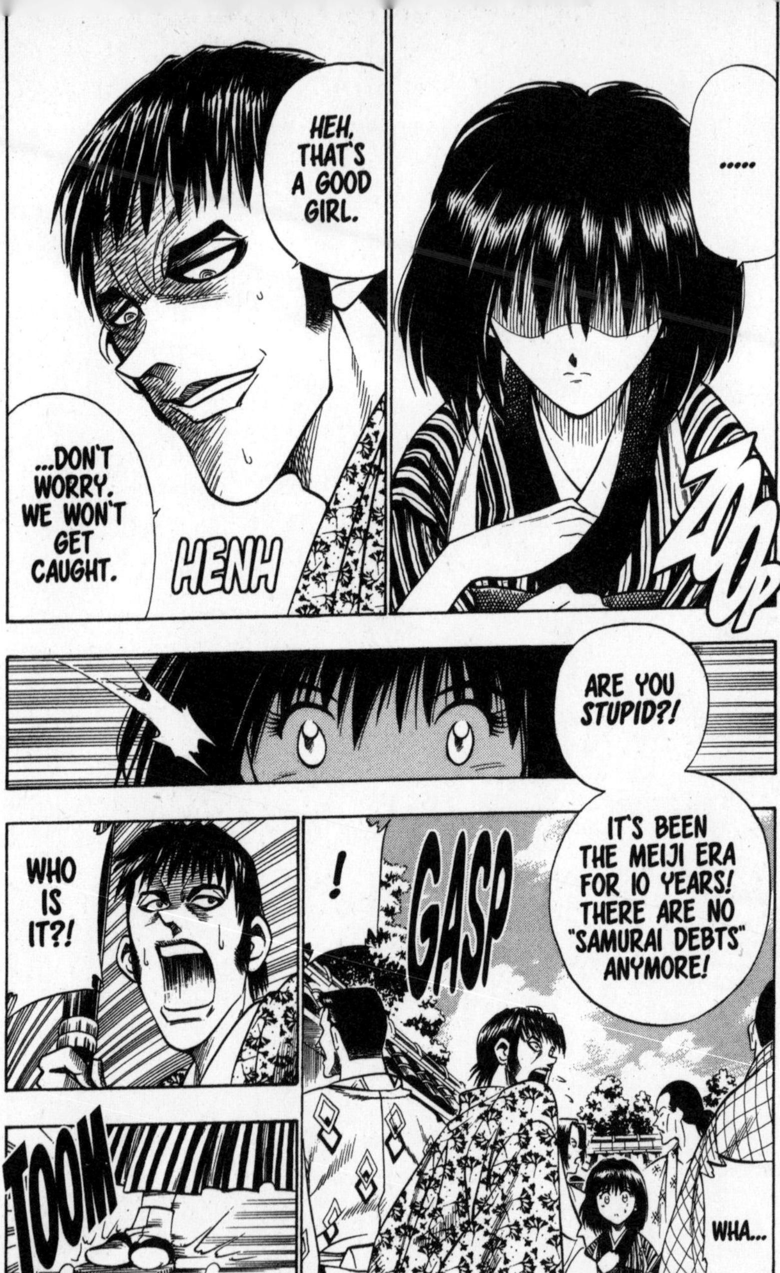
.....
ZOOP
HEH, THAT'S A GOOD GIRL.
...DON'T WORRY. WE WON'T GET CAUGHT.
HENH
ARE YOU STUPID?!
IT'S BEEN THE MEIJI ERA FOR 10 YEARS! THERE ARE NO "SAMURAI DEBTS" ANYMORE!
GASP
!
WHA...
WHO IS IT?!
TOOM

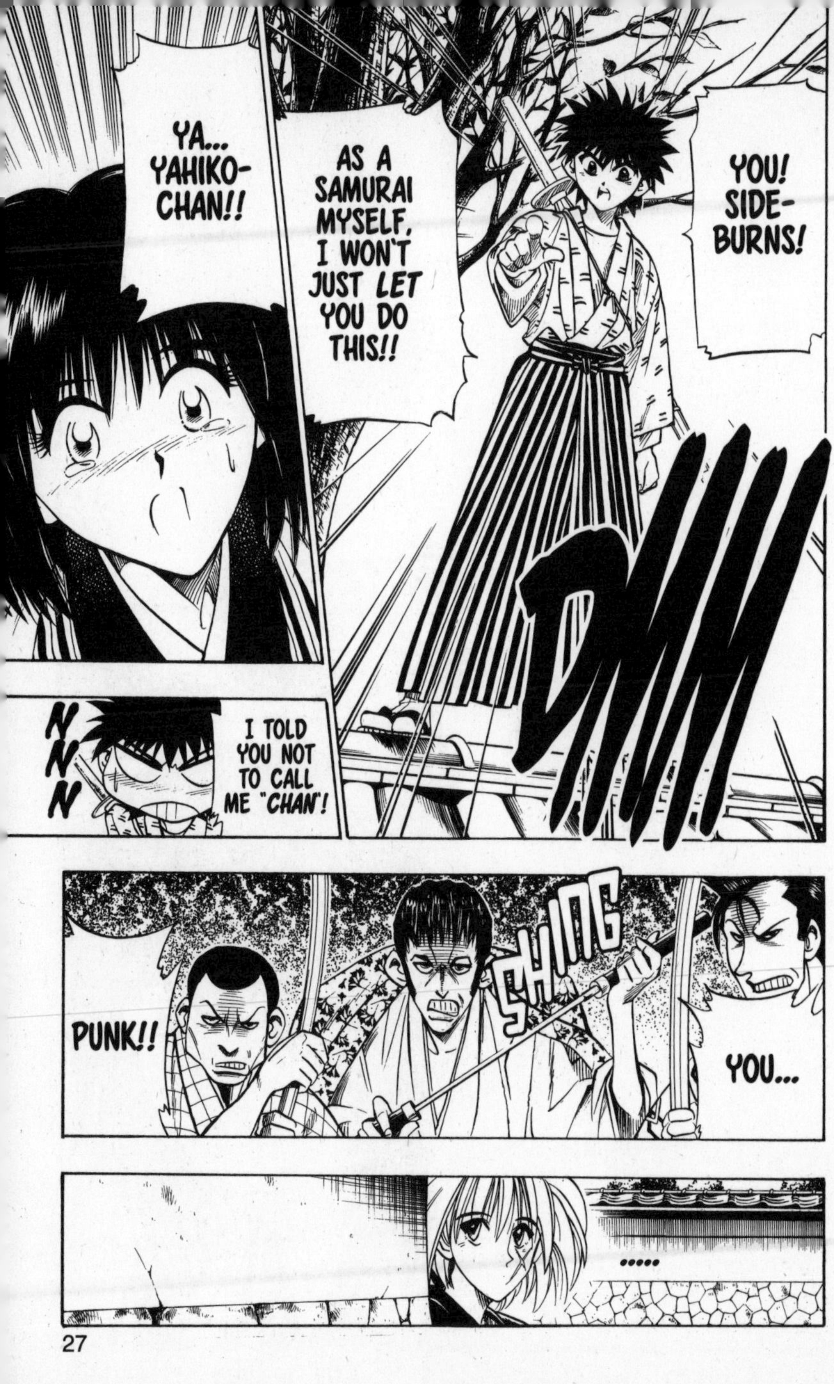
YOU! SIDE-BURNS!
AS A SAMURAI MYSELF, I WON'T JUST *LET* YOU DO THIS!!
DMM
YA... YAHIKO-CHAN!!
NNN
I TOLD YOU NOT TO CALL ME "*CHAN*"!
YOU...
SHING
PUNK!!
.....

Rurouni Kenshin

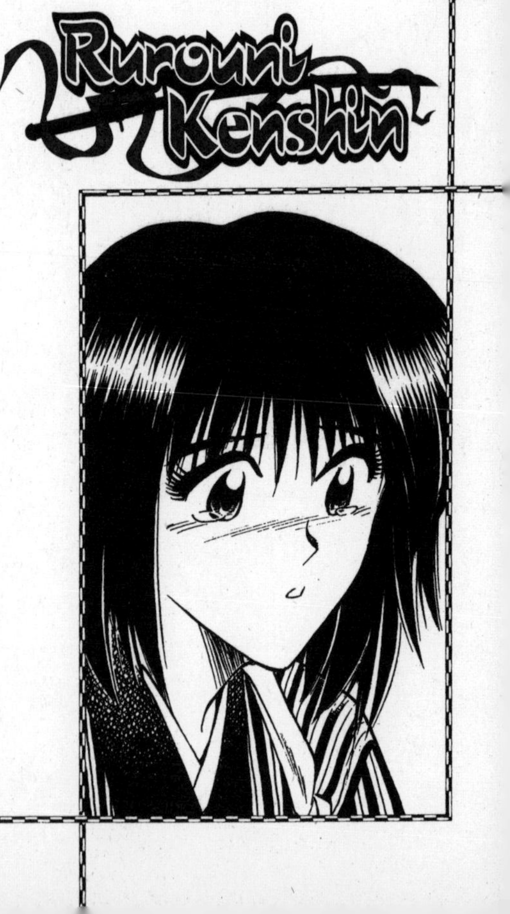

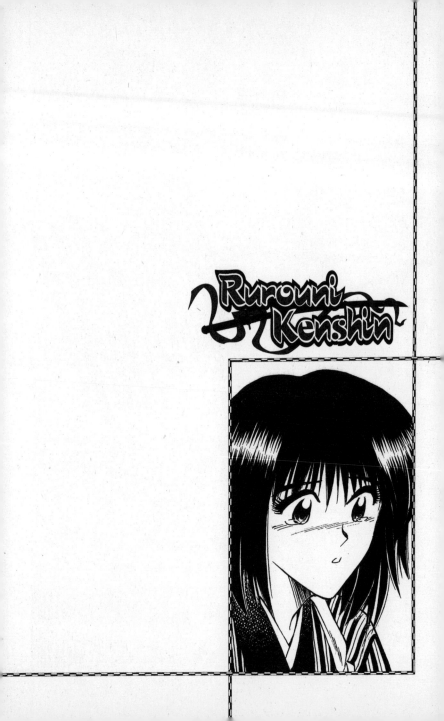

READ THIS WAY

# Act 32

# Bonus Story: Yahiko's Battle (2)

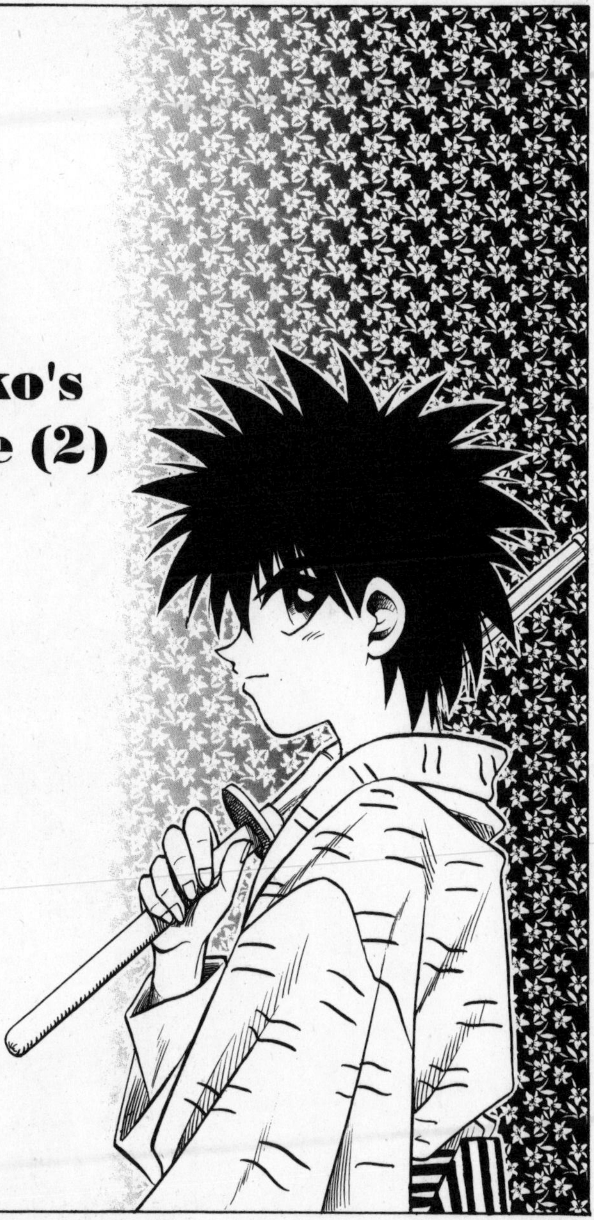

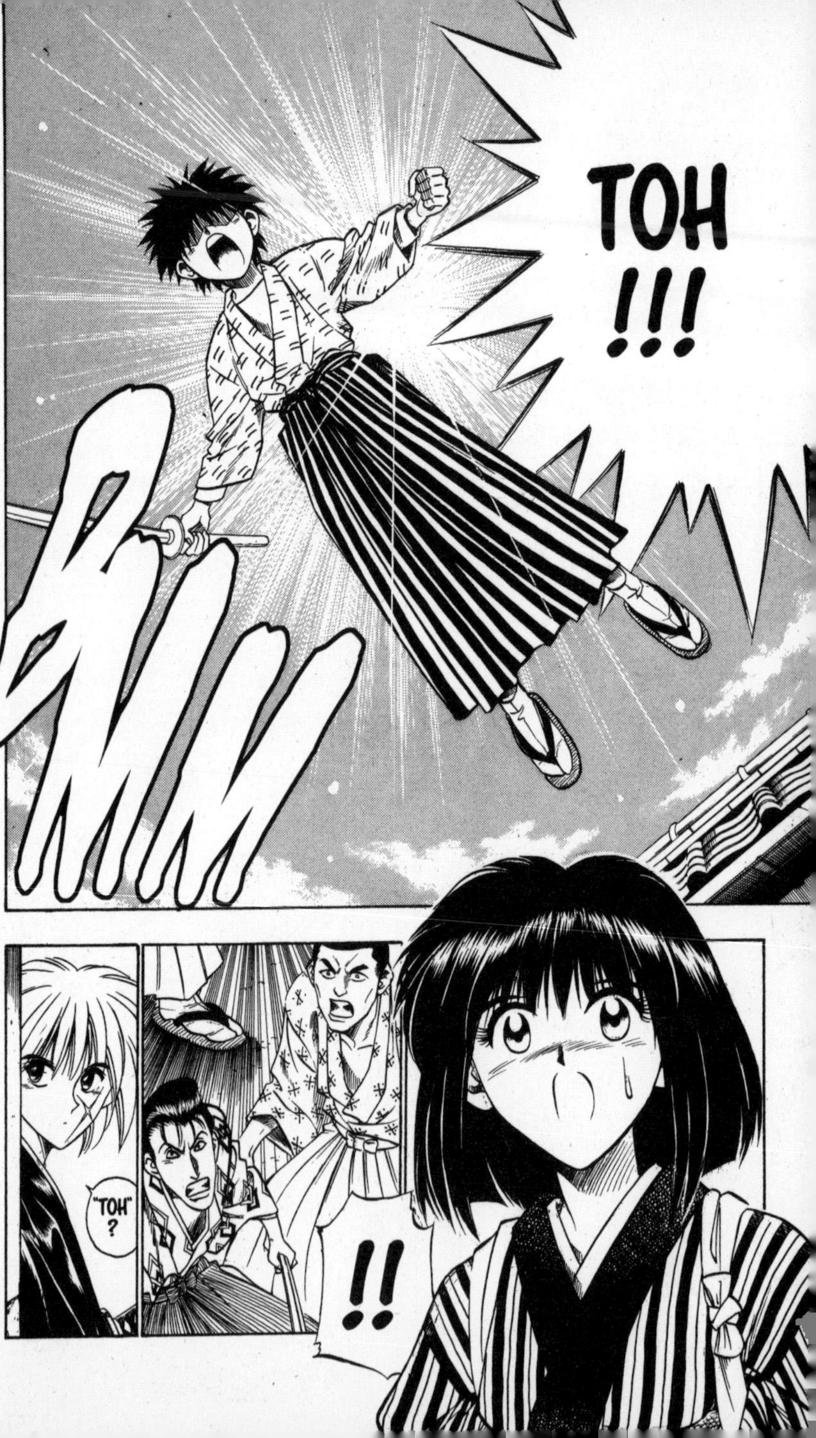
TOH !!!
!!
"TOH" ?

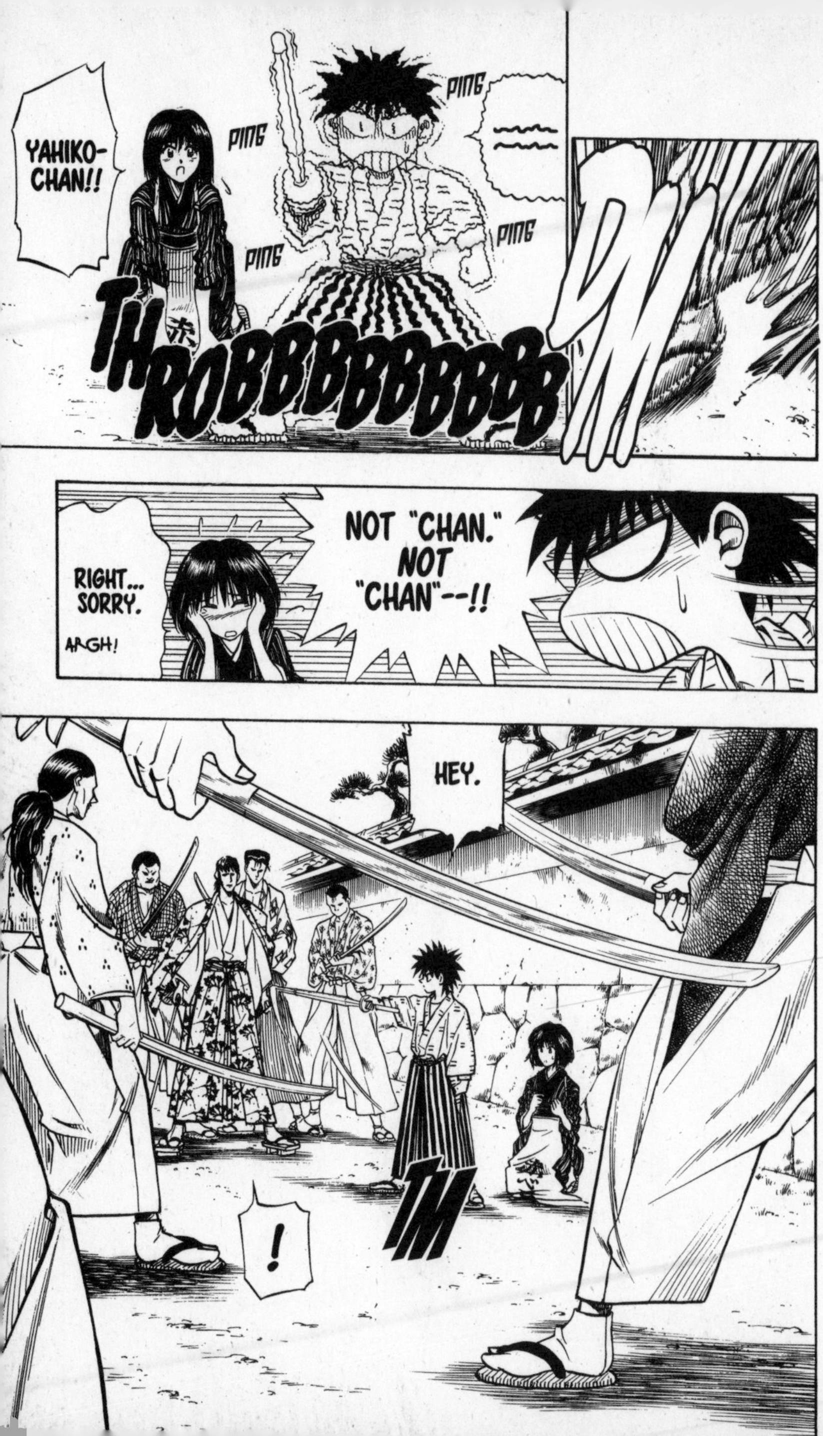
PING
PING
PING
YAHIKO-CHAN!!
PING
THROBBBBBBBBB
NOT "CHAN." NOT "CHAN"--!!
RIGHT... SORRY.
ARGH!
HEY.
!

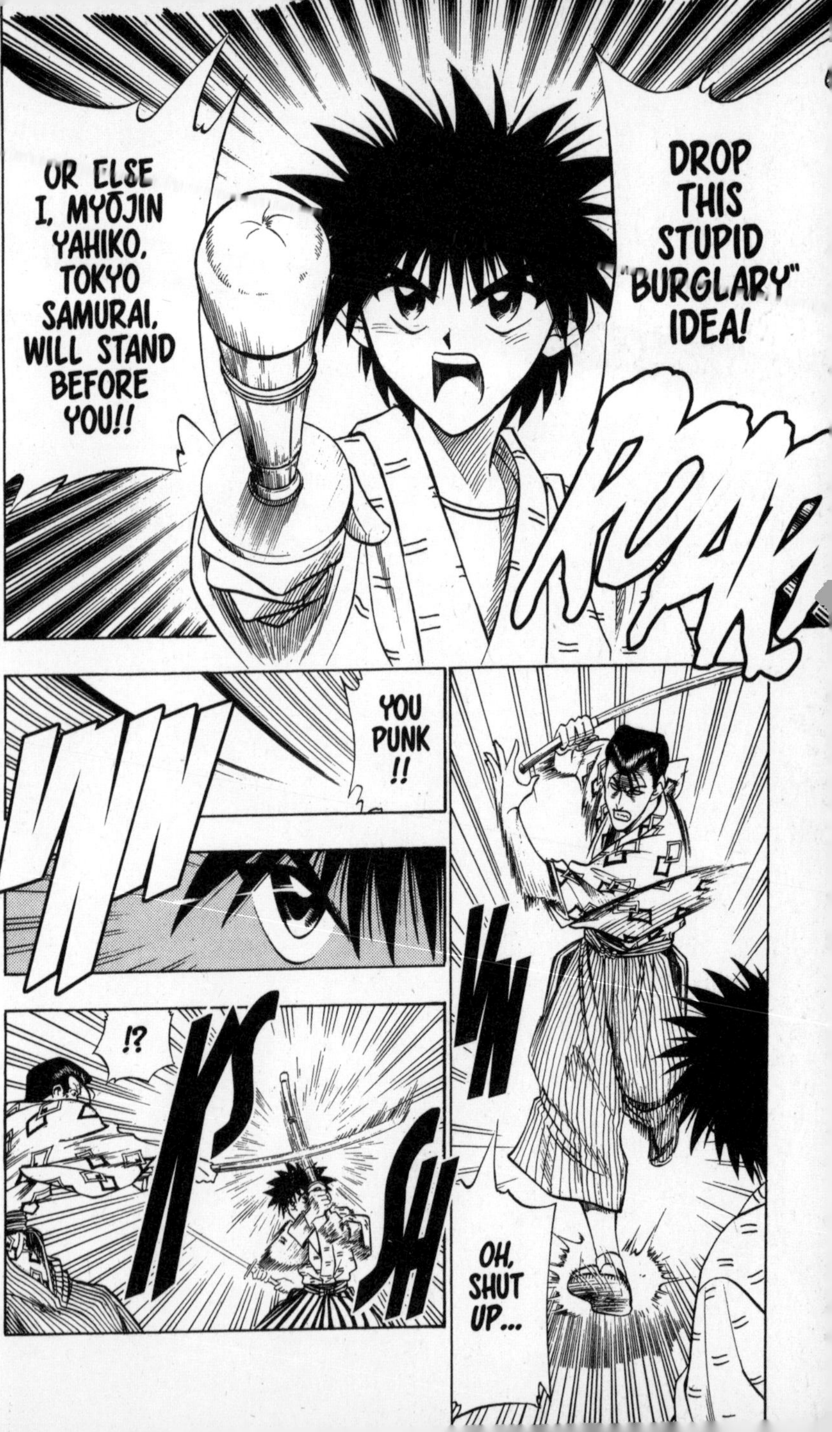
DROP THIS STUPID "BURGLARY" IDEA!
OR ELSE I, MYŌJIN YAHIKO, TOKYO SAMURAI, WILL STAND BEFORE YOU!!
OH, SHUT UP...
YOU PUNK!!
!?

READ THIS WAY

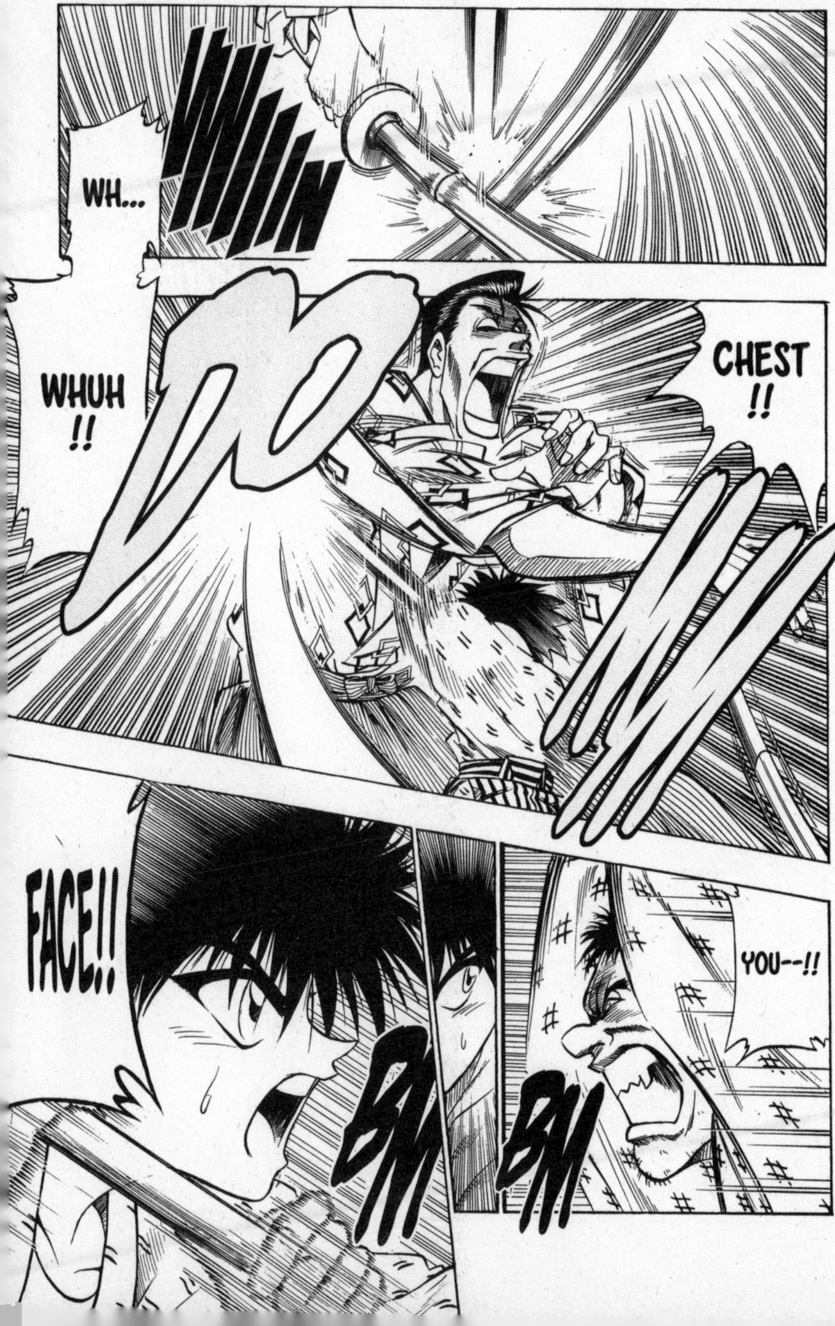
WH...
CHEST!!
WHUH!!
YOU--!!
FACE!!

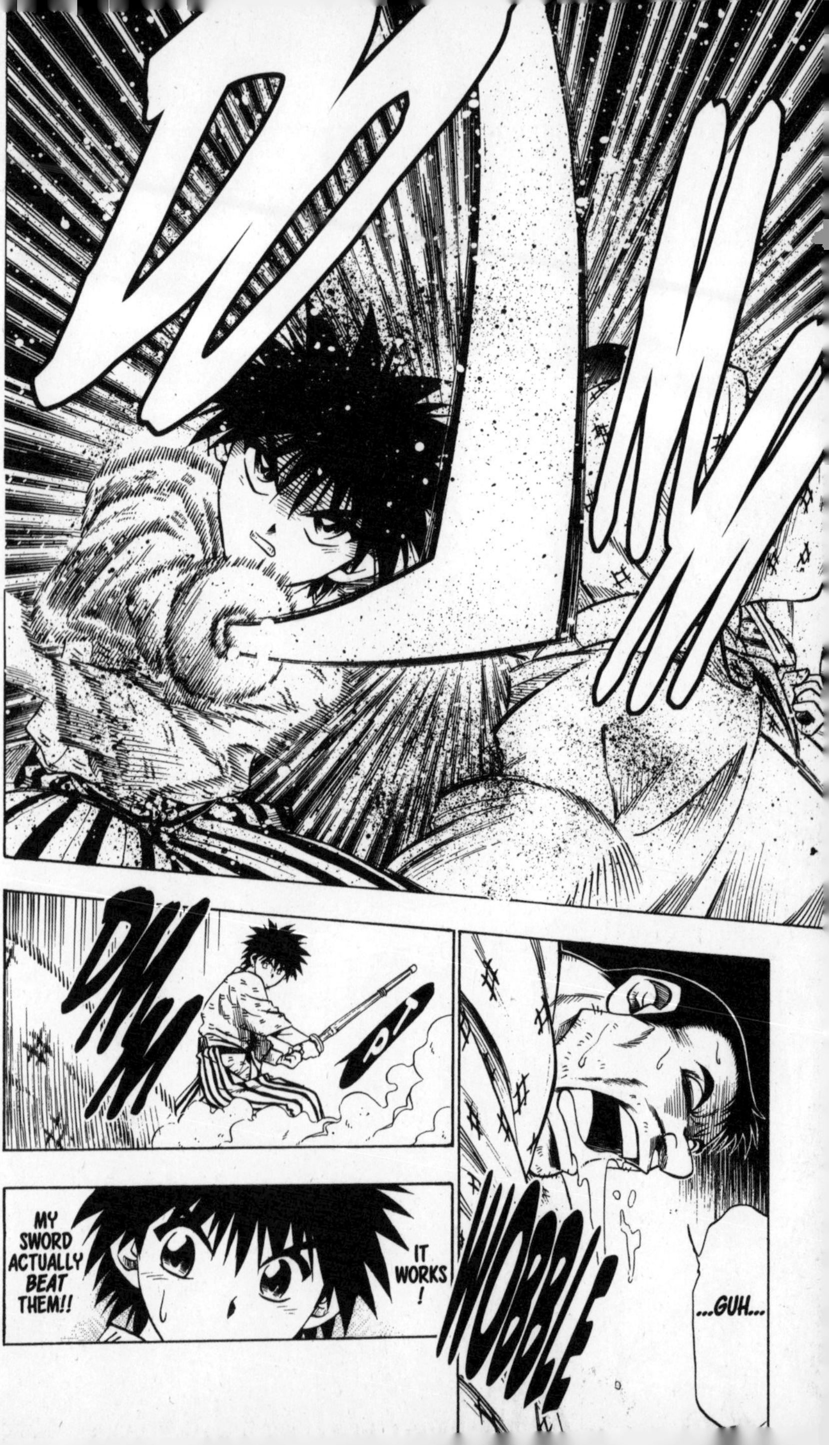
WOBBLE
...GUH...
IT WORKS!
MY SWORD ACTUALLY BEAT THEM!!

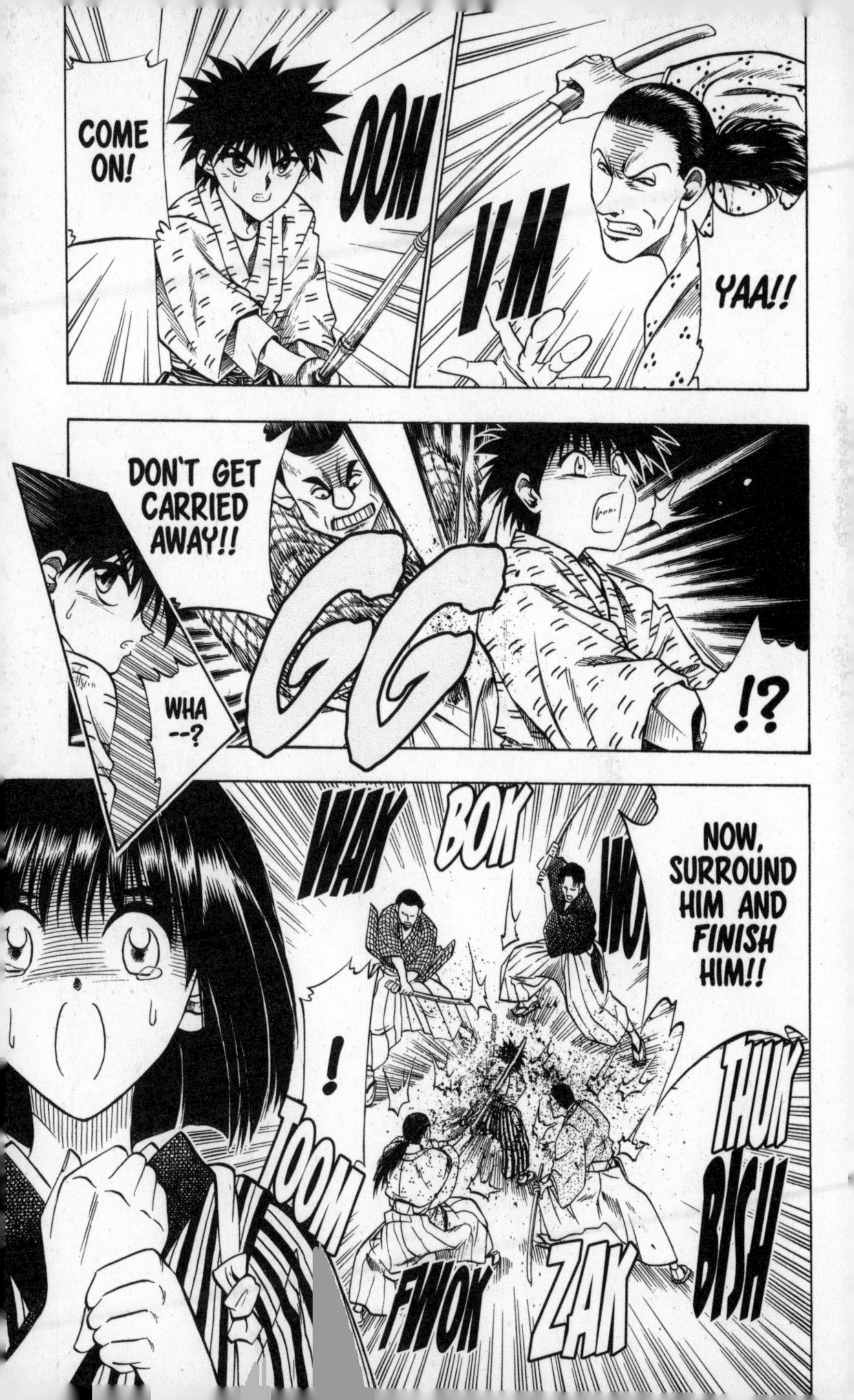
YAA!!
VM
OOM
COME ON!
!?
DON'T GET CARRIED AWAY!!
GG
WHA --?
NOW, SURROUND HIM AND FINISH HIM!!
WO
BOK
WAK
THUK
BISH
ZAK
FWOK
TOOM
!

READ THIS WAY

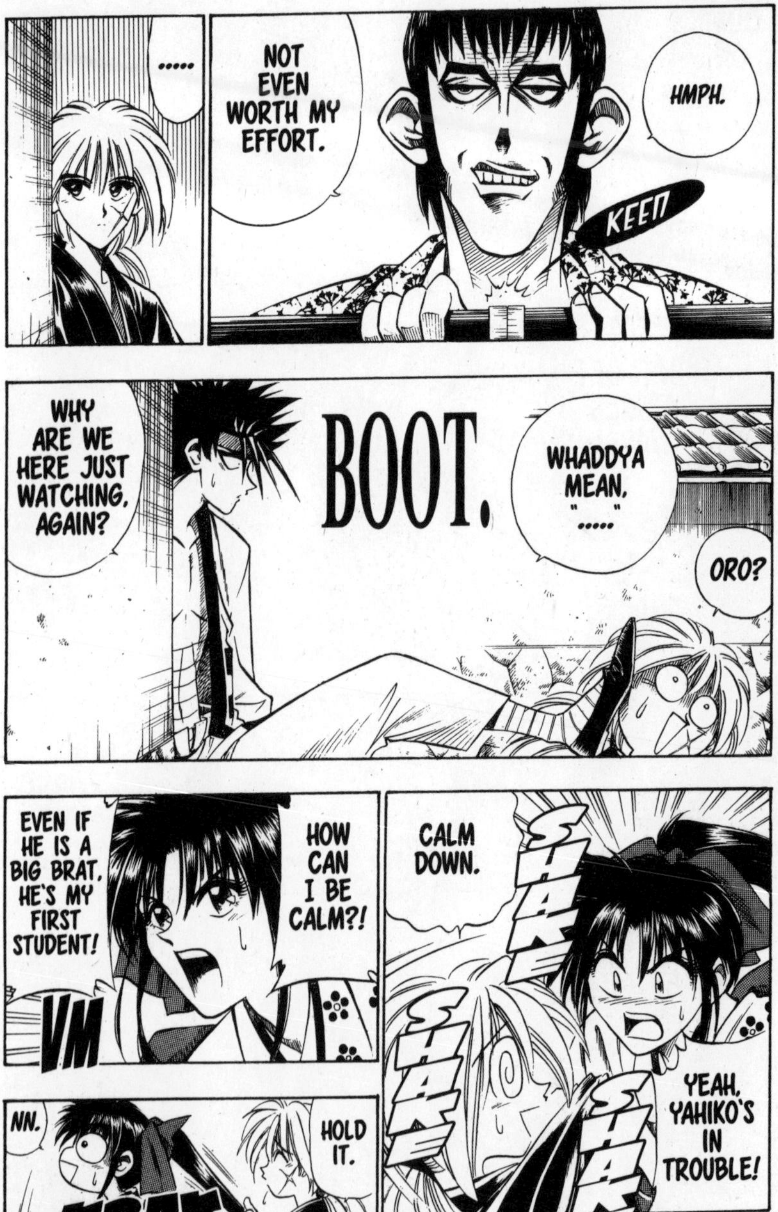
HMPH.
KEEN
NOT EVEN WORTH MY EFFORT.
.....
ORO?
WHADDYA MEAN, "....."
BOOT.
WHY ARE WE HERE JUST WATCHING, AGAIN?
CALM DOWN.
SHAKE
SHAKE
SHAKE
YEAH, YAHIKO'S IN TROUBLE!
HOW CAN I BE CALM?!
EVEN IF HE IS A BIG BRAT, HE'S MY FIRST STUDENT!
VM
HOLD IT.
NN.
KRAK

READ THIS WAY

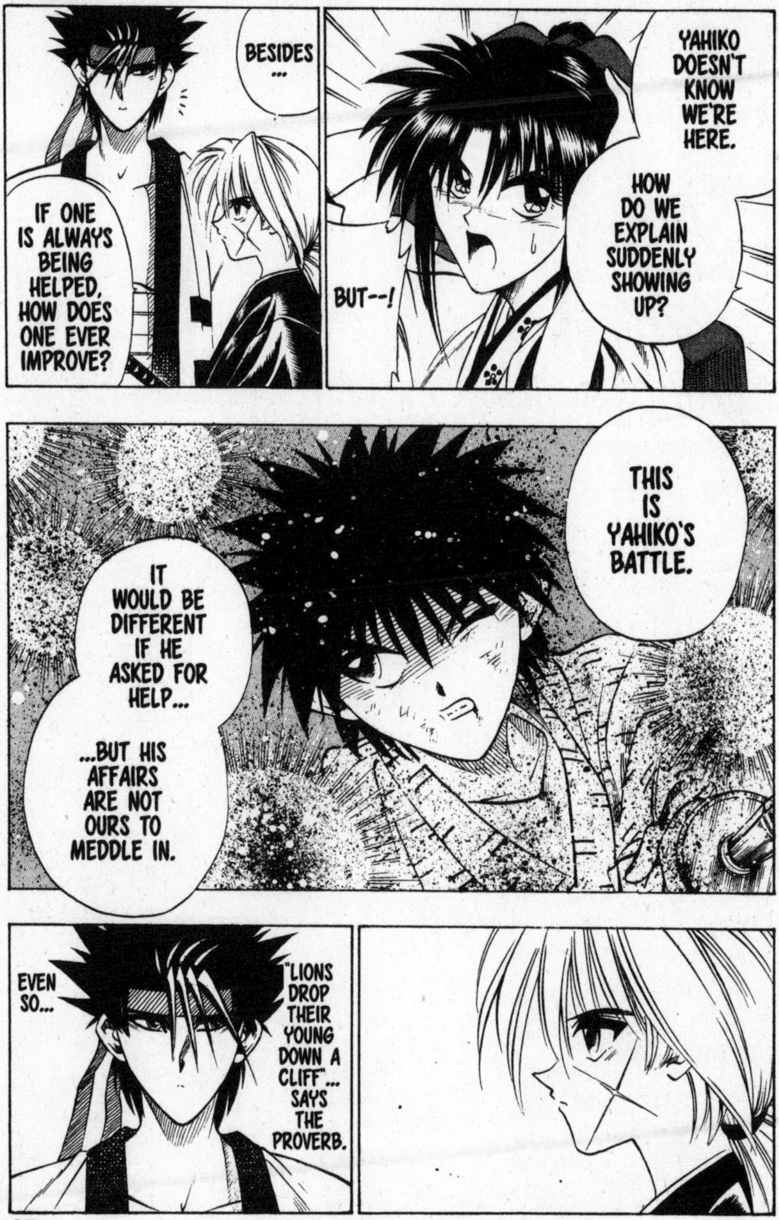

YAHIKO DOESN'T KNOW WE'RE HERE.
HOW DO WE EXPLAIN SUDDENLY SHOWING UP?
BUT--!
BESIDES...
IF ONE IS ALWAYS BEING HELPED, HOW DOES ONE EVER IMPROVE?
THIS IS YAHIKO'S BATTLE.
IT WOULD BE DIFFERENT IF HE ASKED FOR HELP...
...BUT HIS AFFAIRS ARE NOT OURS TO MEDDLE IN.
"LIONS DROP THEIR YOUNG DOWN A CLIFF"... SAYS THE PROVERB.
EVEN SO...

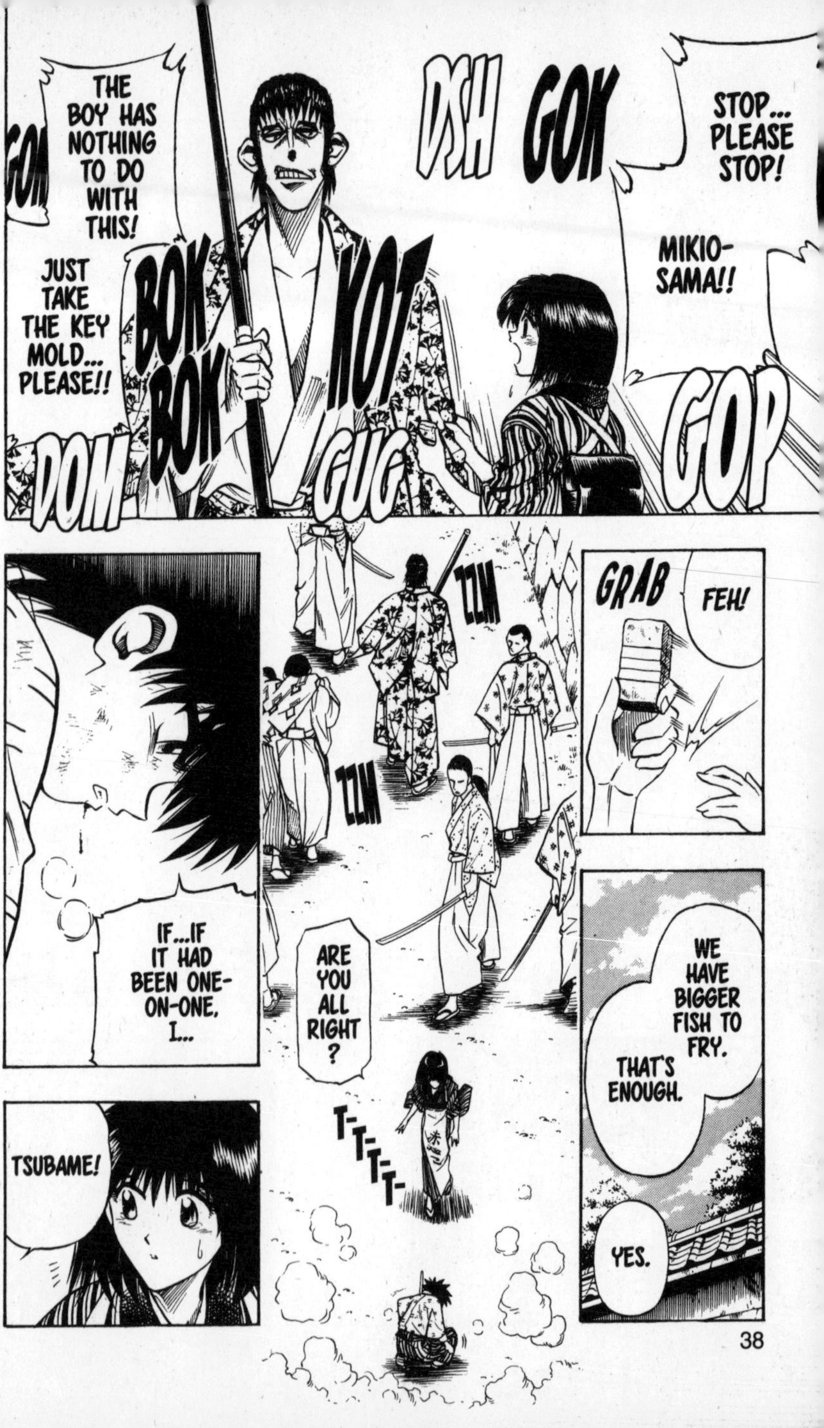
STOP... PLEASE STOP!
DSH
GOK
MIKIO-SAMA!!
GOP
THE BOY HAS NOTHING TO DO WITH THIS!
KOT
GUG
BOK
BOK
JUST TAKE THE KEY MOLD... PLEASE!!
DOM
GRAB
FEH!
WE HAVE BIGGER FISH TO FRY.
THAT'S ENOUGH.
YES.
ZZM
ZZM
ARE YOU ALL RIGHT?
T-T-T-T-
IF...IF IT HAD BEEN ONE-ON-ONE, I...
TSUBAME!

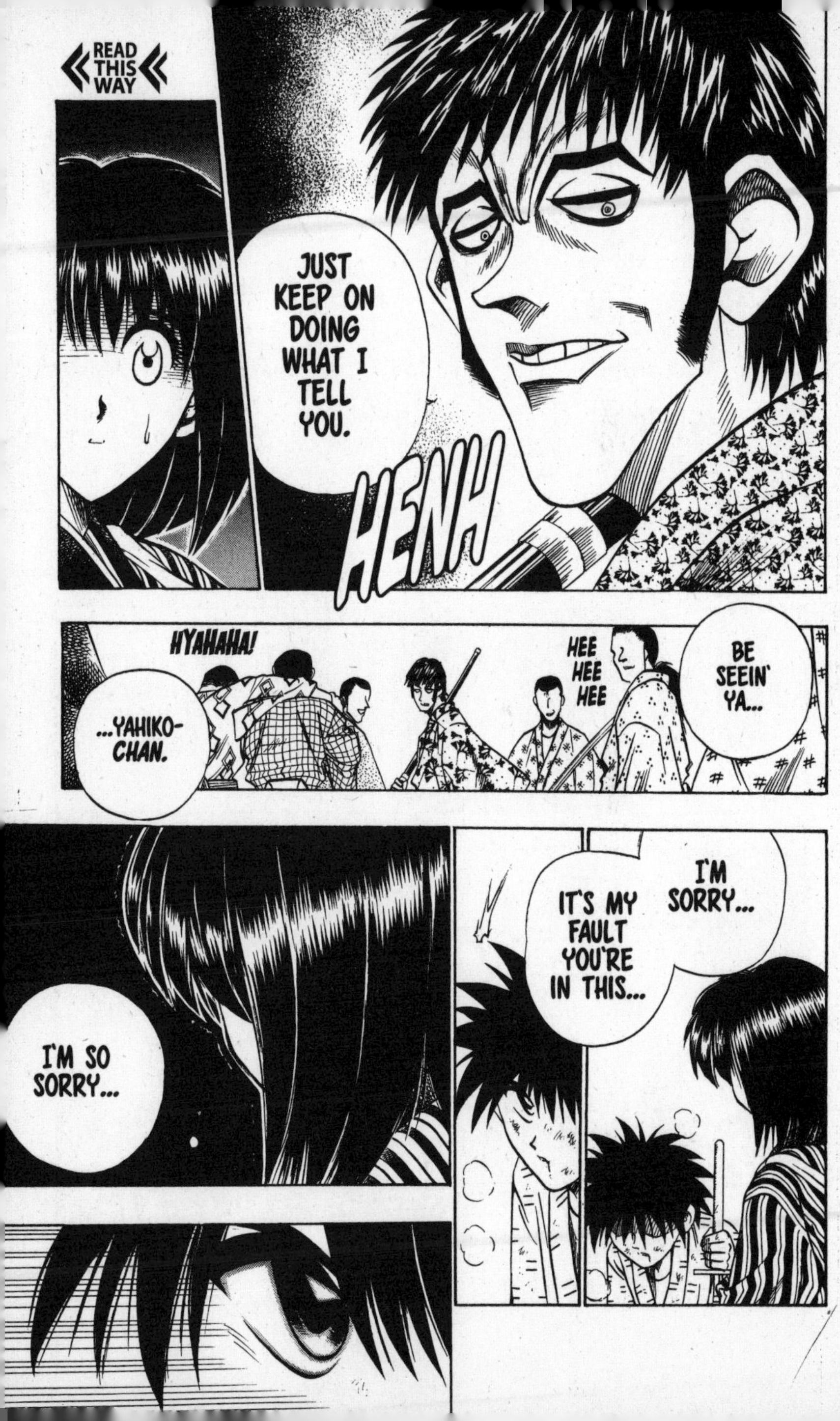
READ THIS WAY
JUST KEEP ON DOING WHAT I TELL YOU.
HENH
BE SEEIN' YA...
HEE HEE HEE
HYAHAHA!
...YAHIKO-CHAN.
I'M SORRY...
IT'S MY FAULT YOU'RE IN THIS...
I'M SO SORRY...

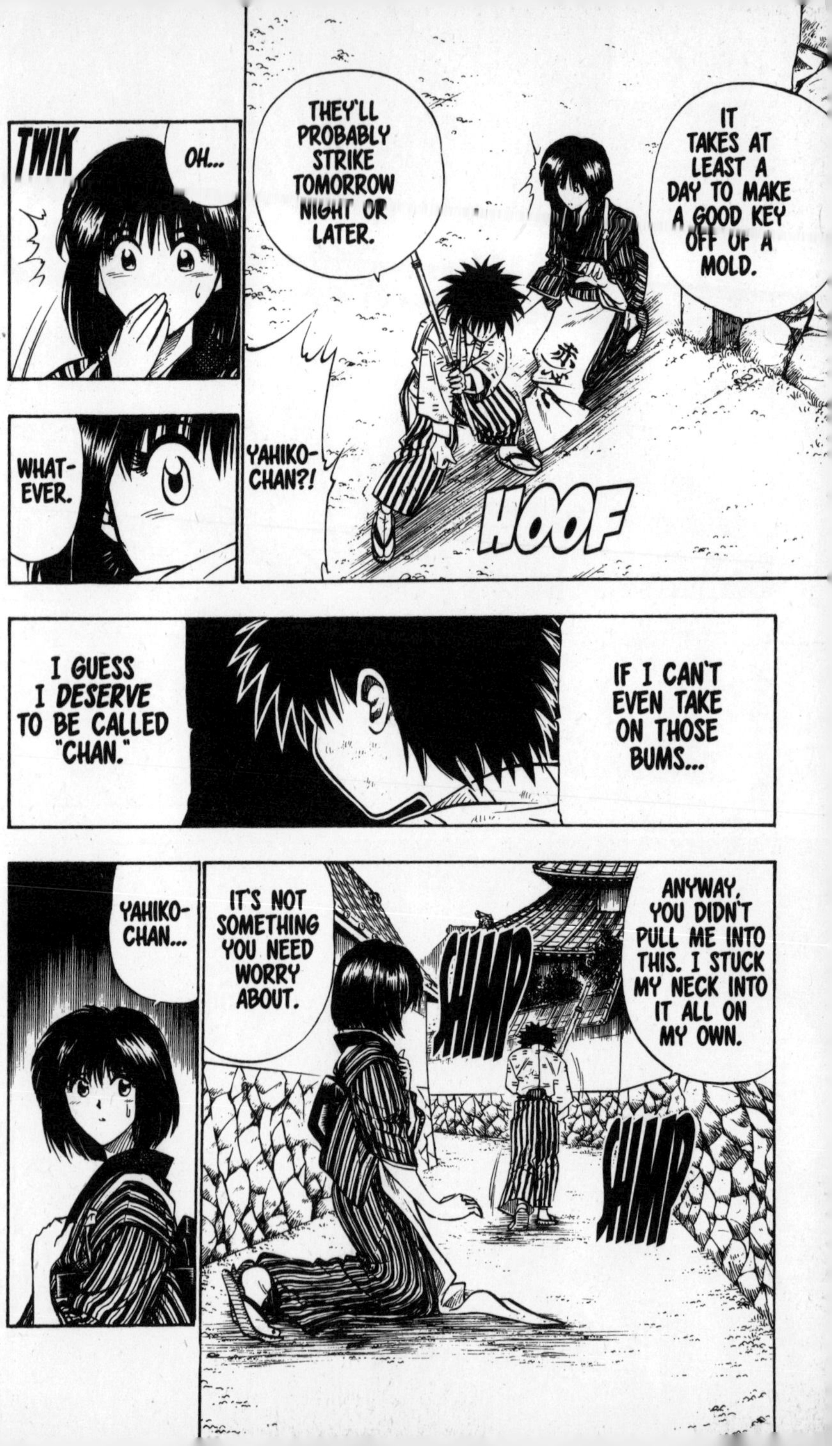
IT TAKES AT LEAST A DAY TO MAKE A GOOD KEY OFF OF A MOLD.
THEY'LL PROBABLY STRIKE TOMORROW NIGHT OR LATER.
HOOF
YAHIKO-CHAN?!
TWIK
OH...
WHAT-EVER.
IF I CAN'T EVEN TAKE ON THOSE BUMS...
I GUESS I *DESERVE* TO BE CALLED "CHAN."
ANYWAY, YOU DIDN'T PULL ME INTO THIS. I STUCK MY NECK INTO IT ALL ON MY OWN.
CHMP
CHMP
IT'S NOT SOMETHING YOU NEED WORRY ABOUT.
YAHIKO-CHAN...

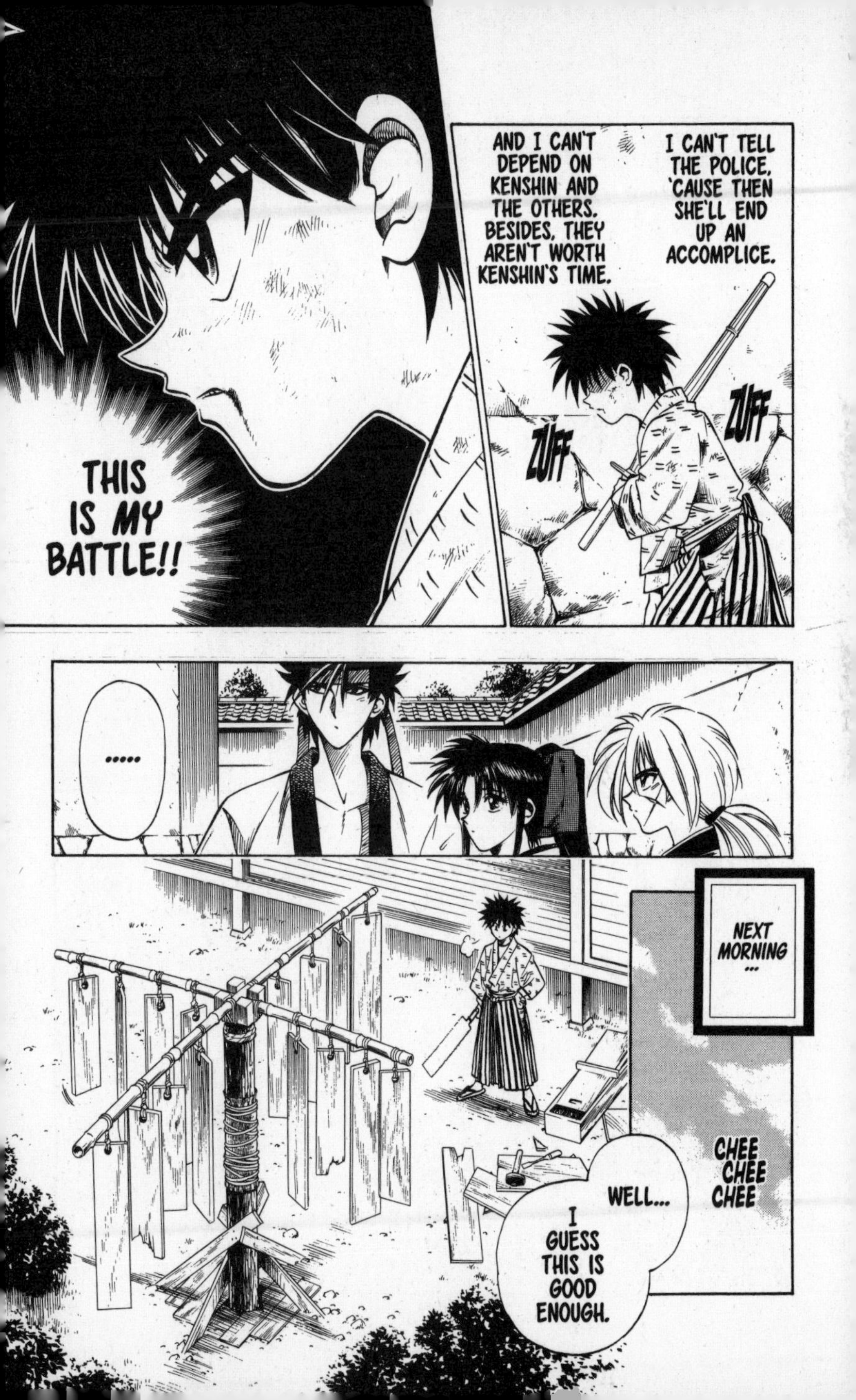
I CAN'T TELL THE POLICE, 'CAUSE THEN SHE'LL END UP AN ACCOMPLICE.
AND I CAN'T DEPEND ON KENSHIN AND THE OTHERS. BESIDES, THEY AREN'T WORTH KENSHIN'S TIME.
ZUFF
ZUFF
THIS IS MY BATTLE!!
......
NEXT MORNING...
CHEE CHEE CHEE
WELL...
I GUESS THIS IS GOOD ENOUGH.

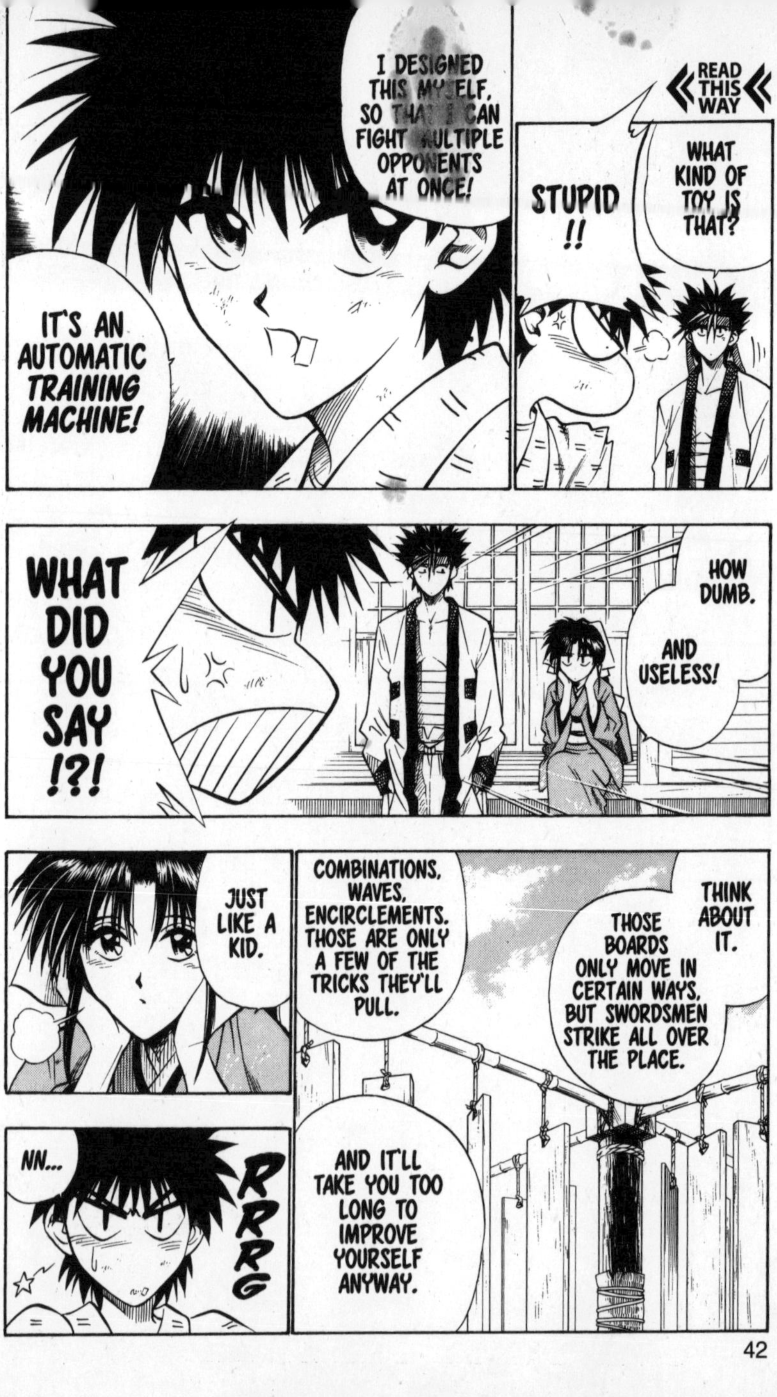
READ THIS WAY
WHAT KIND OF TOY IS THAT?
STUPID !!
I DESIGNED THIS MYSELF, SO THAT I CAN FIGHT MULTIPLE OPPONENTS AT ONCE!
IT'S AN AUTOMATIC TRAINING MACHINE!
HOW DUMB.
AND USELESS!
WHAT DID YOU SAY !?!
THINK ABOUT IT.
THOSE BOARDS ONLY MOVE IN CERTAIN WAYS, BUT SWORDSMEN STRIKE ALL OVER THE PLACE.
COMBINATIONS, WAVES, ENCIRCLEMENTS. THOSE ARE ONLY A FEW OF THE TRICKS THEY'LL PULL.
AND IT'LL TAKE YOU TOO LONG TO IMPROVE YOURSELF ANYWAY.
JUST LIKE A KID.
NN...
RRRG

READ THIS WAY

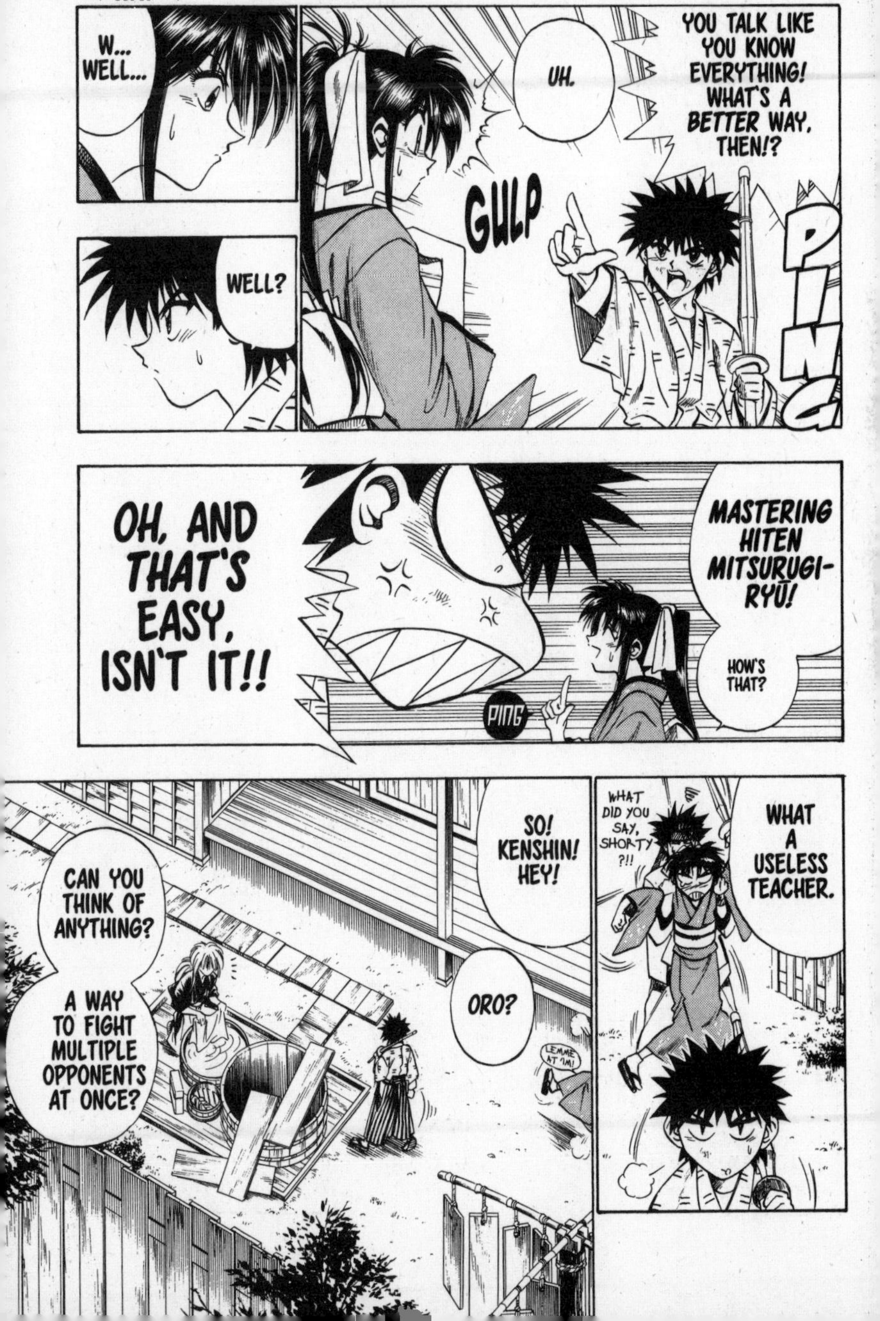
YOU TALK LIKE YOU KNOW EVERYTHING! WHAT'S A BETTER WAY, THEN!?
UH.
GULP
PING
W... WELL...
WELL?
MASTERING HITEN MITSURUGI-RYŪ!
HOW'S THAT?
PING
OH, AND THAT'S EASY, ISN'T IT!!
WHAT A USELESS TEACHER.
WHAT DID YOU SAY, SHORTY?!!
SO! KENSHIN! HEY!
CAN YOU THINK OF ANYTHING?
A WAY TO FIGHT MULTIPLE OPPONENTS AT ONCE?
ORO?
LEMME AT 'IM!

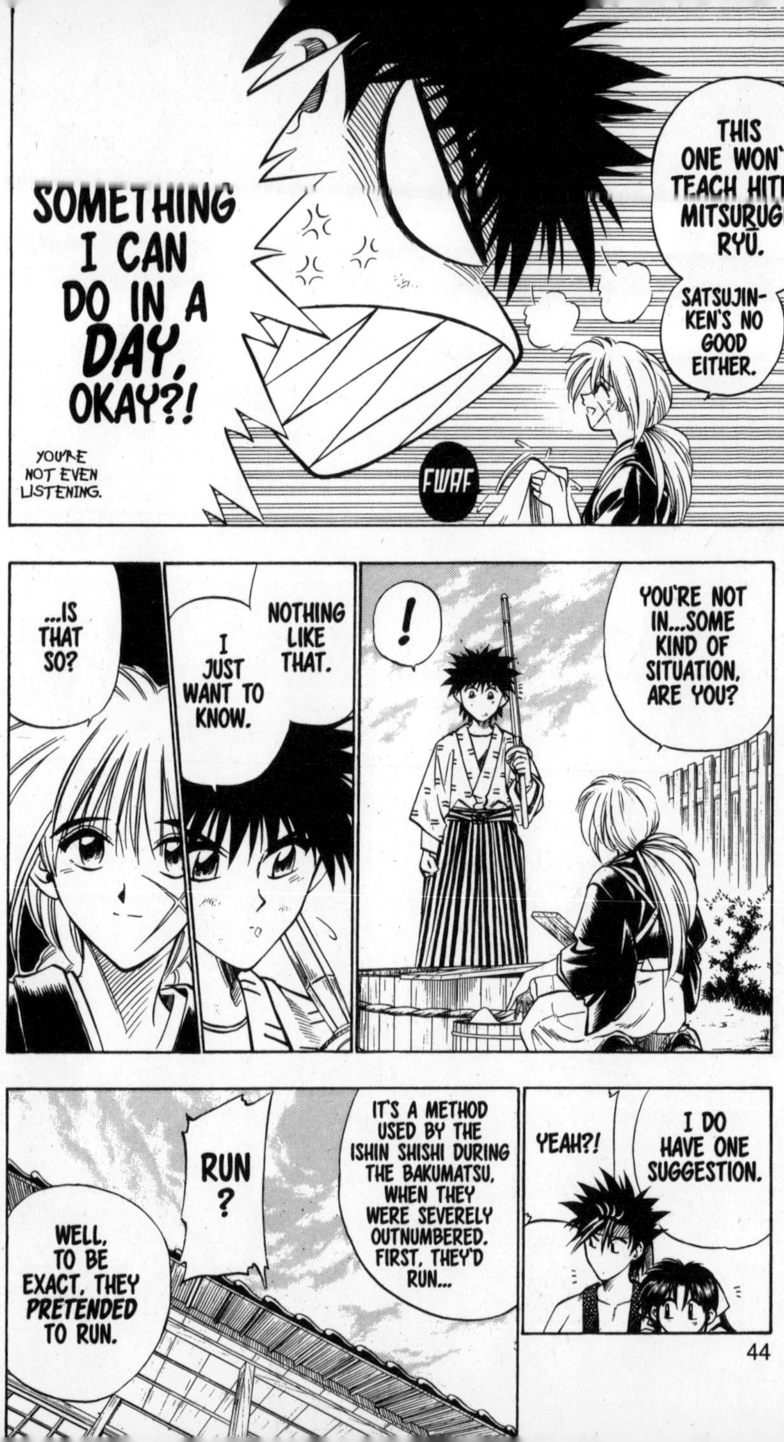
THIS ONE WON'T TEACH HITEN MITSURUGI-RYŪ.
SATSUJIN-KEN'S NO GOOD EITHER.
SOMETHING I CAN DO IN A DAY, OKAY?!
FWAF
YOU'RE NOT EVEN LISTENING.
YOU'RE NOT IN...SOME KIND OF SITUATION, ARE YOU?
!
NOTHING LIKE THAT.
I JUST WANT TO KNOW.
...IS THAT SO?
I DO HAVE ONE SUGGESTION.
YEAH?!
IT'S A METHOD USED BY THE ISHIN SHISHI DURING THE BAKUMATSU, WHEN THEY WERE SEVERELY OUTNUMBERED. FIRST, THEY'D RUN...
RUN?
WELL, TO BE EXACT, THEY PRETENDED TO RUN.

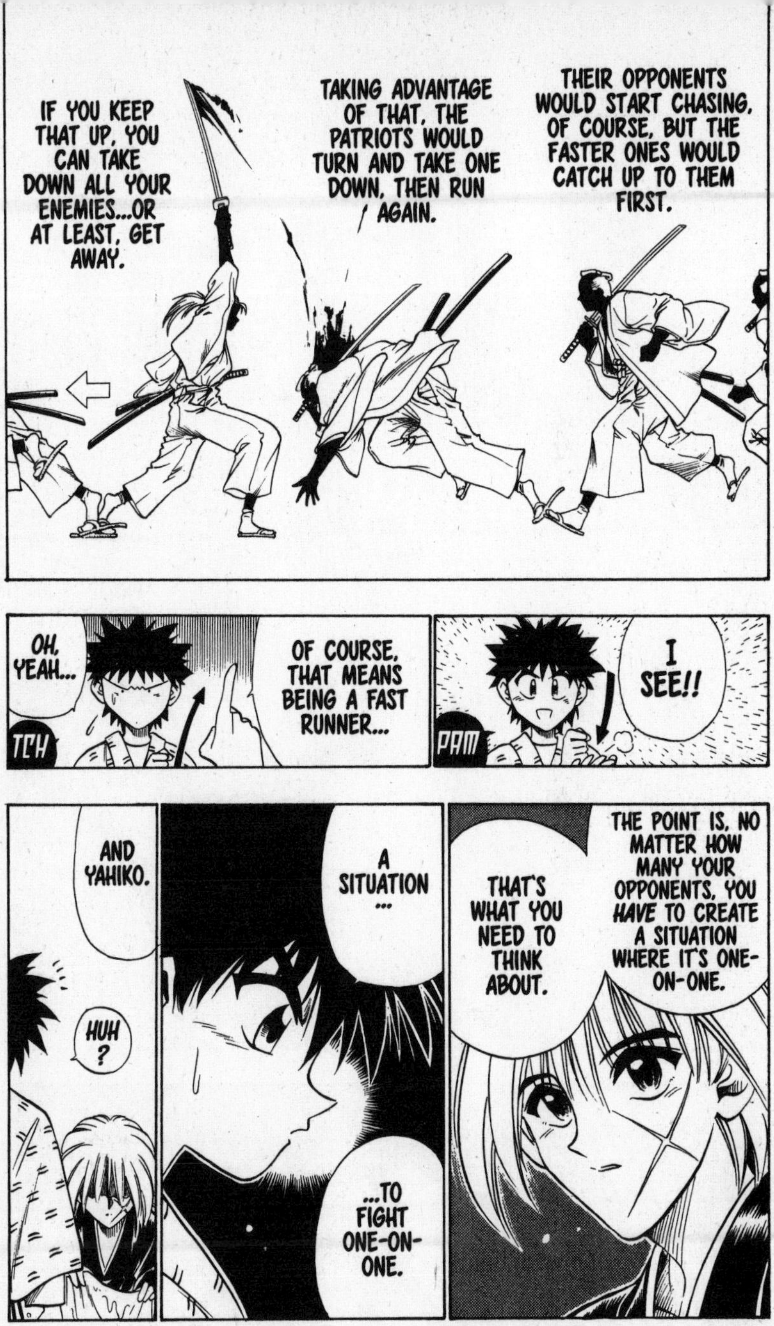
THEIR OPPONENTS WOULD START CHASING, OF COURSE, BUT THE FASTER ONES WOULD CATCH UP TO THEM FIRST.
TAKING ADVANTAGE OF THAT, THE PATRIOTS WOULD TURN AND TAKE ONE DOWN, THEN RUN AGAIN.
IF YOU KEEP THAT UP, YOU CAN TAKE DOWN ALL YOUR ENEMIES...OR AT LEAST, GET AWAY.
I SEE!!
PAM
OF COURSE, THAT MEANS BEING A FAST RUNNER...
OH, YEAH...
TCH
THE POINT IS, NO MATTER HOW MANY YOUR OPPONENTS, YOU *HAVE* TO CREATE A SITUATION WHERE IT'S ONE-ON-ONE.
THAT'S WHAT YOU NEED TO THINK ABOUT.
A SITUATION ...
...TO FIGHT ONE-ON-ONE.
AND YAHIKO.
HUH ?

READ THIS WAY

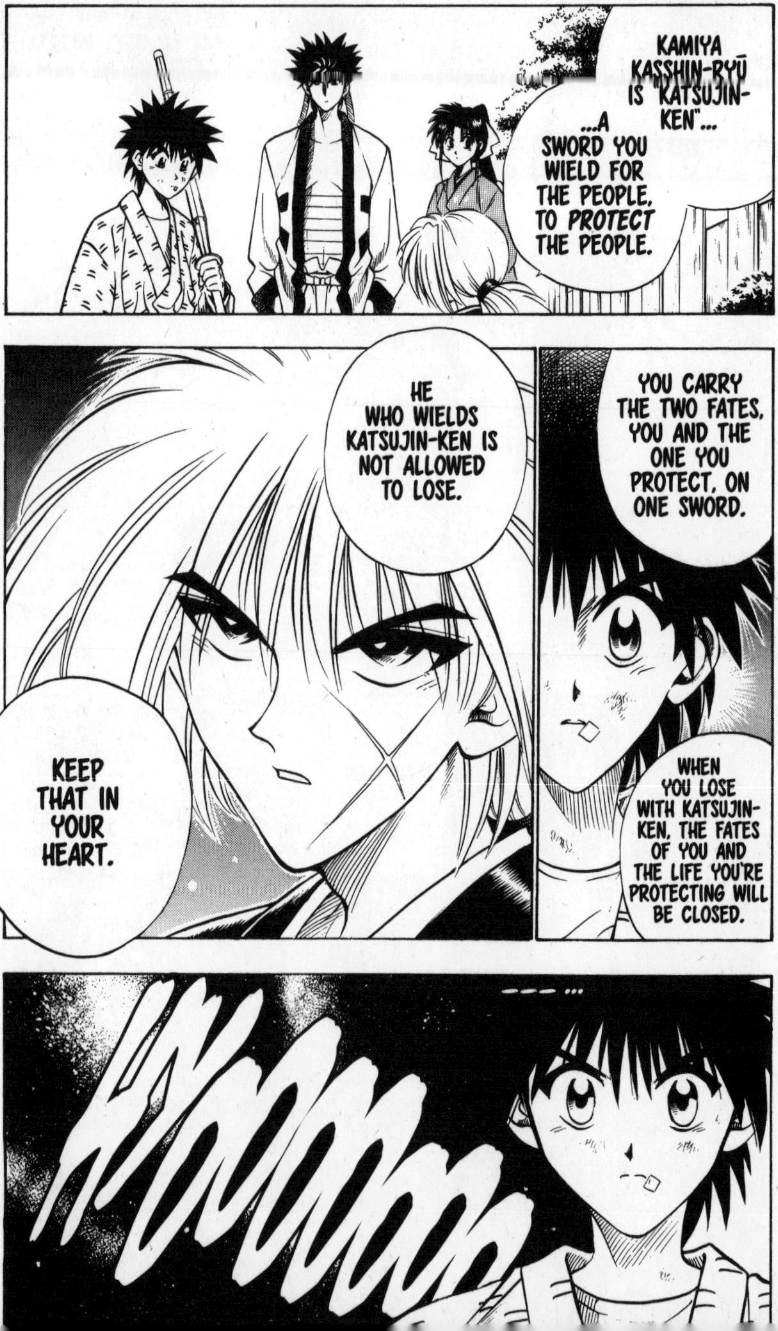
KAMIYA KASSHIN-RYŪ IS "KATSUJIN-KEN"...
...A SWORD YOU WIELD FOR THE PEOPLE, TO PROTECT THE PEOPLE.
YOU CARRY THE TWO FATES, YOU AND THE ONE YOU PROTECT, ON ONE SWORD.
WHEN YOU LOSE WITH KATSUJIN-KEN, THE FATES OF YOU AND THE LIFE YOU'RE PROTECTING WILL BE CLOSED.
HE WHO WIELDS KATSUJIN-KEN IS NOT ALLOWED TO LOSE.
KEEP THAT IN YOUR HEART.

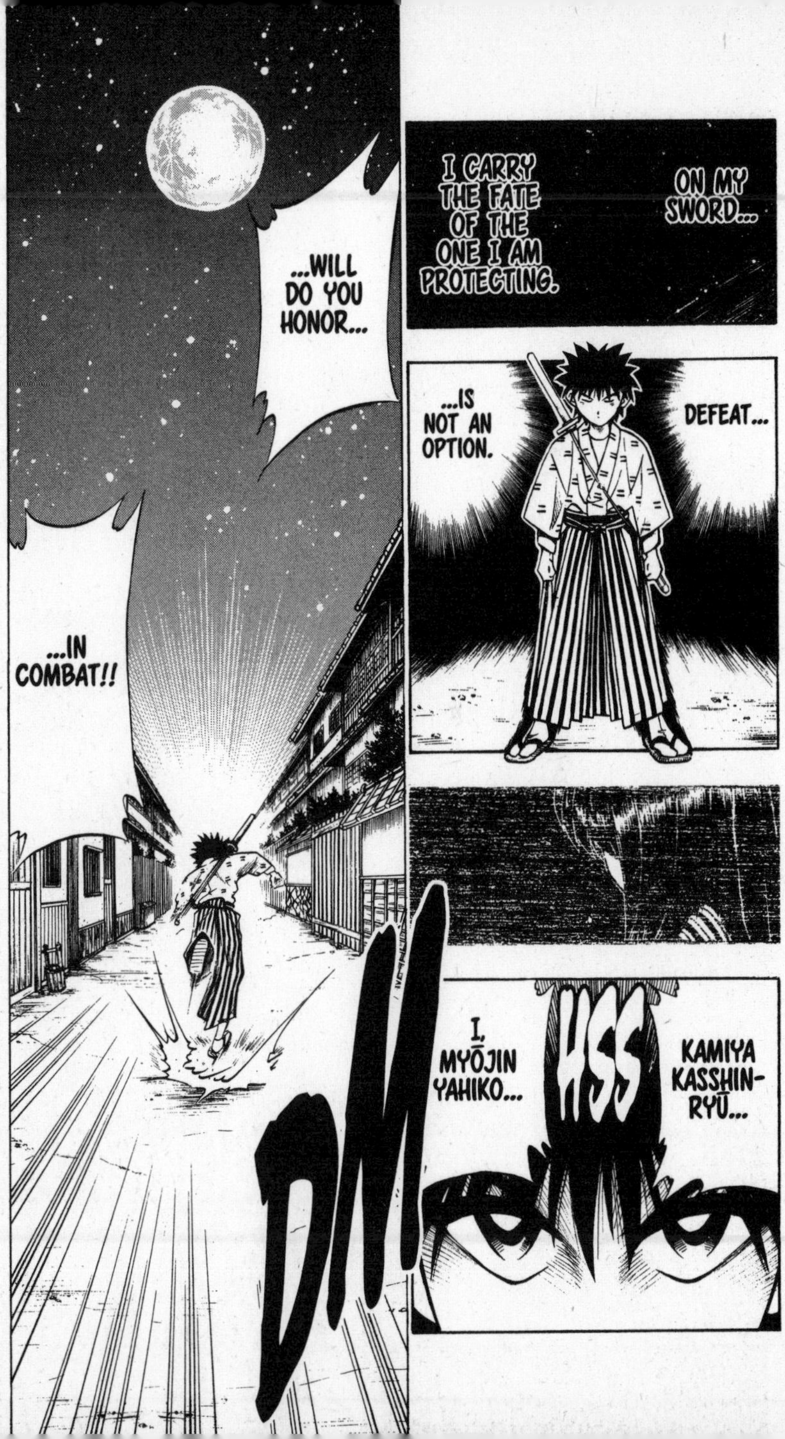
ON MY SWORD...
I CARRY THE FATE OF THE ONE I AM PROTECTING.
DEFEAT...
...IS NOT AN OPTION.
KAMIYA KASSHIN-RYŪ...
HSS
I, MYŌJIN YAHIKO...
DM
...WILL DO YOU HONOR...
...IN COMBAT!!

Rurouni Kenshin

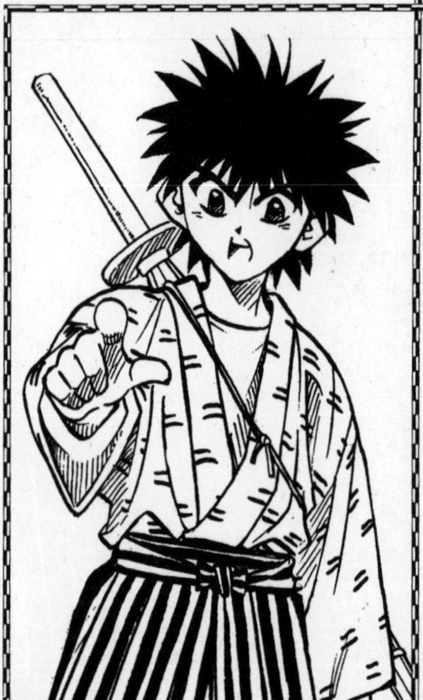

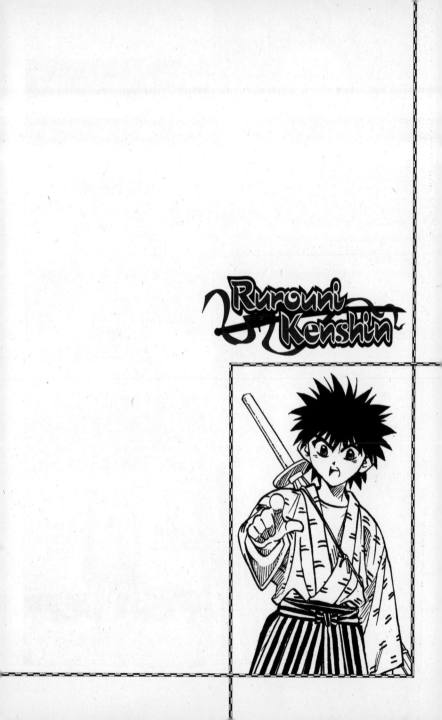

# Act 33 Bonus Story: Yahiko's Battle (3)

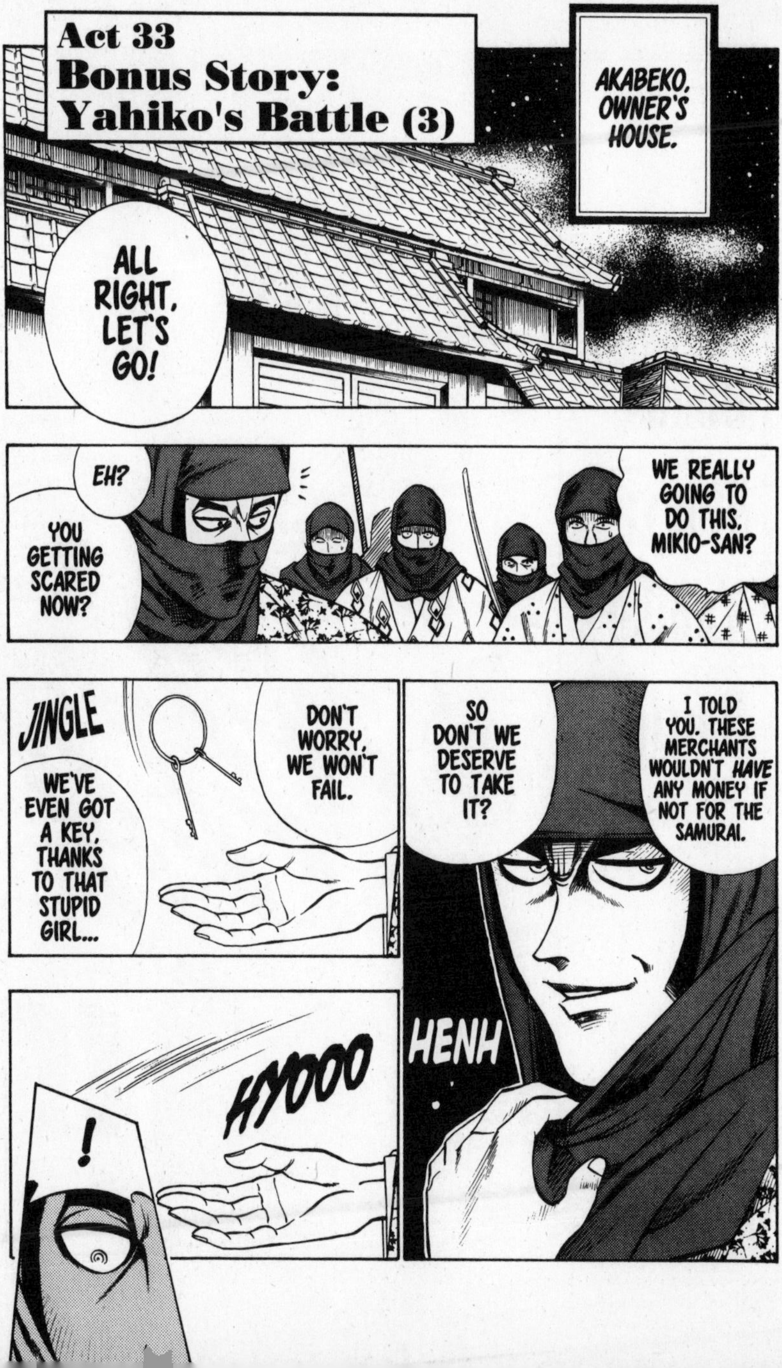
AKABEKO, OWNER'S HOUSE.
ALL RIGHT, LET'S GO!
WE REALLY GOING TO DO THIS, MIKIO-SAN?
EH?
YOU GETTING SCARED NOW?
I TOLD YOU. THESE MERCHANTS WOULDN'T *HAVE* ANY MONEY IF NOT FOR THE SAMURAI.
SO DON'T WE DESERVE TO TAKE IT?
HENH
DON'T WORRY, WE WON'T FAIL.
JINGLE
WE'VE EVEN GOT A KEY, THANKS TO THAT STUPID GIRL...
HYOOO
!

READ THIS WAY

# Act 33 Bonus Story: Yahiko's Battle (3)

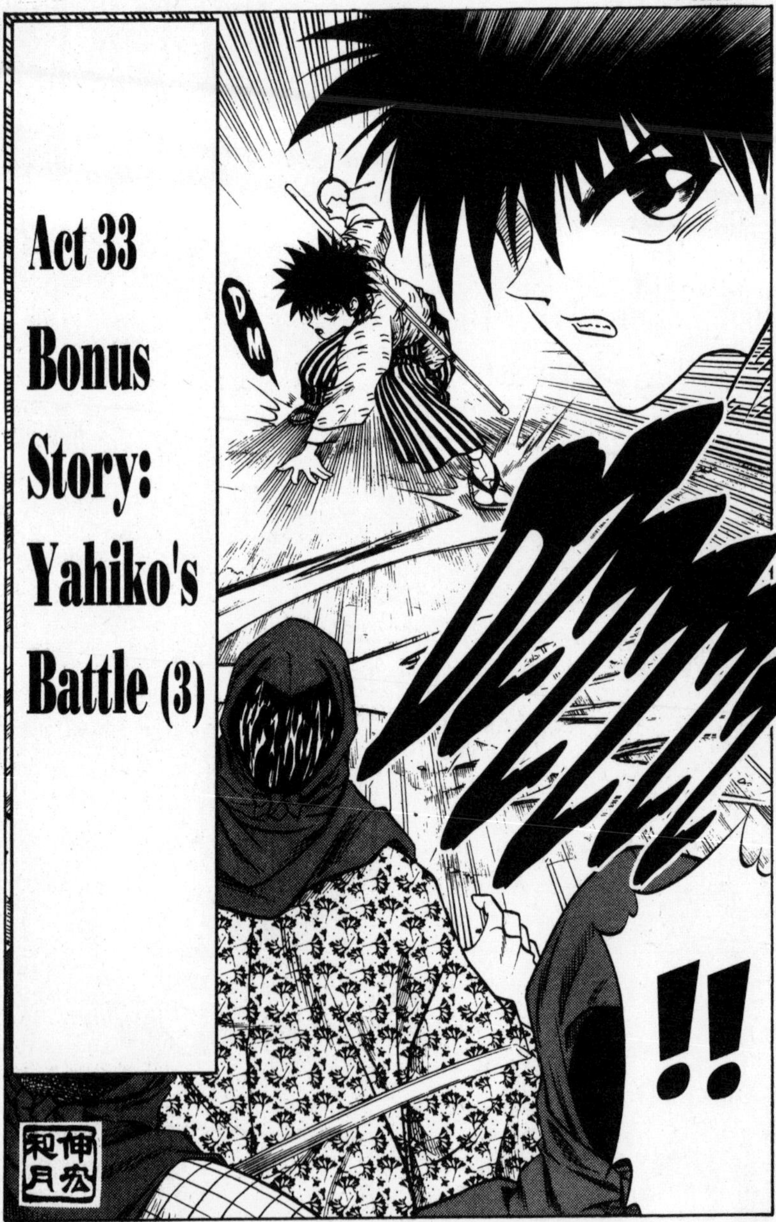
DM
!!

READ THIS WAY

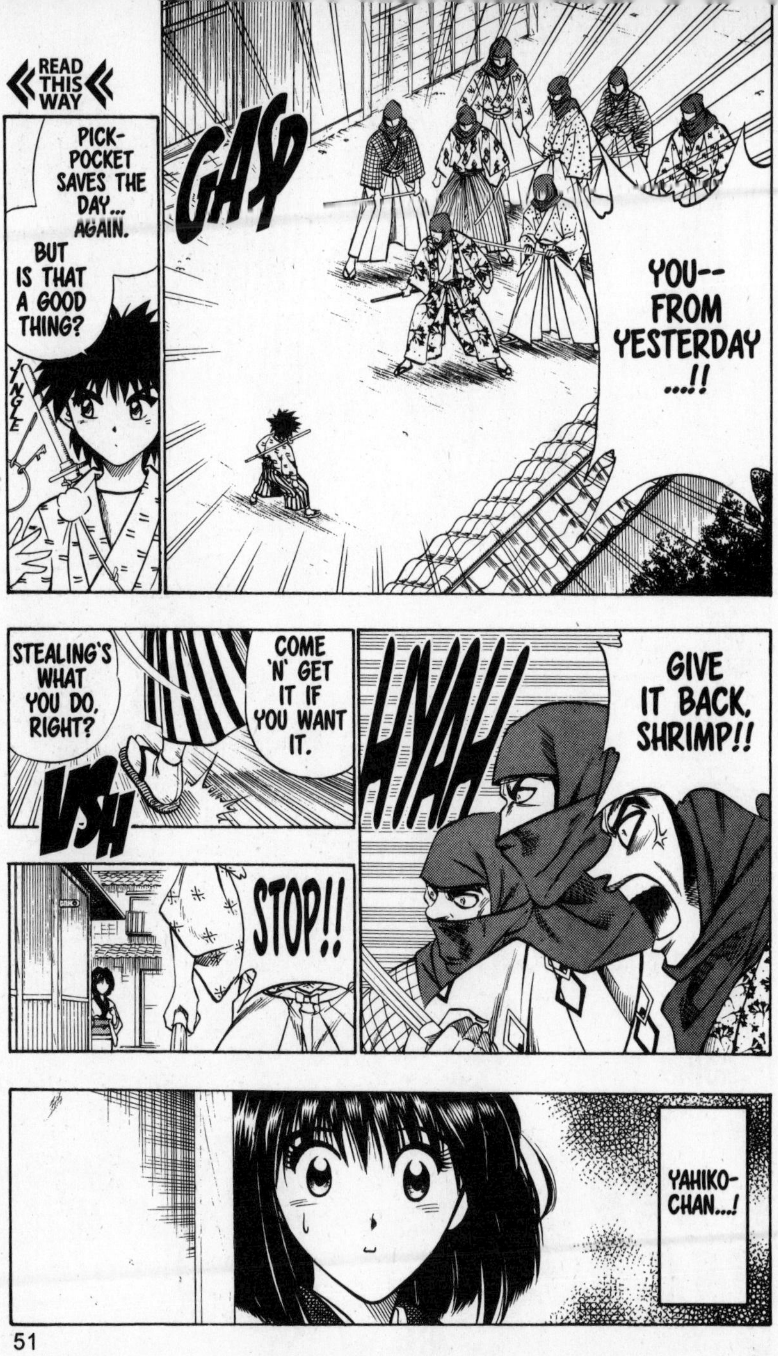

GASP
YOU-- FROM YESTERDAY ...!!
PICK-POCKET SAVES THE DAY... AGAIN.
BUT IS THAT A GOOD THING?
JINGLE
HYAH
GIVE IT BACK, SHRIMP!!
COME 'N' GET IT IF YOU WANT IT.
STEALING'S WHAT YOU DO, RIGHT?
VSH
STOP!!
YAHIKO-CHAN...!

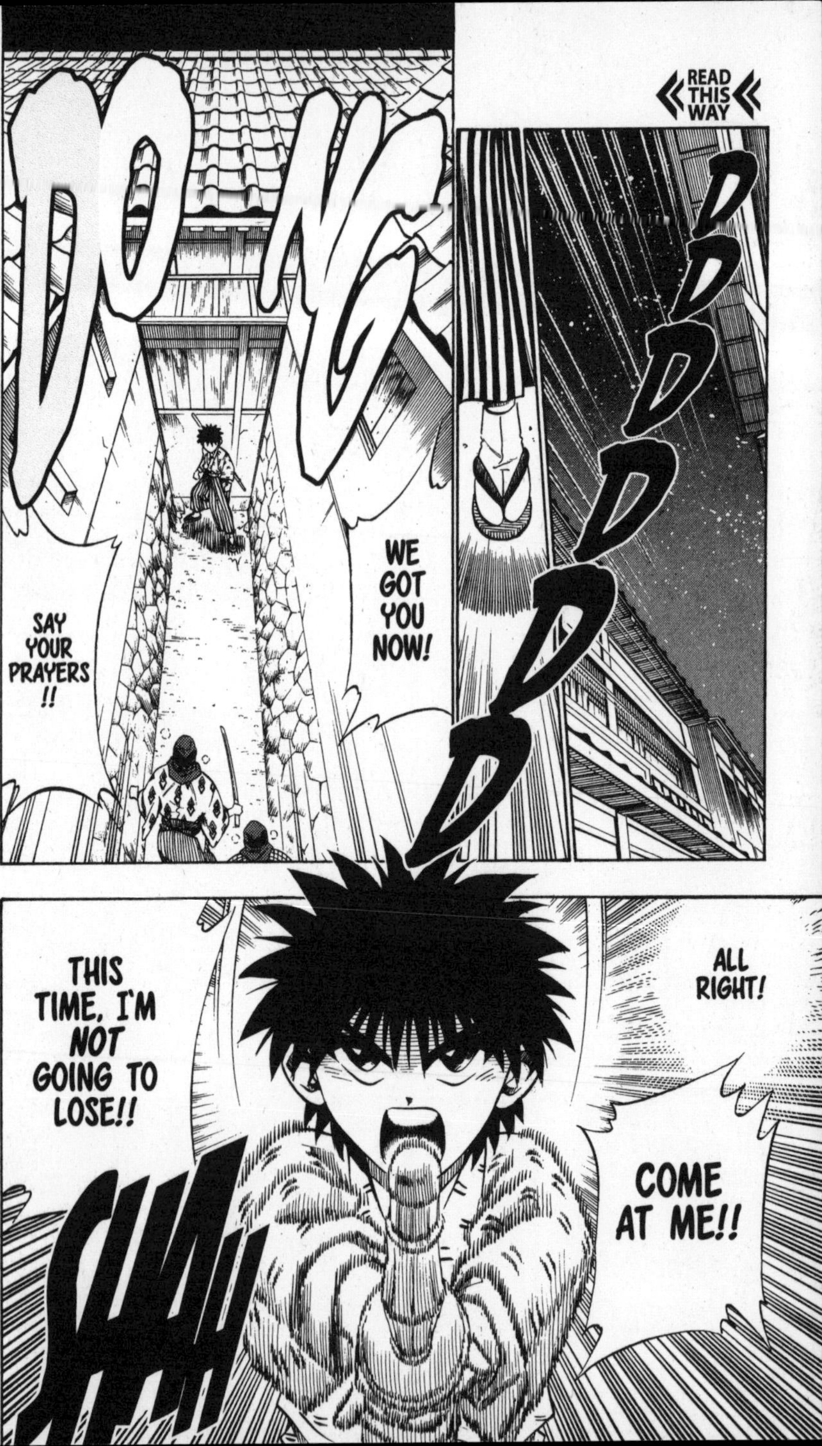
READ THIS WAY
DONG
WE GOT YOU NOW!
SAY YOUR PRAYERS!!
ALL RIGHT!
COME AT ME!!
THIS TIME, I'M NOT GOING TO LOSE!!

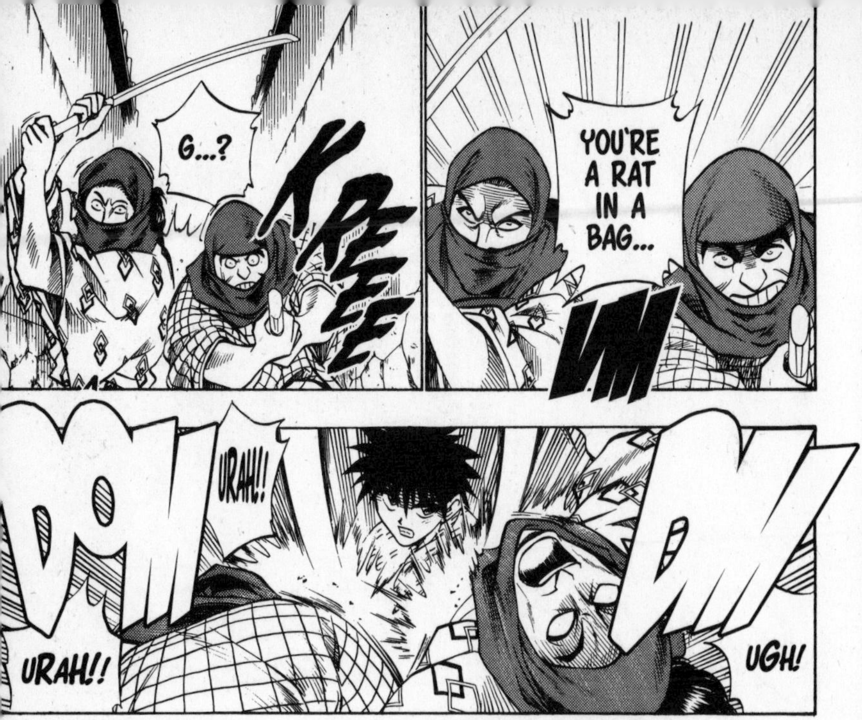
YOU'RE A RAT IN A BAG...
VM
G...?
KREEEE
UGH!
URAH!!
URAH!!

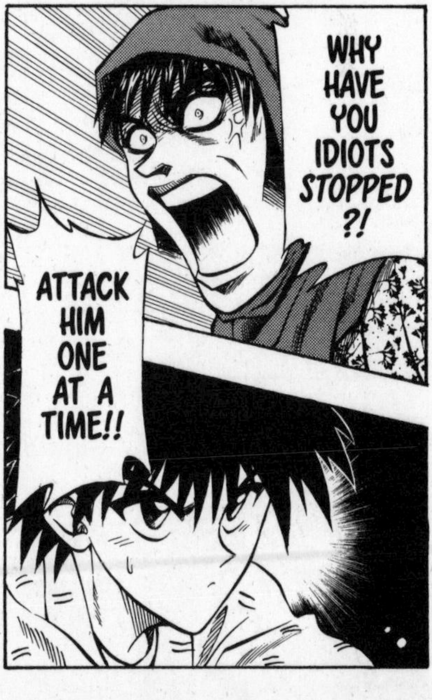
WHY HAVE YOU IDIOTS STOPPED ?!
ATTACK HIM ONE AT A TIME!!

Seems I'll finally have a chance to get to those fan letters. Just a little while longer, please! I haven't even had time to read the letters recently—and that's not something I'm proud of—but I do plan to make time and read them all. Reading them gives me energy, as usual; some even make me want to say to their authors, "Whoa, whoa, take it easy, huh?" (Even those letters put a smile on my face, though.)

伸宏
和月

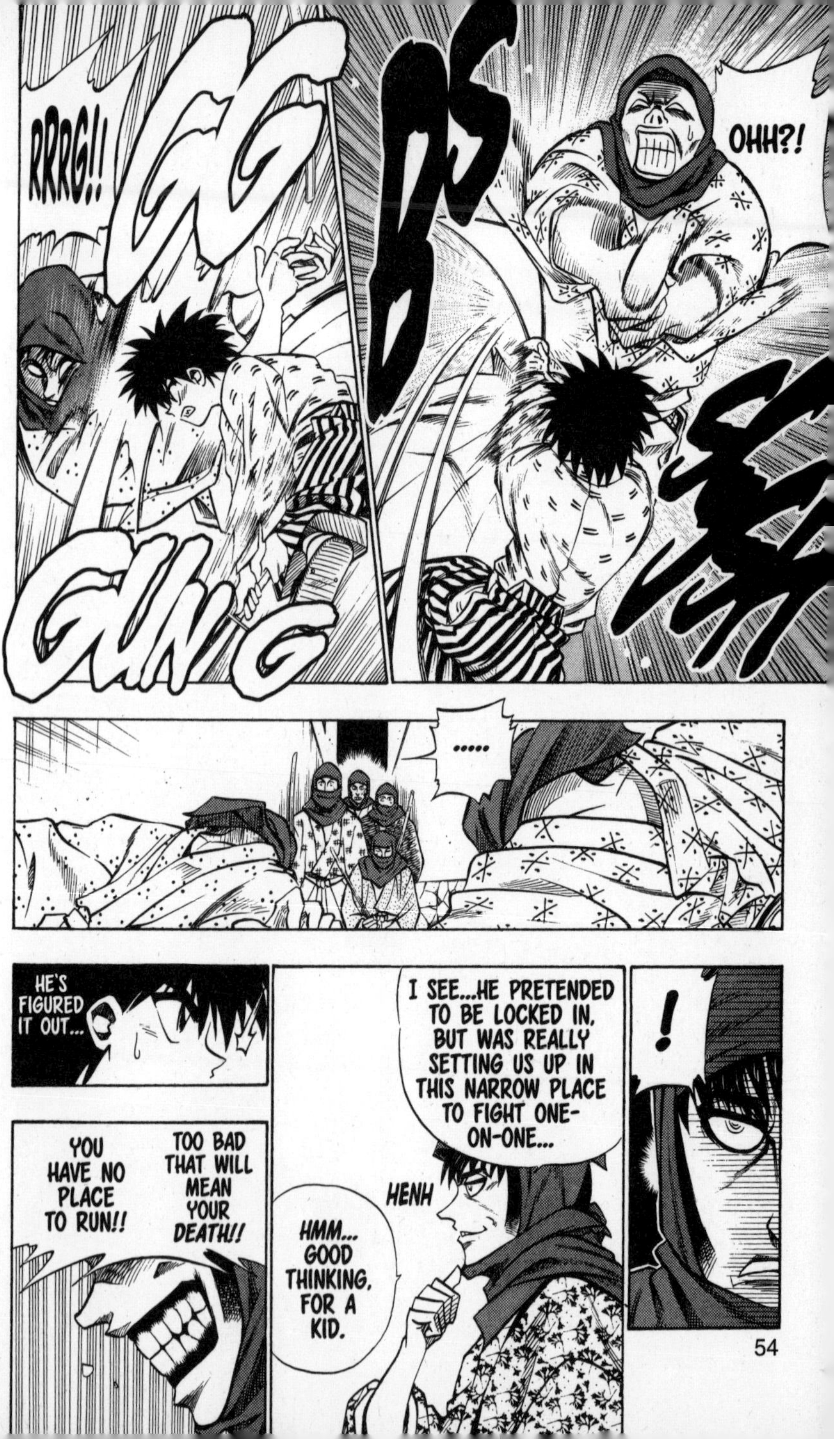
OHH?!
RRRG!!
GUNG
.....
!
I SEE...HE PRETENDED TO BE LOCKED IN, BUT WAS REALLY SETTING US UP IN THIS NARROW PLACE TO FIGHT ONE-ON-ONE...
HENH
HMM... GOOD THINKING, FOR A KID.
HE'S FIGURED IT OUT...
TOO BAD THAT WILL MEAN YOUR DEATH!!
YOU HAVE NO PLACE TO RUN!!

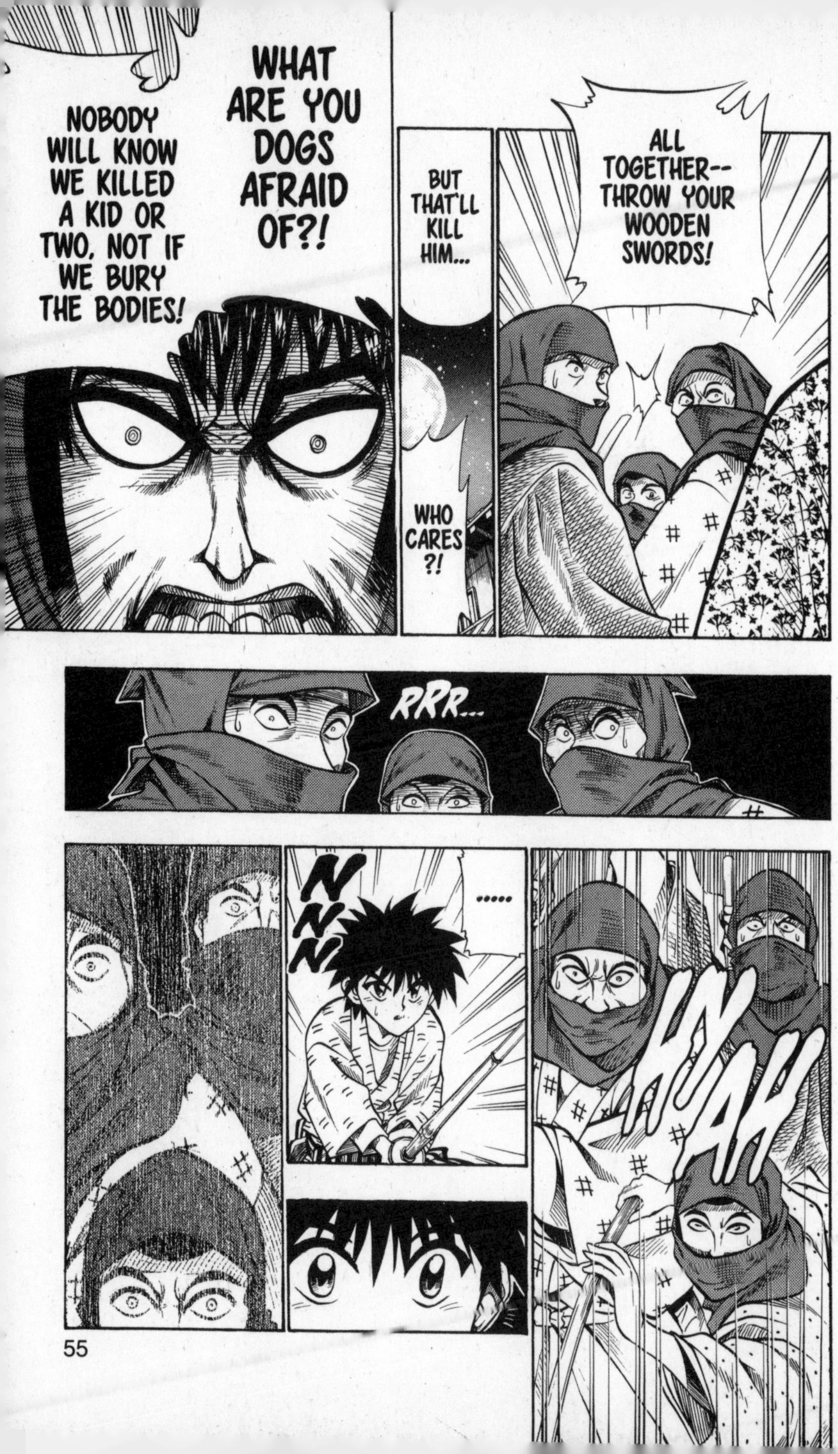
ALL TOGETHER-- THROW YOUR WOODEN SWORDS!
BUT THAT'LL KILL HIM...
WHO CARES?!
WHAT ARE YOU DOGS AFRAID OF?!
NOBODY WILL KNOW WE KILLED A KID OR TWO, NOT IF WE BURY THE BODIES!
RRR...
HN
WAH
NNN
.....

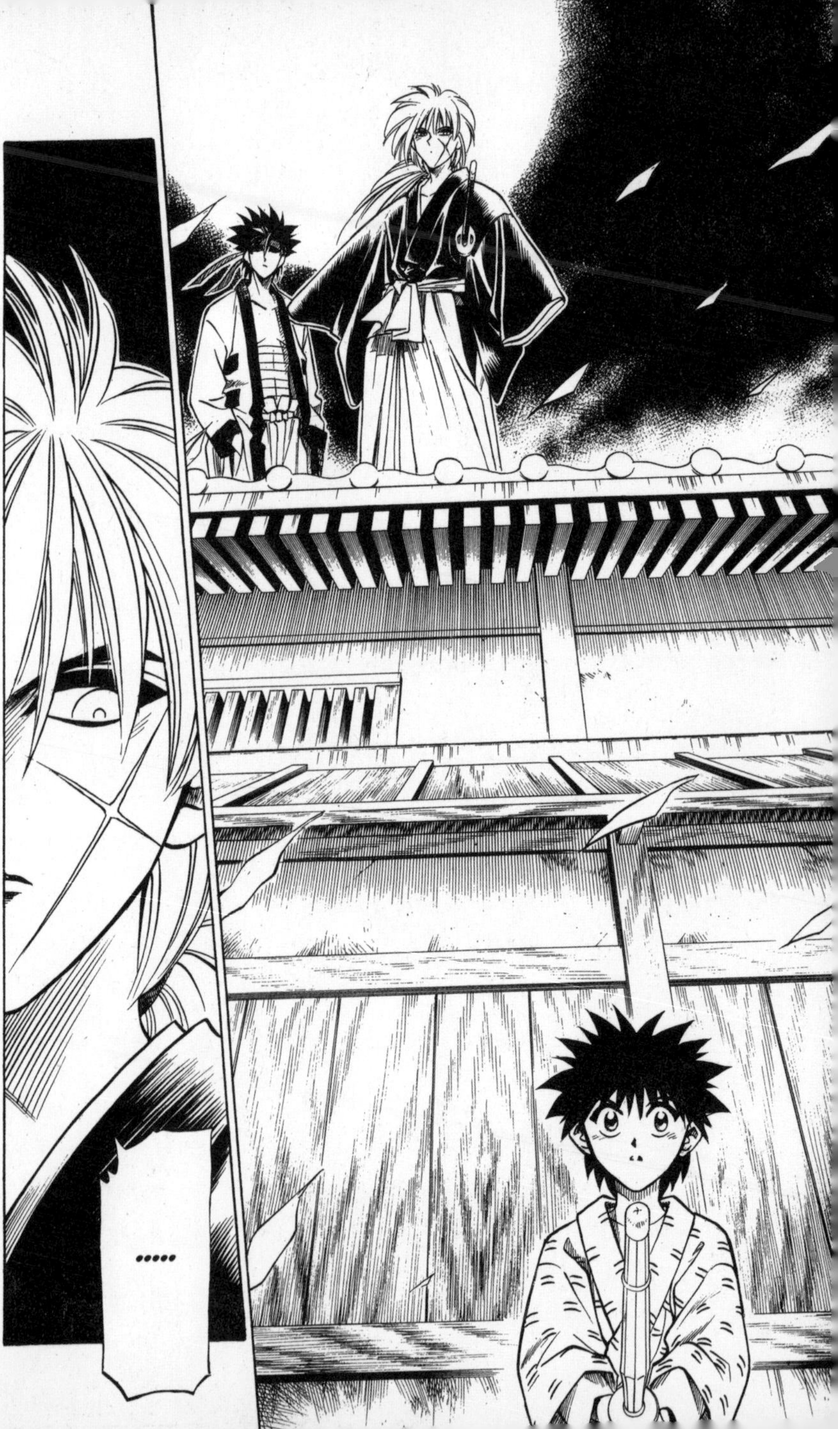
.....

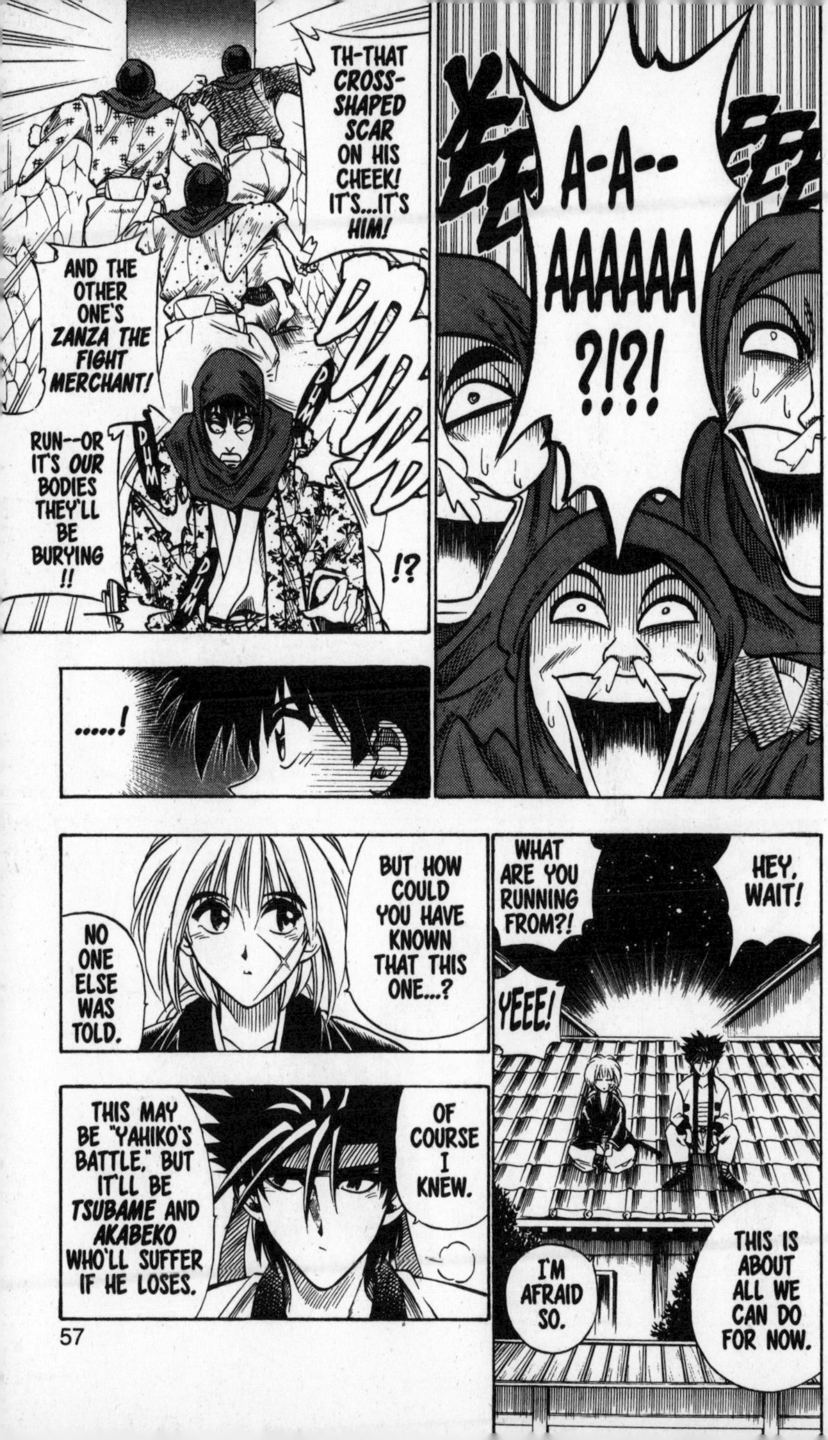
A-A--
AAAAAA
?!?!
TH-THAT CROSS-SHAPED SCAR ON HIS CHEEK! IT'S...IT'S HIM!
AND THE OTHER ONE'S ZANZA THE FIGHT MERCHANT!
RUN--OR IT'S OUR BODIES THEY'LL BE BURYING!!
!?
.....!
HEY, WAIT!
WHAT ARE YOU RUNNING FROM?!
YEEE!
THIS IS ABOUT ALL WE CAN DO FOR NOW.
I'M AFRAID SO.
BUT HOW COULD YOU HAVE KNOWN THAT THIS ONE...?
NO ONE ELSE WAS TOLD.
OF COURSE I KNEW.
THIS MAY BE "YAHIKO'S BATTLE," BUT IT'LL BE TSUBAME AND AKABEKO WHO'LL SUFFER IF HE LOSES.

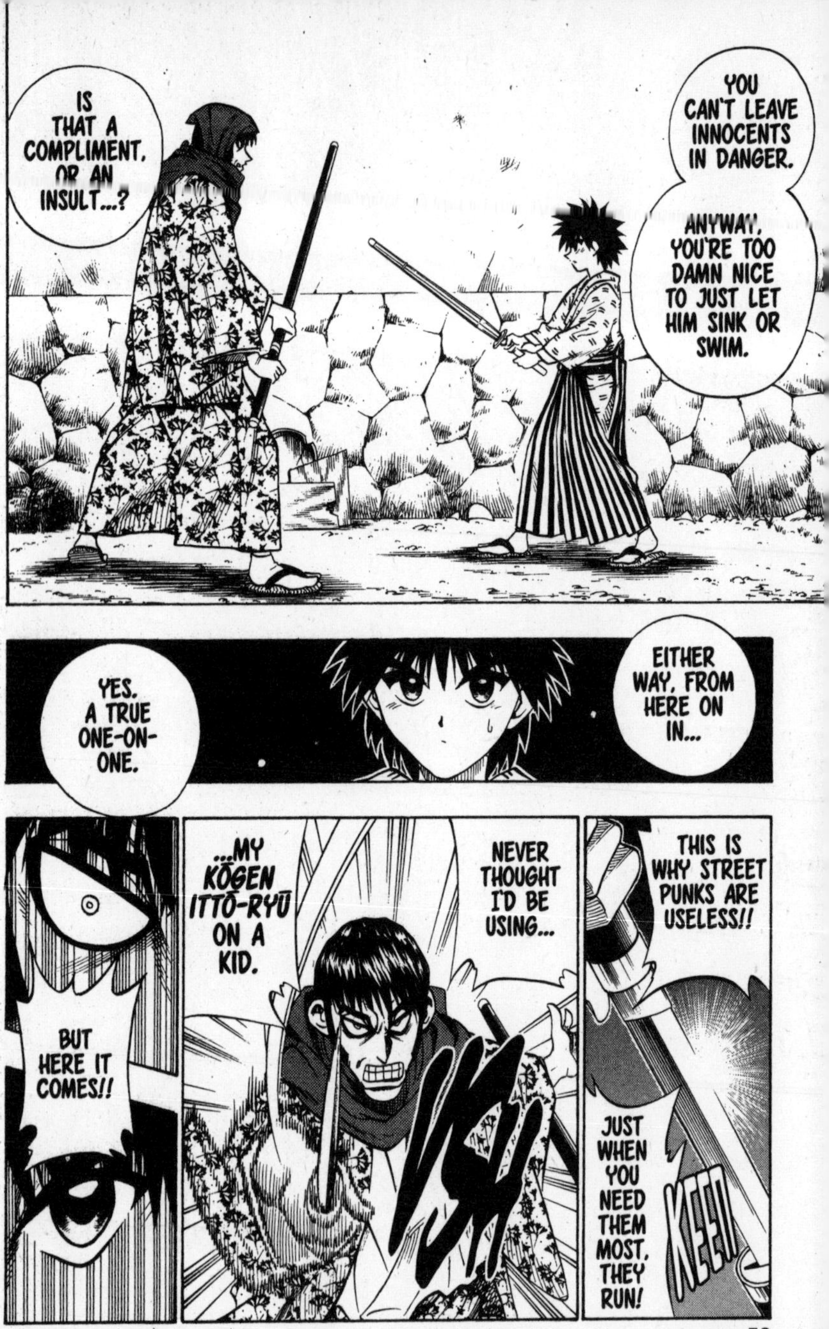
YOU CAN'T LEAVE INNOCENTS IN DANGER.
ANYWAY, YOU'RE TOO DAMN NICE TO JUST LET HIM SINK OR SWIM.
IS THAT A COMPLIMENT, OR AN INSULT...?
EITHER WAY, FROM HERE ON IN...
YES. A TRUE ONE-ON-ONE.
THIS IS WHY STREET PUNKS ARE USELESS!!
JUST WHEN YOU NEED THEM MOST, THEY RUN!
KEEN
NEVER THOUGHT I'D BE USING...
...MY KŌGEN ITTŌ-RYŪ ON A KID.
VSH
BUT HERE IT COMES!!

READ THIS WAY

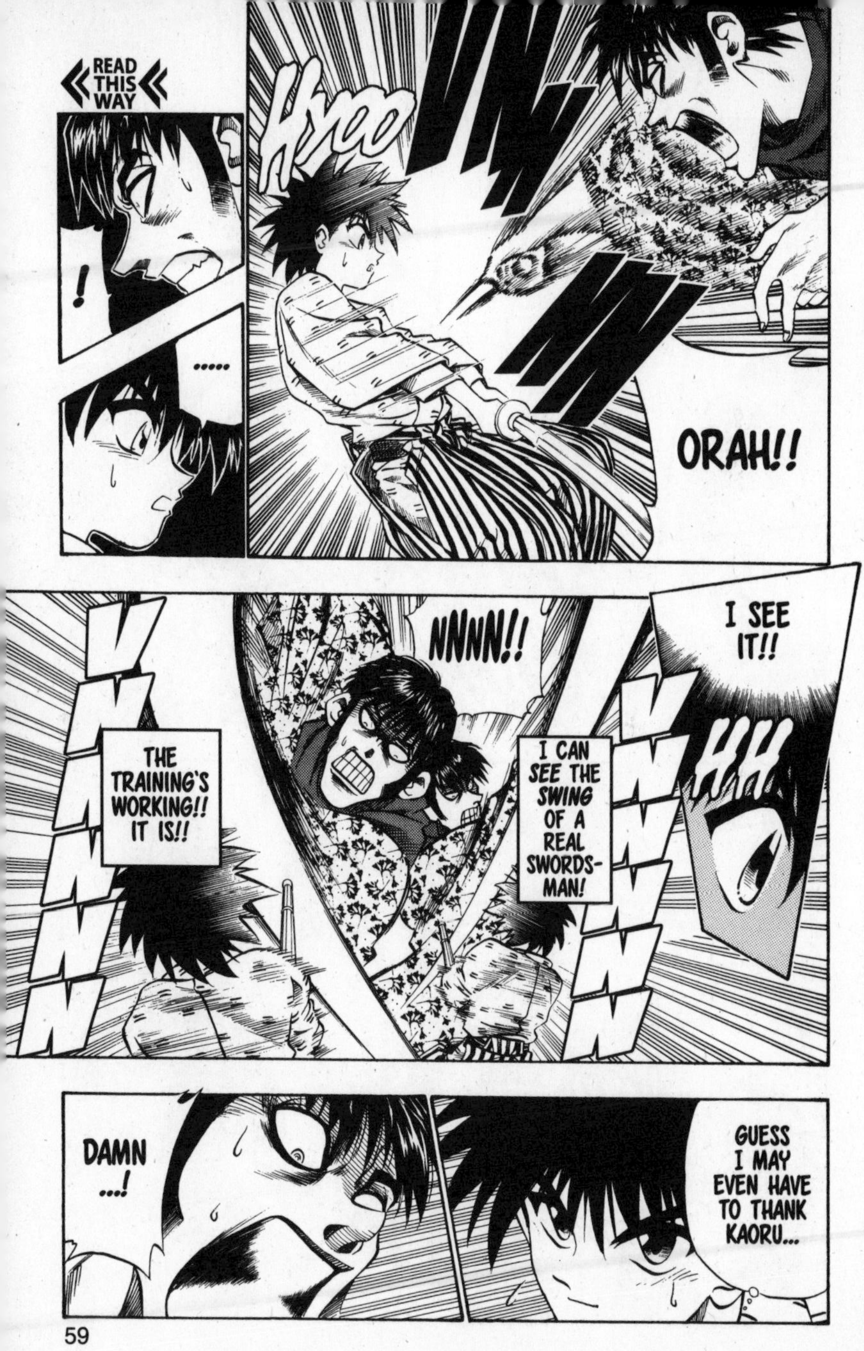
HYOO
VINN
NNN
ORAH!!
!
.....
I SEE IT!!
HH
NNNN!!
I CAN SEE THE SWING OF A REAL SWORDSMAN!
VNNNNNN
THE TRAINING'S WORKING!! IT IS!!
VNNNNN
GUESS I MAY EVEN HAVE TO THANK KAORU...
DAMN ...!

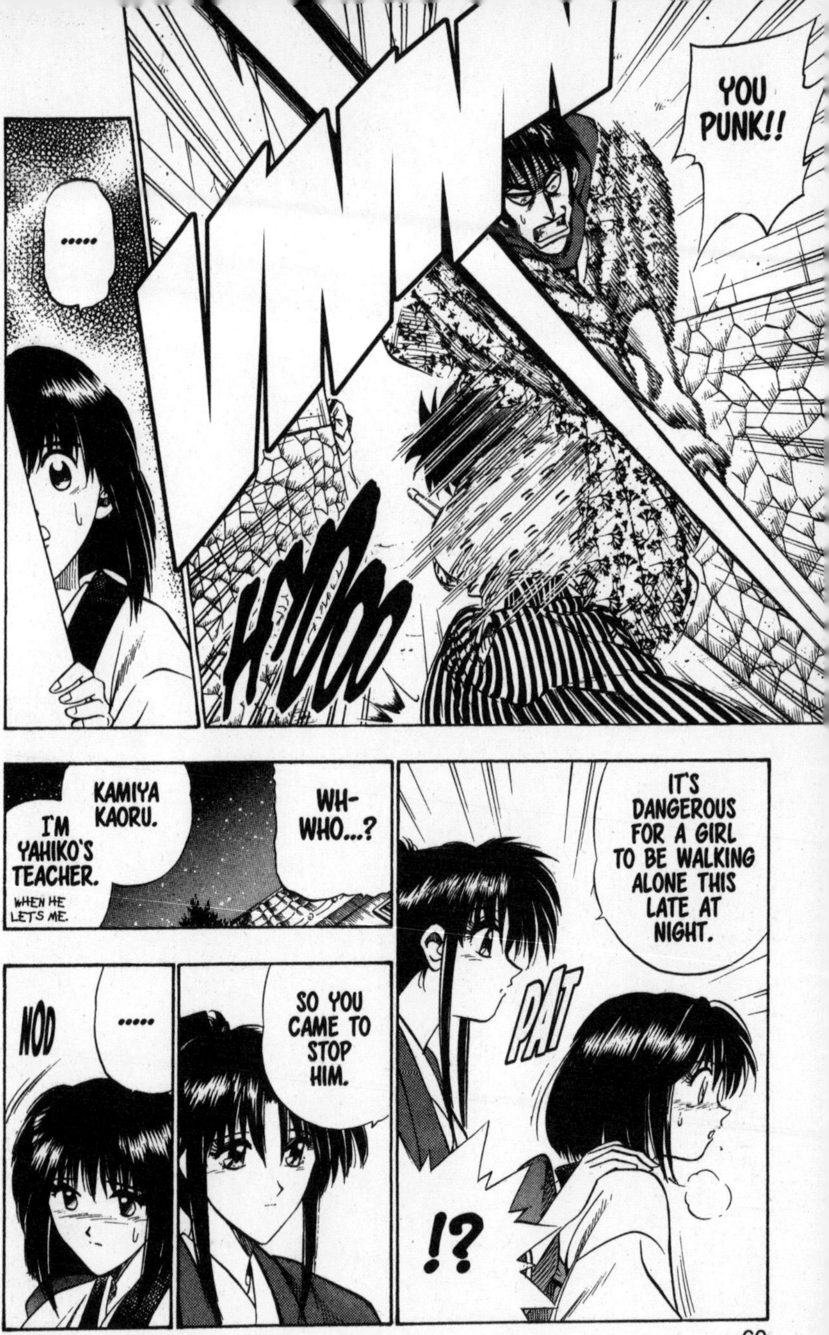
YOU PUNK!!
......
IT'S DANGEROUS FOR A GIRL TO BE WALKING ALONE THIS LATE AT NIGHT.
PAT
!?
WH- WHO...?
KAMIYA KAORU.
I'M YAHIKO'S TEACHER.
WHEN HE LETS ME.
SO YOU CAME TO STOP HIM.
NOD
......

READ THIS WAY

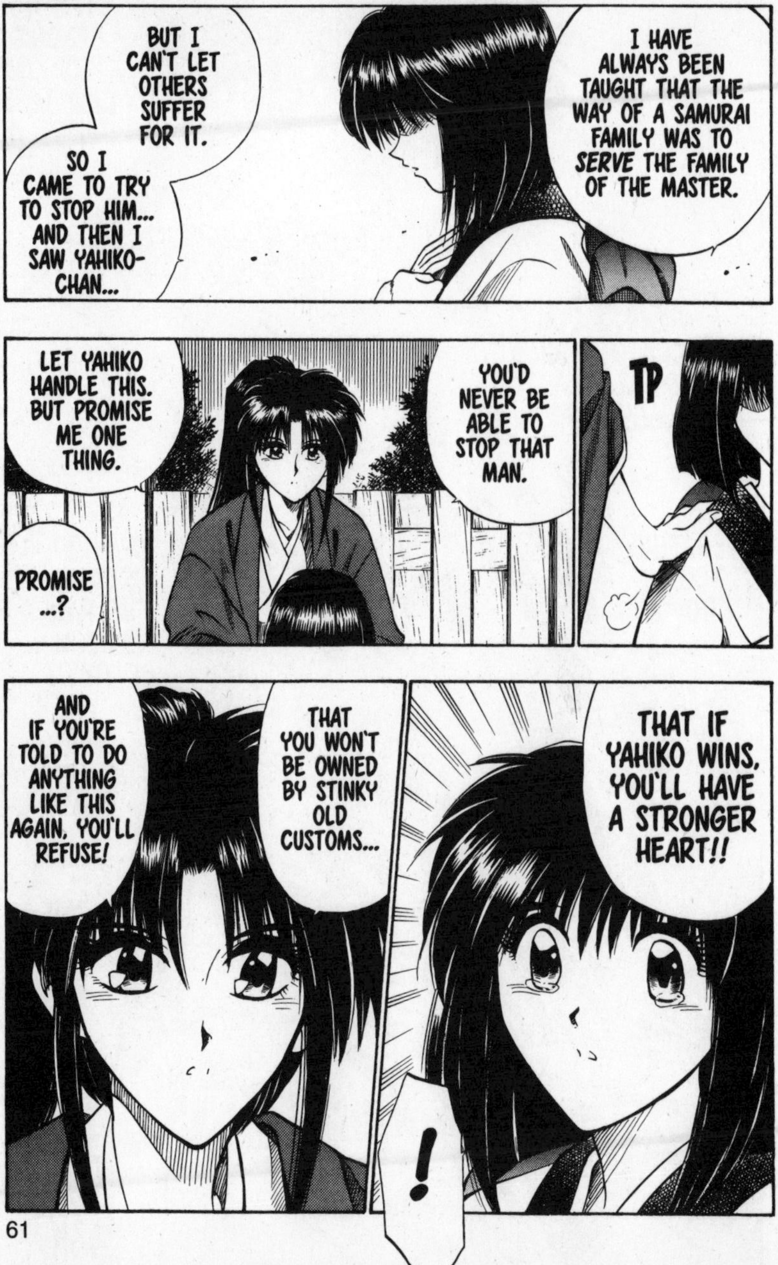
I HAVE ALWAYS BEEN TAUGHT THAT THE WAY OF A SAMURAI FAMILY WAS TO *SERVE* THE FAMILY OF THE MASTER.
BUT I CAN'T LET OTHERS SUFFER FOR IT.
SO I CAME TO TRY TO STOP HIM... AND THEN I SAW YAHIKO-CHAN...
TP
YOU'D NEVER BE ABLE TO STOP THAT MAN.
LET YAHIKO HANDLE THIS. BUT PROMISE ME ONE THING.
PROMISE ...?
THAT IF YAHIKO WINS, YOU'LL HAVE A STRONGER HEART!!
!
THAT YOU WON'T BE OWNED BY STINKY OLD CUSTOMS...
AND IF YOU'RE TOLD TO DO ANYTHING LIKE THIS AGAIN, YOU'LL REFUSE!

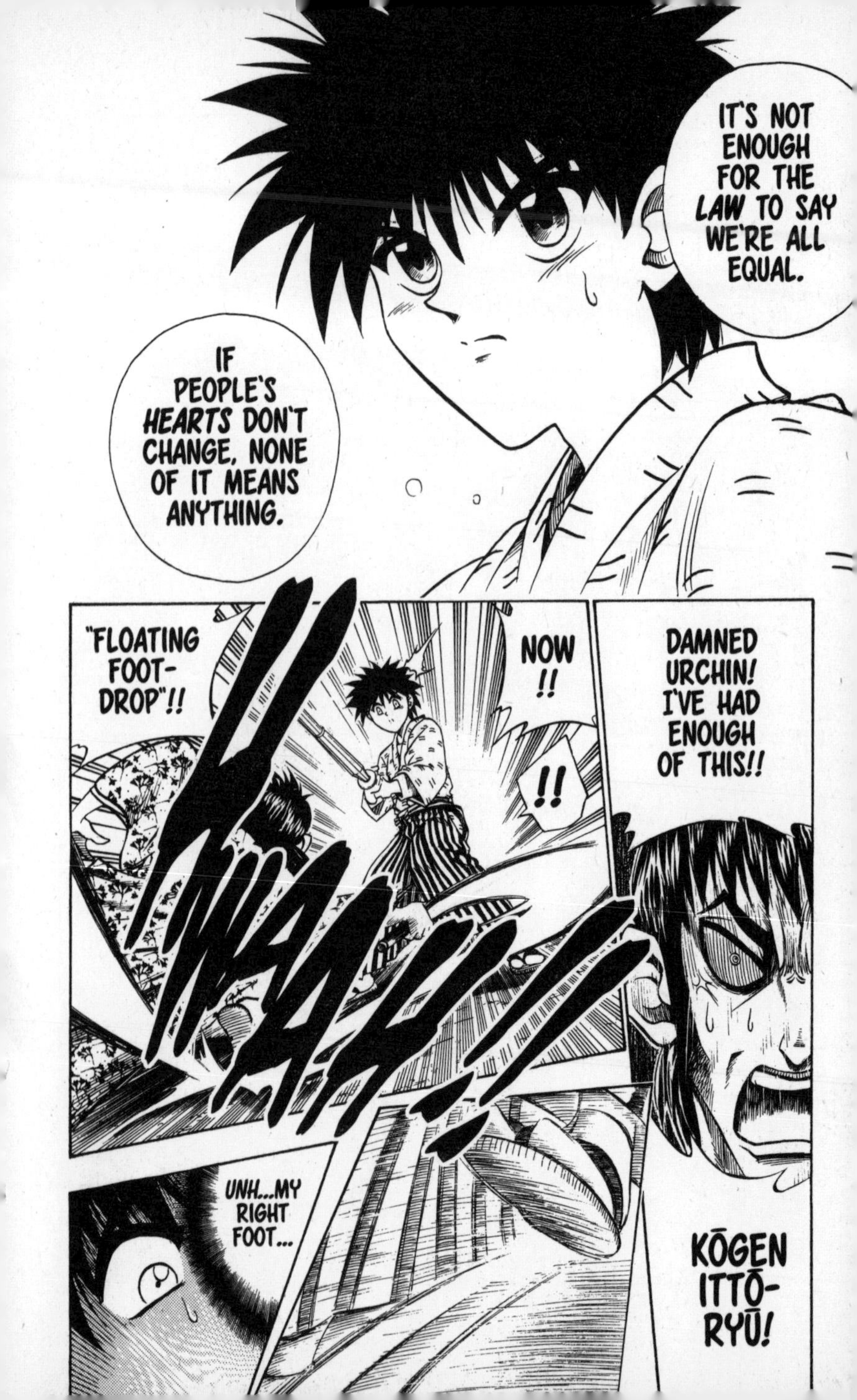
IT'S NOT ENOUGH FOR THE LAW TO SAY WE'RE ALL EQUAL.
IF PEOPLE'S HEARTS DON'T CHANGE, NONE OF IT MEANS ANYTHING.
DAMNED URCHIN! I'VE HAD ENOUGH OF THIS!!
KŌGEN ITTŌ-RYŪ!
!!
NOW !!
"FLOATING FOOT-DROP"!!
UNH...MY RIGHT FOOT...

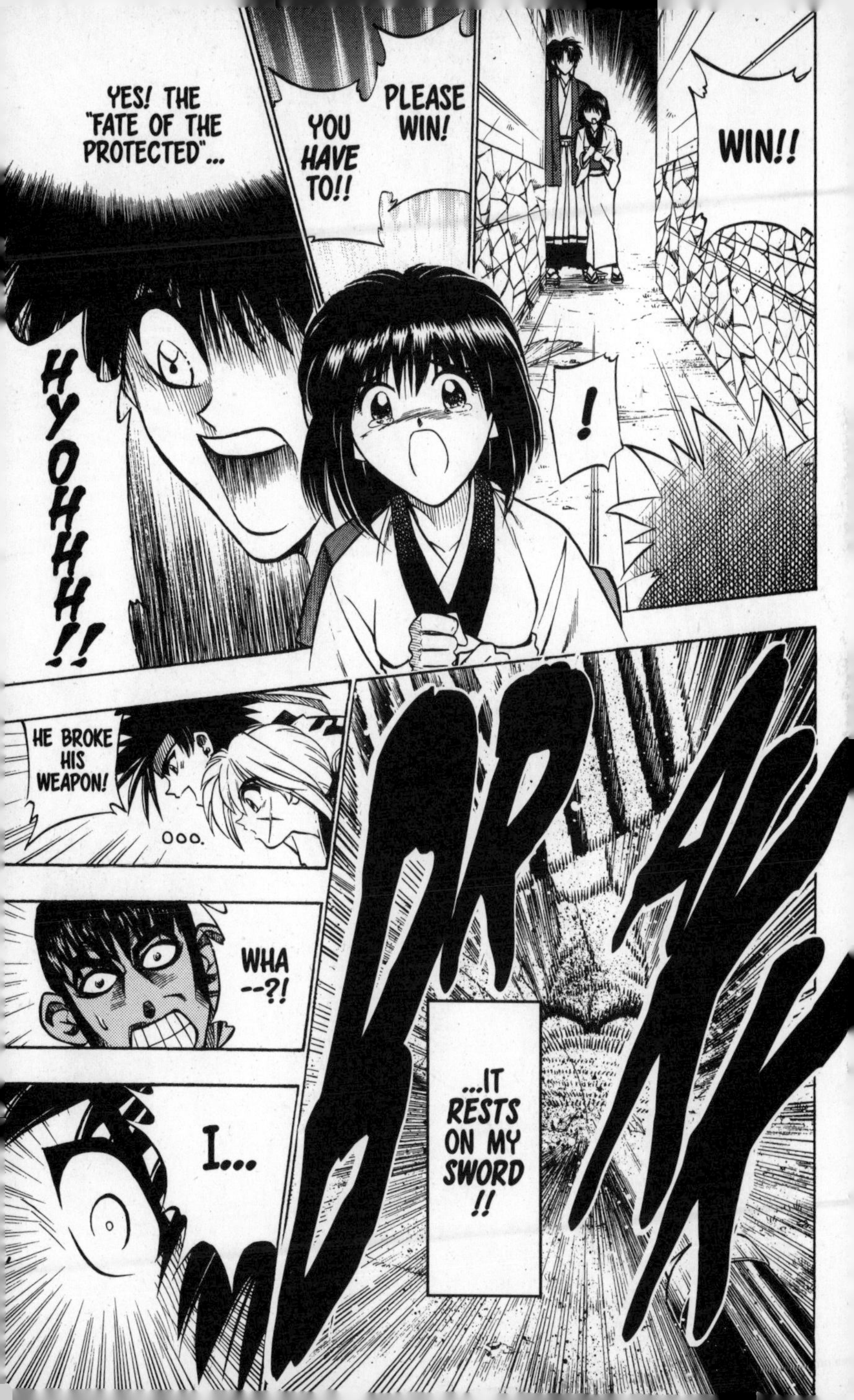
WIN!!
PLEASE WIN!
YOU HAVE TO!!
!
YES! THE "FATE OF THE PROTECTED"...
HYOHHHH!!
...IT RESTS ON MY SWORD !!
HE BROKE HIS WEAPON!
ooo.
WHA --?!
I...

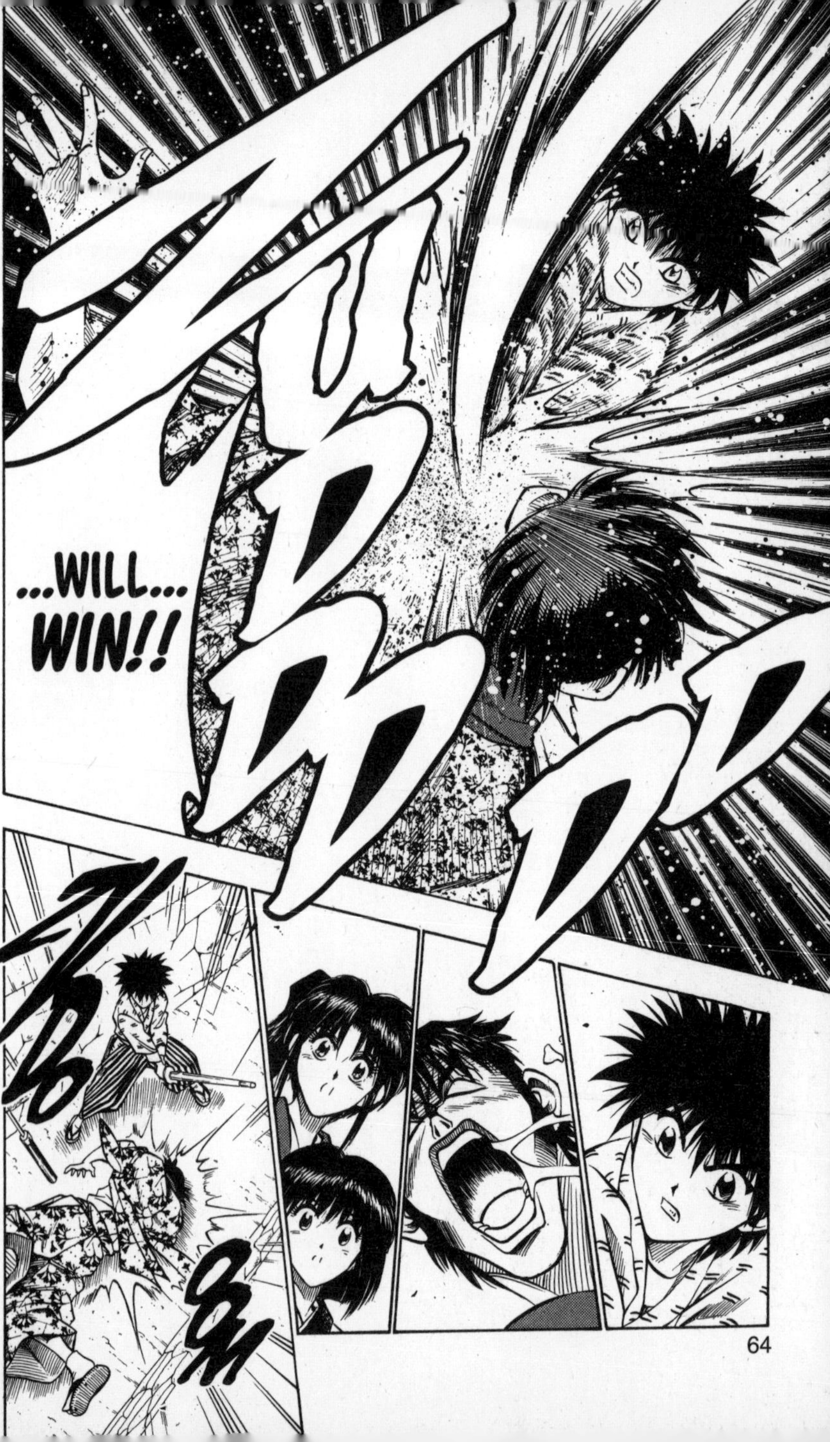
...WILL... WIN!!

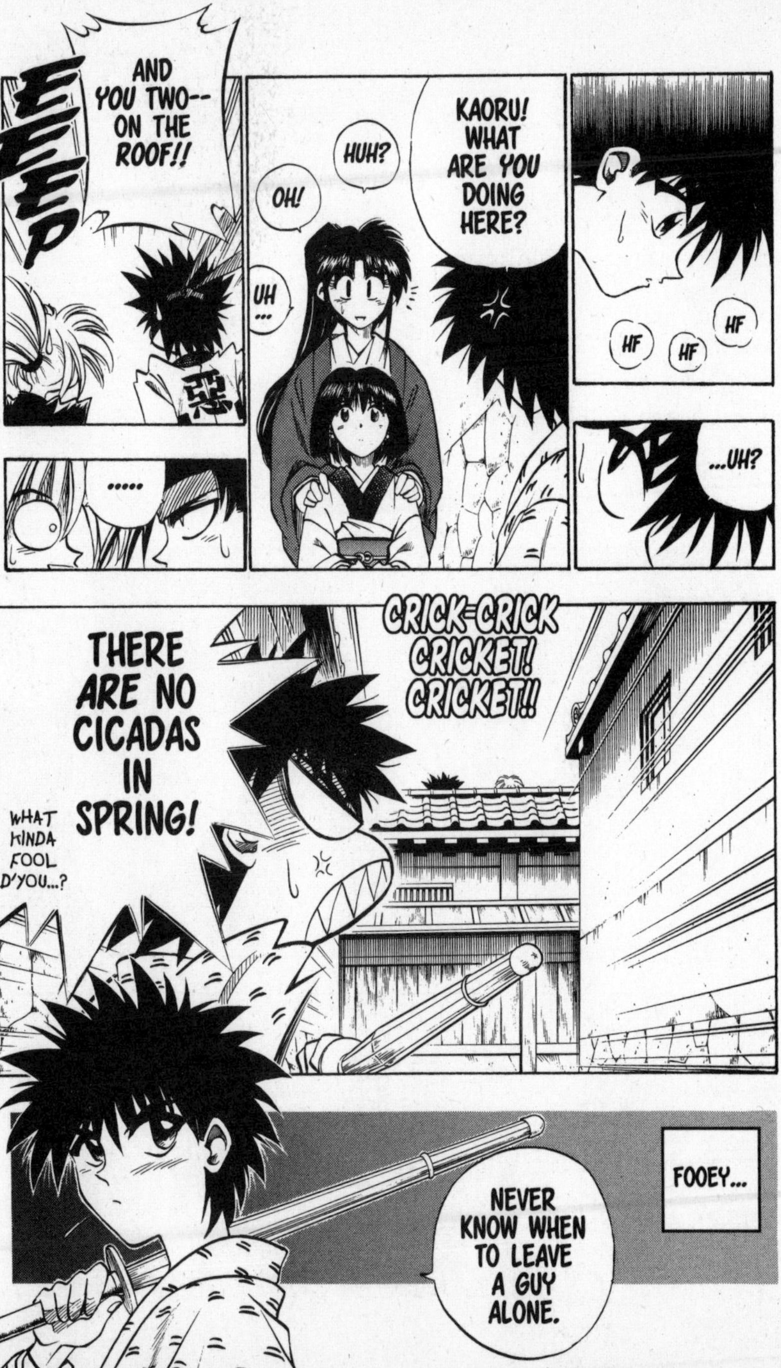
HF
HF
HF
...UH?
KAORU! WHAT ARE YOU DOING HERE?
HUH?
OH!
UH...
AND YOU TWO-- ON THE ROOF!!
EEEEP
.....
CRICK-CRICK CRICKET! CRICKET!!
THERE ARE NO CICADAS IN SPRING!
WHAT KINDA FOOL D'YOU...?
FOOEY...
NEVER KNOW WHEN TO LEAVE A GUY ALONE.

READ THIS WAY

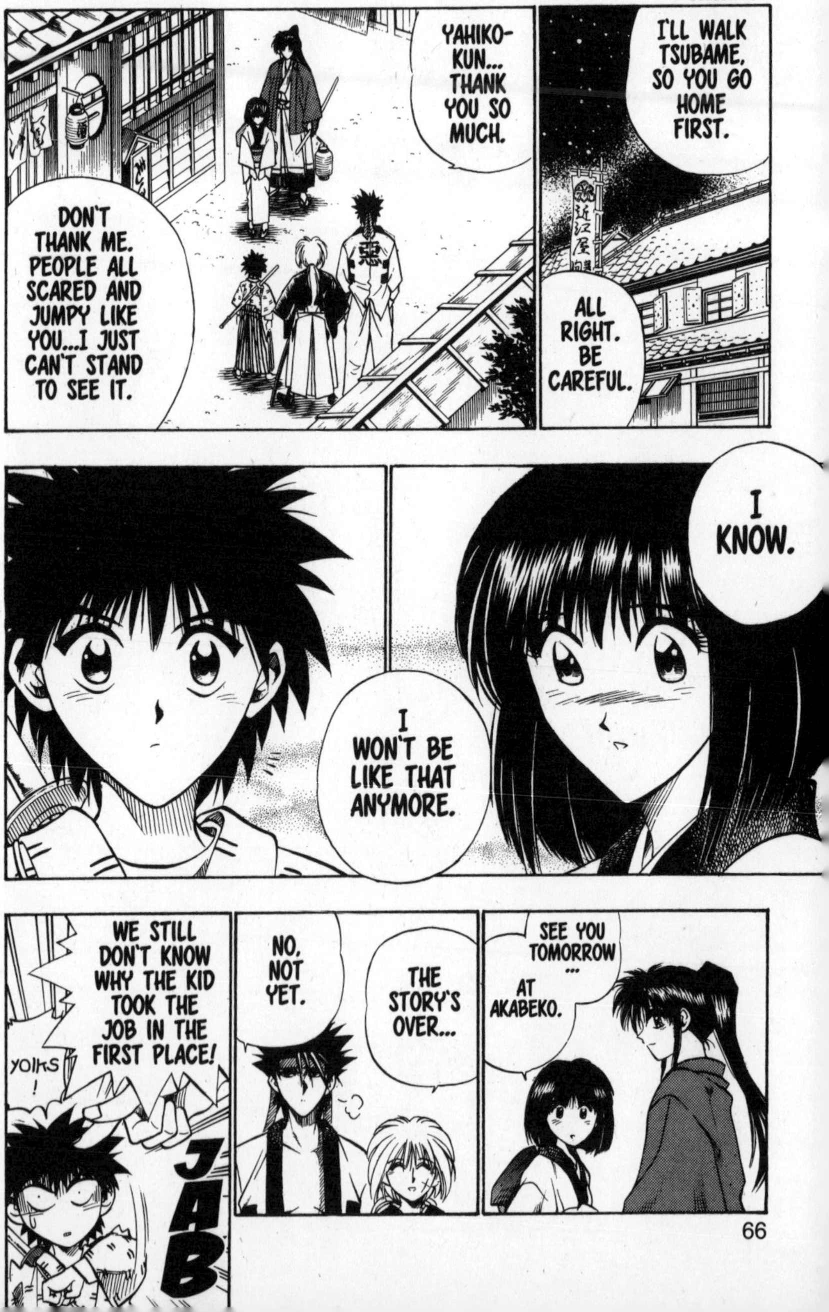
I'LL WALK TSUBAME, SO YOU GO HOME FIRST.
ALL RIGHT. BE CAREFUL.
YAHIKO-KUN... THANK YOU SO MUCH.
DON'T THANK ME. PEOPLE ALL SCARED AND JUMPY LIKE YOU...I JUST CAN'T STAND TO SEE IT.
I KNOW.
I WON'T BE LIKE THAT ANYMORE.
SEE YOU TOMORROW ...
AT AKABEKO.
THE STORY'S OVER...
NO, NOT YET.
WE STILL DON'T KNOW WHY THE KID TOOK THE JOB IN THE FIRST PLACE!
YOIKS!
JAB

READ THIS WAY

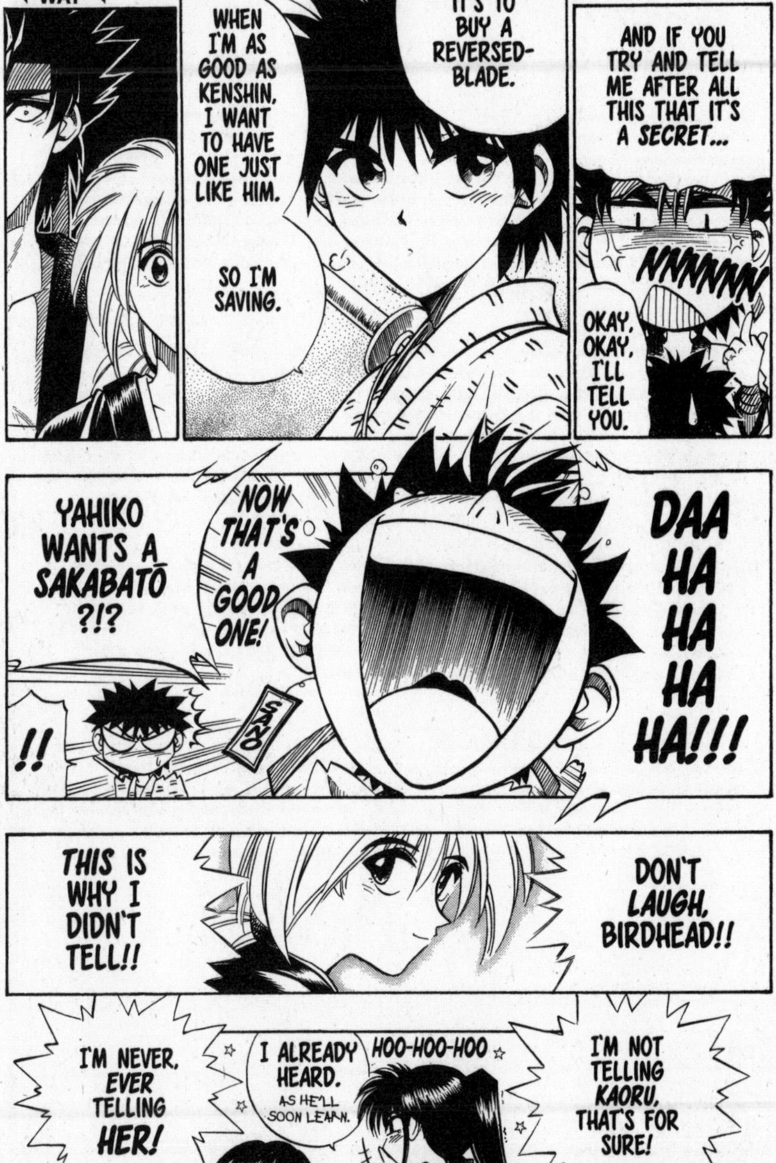
AND IF YOU TRY AND TELL ME AFTER ALL THIS THAT IT'S A SECRET...
NNNNNN
OKAY, OKAY, I'LL TELL YOU.
IT'S TO BUY A REVERSED-BLADE.
WHEN I'M AS GOOD AS KENSHIN, I WANT TO HAVE ONE JUST LIKE HIM.
SO I'M SAVING.
DAA HA HA HA HA HA!!!
NOW THAT'S A GOOD ONE!
YAHIKO WANTS A SAKABATŌ?!?
SANO
!!
DON'T LAUGH, BIRDHEAD!!
THIS IS WHY I DIDN'T TELL!!
I'M NOT TELLING KAORU, THAT'S FOR SURE!
HOO-HOO-HOO
I ALREADY HEARD.
AS HE'LL SOON LEARN.
I'M NEVER, EVER TELLING HER!
?

## The Secret Life of Characters (15)

# —Sanjō Tsubame—

**In terms of personality, there's no real model. Created more as a bridge to the "Raijūta" episodes, the main point of the "sidestory" in this volume was to shine the spotlight on Yahiko—"a young girl being a young man's motivation to act" the weird thought I found myself having—and thus was the story crafted to provide an opportunity for Tsubame to appear as its heroine. Some cling to their beliefs because of pride or conviction; some because they're just too weak-willed to change. Tsubame's character is testament to the wrong thinking of a previous age...that, and as a direct contrast to "acts-before-he-thinks" Yahiko.**

**As mentioned above, the Yahiko sidestory was meant mainly as a bridge and yet, once begun, it also raised all sorts of problems. There was the possibility that it could go longer than three episodes...the desire to focus more on Kenshin and the others...the rapid shuttling, back and forth, of the action. It was a really tiring story to tell! It was all worth it in the end, though, since the readers liked it, and even though it was short, it managed to successfully capture the world of "*RuroKen*." On the other hand, psychological fatigue-wise, the stress of it would drag behind me long after...**

**In terms of design, you could say the model came from a certain wildly popular "planet-themed" anime show—from the character symbolized by a "ringed-planet" in particular. Tsubame's just an average girl, so her hair had to be either a bowl-cut, or in pigtails. While working on a draft of a draft, I chanced to see the show and decided "Right! A bowl-cut it is!" (Why I'd say "Right!" to myself, I've no idea.)**

**Watsuki doesn't make a habit of watching this kind of anime, mind you, but during his period of apprenticeship, it was suggested to him by the *sensei's* chief assistant that he do so, and so he has, on and off, ever since. The "fire-planet" one is cool...the "ringed-planet" one is cool...straight black hair is cool...you see before you one Watsuki Nobuhiro, falling to pieces....**

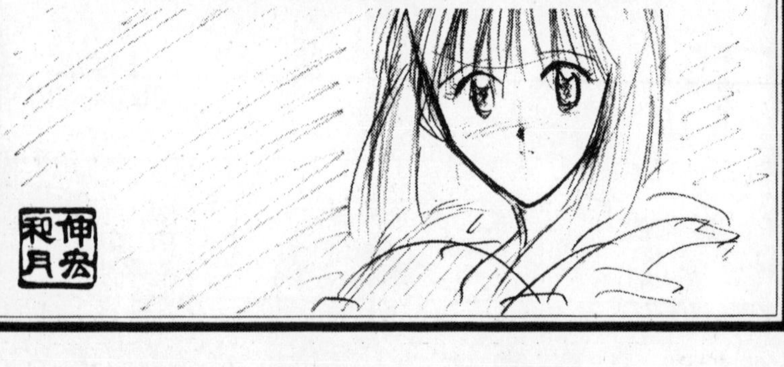
伸宏
和月

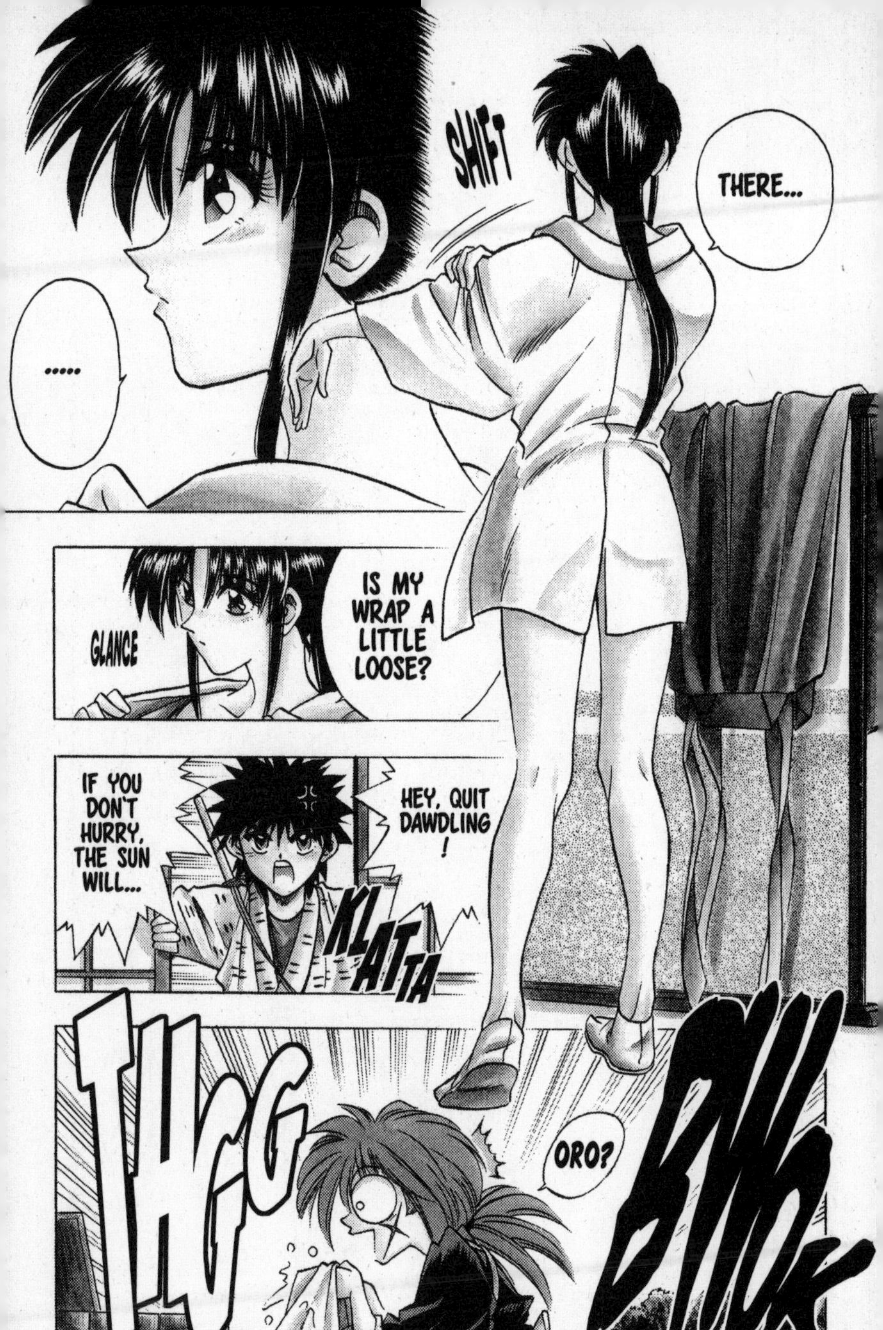
SHIFT
THERE...
......
IS MY WRAP A LITTLE LOOSE?
GLANCE
HEY, QUIT DAWDLING!
IF YOU DON'T HURRY, THE SUN WILL...
KLATTA
ORO?

**Act 34—The State of Meiji Swordsmanship**

# Act 34
# The State of Meiji Swordsmanship

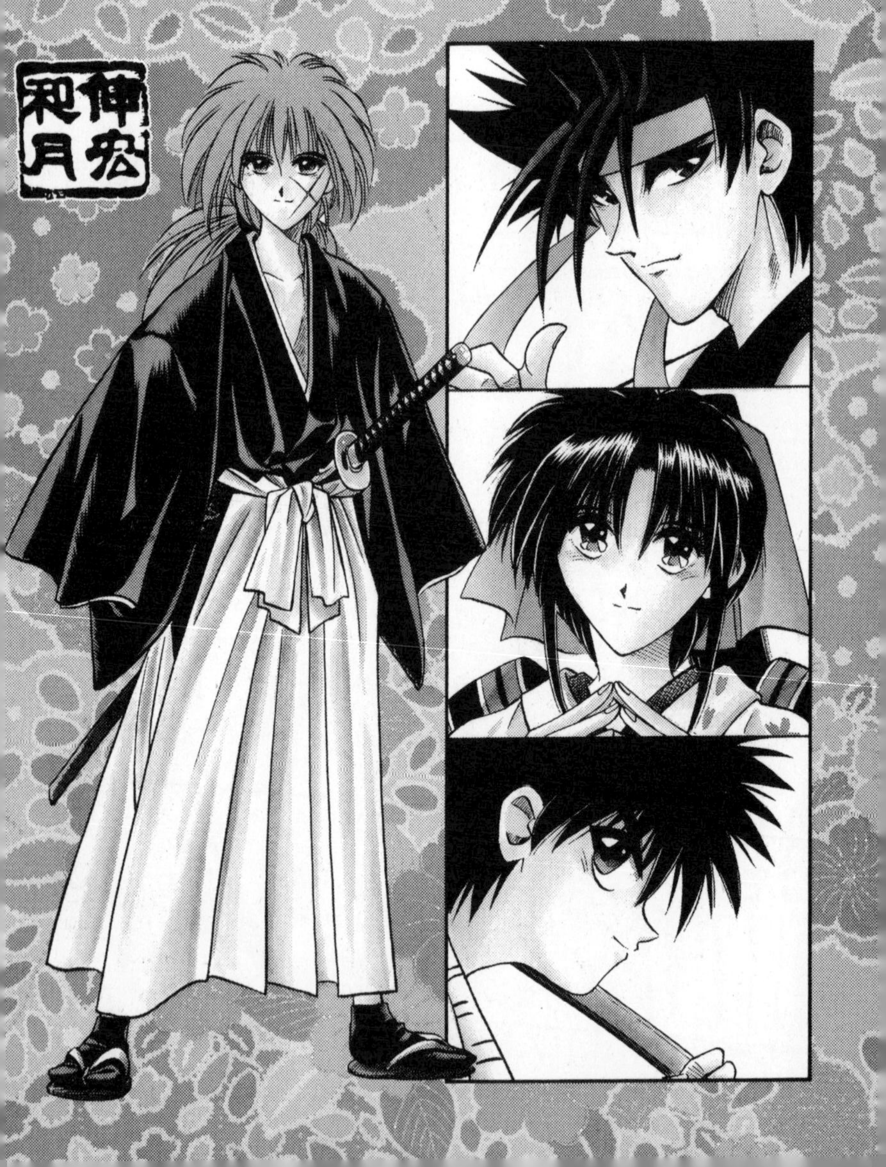
和月伸宏

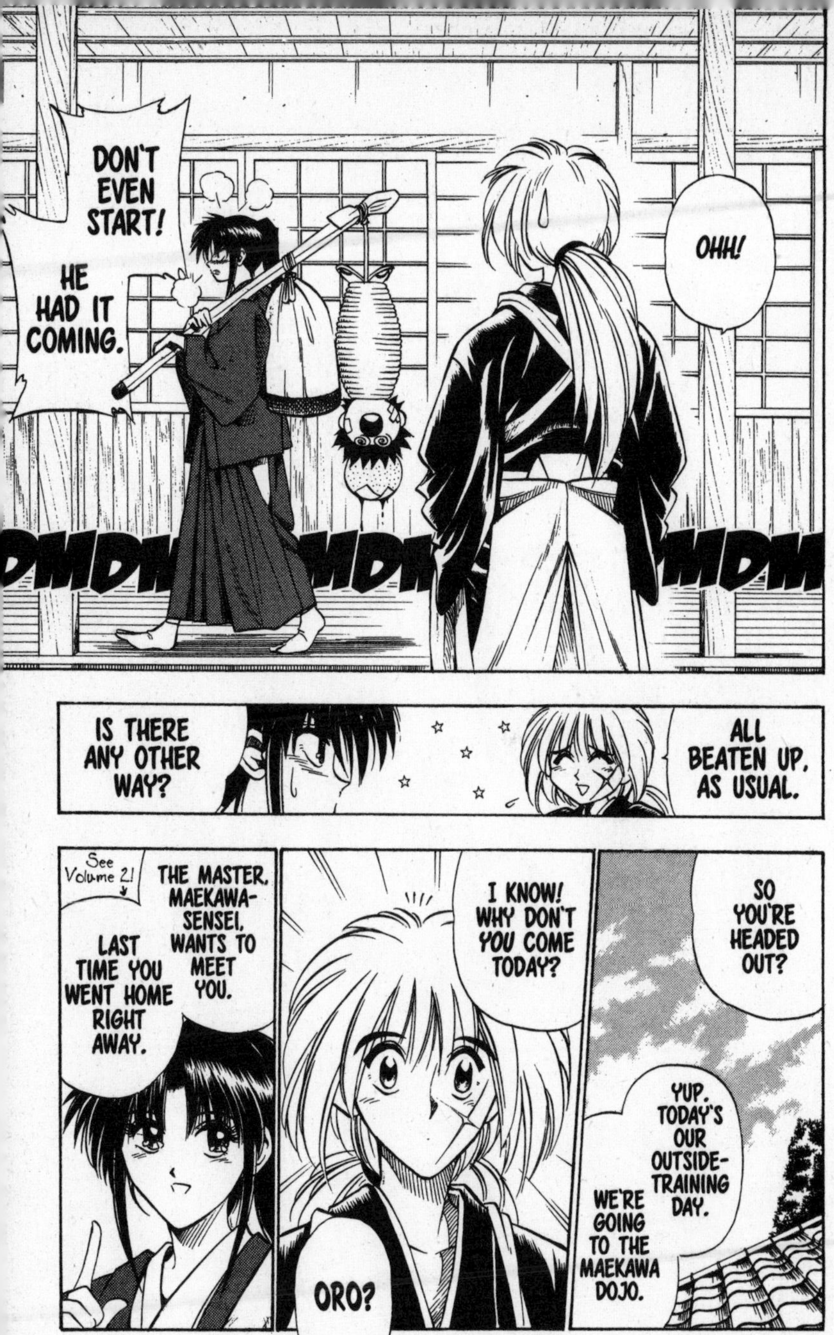
OHH!
DON'T EVEN START!
HE HAD IT COMING.
DMDM
ALL BEATEN UP, AS USUAL.
IS THERE ANY OTHER WAY?
SO YOU'RE HEADED OUT?
YUP. TODAY'S OUR OUTSIDE-TRAINING DAY.
WE'RE GOING TO THE MAEKAWA DOJO.
I KNOW! WHY DON'T YOU COME TODAY?
ORO?
THE MASTER, MAEKAWA-SENSEI, WANTS TO MEET YOU.
LAST TIME YOU WENT HOME RIGHT AWAY.
See Volume 2!

READ THIS WAY

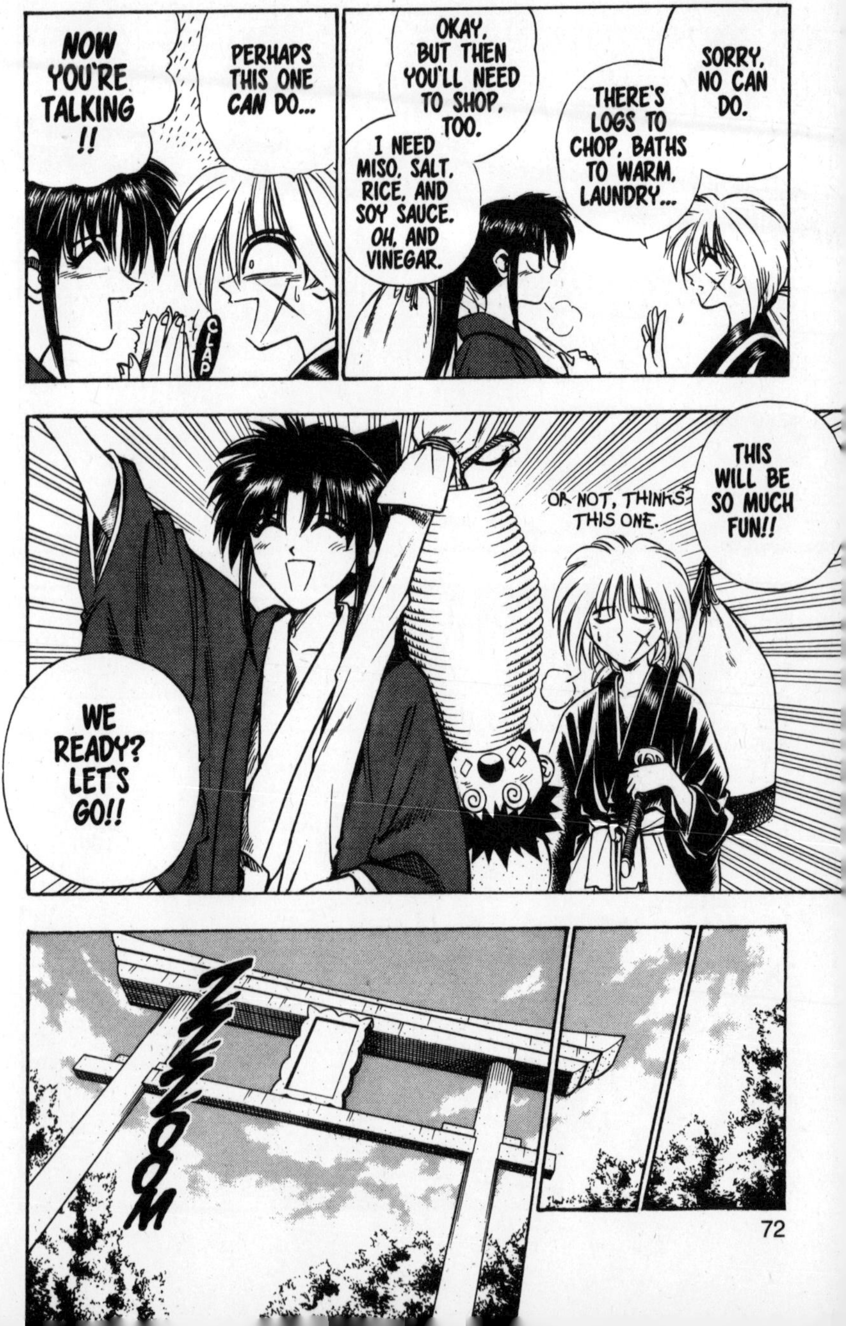
SORRY, NO CAN DO.
THERE'S LOGS TO CHOP, BATHS TO WARM, LAUNDRY...
OKAY, BUT THEN YOU'LL NEED TO SHOP, TOO.
I NEED MISO, SALT, RICE, AND SOY SAUCE. OH, AND VINEGAR.
PERHAPS THIS ONE CAN DO...
NOW YOU'RE TALKING!!
CLAP
THIS WILL BE SO MUCH FUN!!
OR NOT, THINKS THIS ONE.
WE READY? LET'S GO!!

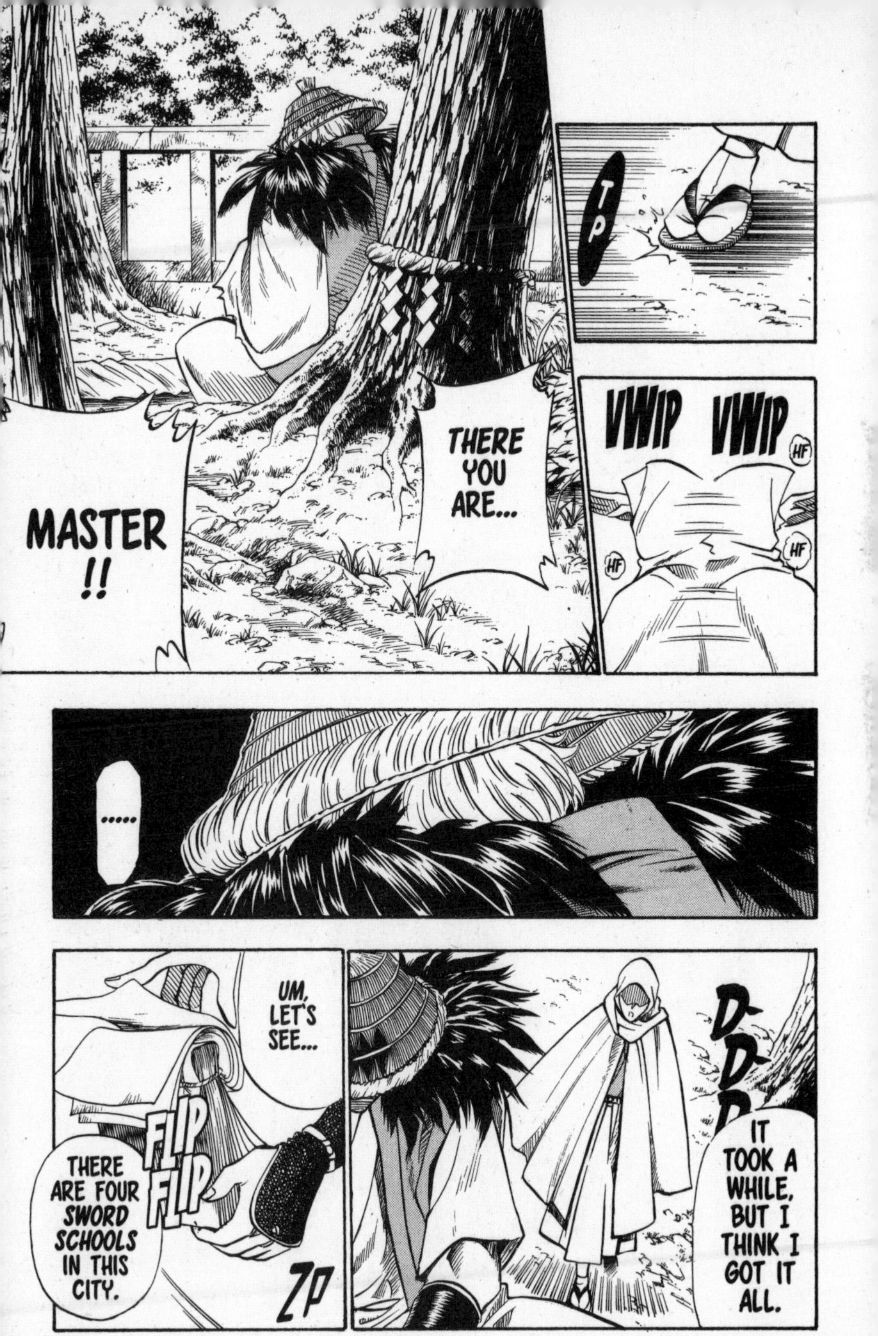
TP
VWIP VWIP
HF
HF
HF
THERE YOU ARE...
MASTER !!
......
D D D
IT TOOK A WHILE, BUT I THINK I GOT IT ALL.
UM, LET'S SEE...
FLIP FLIP
THERE ARE FOUR SWORD SCHOOLS IN THIS CITY.
ZP

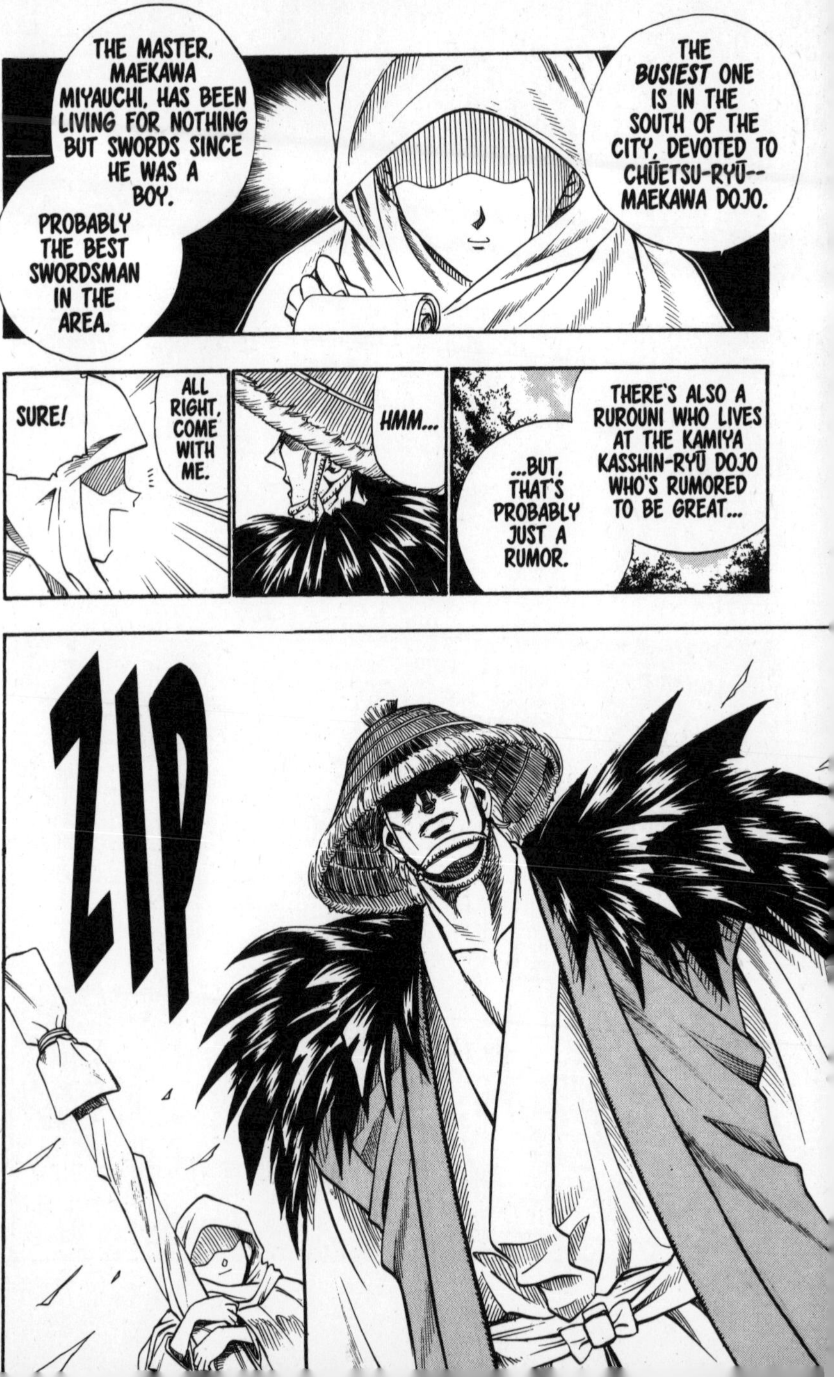
THE *BUSIEST* ONE IS IN THE SOUTH OF THE CITY, DEVOTED TO CHŪETSU-RYŪ-- MAEKAWA DOJO.
THE MASTER, MAEKAWA MIYAUCHI, HAS BEEN LIVING FOR NOTHING BUT SWORDS SINCE HE WAS A BOY.
PROBABLY THE BEST SWORDSMAN IN THE AREA.
THERE'S ALSO A RUROUNI WHO LIVES AT THE KAMIYA KASSHIN-RYŪ DOJO WHO'S RUMORED TO BE GREAT...
...BUT, THAT'S PROBABLY JUST A RUMOR.
HMM...
ALL RIGHT, COME WITH ME.
SURE!
ZIP

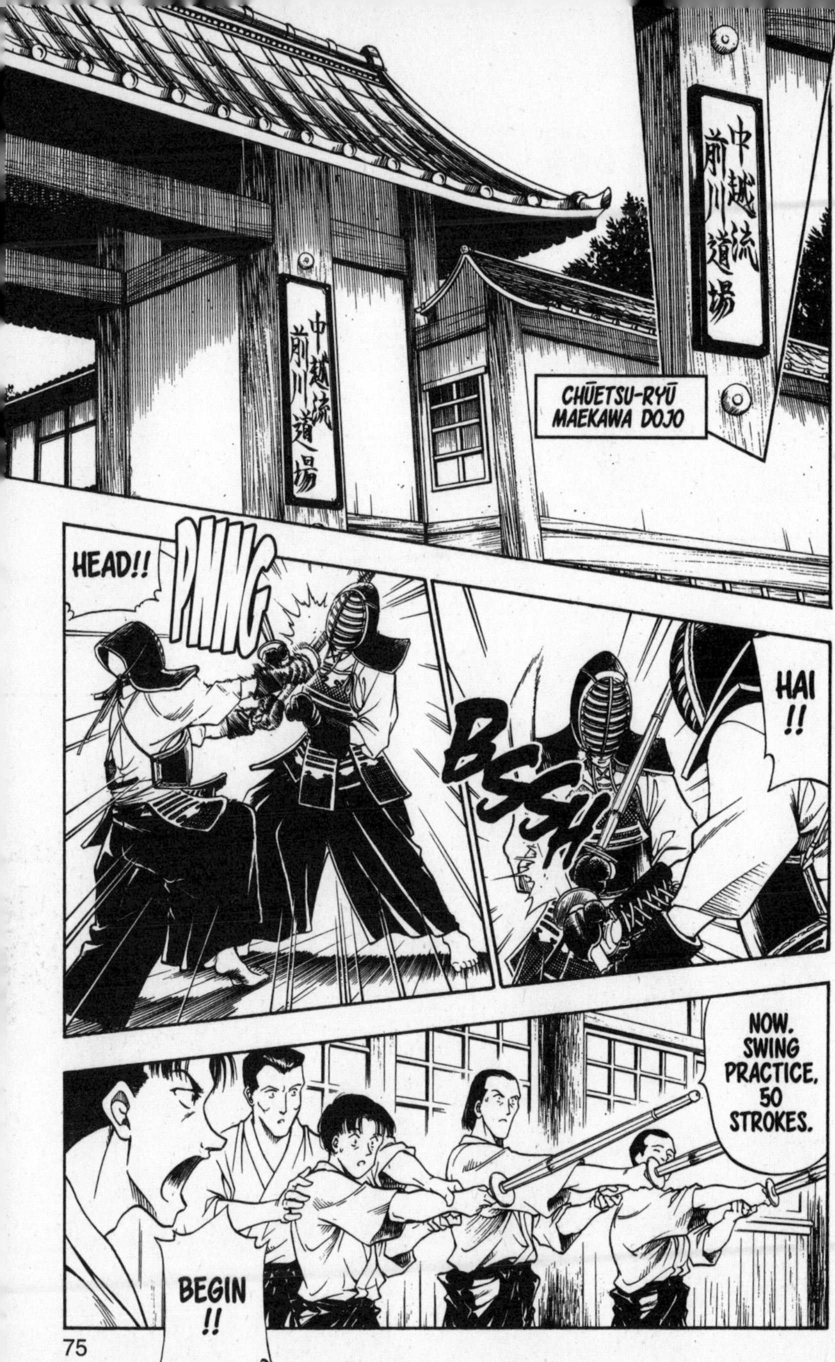
中越流前川道場
中越流前川道場
CHŪETSU-RYŪ MAEKAWA DOJO
HAI !!
BSSH
HEAD!!
PWNG
NOW. SWING PRACTICE, 50 STROKES.
BEGIN !!

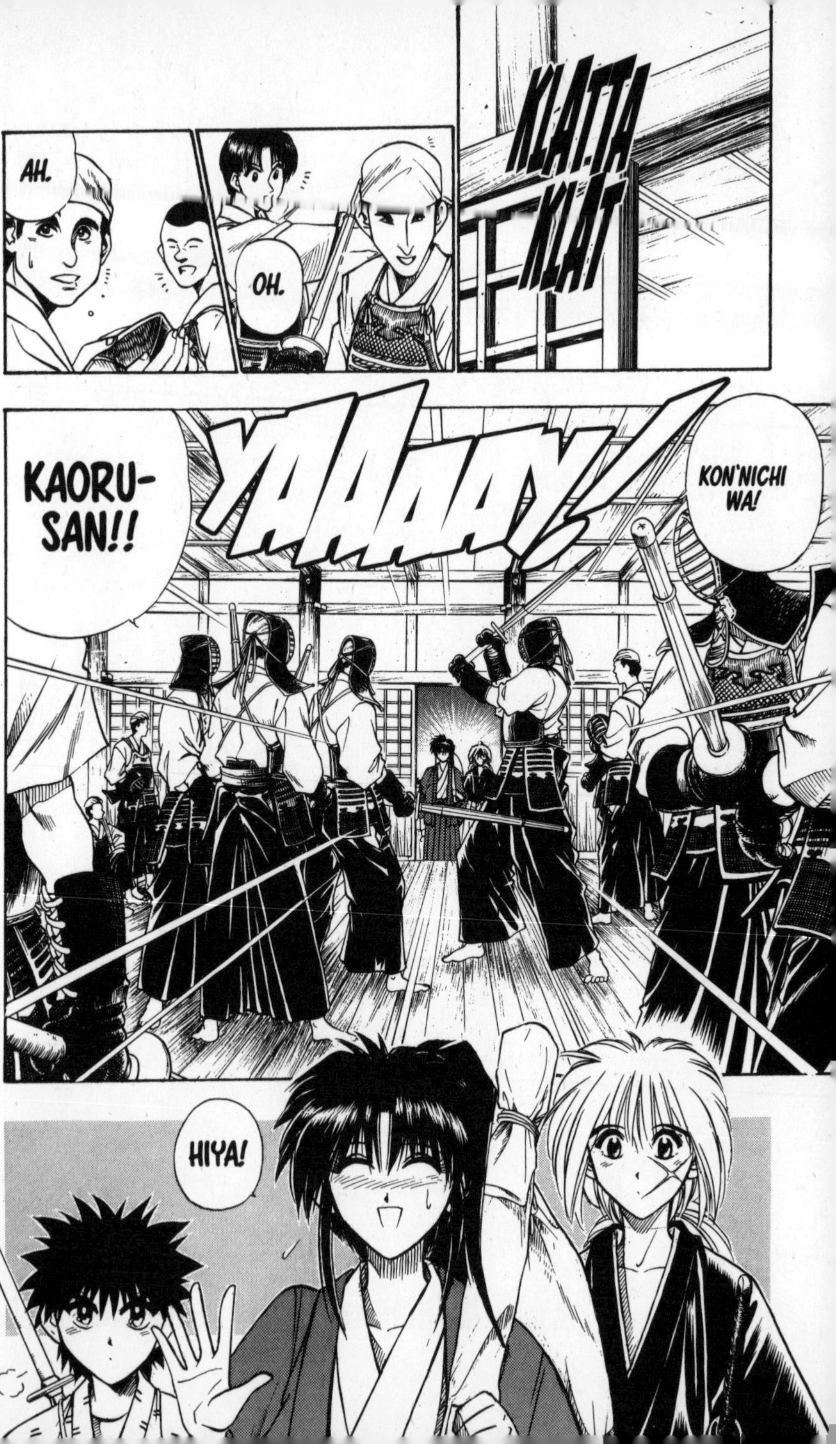
KLATA KLAT
OH.
AH.
KON'NICHI WA!
YAAAAY!
KAORU-SAN!!
HIYA!

READ THIS WAY

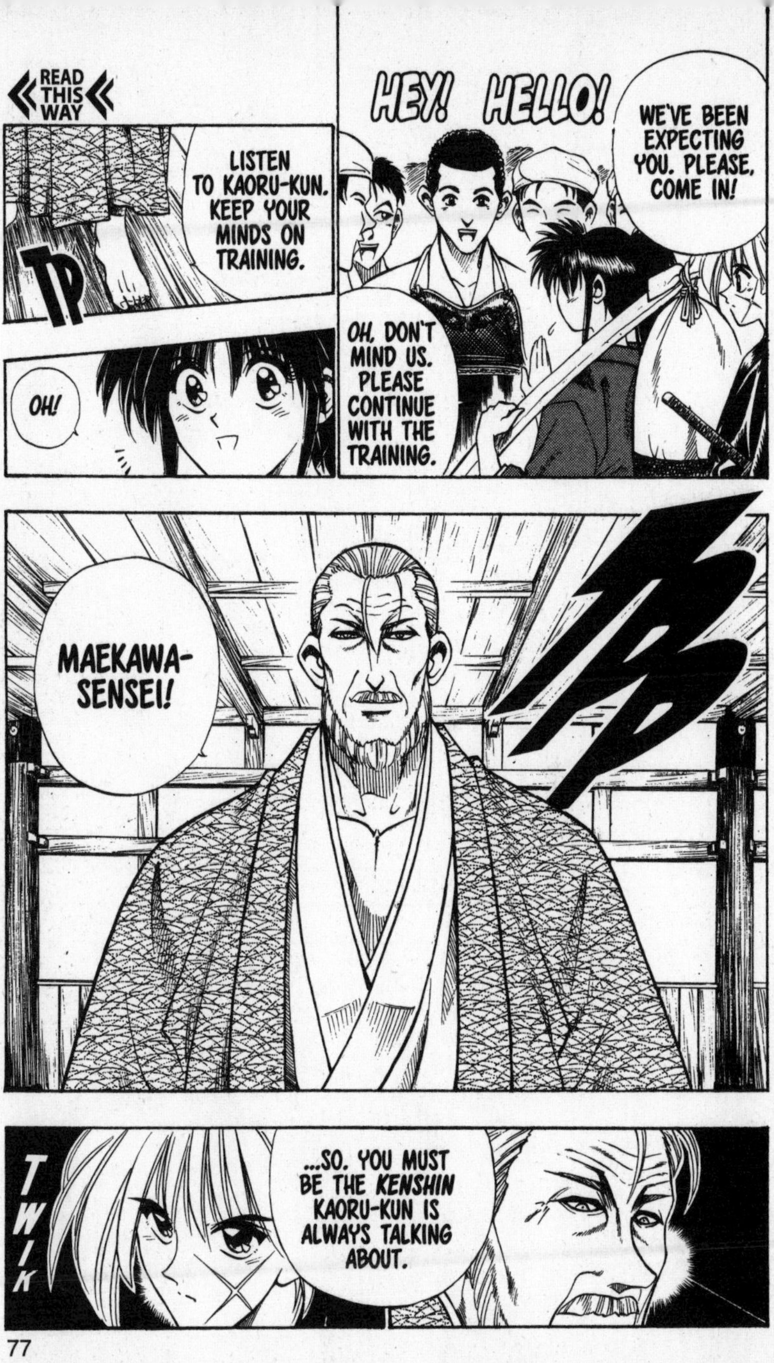

HEY! HELLO!
WE'VE BEEN EXPECTING YOU. PLEASE, COME IN!
OH, DON'T MIND US. PLEASE CONTINUE WITH THE TRAINING.
LISTEN TO KAORU-KUN. KEEP YOUR MINDS ON TRAINING.
TP
OH!
MAEKAWA-SENSEI!
...SO. YOU MUST BE THE *KENSHIN* KAORU-KUN IS ALWAYS TALKING ABOUT.
TWIK

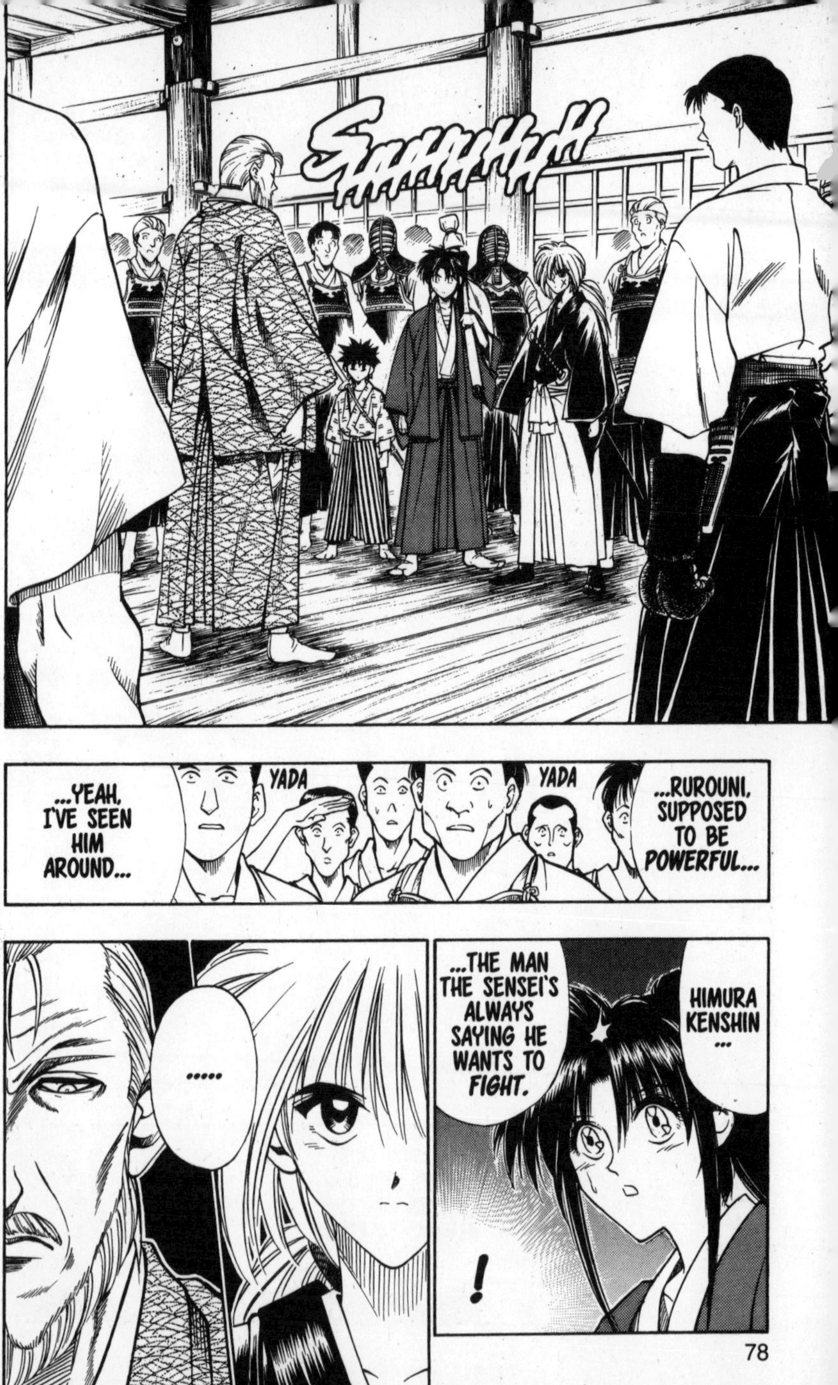
...RUROUNI, SUPPOSED TO BE POWERFUL...
YADA
YADA
...YEAH, I'VE SEEN HIM AROUND...
HIMURA KENSHIN ...
...THE MAN THE SENSEI'S ALWAYS SAYING HE WANTS TO FIGHT.
!
.....

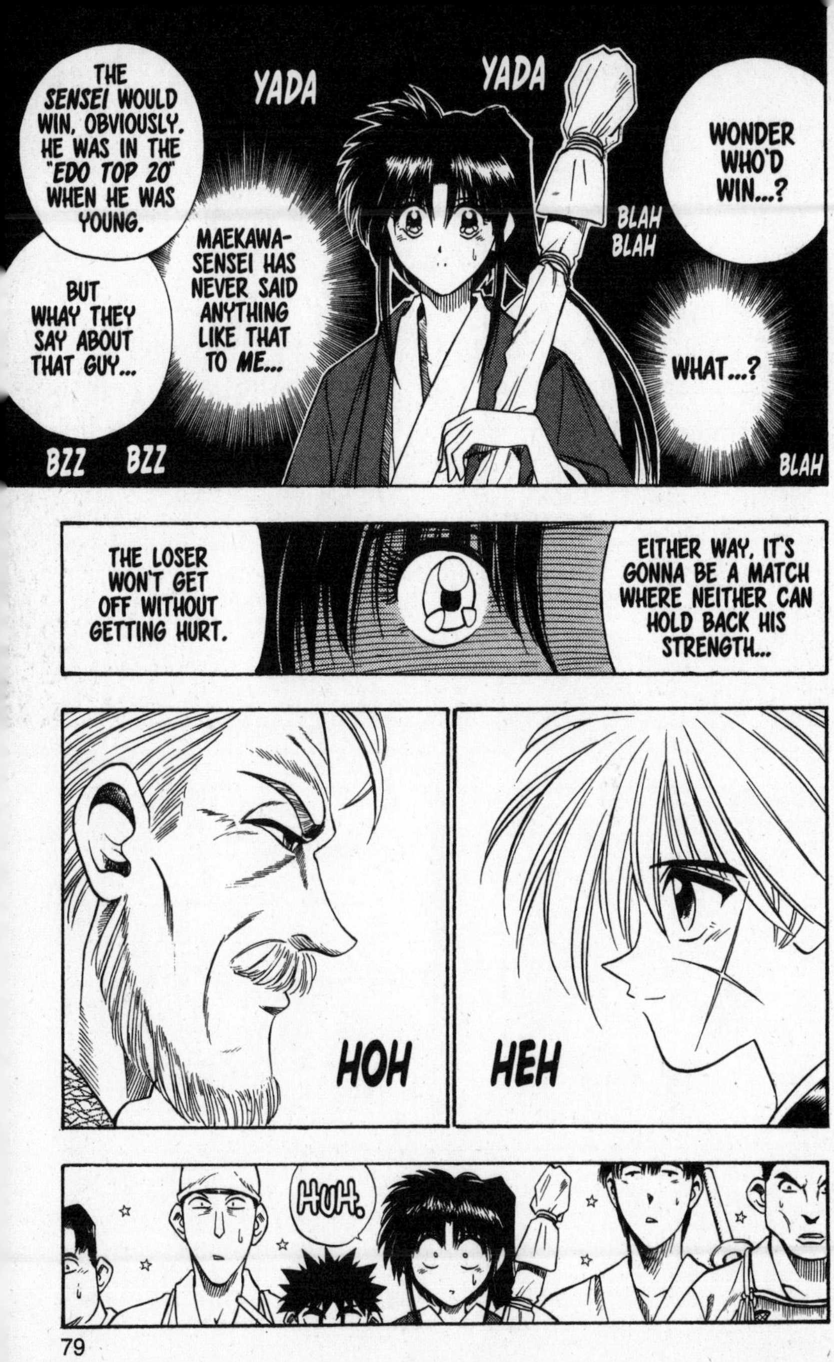

WONDER WHO'D WIN...?
YADA
BLAH BLAH
WHAT...?
BLAH
YADA
THE *SENSEI* WOULD WIN, OBVIOUSLY. HE WAS IN THE "*EDO TOP 20*" WHEN HE WAS YOUNG.
MAEKAWA-SENSEI HAS NEVER SAID ANYTHING LIKE THAT TO *ME*...
BUT WHAY THEY SAY ABOUT THAT GUY...
BZZ
BZZ
EITHER WAY, IT'S GONNA BE A MATCH WHERE NEITHER CAN HOLD BACK HIS STRENGTH...
THE LOSER WON'T GET OFF WITHOUT GETTING HURT.
HEH
HOH
HUH.

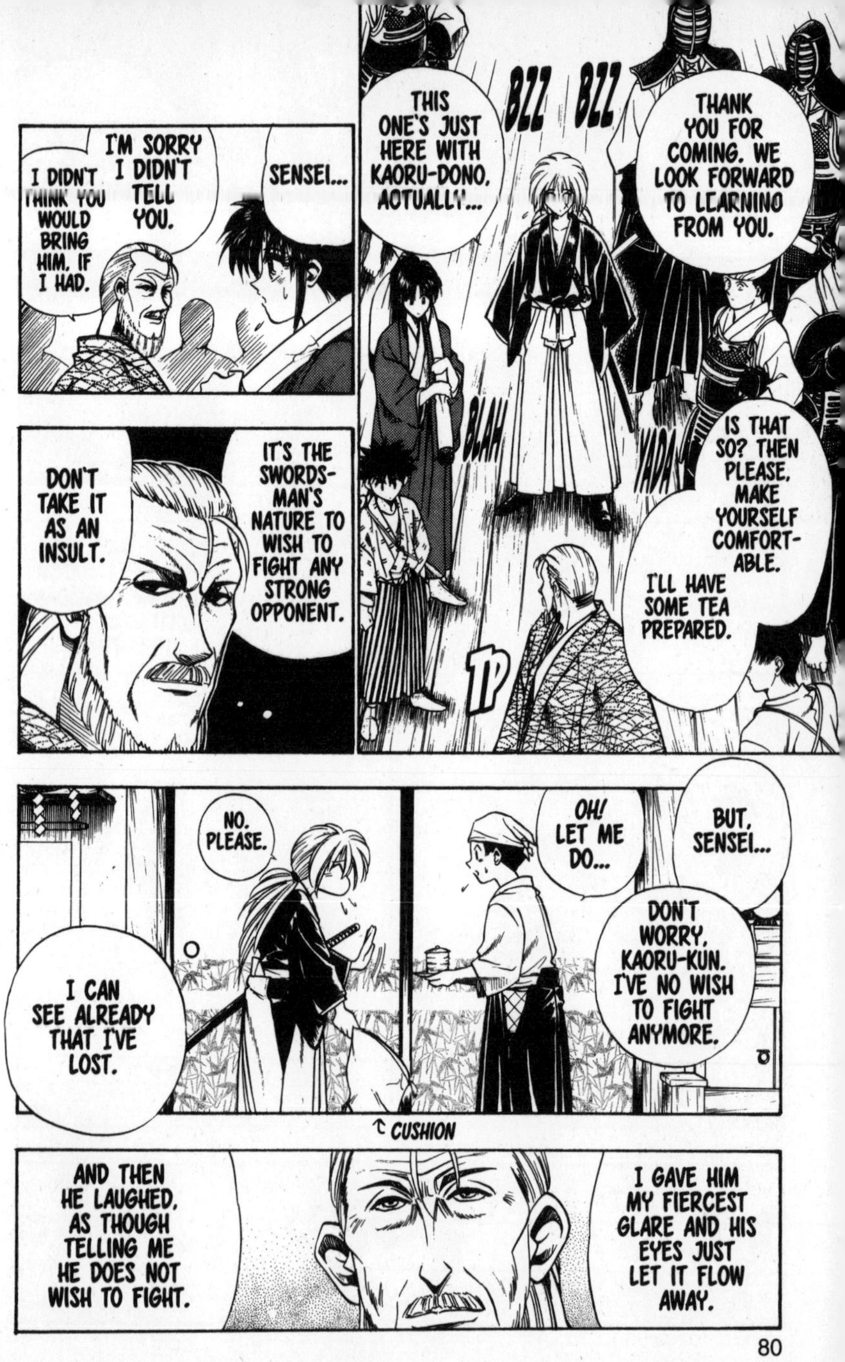
THANK YOU FOR COMING. WE LOOK FORWARD TO LEARNING FROM YOU.
BZZ BZZ
THIS ONE'S JUST HERE WITH KAORU-DONO, ACTUALLY...
IS THAT SO? THEN PLEASE, MAKE YOURSELF COMFORTABLE.
I'LL HAVE SOME TEA PREPARED.
YADA
BLAH
TP
SENSEI...
I'M SORRY I DIDN'T TELL YOU.
I DIDN'T THINK YOU WOULD BRING HIM, IF I HAD.
IT'S THE SWORDSMAN'S NATURE TO WISH TO FIGHT ANY STRONG OPPONENT.
DON'T TAKE IT AS AN INSULT.
BUT, SENSEI...
OH! LET ME DO...
DON'T WORRY, KAORU-KUN. I'VE NO WISH TO FIGHT ANYMORE.
NO. PLEASE.
I CAN SEE ALREADY THAT I'VE LOST.
CUSHION
I GAVE HIM MY FIERCEST GLARE AND HIS EYES JUST LET IT FLOW AWAY.
AND THEN HE LAUGHED, AS THOUGH TELLING ME HE DOES NOT WISH TO FIGHT.

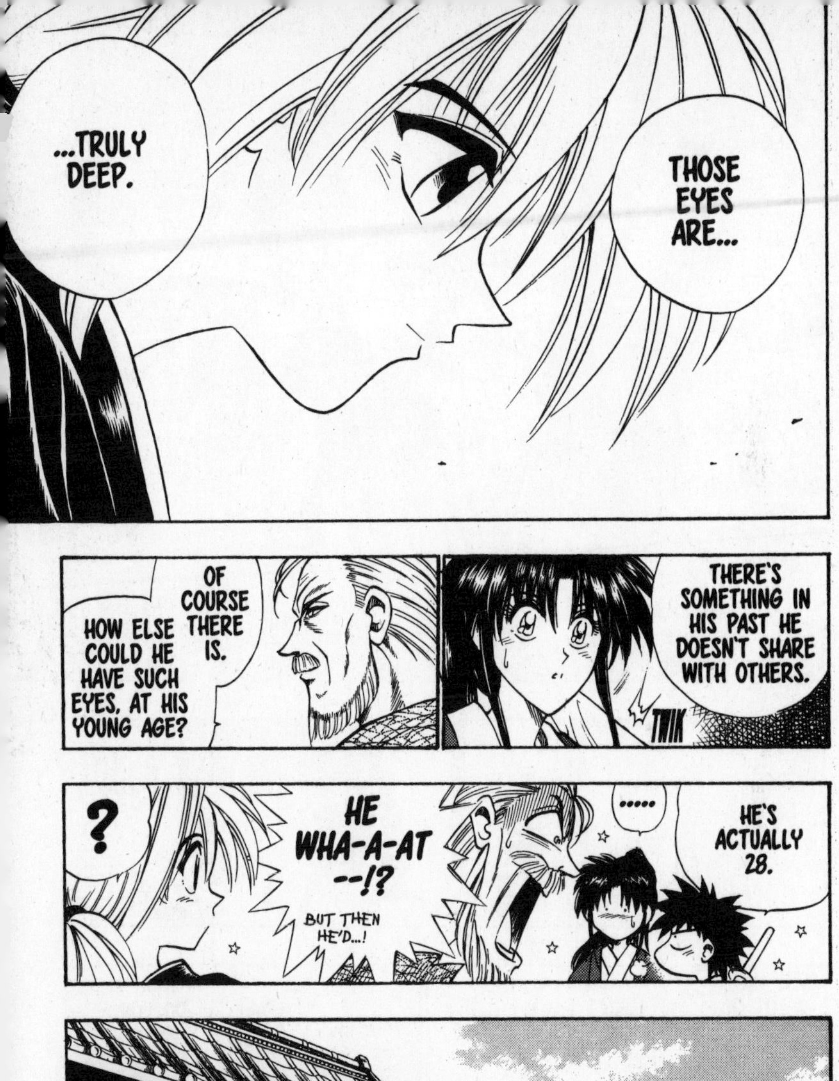
THOSE EYES ARE...
...TRULY DEEP.
THERE'S SOMETHING IN HIS PAST HE DOESN'T SHARE WITH OTHERS.
TWIK
OF COURSE THERE IS.
HOW ELSE COULD HE HAVE SUCH EYES, AT HIS YOUNG AGE?
HE'S ACTUALLY 28.
.....
HE WHA-A-AT--!?
BUT THEN HE'D...!
?

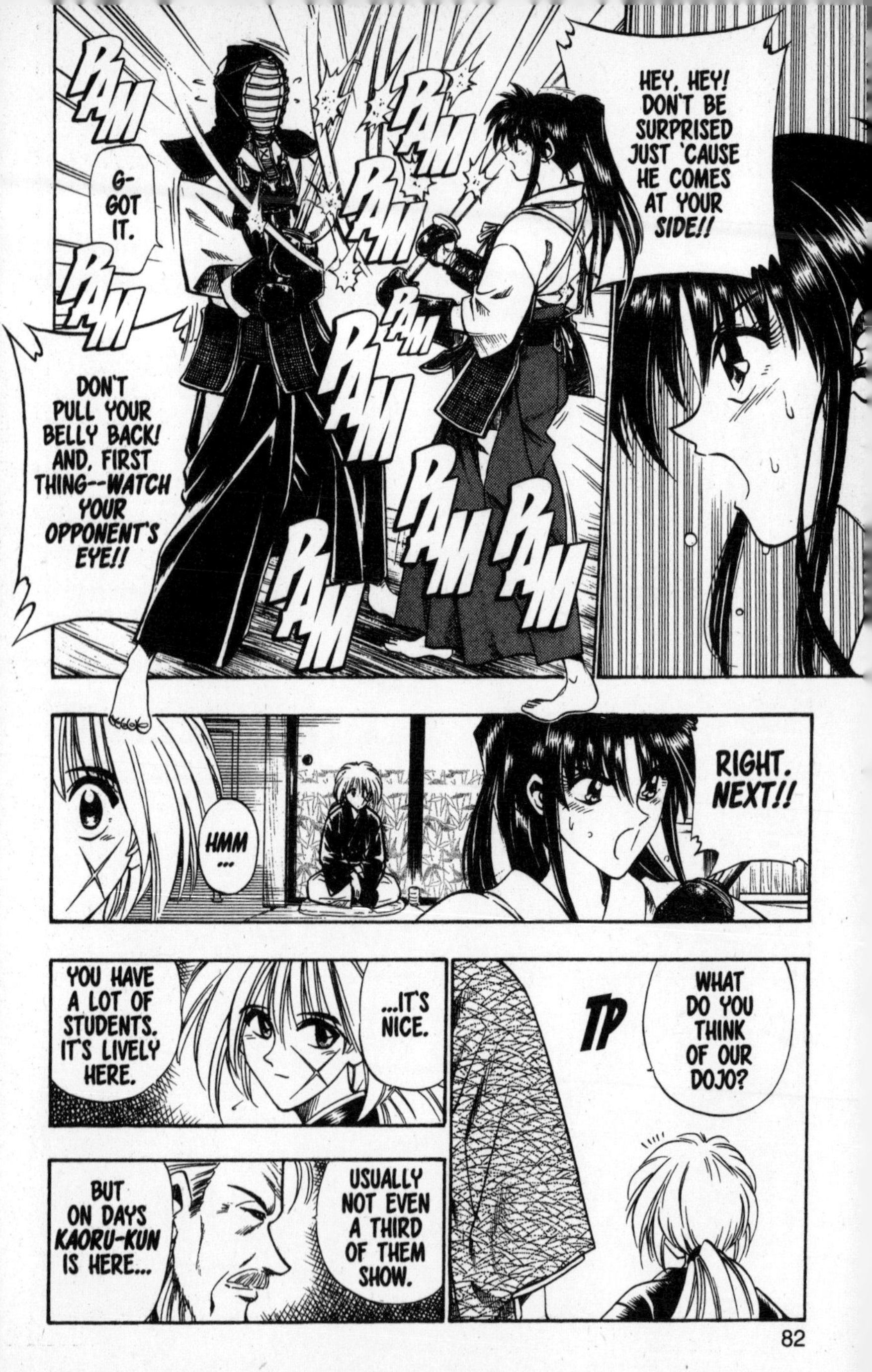

HEY, HEY! DON'T BE SURPRISED JUST 'CAUSE HE COMES AT YOUR SIDE!!
RAM RAM RAM RAM RAM RAM RAM RAM RAM
G-GOT IT.
DON'T PULL YOUR BELLY BACK! AND, FIRST THING--WATCH YOUR OPPONENT'S EYE!!
RIGHT. NEXT!!
HMM...
TP
WHAT DO YOU THINK OF OUR DOJO?
YOU HAVE A LOT OF STUDENTS. IT'S LIVELY HERE.
...IT'S NICE.
USUALLY NOT EVEN A THIRD OF THEM SHOW.
BUT ON DAYS KAORU-KUN IS HERE...

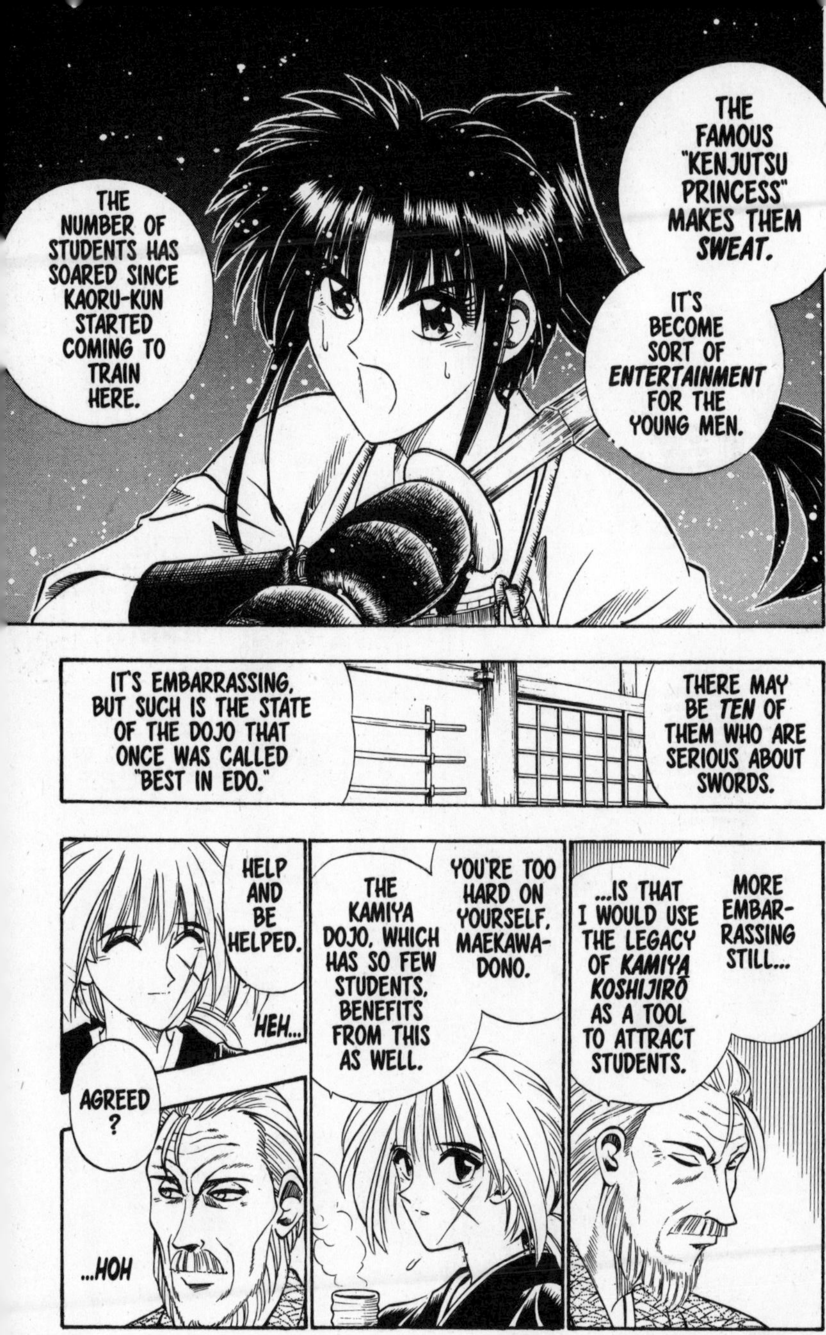
THE FAMOUS "KENJUTSU PRINCESS" MAKES THEM *SWEAT.*
IT'S BECOME SORT OF *ENTERTAINMENT* FOR THE YOUNG MEN.
THE NUMBER OF STUDENTS HAS SOARED SINCE KAORU-KUN STARTED COMING TO TRAIN HERE.
THERE MAY BE *TEN* OF THEM WHO ARE SERIOUS ABOUT SWORDS.
IT'S EMBARRASSING, BUT SUCH IS THE STATE OF THE DOJO THAT ONCE WAS CALLED "BEST IN EDO."
MORE EMBAR-RASSING STILL...
...IS THAT I WOULD USE THE LEGACY OF *KAMIYA KOSHIJIRŌ* AS A TOOL TO ATTRACT STUDENTS.
YOU'RE TOO HARD ON YOURSELF, MAEKAWA-DONO.
THE KAMIYA DOJO, WHICH HAS SO FEW STUDENTS, BENEFITS FROM THIS AS WELL.
HELP AND BE HELPED.
HEH...
AGREED?
...HOH

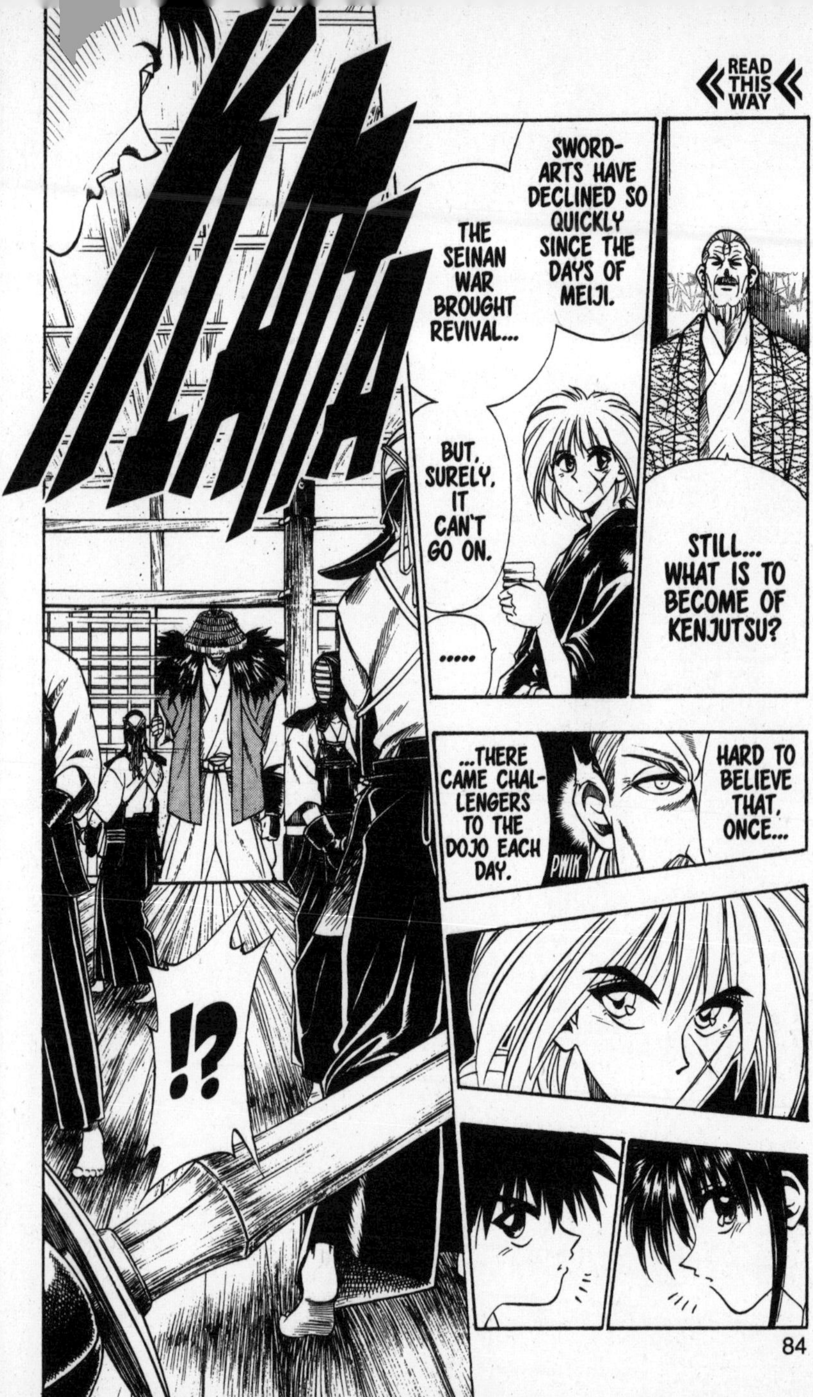
READ THIS WAY
STILL... WHAT IS TO BECOME OF KENJUTSU?
SWORD-ARTS HAVE DECLINED SO QUICKLY SINCE THE DAYS OF MEIJI.
THE SEINAN WAR BROUGHT REVIVAL...
BUT, SURELY, IT CAN'T GO ON.
.....
HARD TO BELIEVE THAT, ONCE...
...THERE CAME CHAL-LENGERS TO THE DOJO EACH DAY.
PWIK
!?

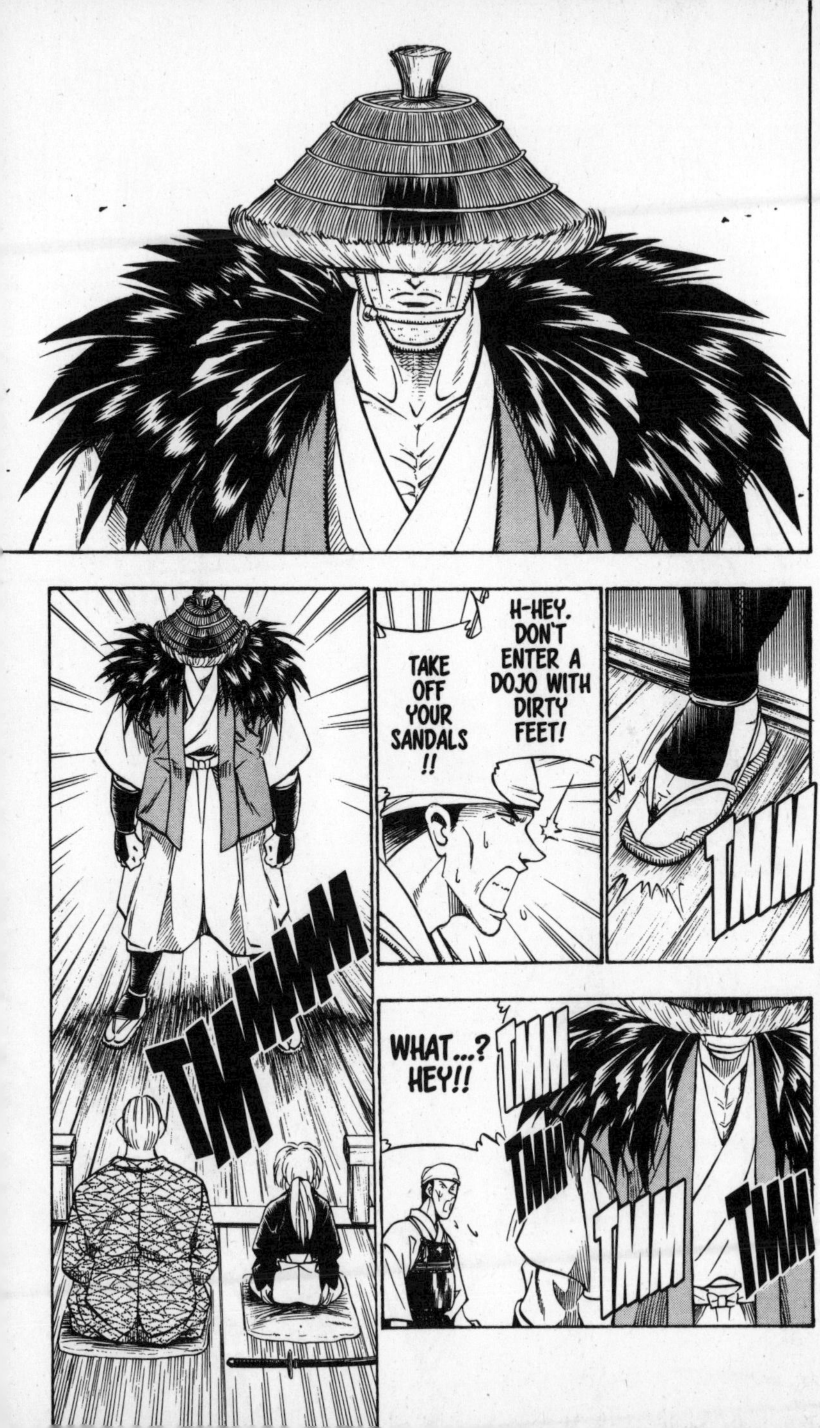
TMM
H-HEY. DON'T ENTER A DOJO WITH DIRTY FEET!
TAKE OFF YOUR SANDALS!!
TMM
TMM
TMM
TMM
WHAT...? HEY!!
TMMMM

READ THIS WAY

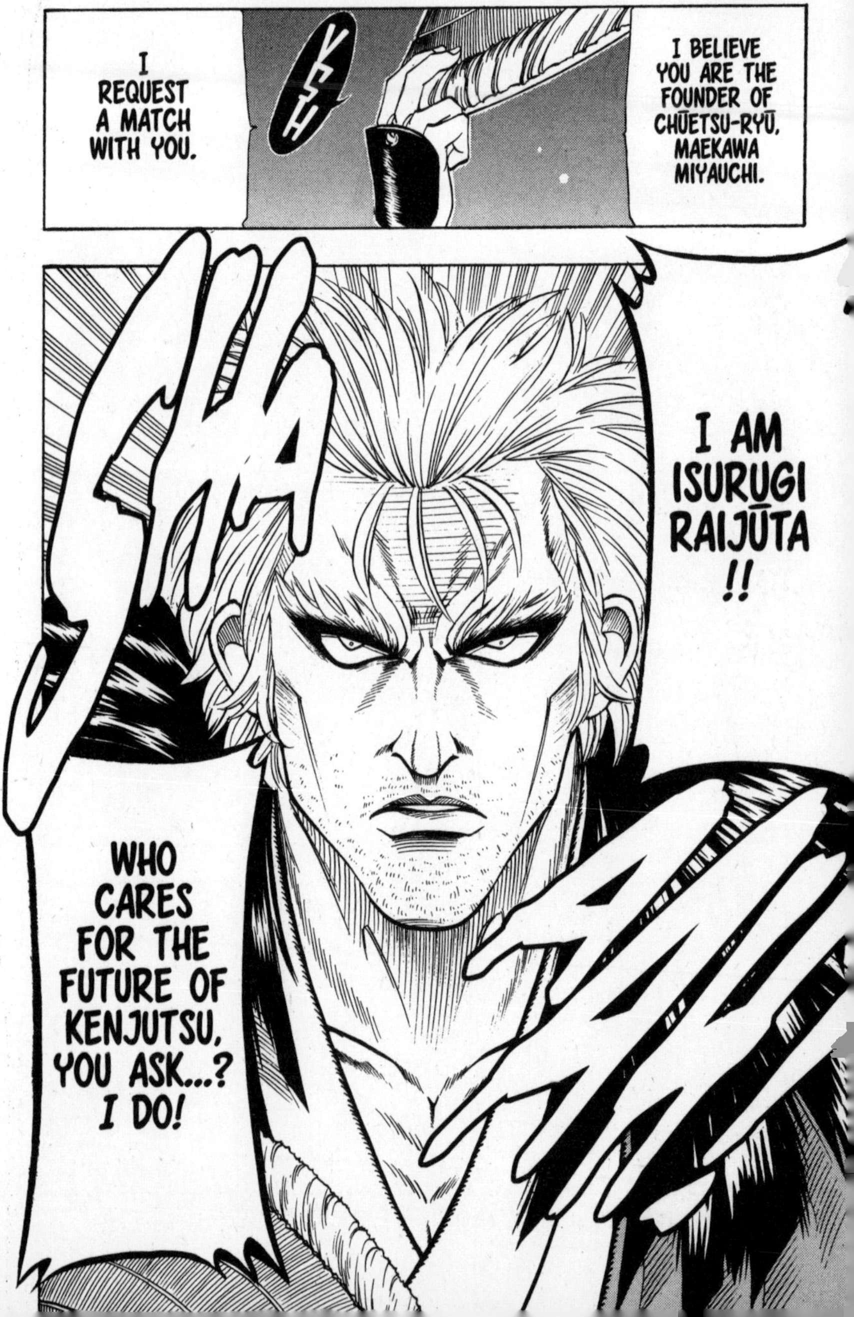

I BELIEVE YOU ARE THE FOUNDER OF CHŪETSU-RYŪ, MAEKAWA MIYAUCHI.
VSH
I REQUEST A MATCH WITH YOU.
I AM ISURUGI RAIJŪTA!!
SHA
WHO CARES FOR THE FUTURE OF KENJUTSU, YOU ASK...? I DO!

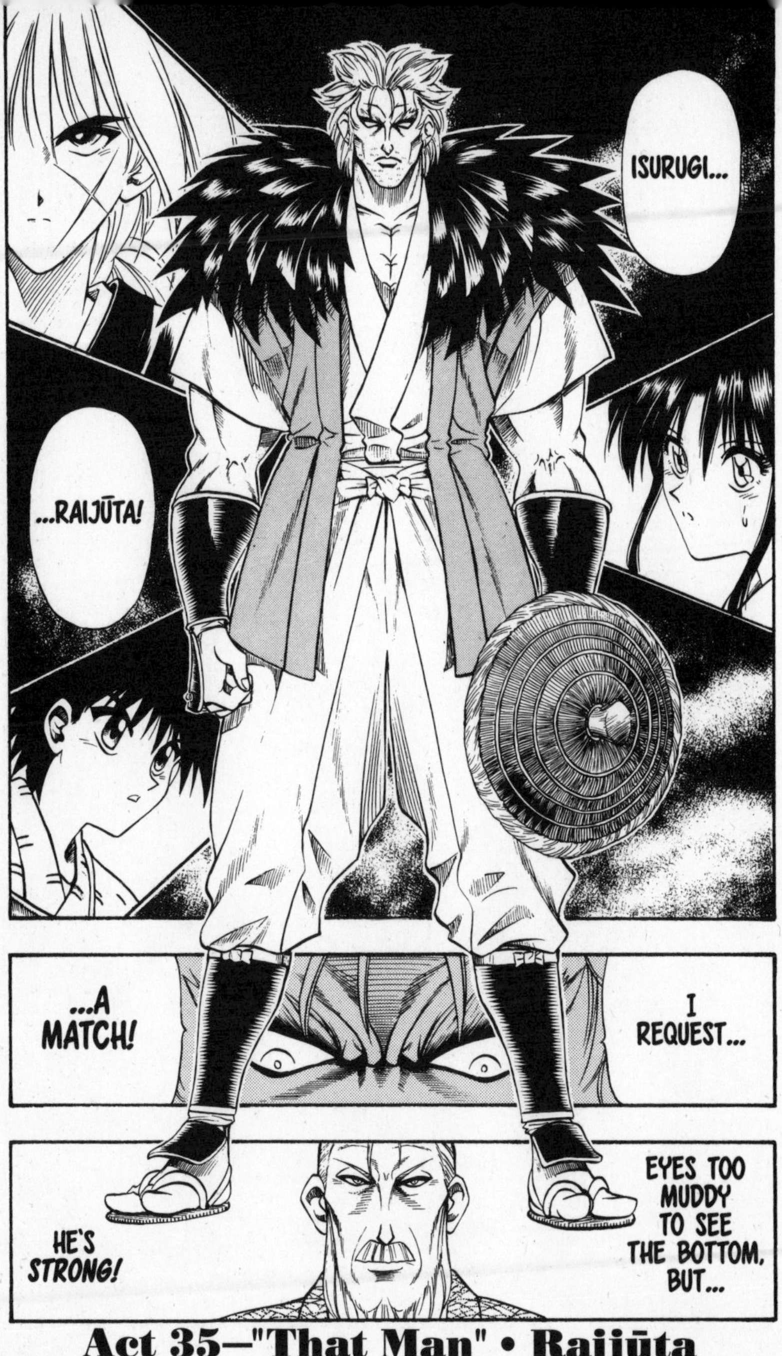
ISURUGI...
...RAIJŪTA!
I REQUEST...
...A MATCH!
EYES TOO MUDDY TO SEE THE BOTTOM, BUT...
HE'S STRONG!

# Act 35—"That Man" • Raijūta

READ THIS WAY

# Act 35
# "That Man" • Raijūta

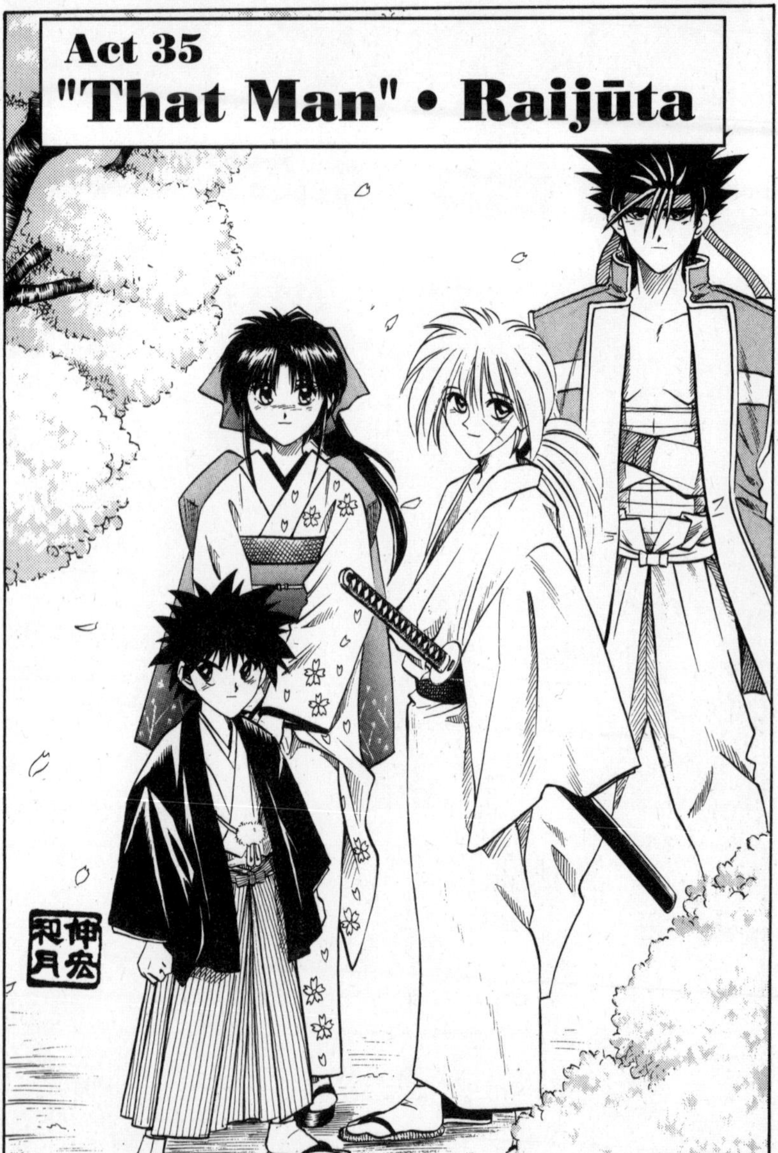

READ THIS WAY

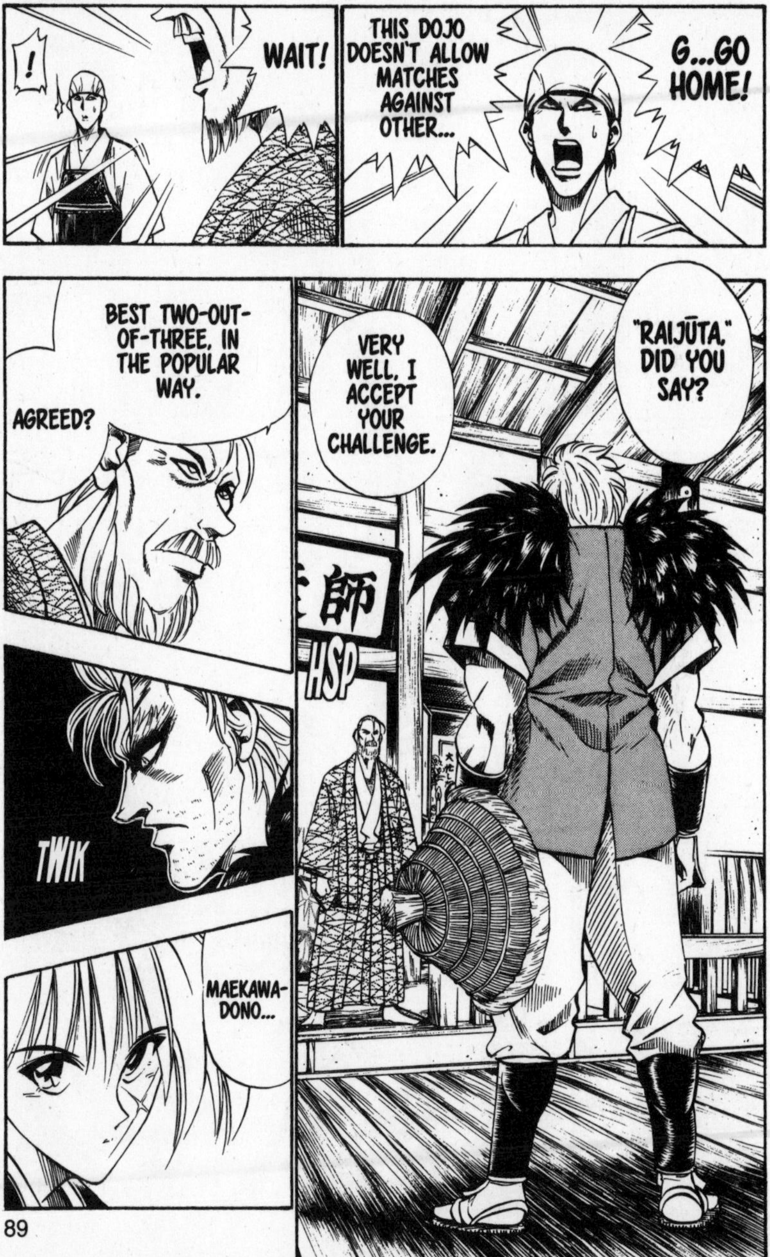
THIS DOJO DOESN'T ALLOW MATCHES AGAINST OTHER...
G...GO HOME!
WAIT!
!
"RAIJŪTA," DID YOU SAY?
VERY WELL, I ACCEPT YOUR CHALLENGE.
師
HSP
BEST TWO-OUT-OF-THREE, IN THE POPULAR WAY.
AGREED?
TWIK
MAEKAWA-DONO...

READ THIS WAY

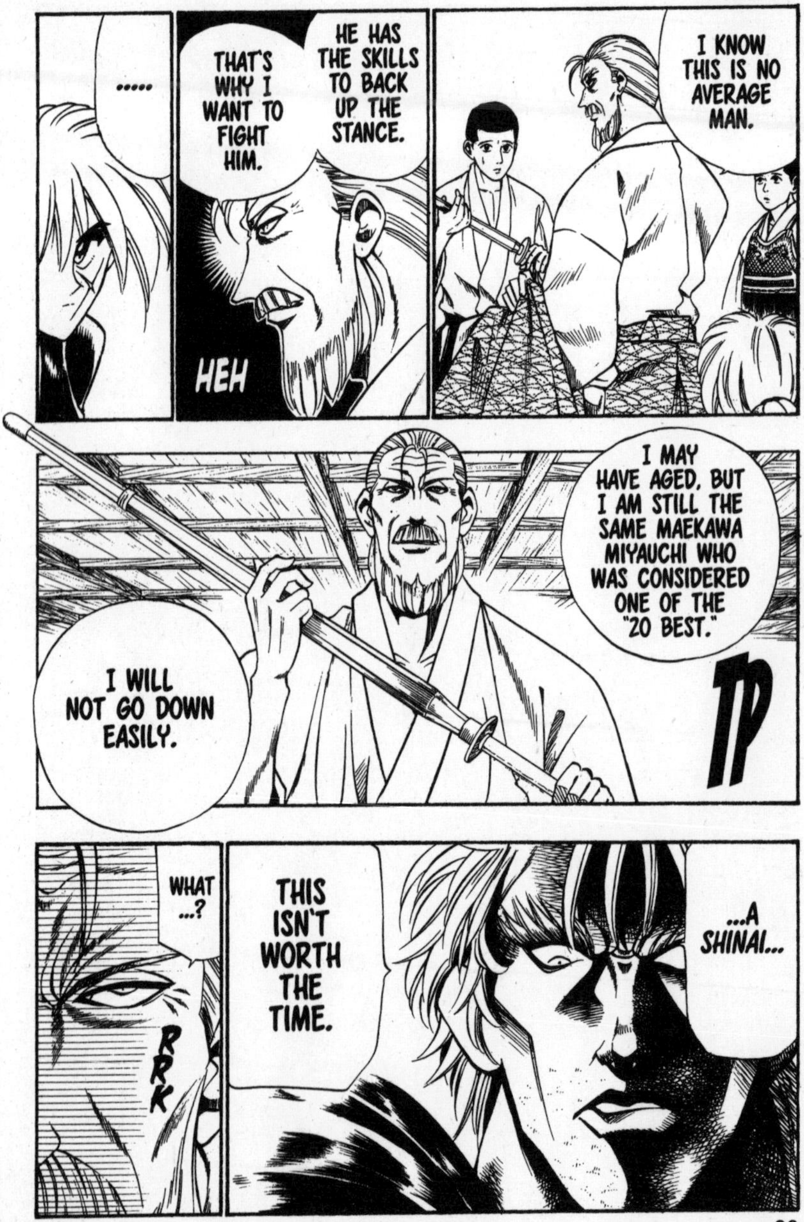

I KNOW THIS IS NO AVERAGE MAN.
HE HAS THE SKILLS TO BACK UP THE STANCE.
THAT'S WHY I WANT TO FIGHT HIM.
HEH
.....
I MAY HAVE AGED, BUT I AM STILL THE SAME MAEKAWA MIYAUCHI WHO WAS CONSIDERED ONE OF THE "20 BEST."
TP
I WILL NOT GO DOWN EASILY.
...A SHINAI...
THIS ISN'T WORTH THE TIME.
WHAT ...?
RRK

READ THIS WAY

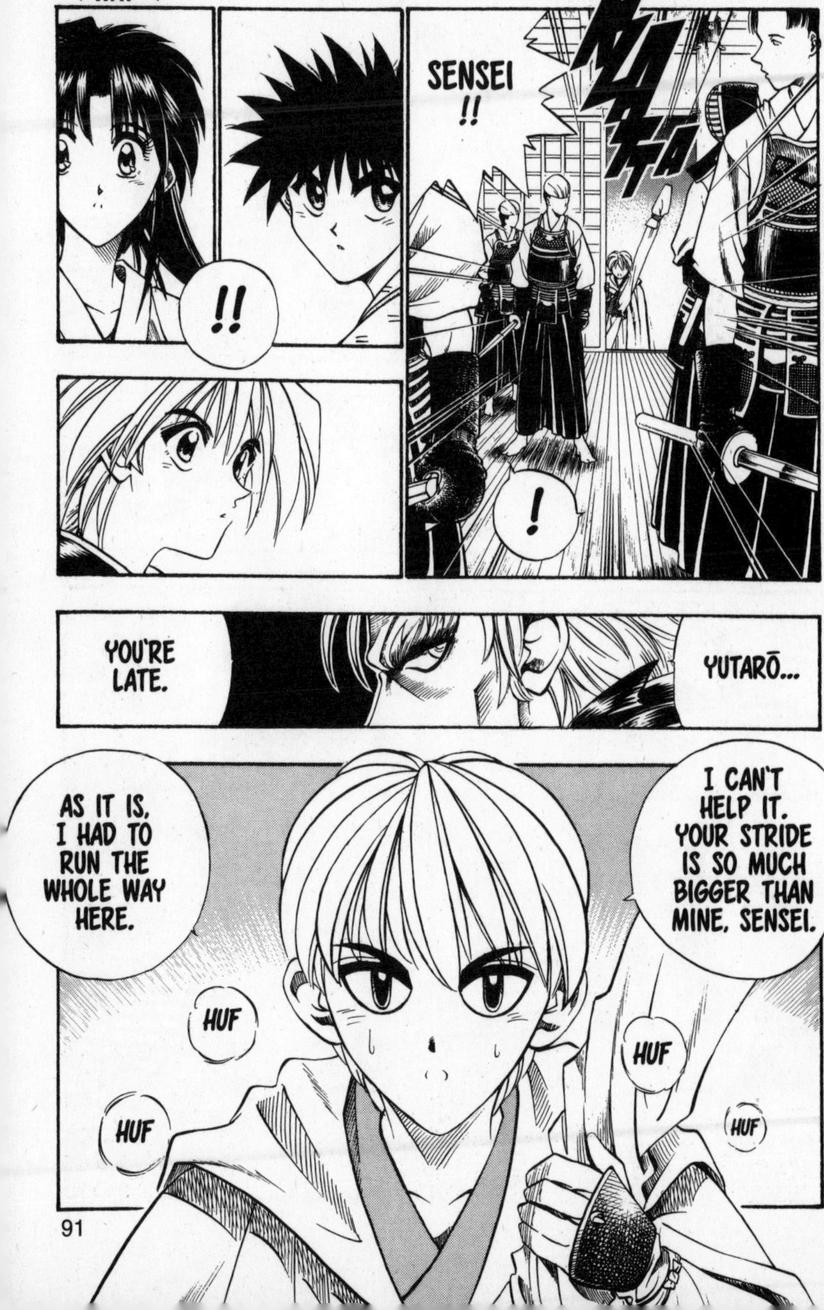
SENSEI !!
!
!!
YUTARŌ...
YOU'RE LATE.
I CAN'T HELP IT. YOUR STRIDE IS SO MUCH BIGGER THAN MINE, SENSEI.
AS IT IS, I HAD TO RUN THE WHOLE WAY HERE.
HUF
HUF
HUF
HUF

READ THIS WAY

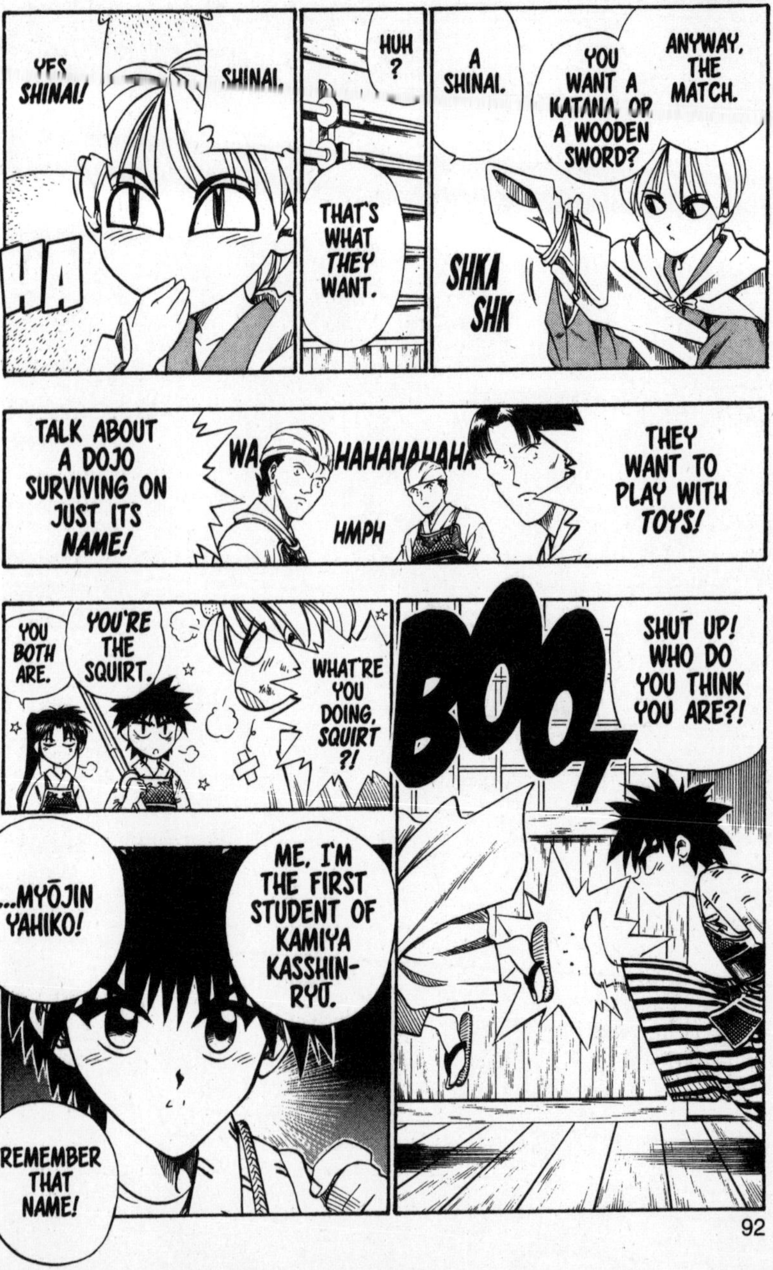
ANYWAY, THE MATCH.
YOU WANT A KATANA, OR A WOODEN SWORD?
A SHINAI.
SHKA SHK
HUH?
THAT'S WHAT THEY WANT.
SHINAI.
YES SHINAI!
HA
THEY WANT TO PLAY WITH TOYS!
WA HAHAHAHAHA
HMPH
TALK ABOUT A DOJO SURVIVING ON JUST ITS NAME!
SHUT UP! WHO DO YOU THINK YOU ARE?!
BOO
WHAT'RE YOU DOING, SQUIRT?!
YOU'RE THE SQUIRT.
YOU BOTH ARE.
ME, I'M THE FIRST STUDENT OF KAMIYA KASSHIN-RYŪ.
...MYŌJIN YAHIKO!
REMEMBER THAT NAME!

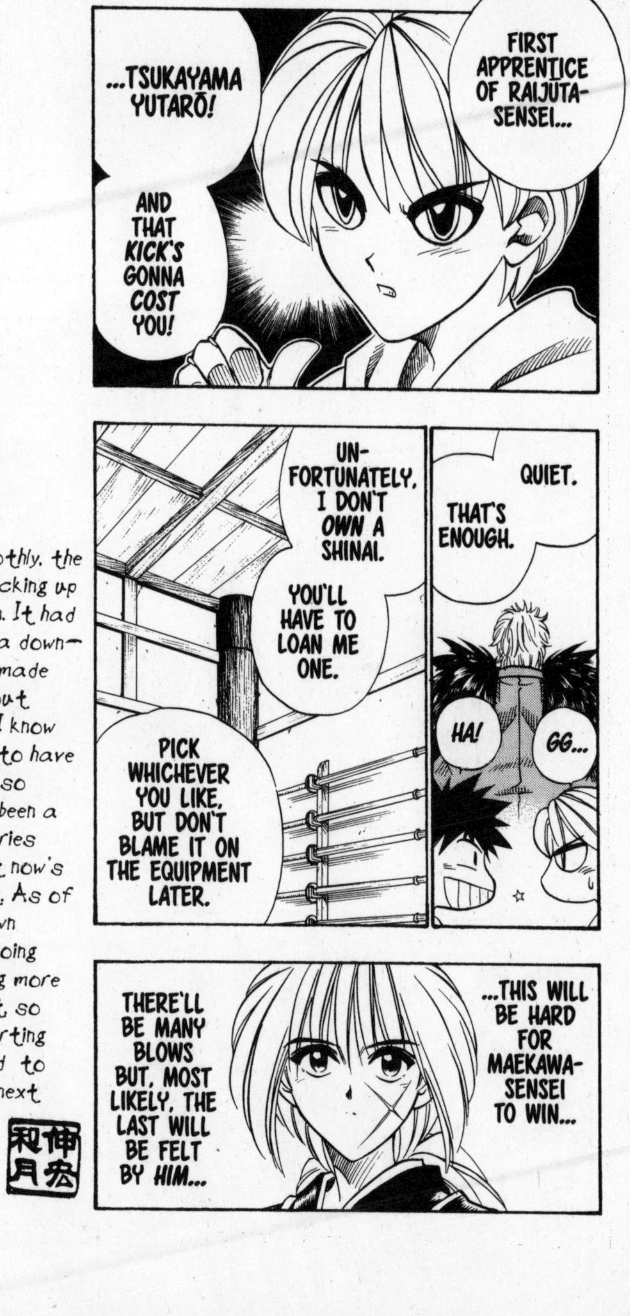
FIRST APPRENTICE OF RAIJŪTA-SENSEI...
...TSUKAYAMA YUTARŌ!
AND THAT KICK'S GONNA COST YOU!
QUIET.
THAT'S ENOUGH.
GG...
HA!
UN-FORTUNATELY, I DON'T OWN A SHINAI.
YOU'LL HAVE TO LOAN ME ONE.
PICK WHICHEVER YOU LIKE, BUT DON'T BLAME IT ON THE EQUIPMENT LATER.
...THIS WILL BE HARD FOR MAEKAWA-SENSEI TO WIN...
THERE'LL BE MANY BLOWS BUT, MOST LIKELY, THE LAST WILL BE FELT BY HIM...

If things go smoothly, the pace will start picking up in the series soon. It had been heading into a down-beat mode, which made me concerned about reader response. I know "RuroKen" ought to have an upbeat ending, so don't worry! It's been a year since the series started, so right now's the critical point. As of this volume, my own quibbles end—I'm going to start putting more "strength" into it, so please keep supporting me. I look forward to seeing you in the next volume!

和月伸宏

READ THIS WAY

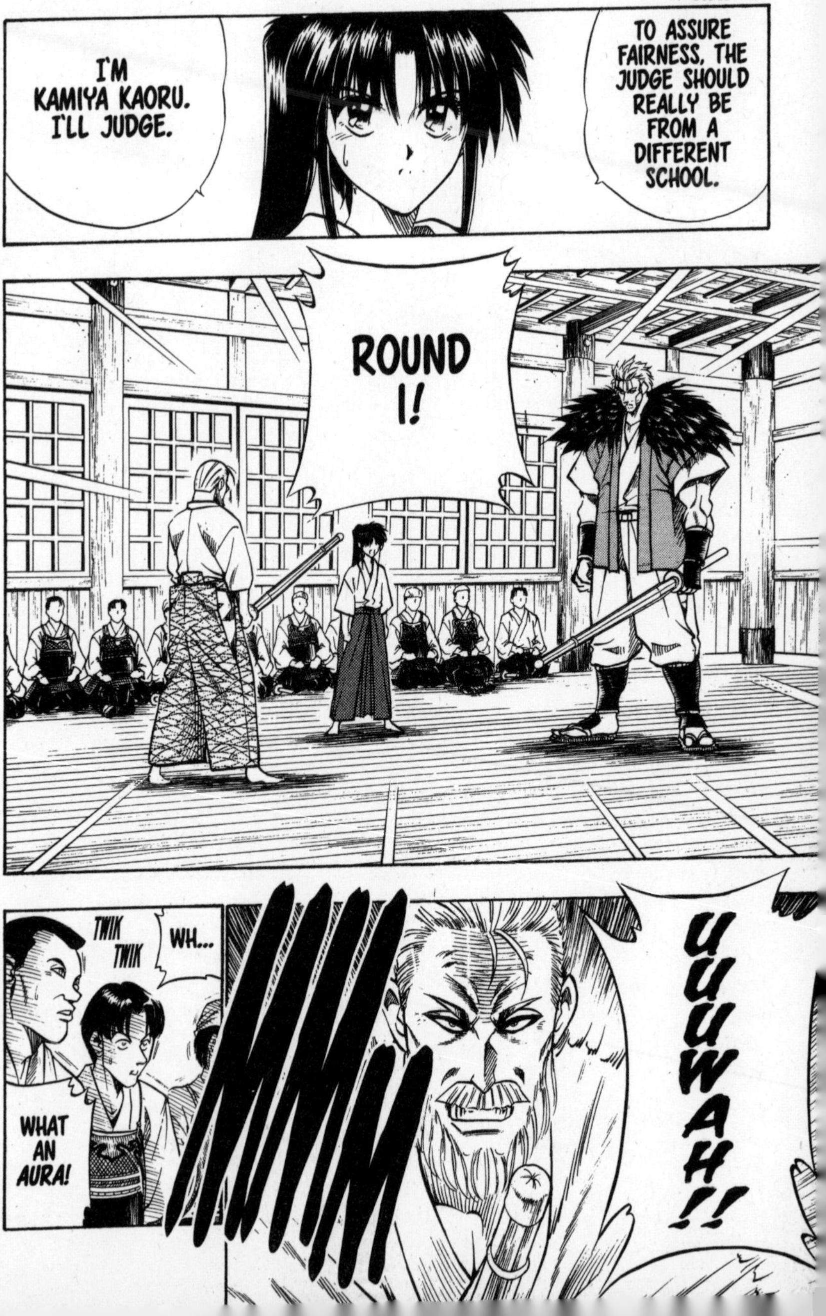
TO ASSURE FAIRNESS, THE JUDGE SHOULD REALLY BE FROM A DIFFERENT SCHOOL.
I'M KAMIYA KAORU. I'LL JUDGE.
ROUND 1!
UUUWAH!!
WH...
TWIK TWIK
WHAT AN AURA!

READ THIS WAY

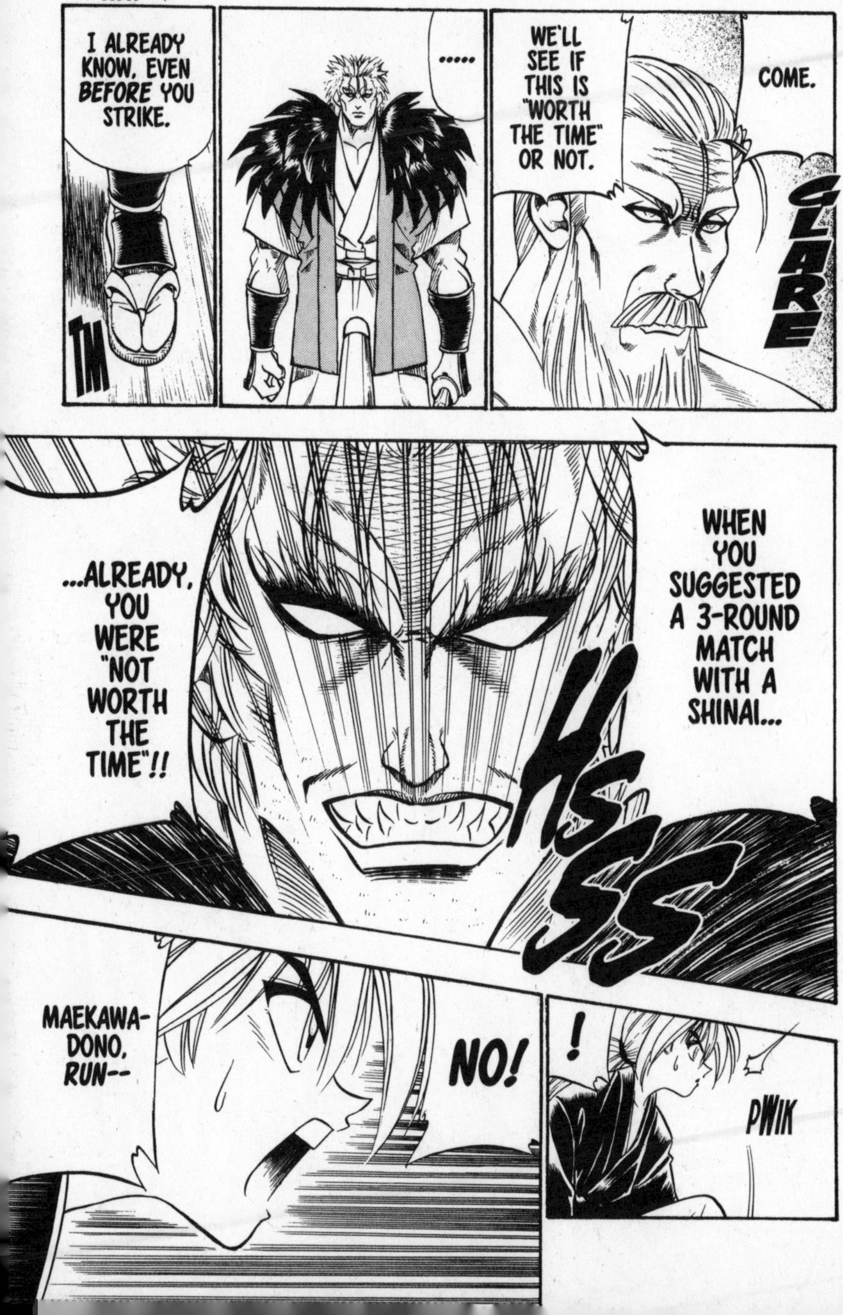
COME.
WE'LL SEE IF THIS IS "WORTH THE TIME" OR NOT.
GLARE
.....
I ALREADY KNOW, EVEN BEFORE YOU STRIKE.
TM
WHEN YOU SUGGESTED A 3-ROUND MATCH WITH A SHINAI...
...ALREADY, YOU WERE "NOT WORTH THE TIME"!!
HSSS
!
PWIK
NO!
MAEKAWA-DONO, RUN--

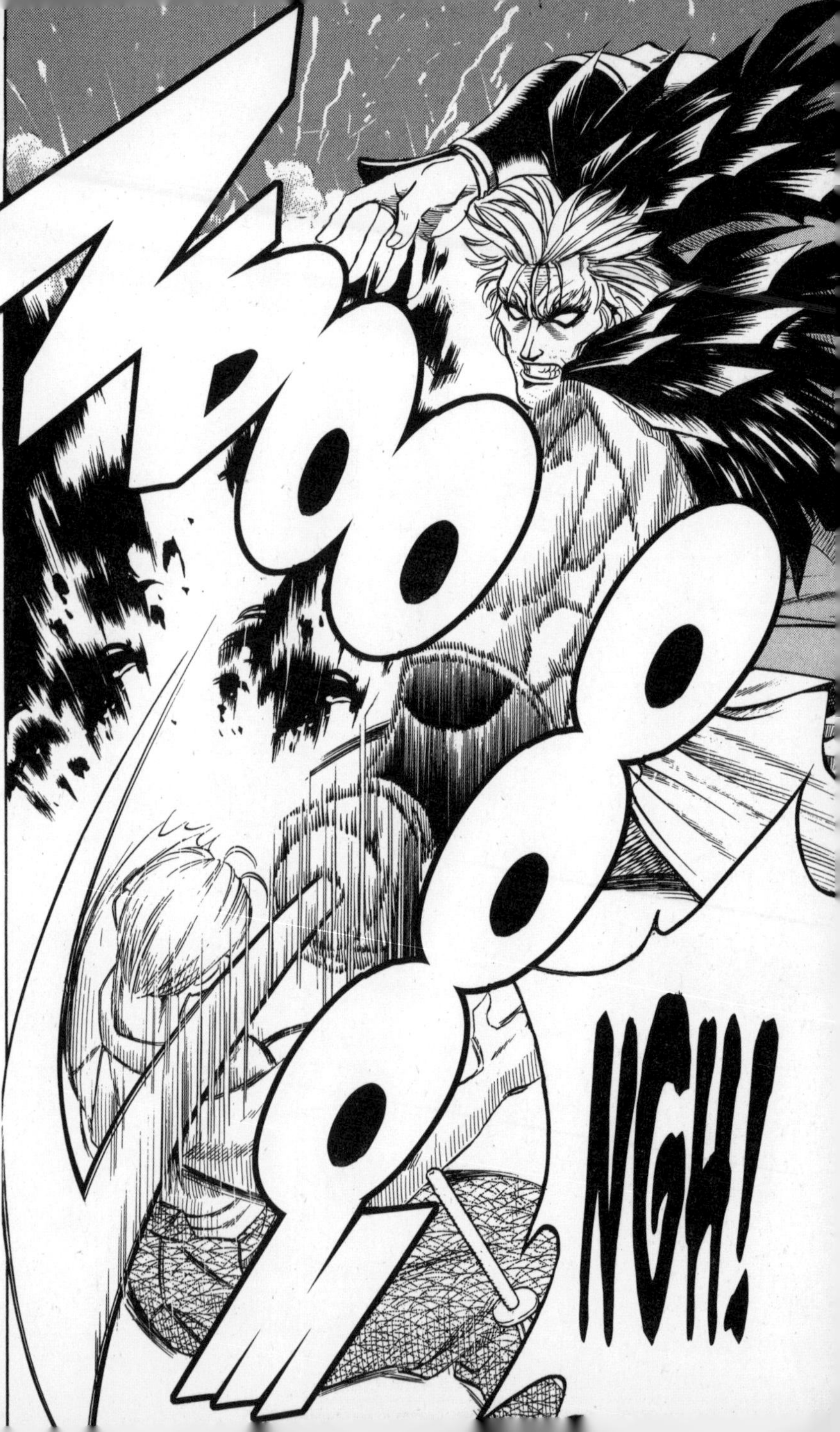
ZOOOOOM
NGH!

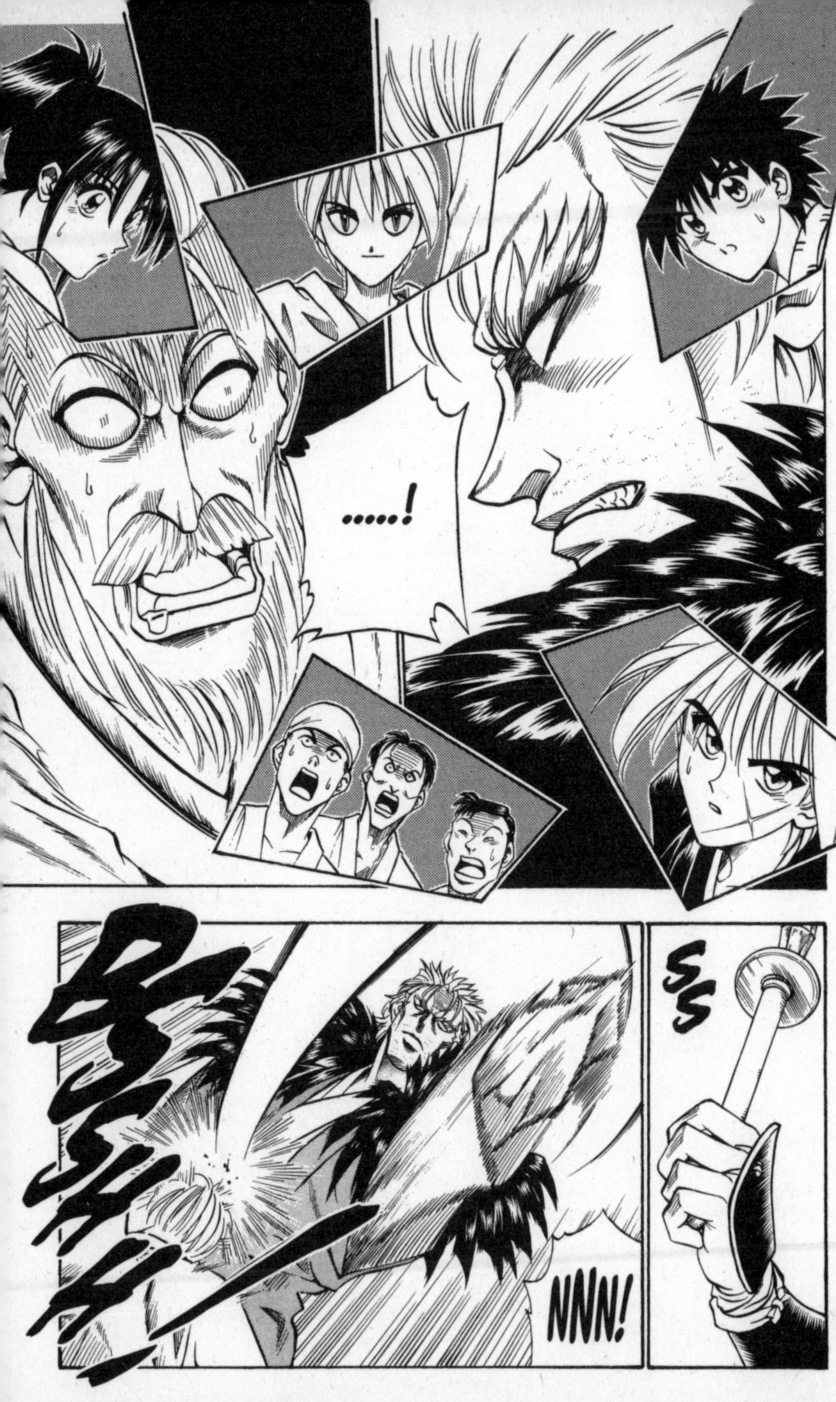
.....!
SS
BASHH!
NNN!

READ THIS WAY

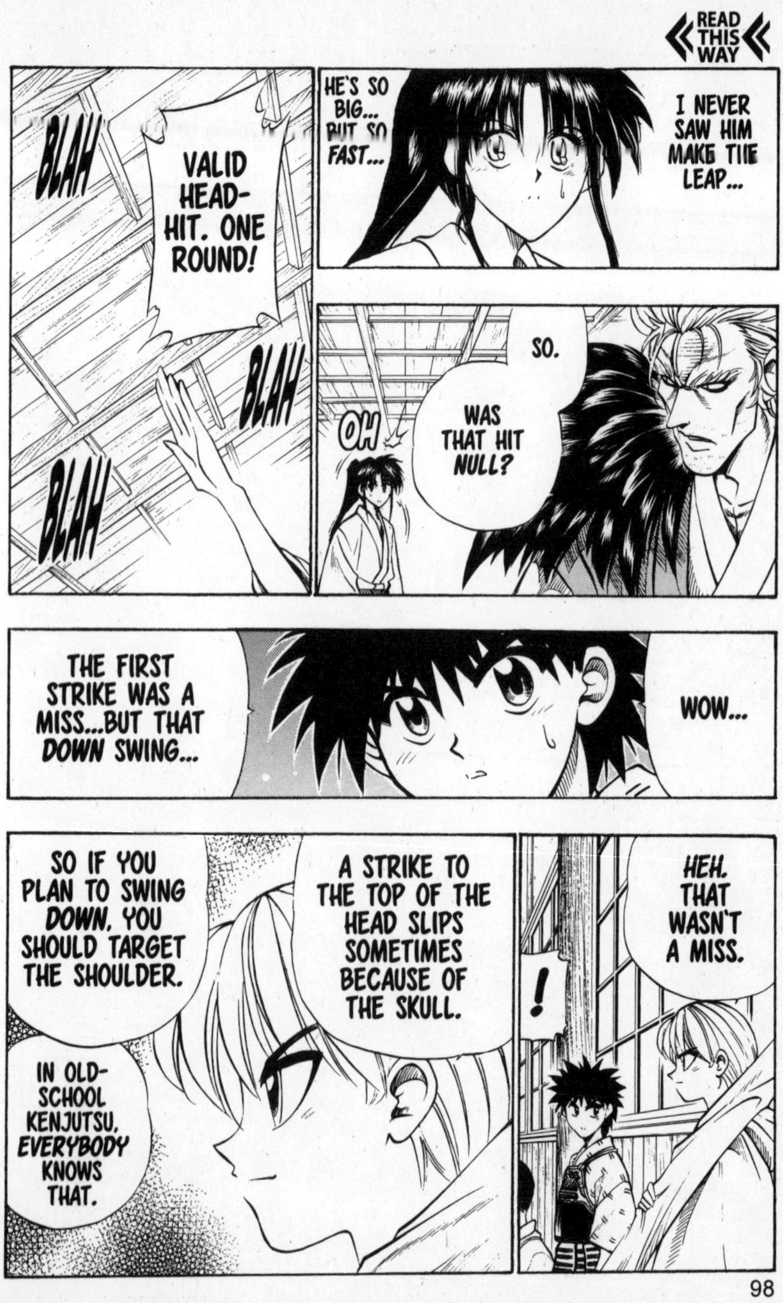
I NEVER SAW HIM MAKE THE LEAP...
HE'S SO BIG... BUT SO FAST...
SO.
WAS THAT HIT NULL?
OH
VALID HEAD-HIT. ONE ROUND!
BLAH
BLAH
BLAH
WOW...
THE FIRST STRIKE WAS A MISS...BUT THAT DOWN SWING...
HEH. THAT WASN'T A MISS.
!
A STRIKE TO THE TOP OF THE HEAD SLIPS SOMETIMES BECAUSE OF THE SKULL.
SO IF YOU PLAN TO SWING DOWN, YOU SHOULD TARGET THE SHOULDER.
IN OLD-SCHOOL KENJUTSU, EVERYBODY KNOWS THAT.

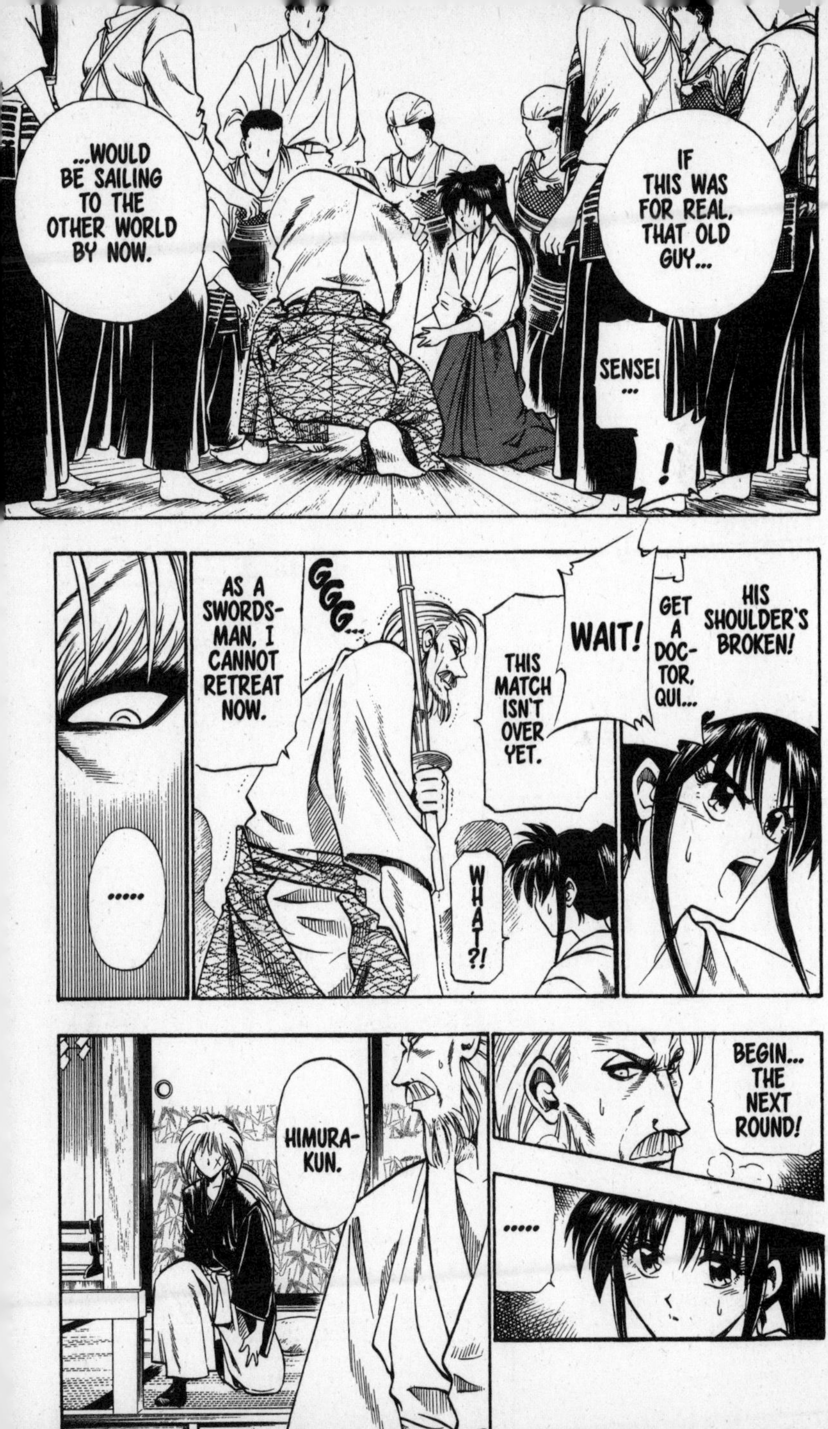
IF THIS WAS FOR REAL, THAT OLD GUY...
...WOULD BE SAILING TO THE OTHER WORLD BY NOW.
SENSEI ...
!
HIS SHOULDER'S BROKEN!
GET A DOC-TOR, QUI...
WAIT!
THIS MATCH ISN'T OVER YET.
AS A SWORDS-MAN, I CANNOT RETREAT NOW.
GGG...
WHAT?!
......
BEGIN... THE NEXT ROUND!
......
HIMURA-KUN.

READ THIS WAY

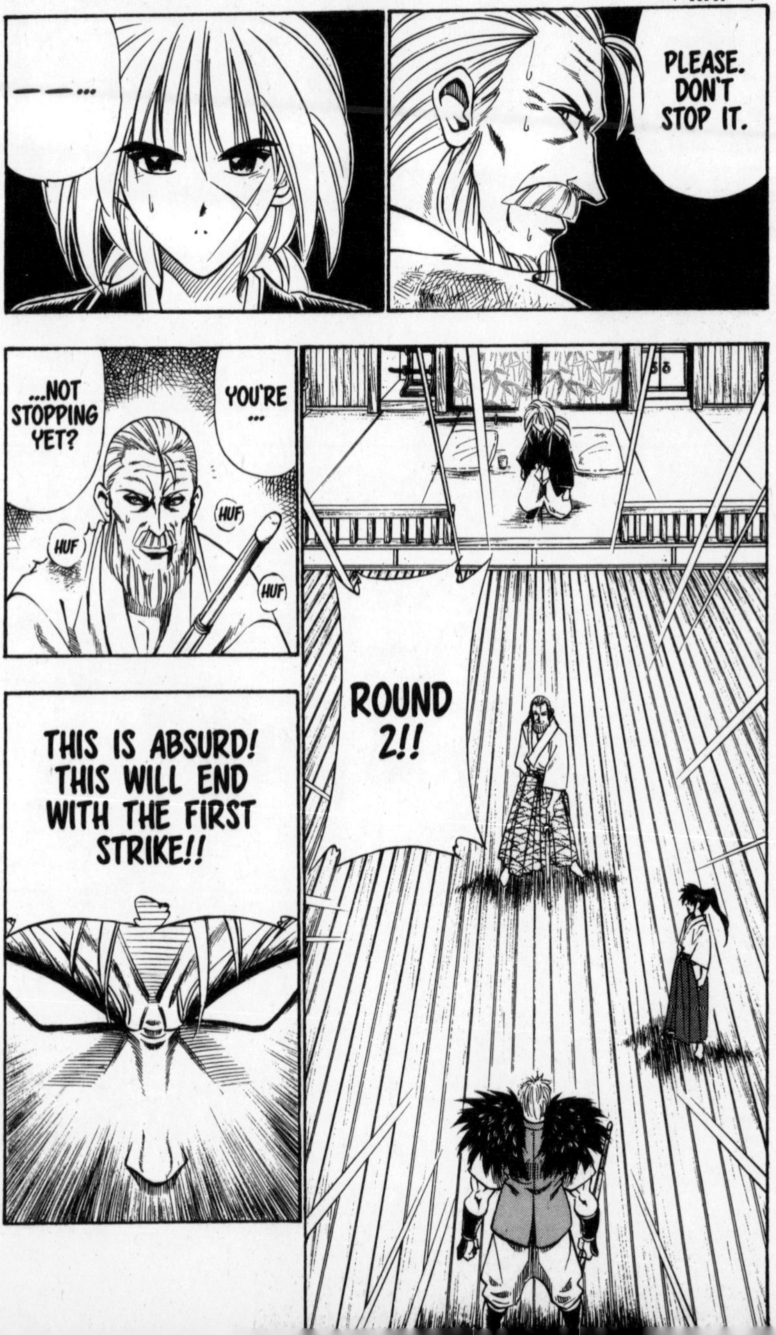

PLEASE. DON'T STOP IT.
——...
ROUND 2!!
YOU'RE ...
...NOT STOPPING YET?
HUF
HUF
HUF
THIS IS ABSURD! THIS WILL END WITH THE FIRST STRIKE!!

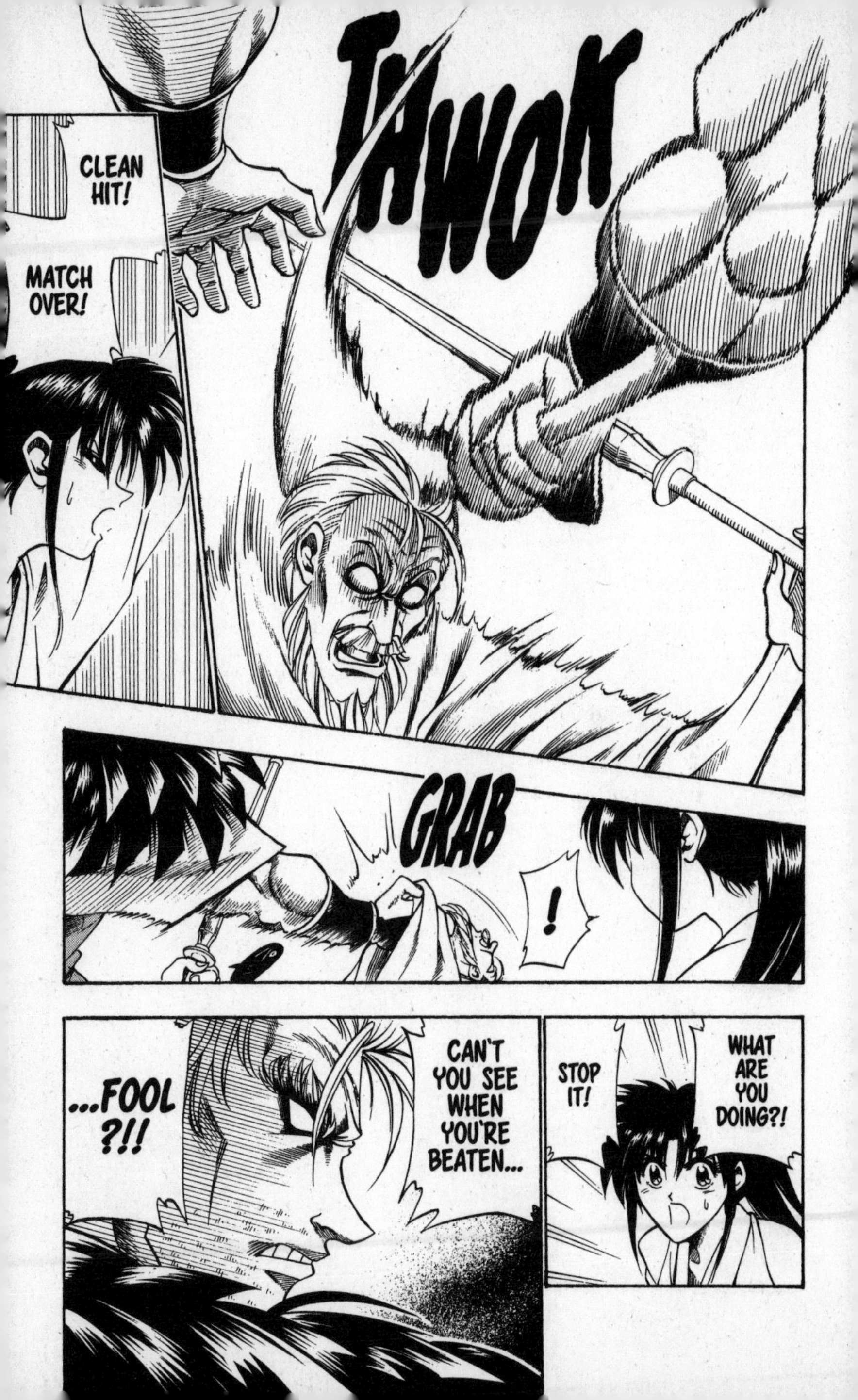
THWOK
CLEAN HIT!
MATCH OVER!
GRAB
!
WHAT ARE YOU DOING?!
STOP IT!
CAN'T YOU SEE WHEN YOU'RE BEATEN...
...FOOL ?!!

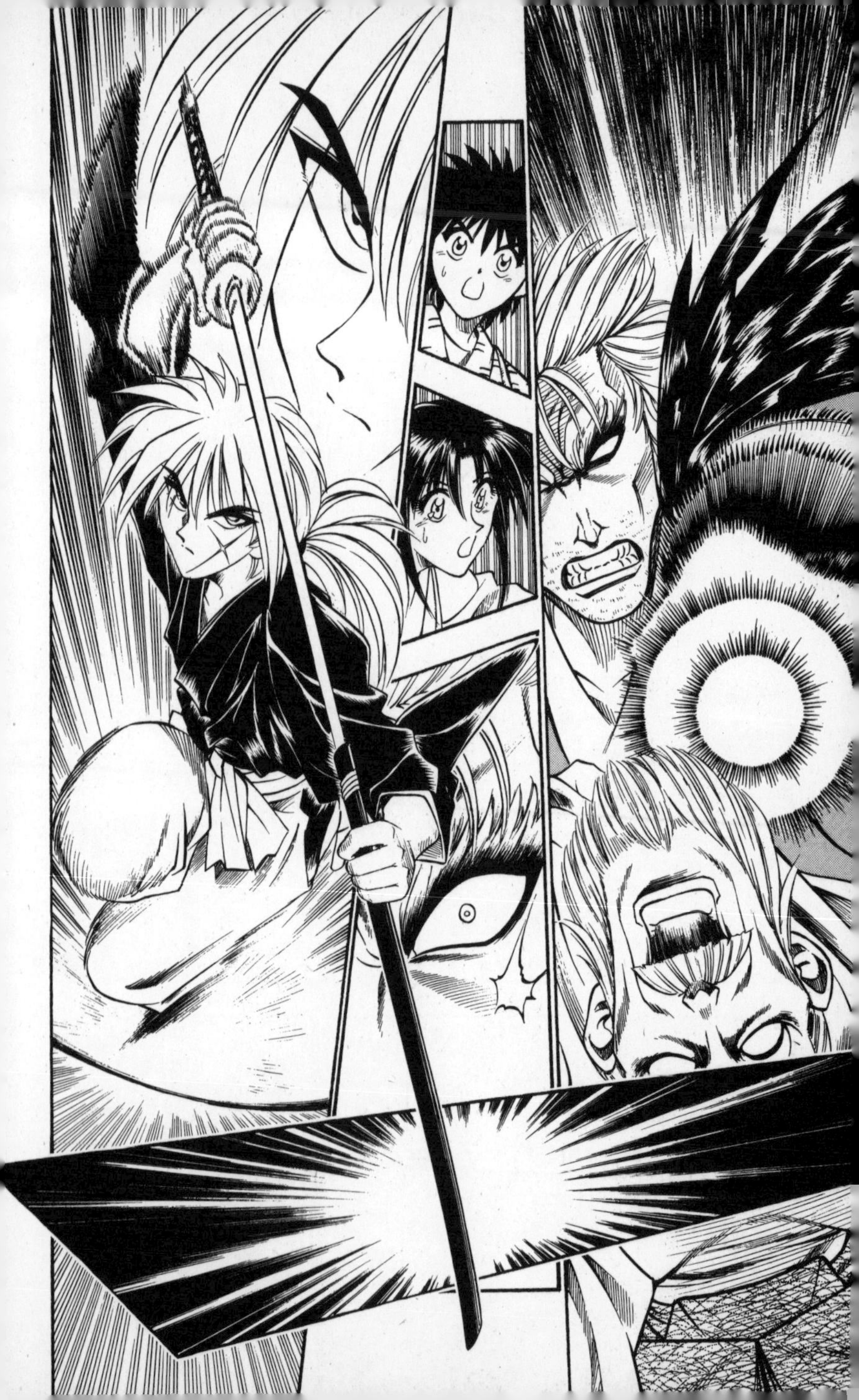

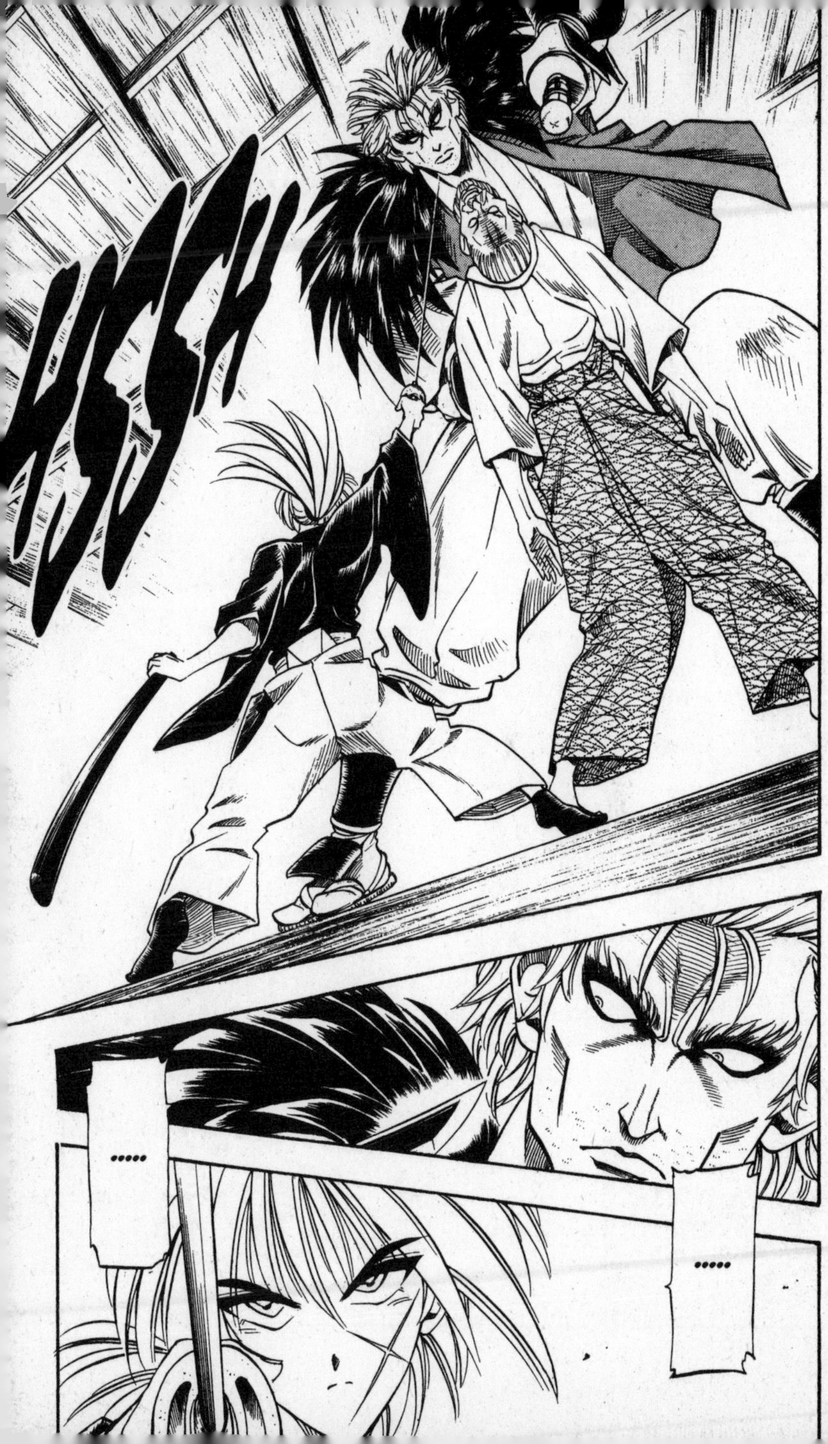

.....
.....

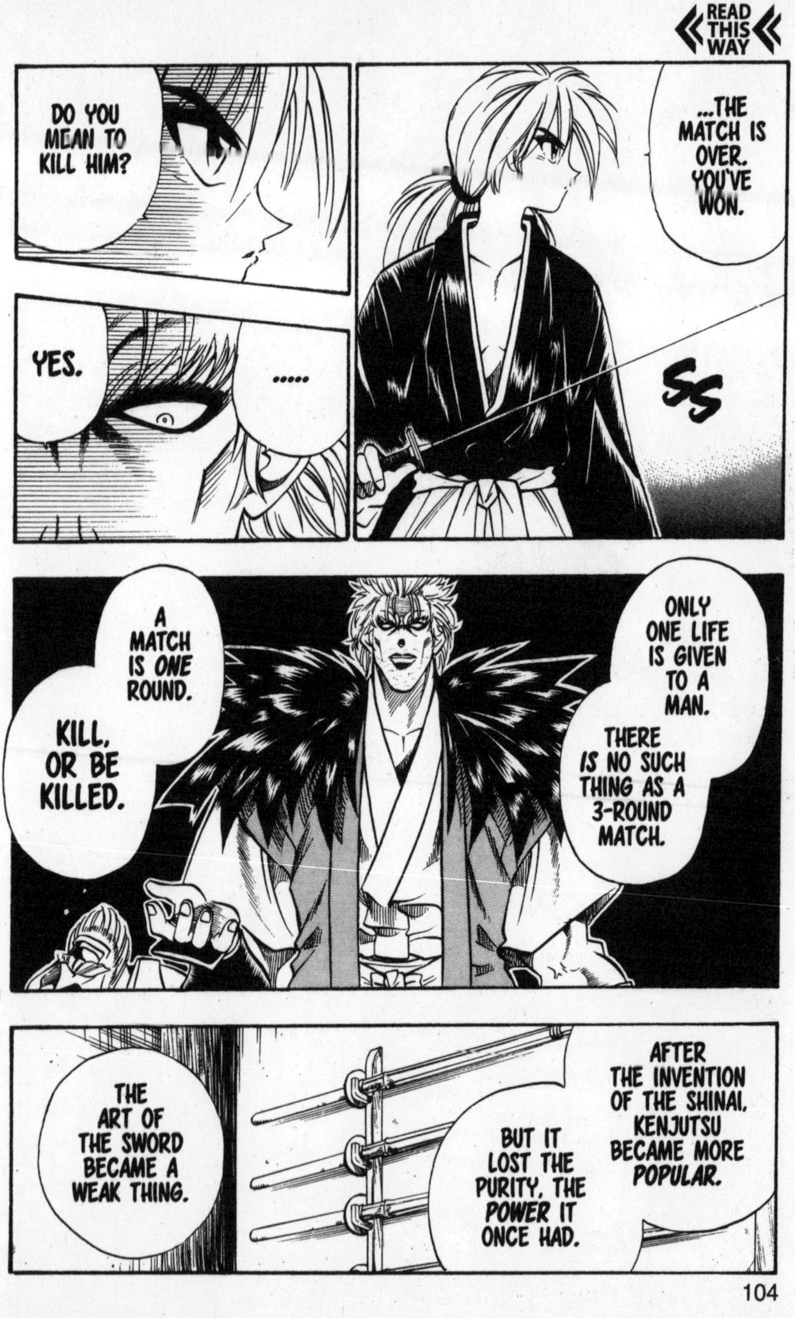
READ THIS WAY
...THE MATCH IS OVER. YOU'VE WON.
SS
DO YOU MEAN TO KILL HIM?
.....
YES.
ONLY ONE LIFE IS GIVEN TO A MAN.
THERE IS NO SUCH THING AS A 3-ROUND MATCH.
A MATCH IS *ONE* ROUND.
KILL, OR BE KILLED.
AFTER THE INVENTION OF THE SHINAI, KENJUTSU BECAME MORE *POPULAR*.
BUT IT LOST THE PURITY, THE *POWER* IT ONCE HAD.
THE ART OF THE SWORD BECAME A WEAK THING.

READ THIS WAY

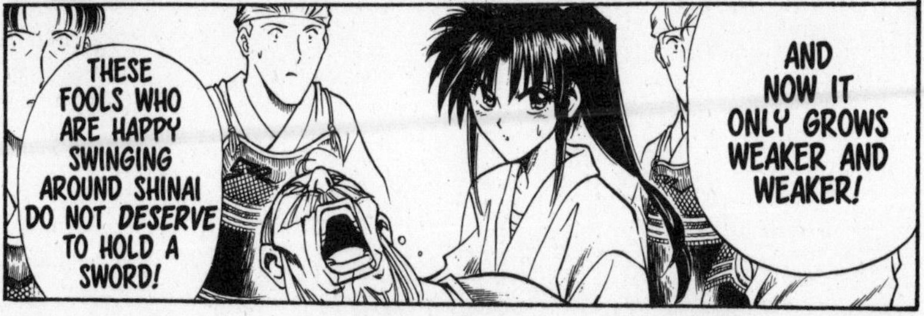
AND NOW IT ONLY GROWS WEAKER AND WEAKER!
THESE FOOLS WHO ARE HAPPY SWINGING AROUND SHINAI DO NOT DESERVE TO HOLD A SWORD!

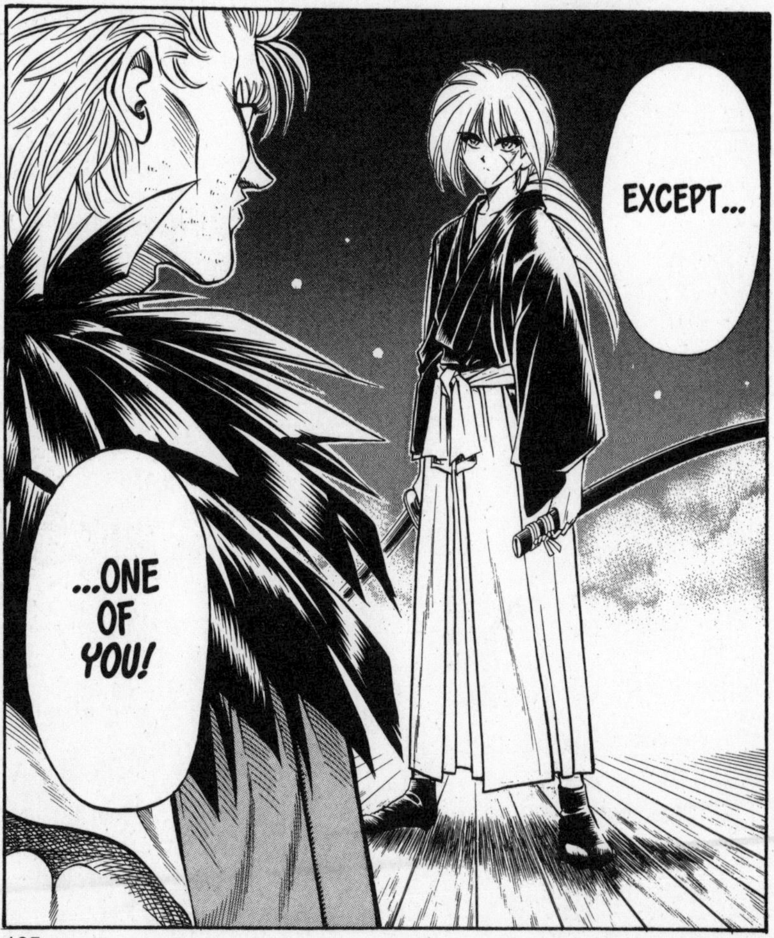
EXCEPT...
...ONE OF YOU!

Rurouni Kenshin

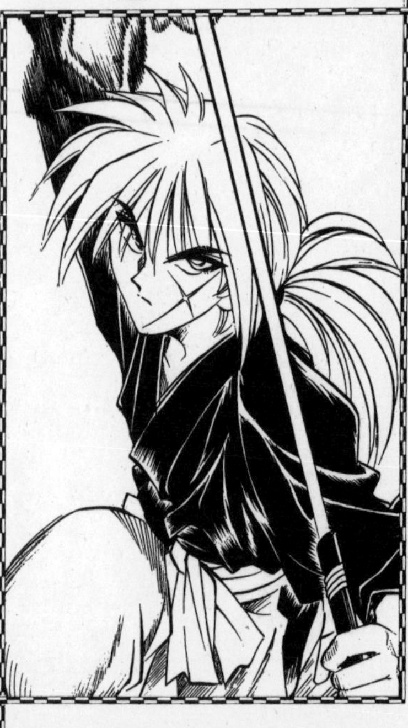

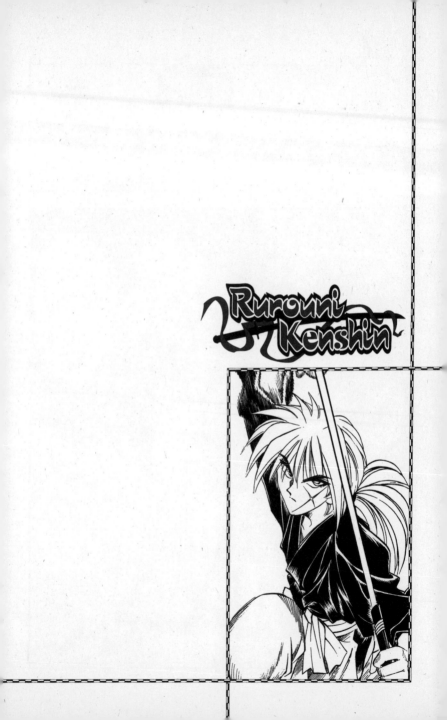

READ THIS WAY

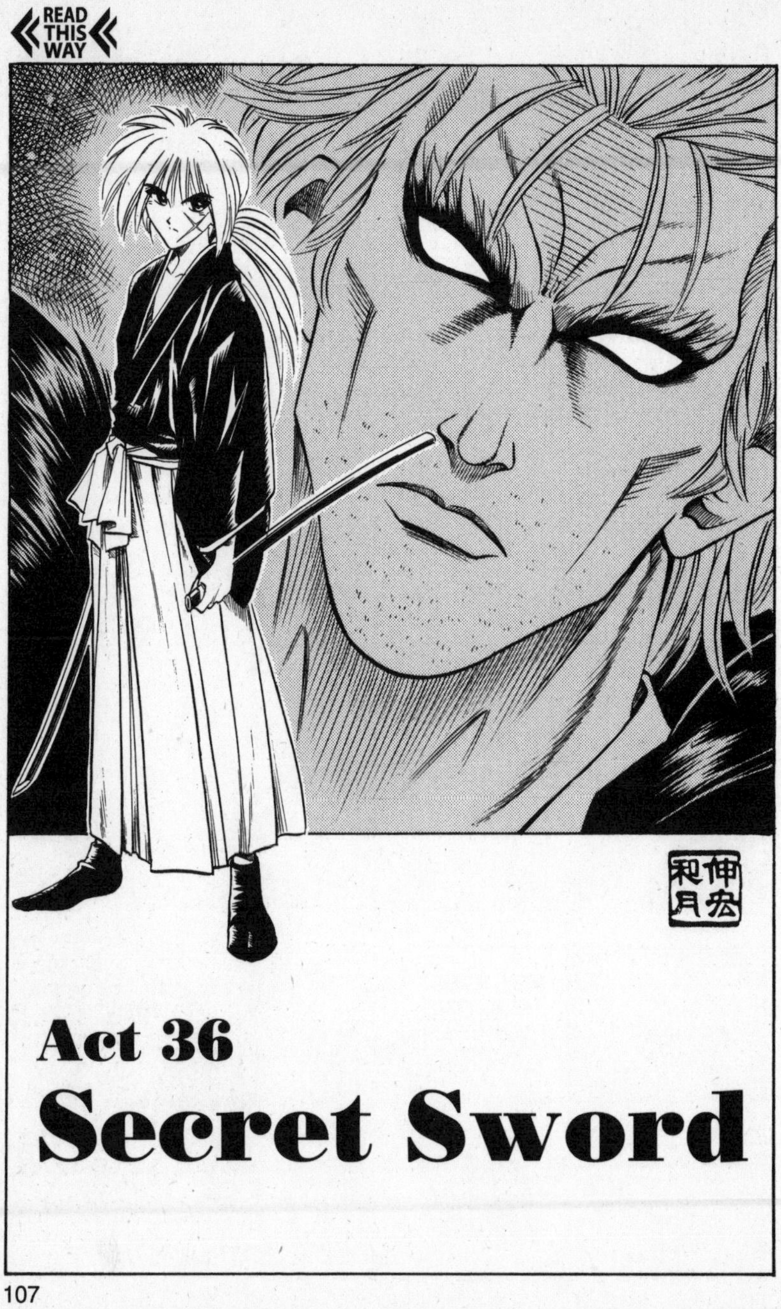
伸宏和月

# Act 36
# Secret Sword

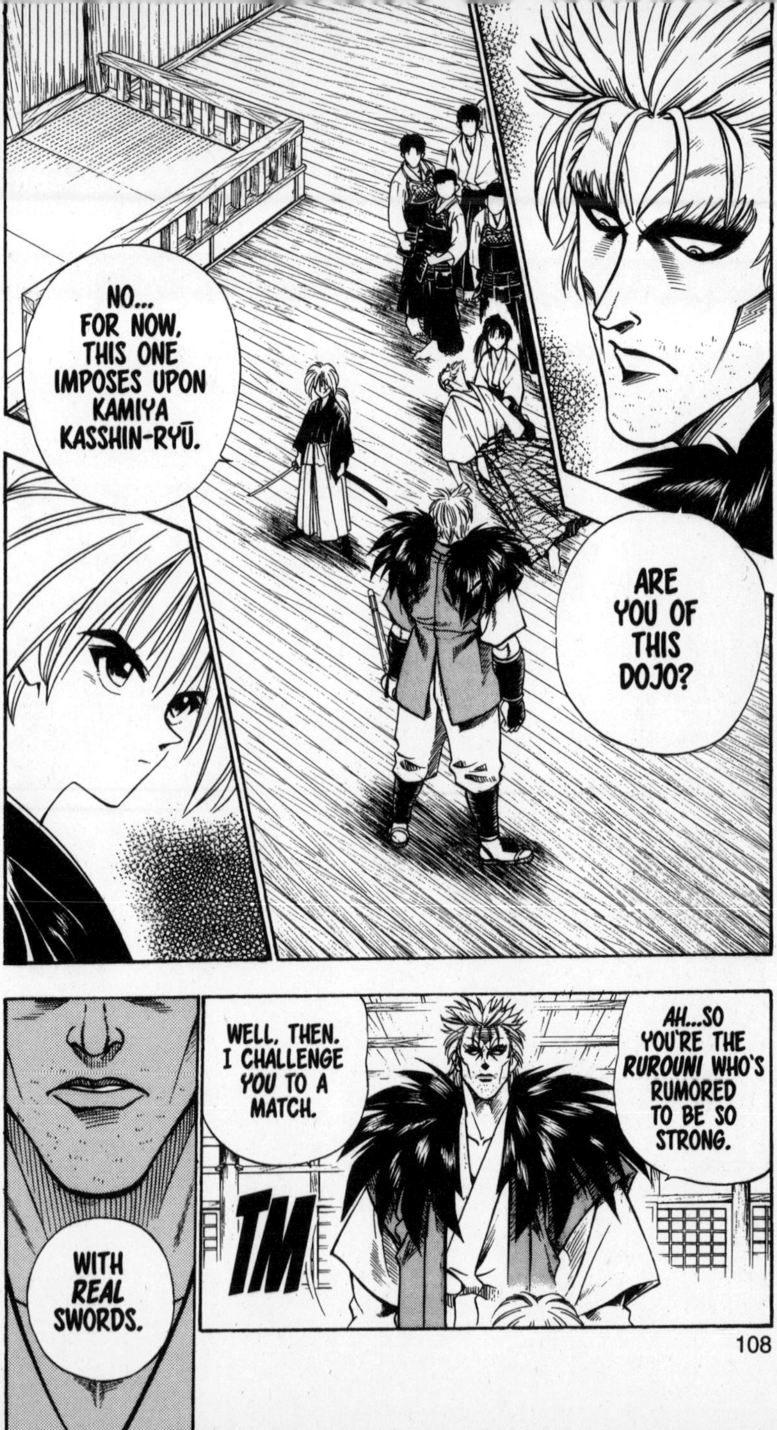
ARE YOU OF THIS DOJO?
NO... FOR NOW, THIS ONE IMPOSES UPON KAMIYA KASSHIN-RYŪ.
AH...SO YOU'RE THE RUROUNI WHO'S RUMORED TO BE SO STRONG.
WELL, THEN. I CHALLENGE YOU TO A MATCH.
TM
WITH REAL SWORDS.

READ THIS WAY

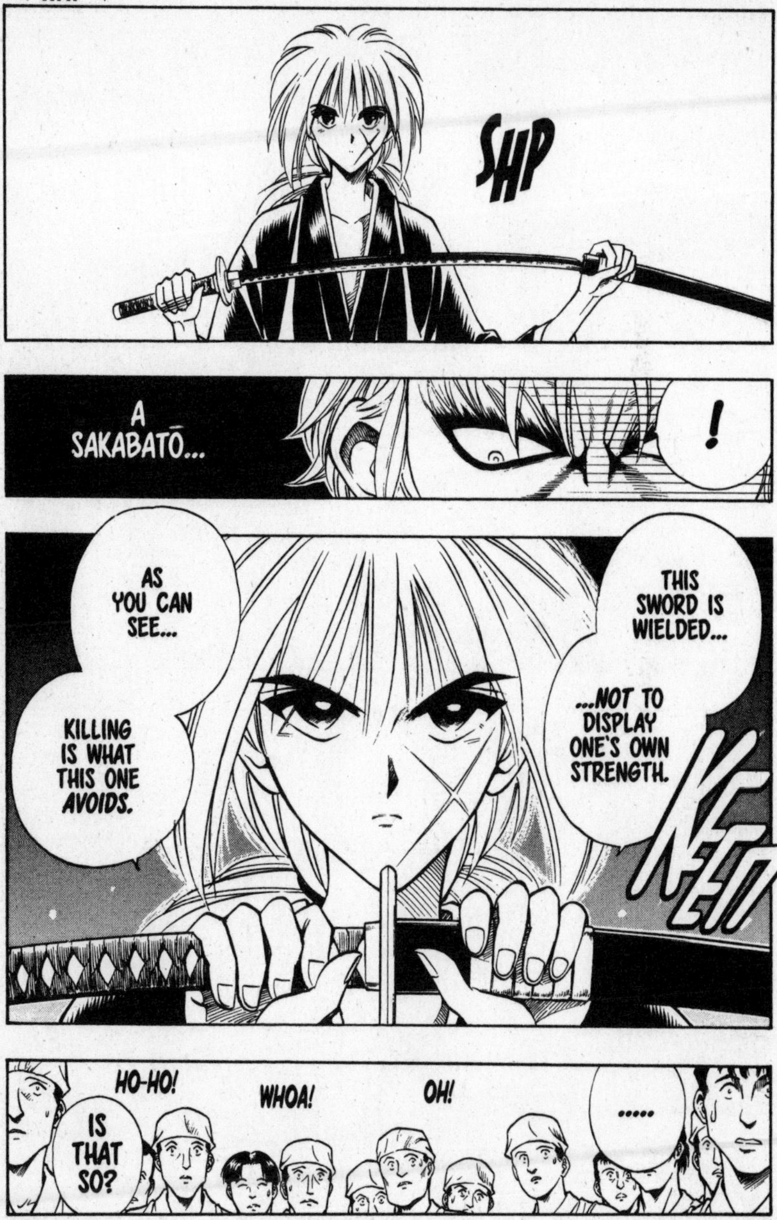
SHP
!
A SAKABATŌ...
THIS SWORD IS WIELDED...
...NOT TO DISPLAY ONE'S OWN STRENGTH.
AS YOU CAN SEE...
KILLING IS WHAT THIS ONE AVOIDS.
.....
OH!
WHOA!
HO-HO!
IS THAT SO?

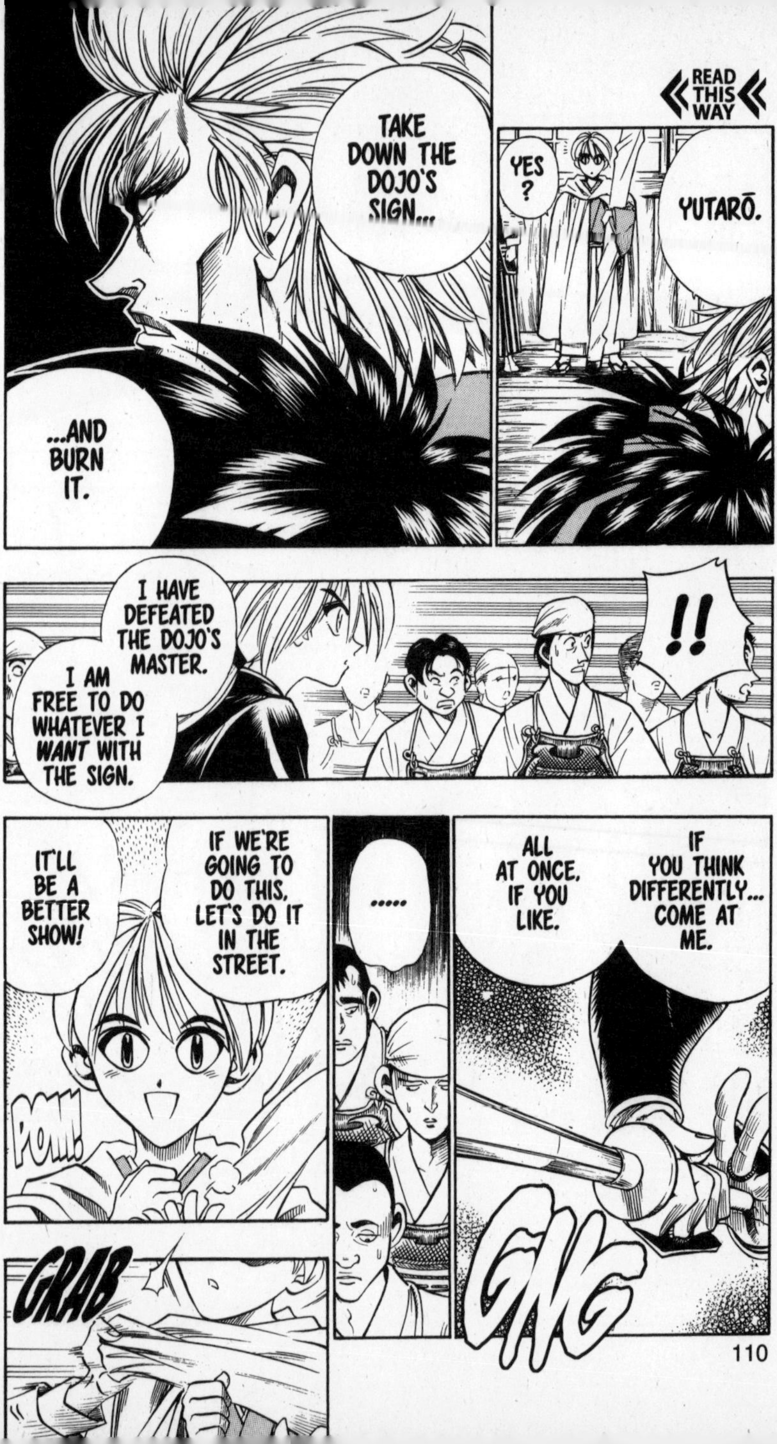
READ THIS WAY
YUTARŌ.
YES?
TAKE DOWN THE DOJO'S SIGN...
...AND BURN IT.
!!
I HAVE DEFEATED THE DOJO'S MASTER.
I AM FREE TO DO WHATEVER I *WANT* WITH THE SIGN.
IF YOU THINK DIFFERENTLY... COME AT ME.
ALL AT ONCE, IF YOU LIKE.
GNG
.....
IF WE'RE GOING TO DO THIS, LET'S DO IT IN THE STREET.
IT'LL BE A BETTER SHOW!
POM!
GRAB

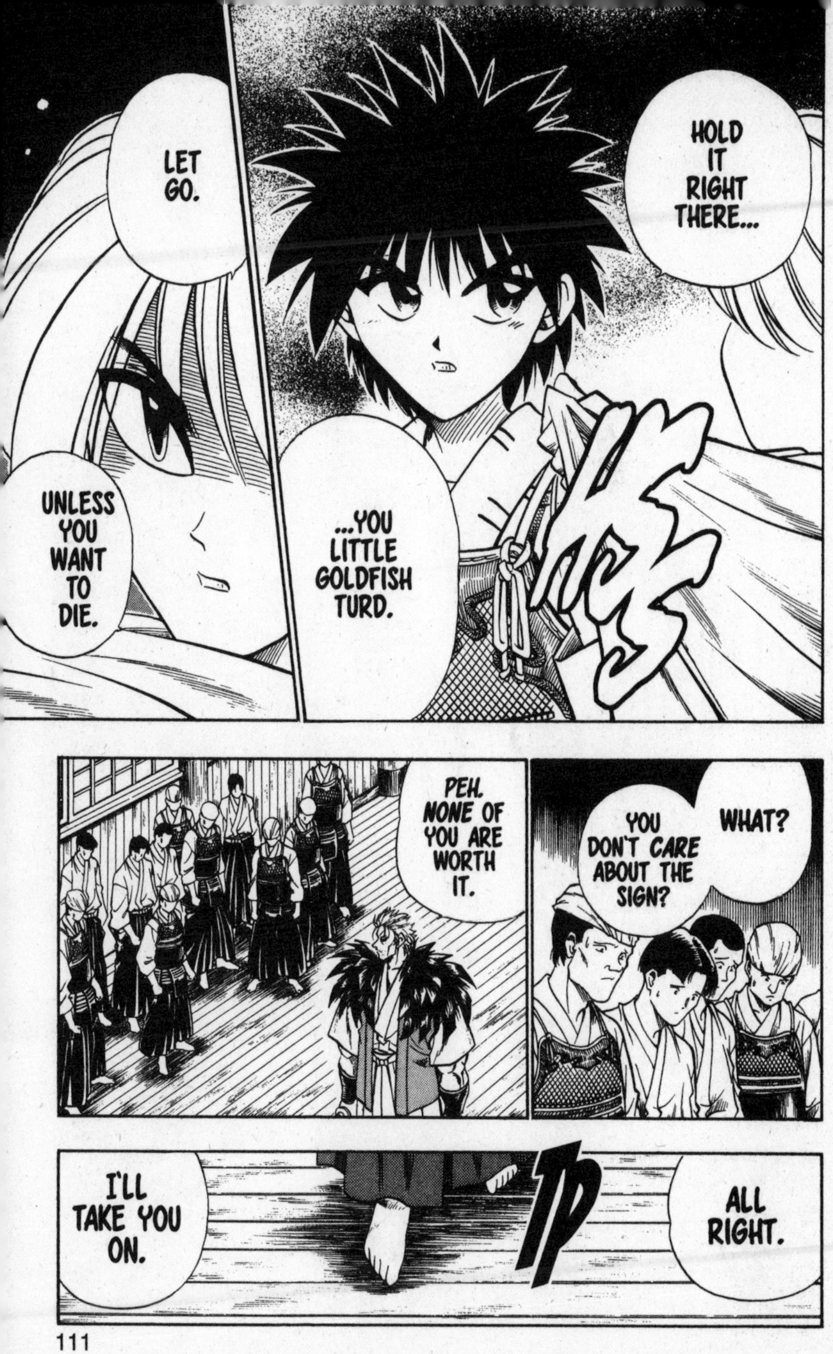
HOLD IT RIGHT THERE...
...YOU LITTLE GOLDFISH TURD.
LET GO.
UNLESS YOU WANT TO DIE.
WHAT?
YOU DON'T CARE ABOUT THE SIGN?
PEH. NONE OF YOU ARE WORTH IT.
ALL RIGHT.
TP
I'LL TAKE YOU ON.

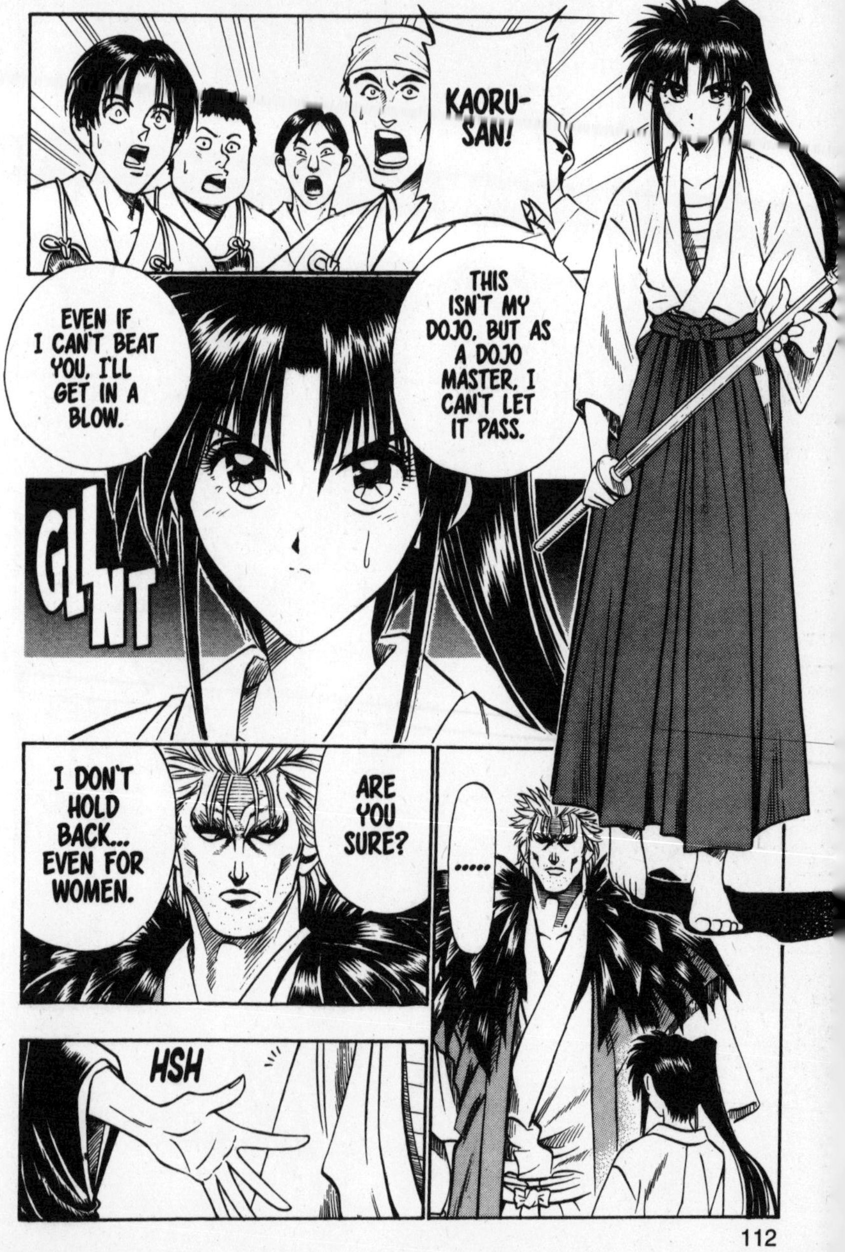
KAORU-SAN!
THIS ISN'T MY DOJO, BUT AS A DOJO MASTER, I CAN'T LET IT PASS.
EVEN IF I CAN'T BEAT YOU, I'LL GET IN A BLOW.
GLINT
.....
ARE YOU SURE?
I DON'T HOLD BACK... EVEN FOR WOMEN.
HSH

READ THIS WAY

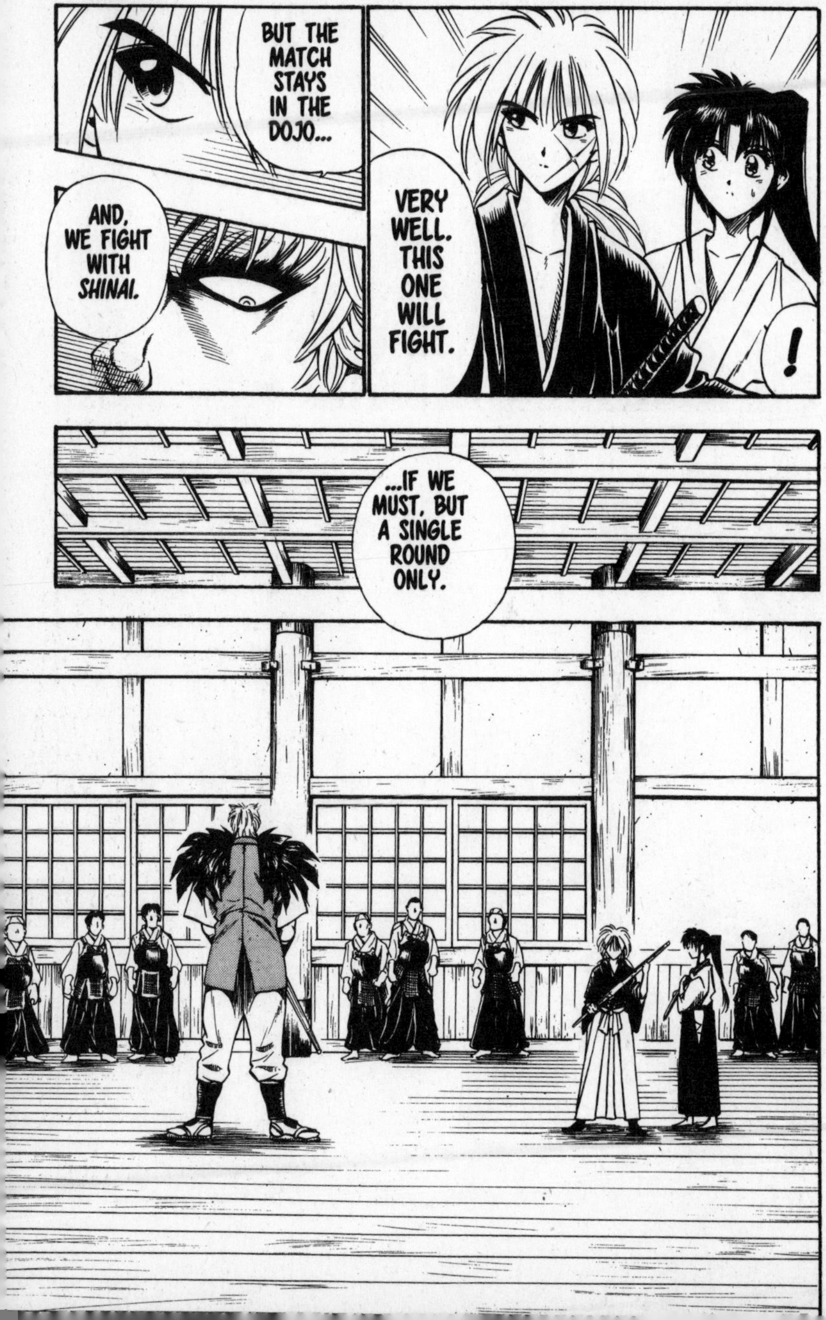
VERY WELL. THIS ONE WILL FIGHT.
!
BUT THE MATCH STAYS IN THE DOJO...
AND, WE FIGHT WITH SHINAI.
...IF WE MUST, BUT A SINGLE ROUND ONLY.

READ THIS WAY

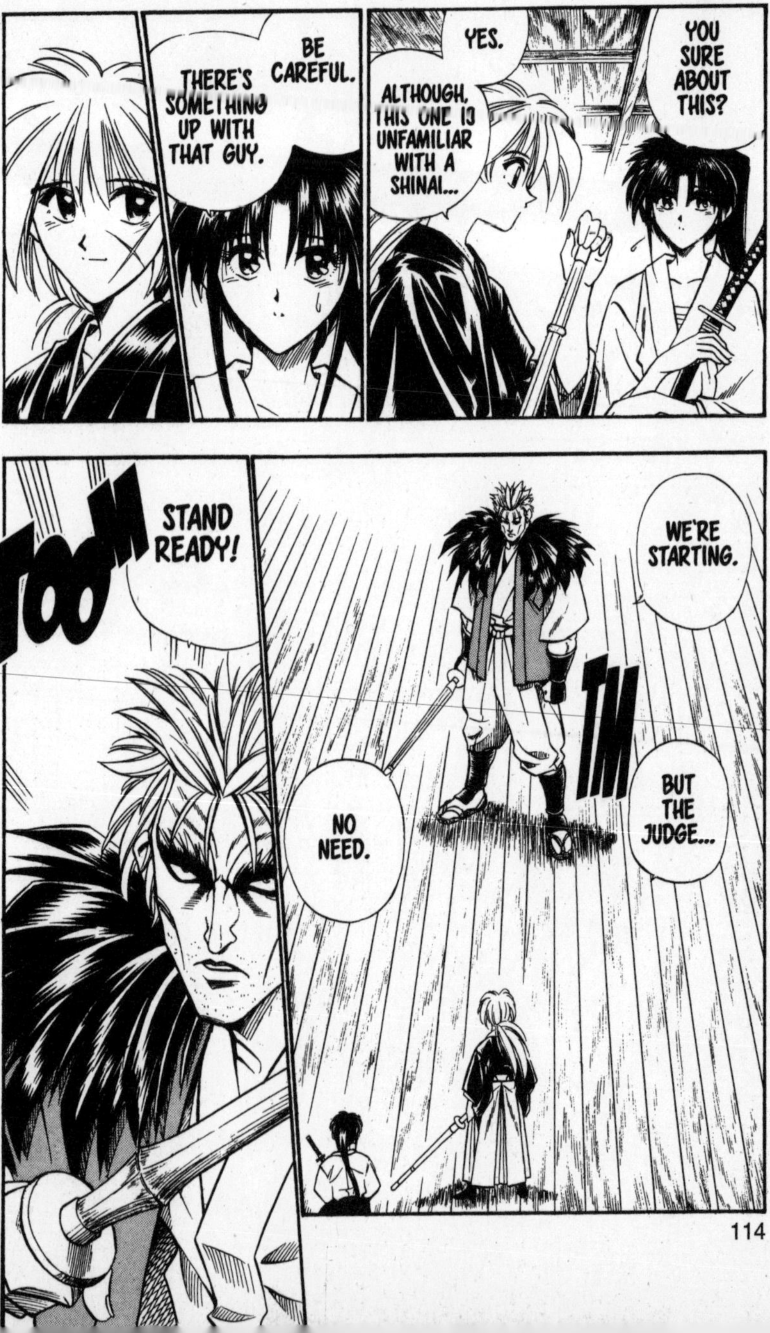

YOU SURE ABOUT THIS?
YES.
ALTHOUGH, THIS ONE IS UNFAMILIAR WITH A SHINAI...
BE CAREFUL.
THERE'S SOMETHING UP WITH THAT GUY.
WE'RE STARTING.
TM
BUT THE JUDGE...
NO NEED.
STAND READY!
TOOM

READ THIS WAY

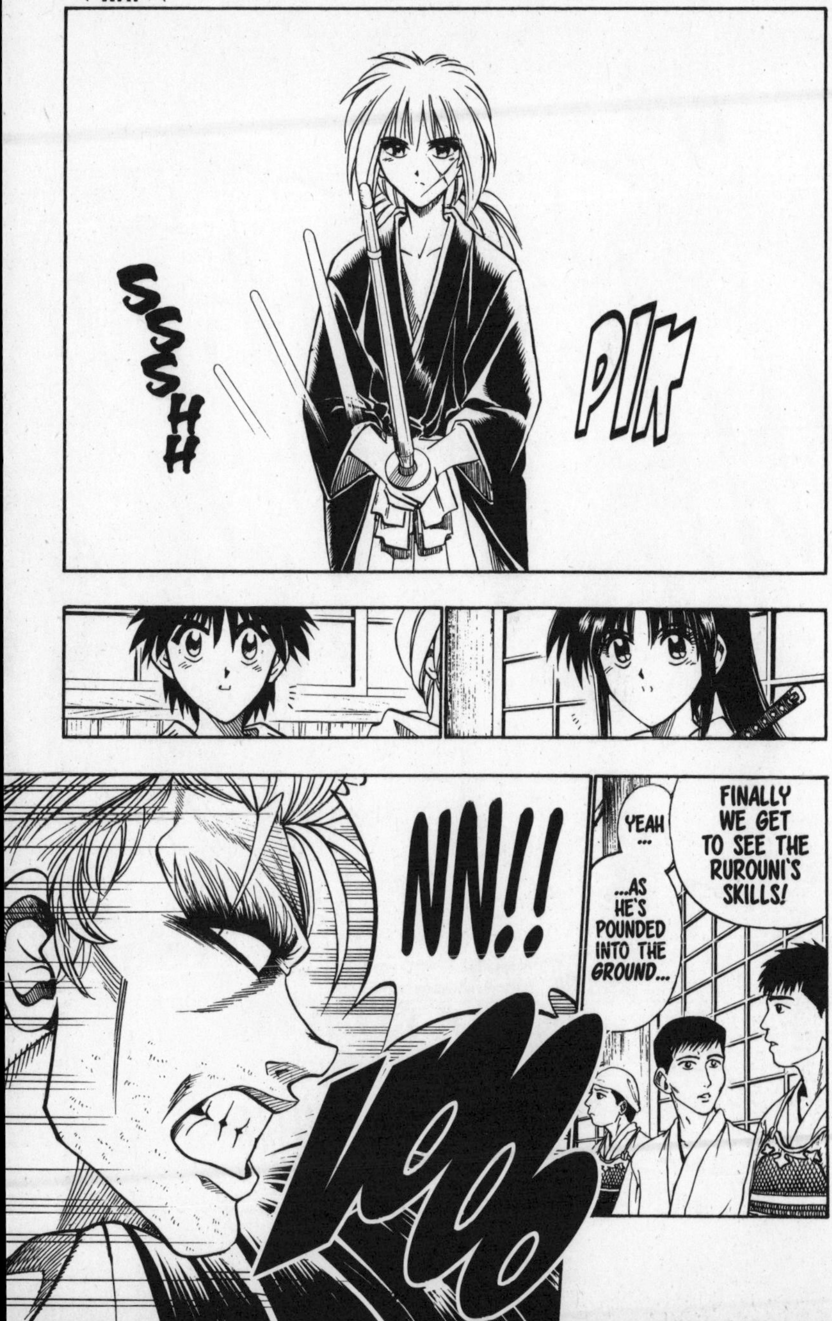
PIN
SSSHH
FINALLY WE GET TO SEE THE RUROUNI'S SKILLS!
YEAH...
...AS HE'S POUNDED INTO THE GROUND...
NN!!

READ THIS WAY

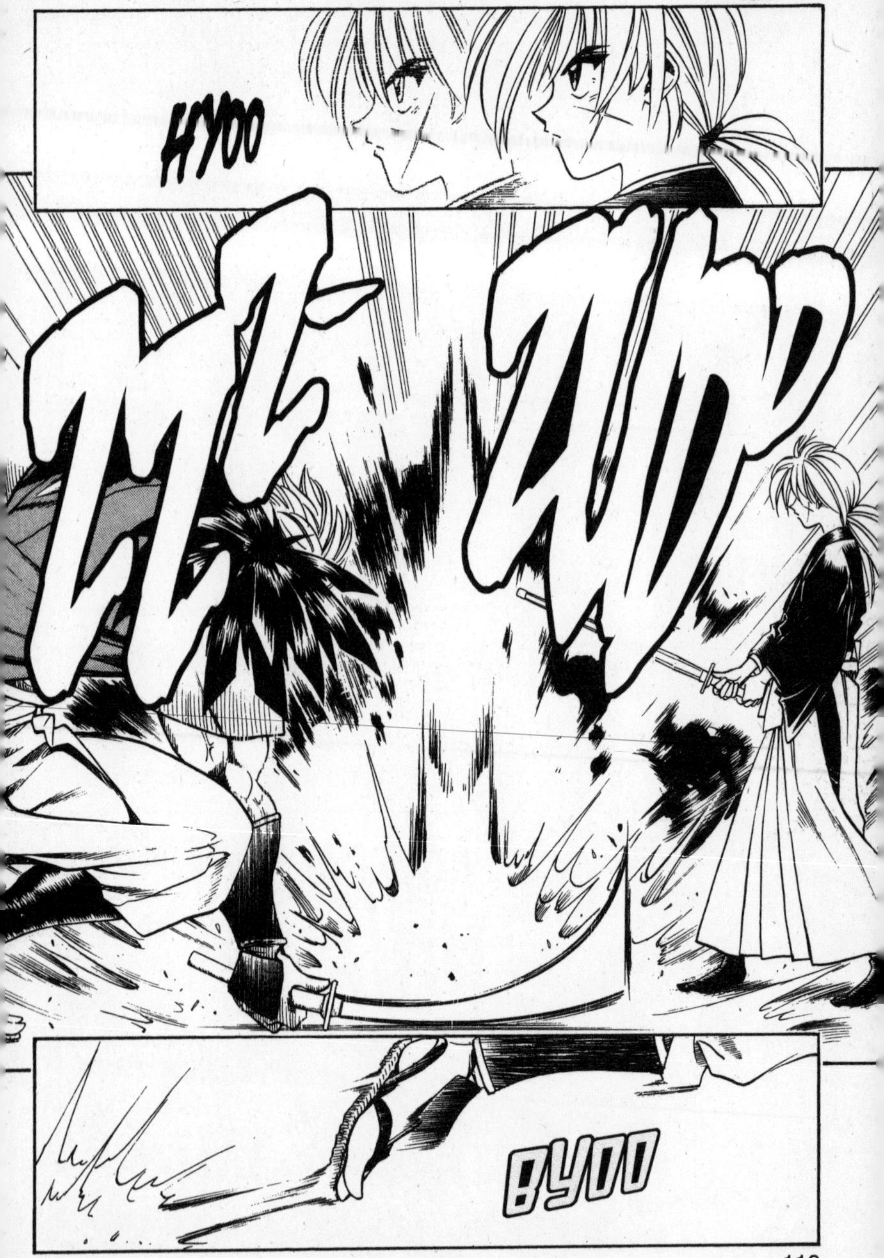
HYOO
ZZ ZUP
BYOO

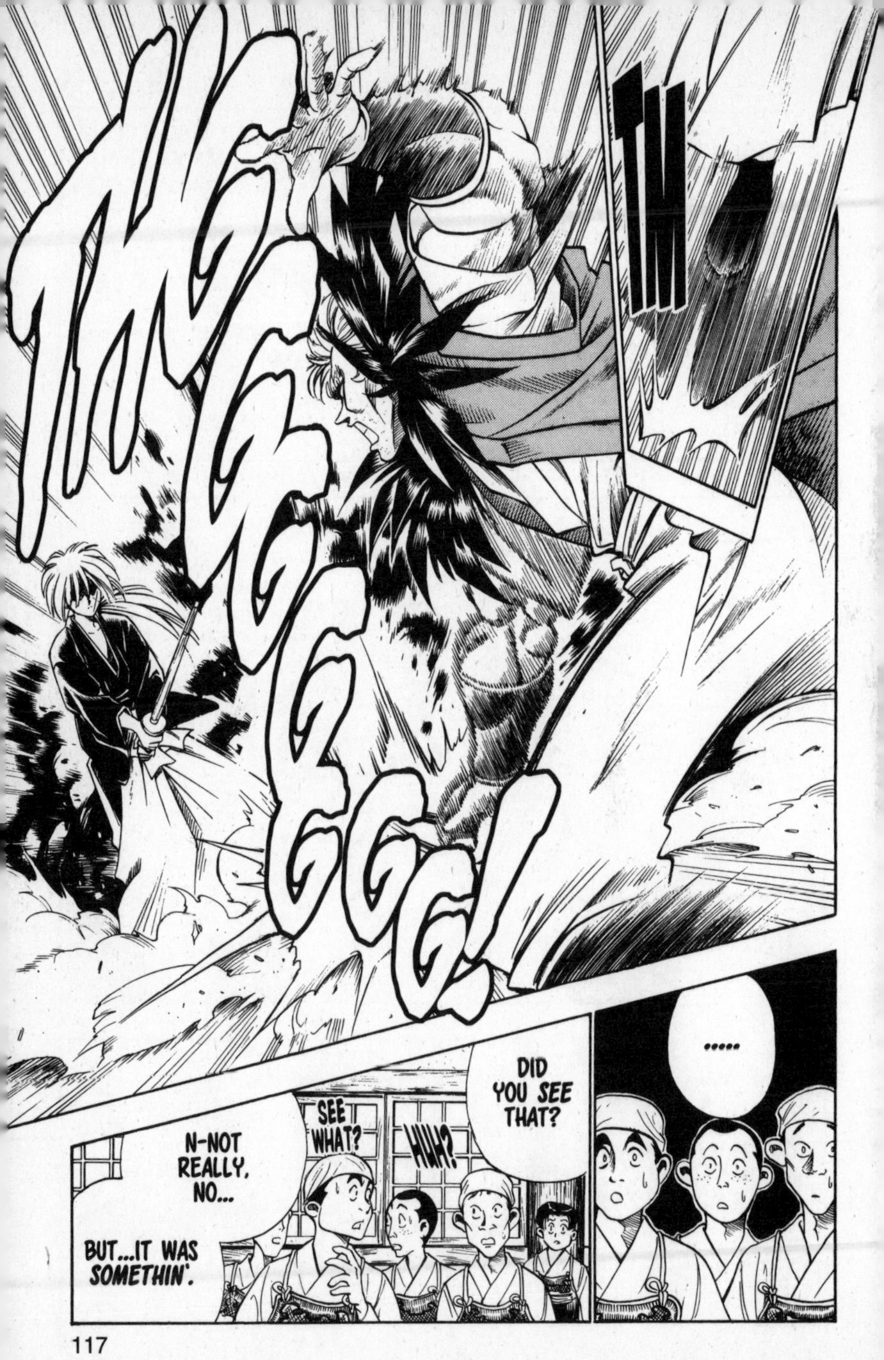
......
DID YOU SEE THAT?
HUH?
SEE WHAT?
N-NOT REALLY, NO...
BUT...IT WAS SOMETHIN'.

READ THIS WAY

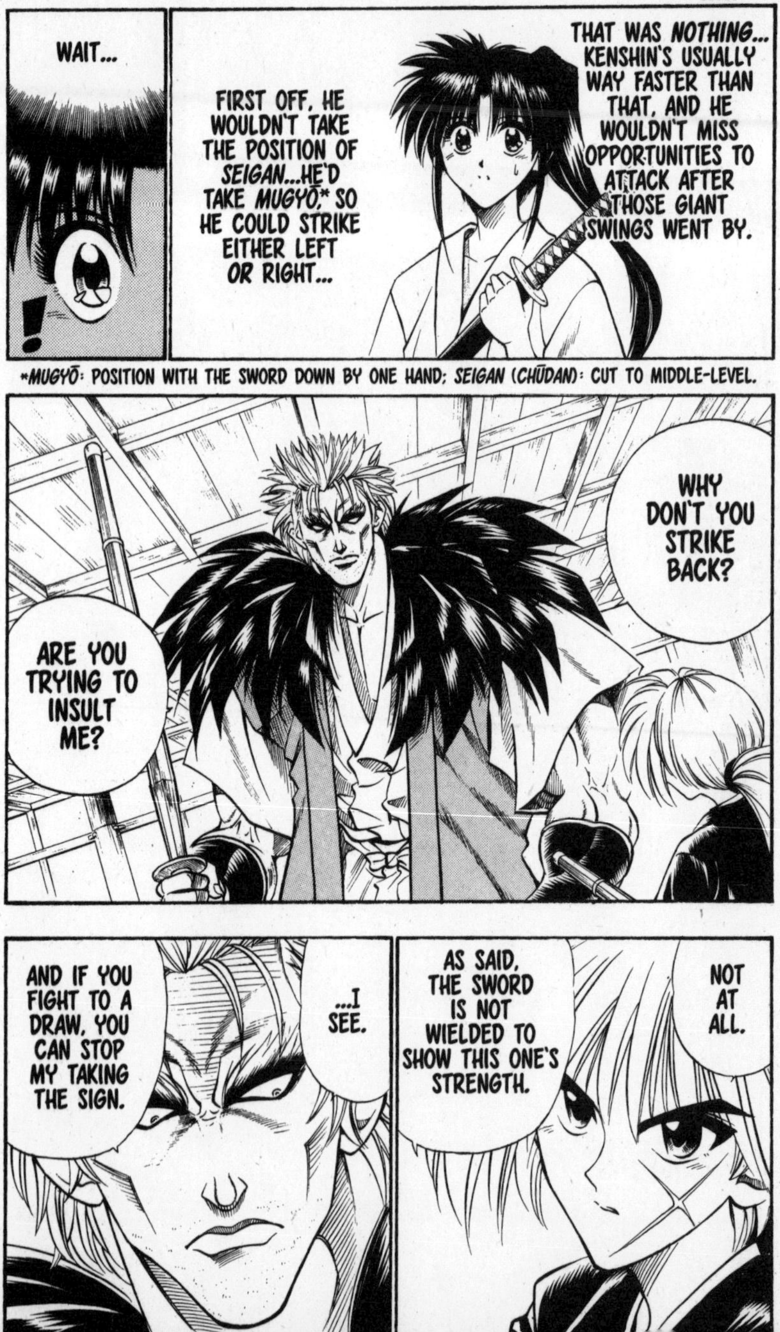
THAT WAS *NOTHING*... KENSHIN'S USUALLY WAY FASTER THAN THAT, AND HE WOULDN'T MISS OPPORTUNITIES TO ATTACK AFTER THOSE GIANT SWINGS WENT BY.
FIRST OFF, HE WOULDN'T TAKE THE POSITION OF *SEIGAN*...HE'D TAKE *MUGYŌ*,* SO HE COULD STRIKE EITHER LEFT *OR* RIGHT...
WAIT...
!
WHY DON'T YOU STRIKE BACK?
ARE YOU TRYING TO INSULT ME?
NOT AT ALL.
AS SAID, THE SWORD IS NOT WIELDED TO SHOW THIS ONE'S STRENGTH.
...I SEE.
AND IF YOU FIGHT TO A DRAW, YOU CAN STOP MY TAKING THE SIGN.

**MUGYŌ*: POSITION WITH THE SWORD DOWN BY ONE HAND; *SEIGAN* (*CHŪDAN*): CUT TO MIDDLE-LEVEL.

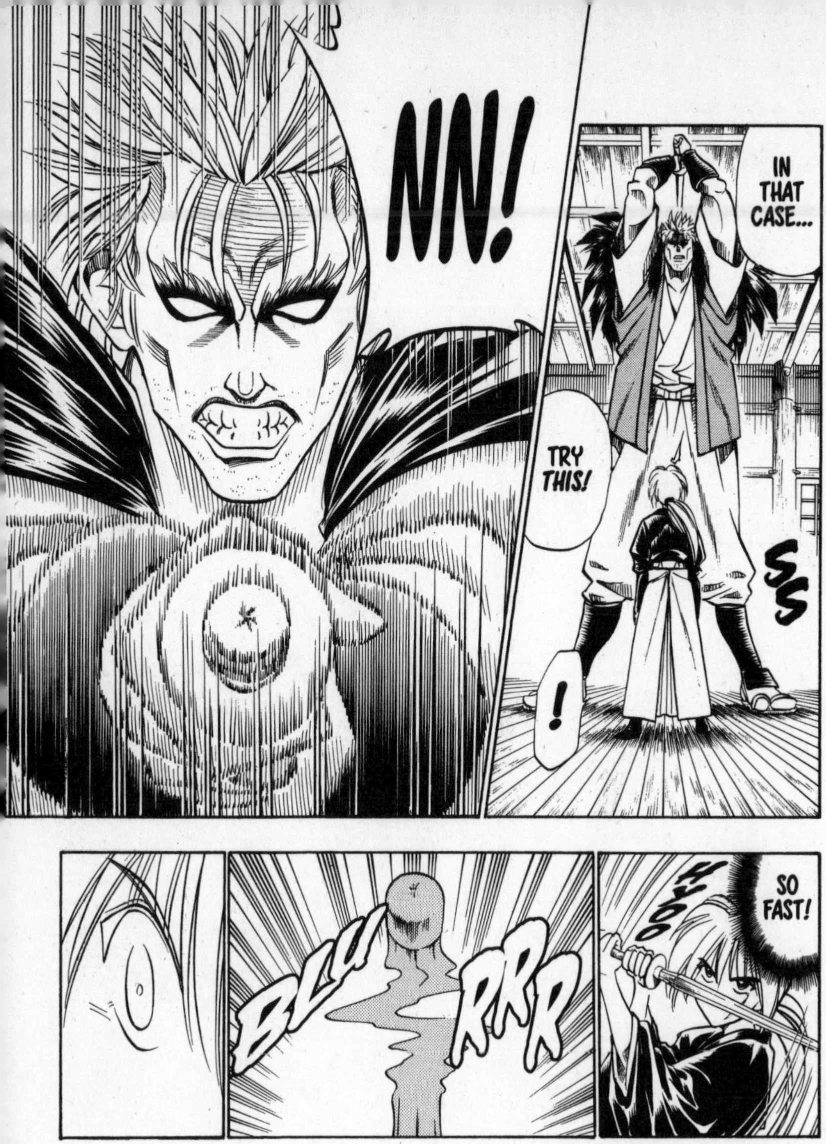
IN THAT CASE...
TRY THIS!
SS
!
NN!
SO FAST!
HYOO
BLURRR
WHAT...
...IS THIS?

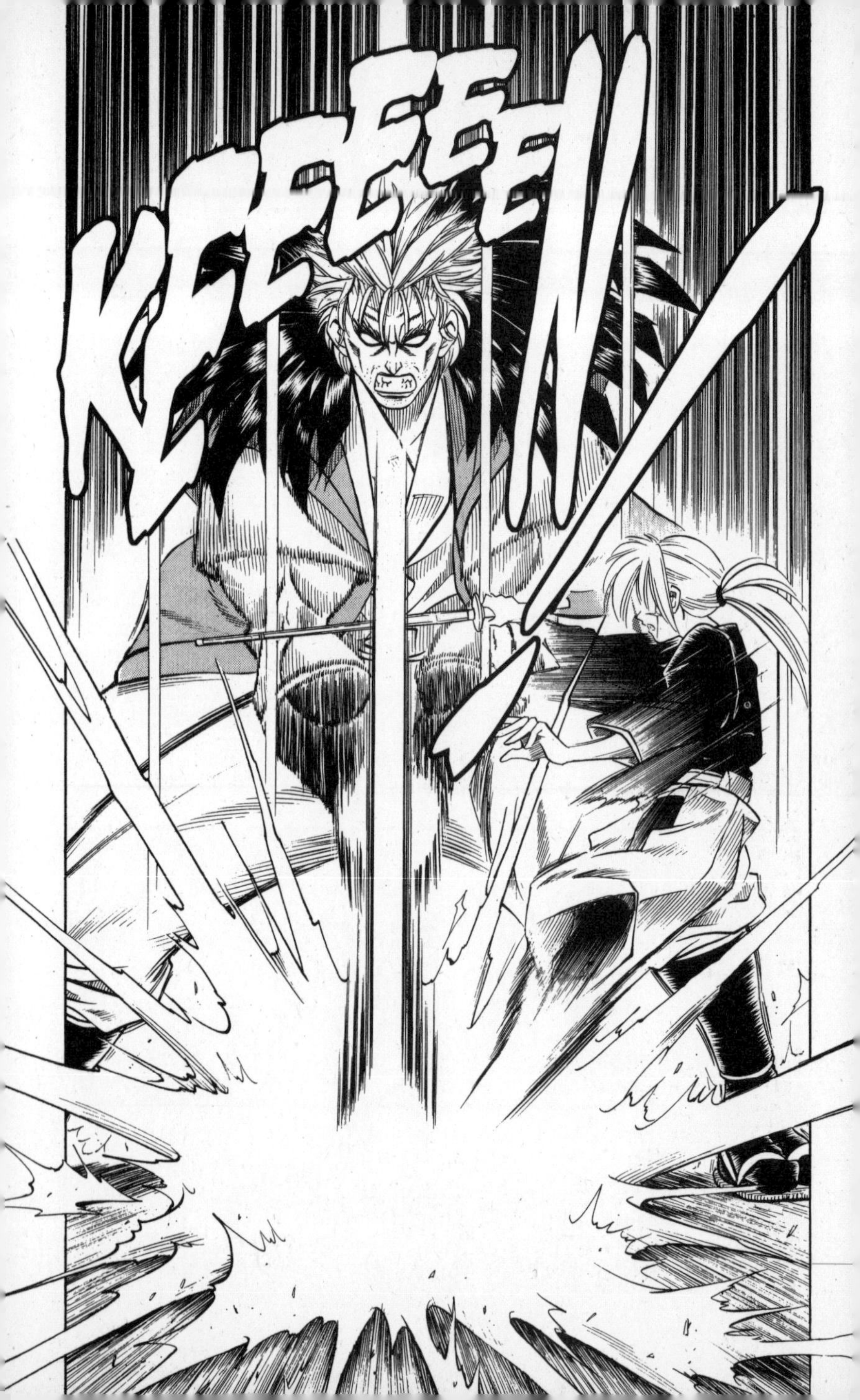
KEEEEN!

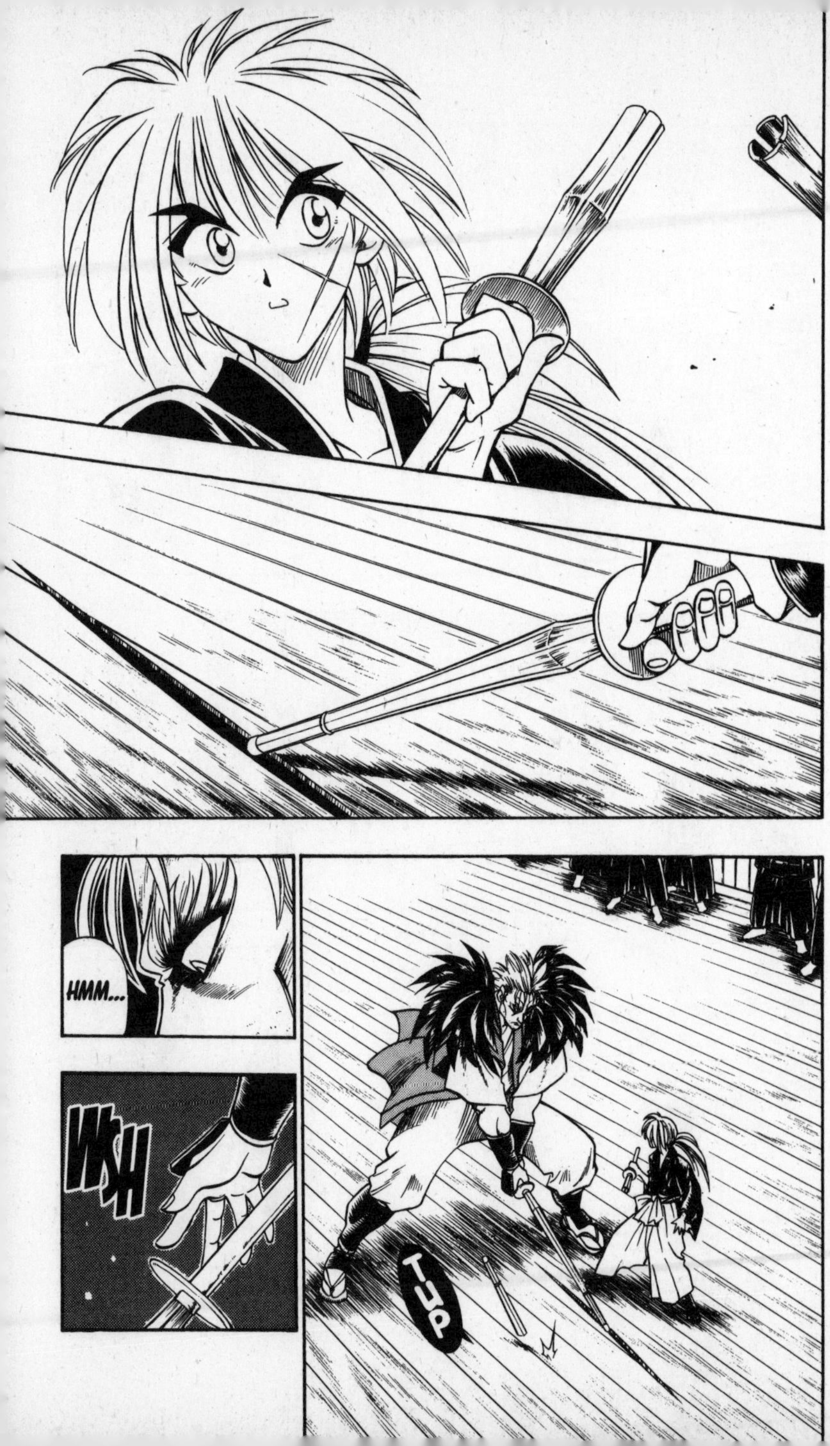
TUP
HMM...
WSH

READ THIS WAY

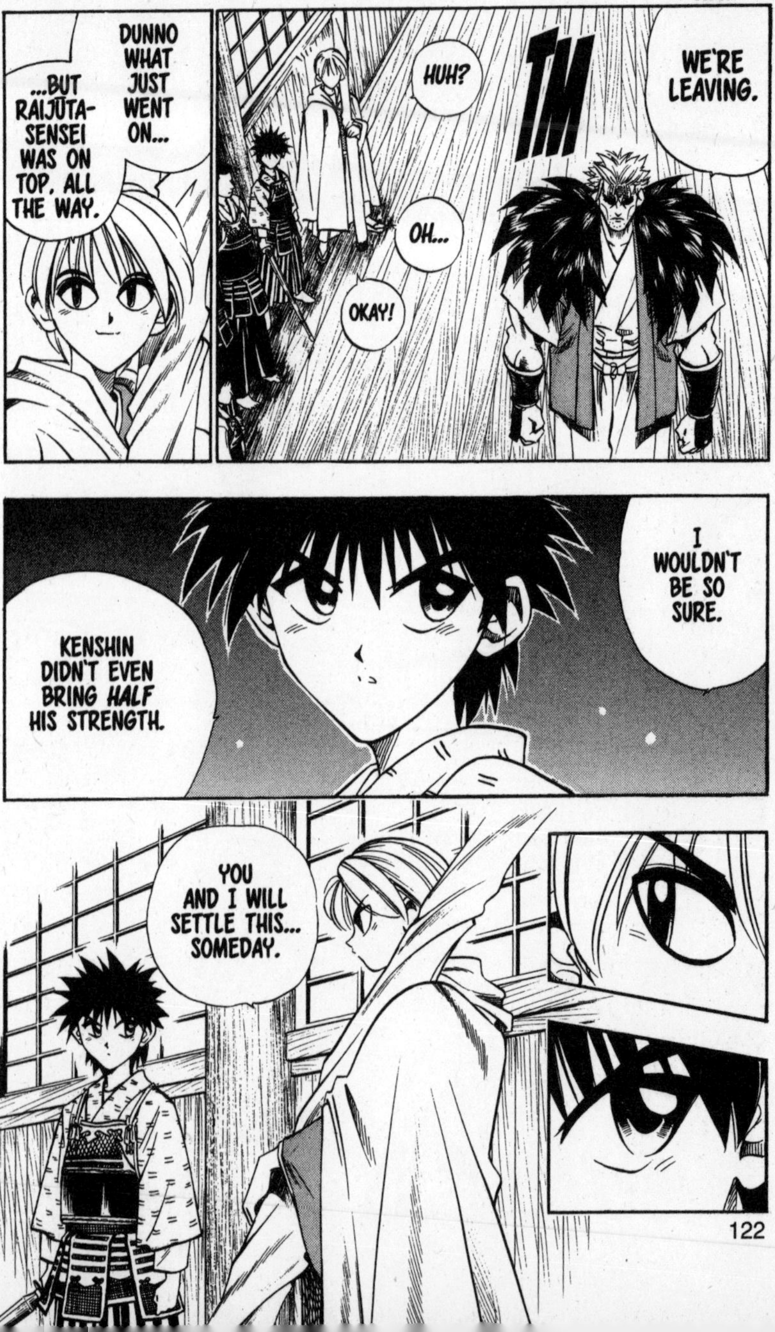
WE'RE LEAVING.
TM
HUH?
OH...
OKAY!
DUNNO WHAT JUST WENT ON...
...BUT RAIJŪTA-SENSEI WAS ON TOP, ALL THE WAY.
I WOULDN'T BE SO SURE.
KENSHIN DIDN'T EVEN BRING *HALF* HIS STRENGTH.
YOU AND I WILL SETTLE THIS... SOMEDAY.

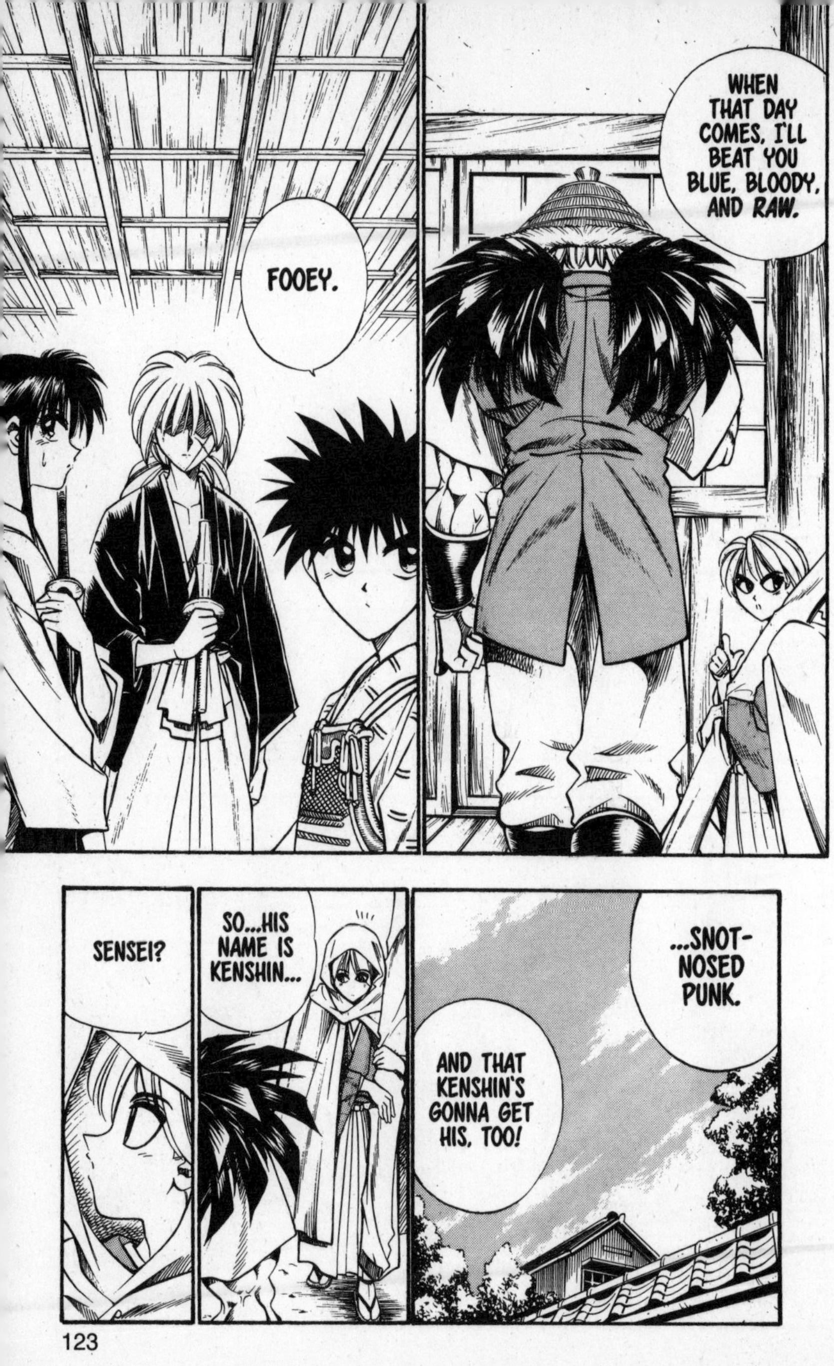
WHEN THAT DAY COMES, I'LL BEAT YOU BLUE, BLOODY, AND RAW.
FOOEY.
...SNOT-NOSED PUNK.
AND THAT KENSHIN'S GONNA GET HIS, TOO!
SO...HIS NAME IS KENSHIN...
SENSEI?

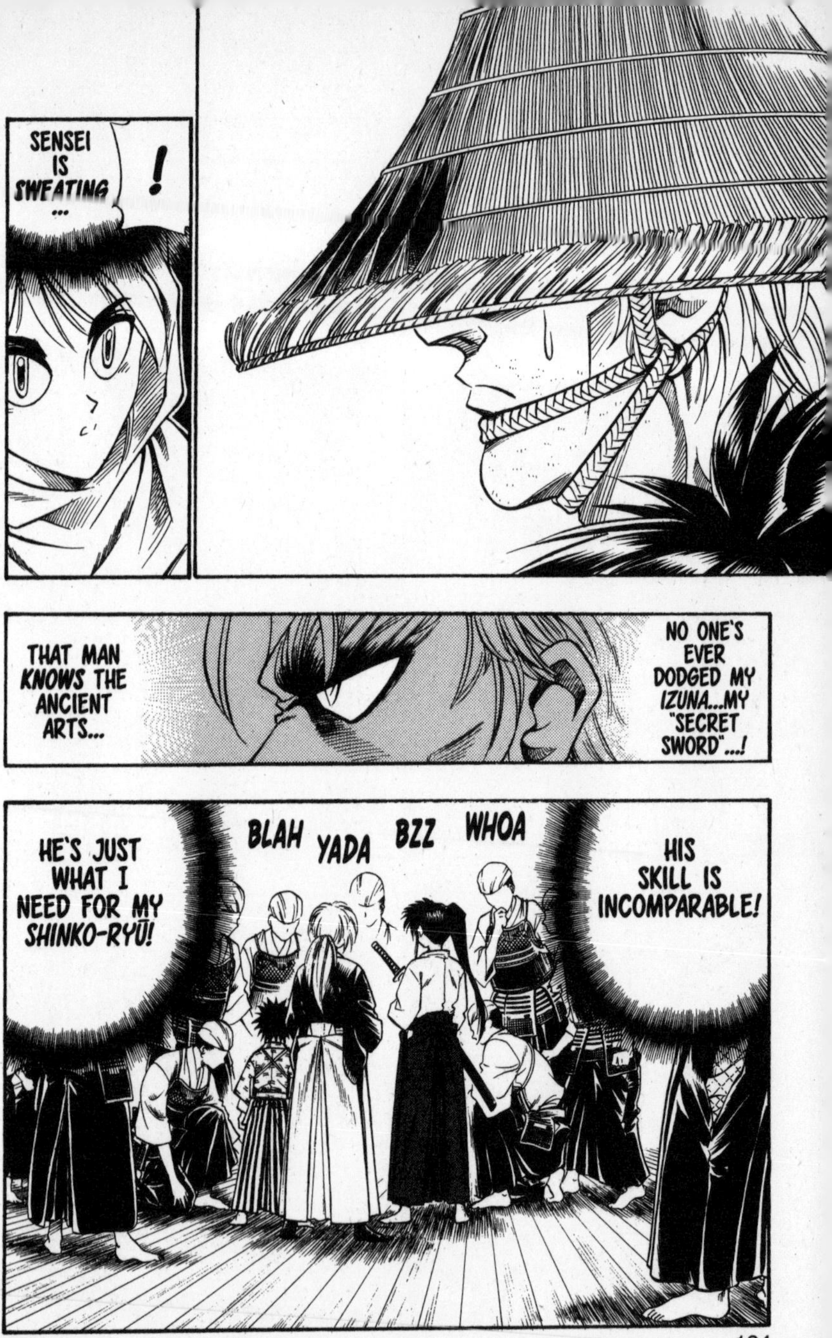
!
SENSEI IS SWEATING...
NO ONE'S EVER DODGED MY IZUNA...MY "SECRET SWORD"...!
THAT MAN KNOWS THE ANCIENT ARTS...
HIS SKILL IS INCOMPARABLE!
WHOA
BZZ
YADA
BLAH
HE'S JUST WHAT I NEED FOR MY SHINKO-RYŪ!

READ THIS WAY

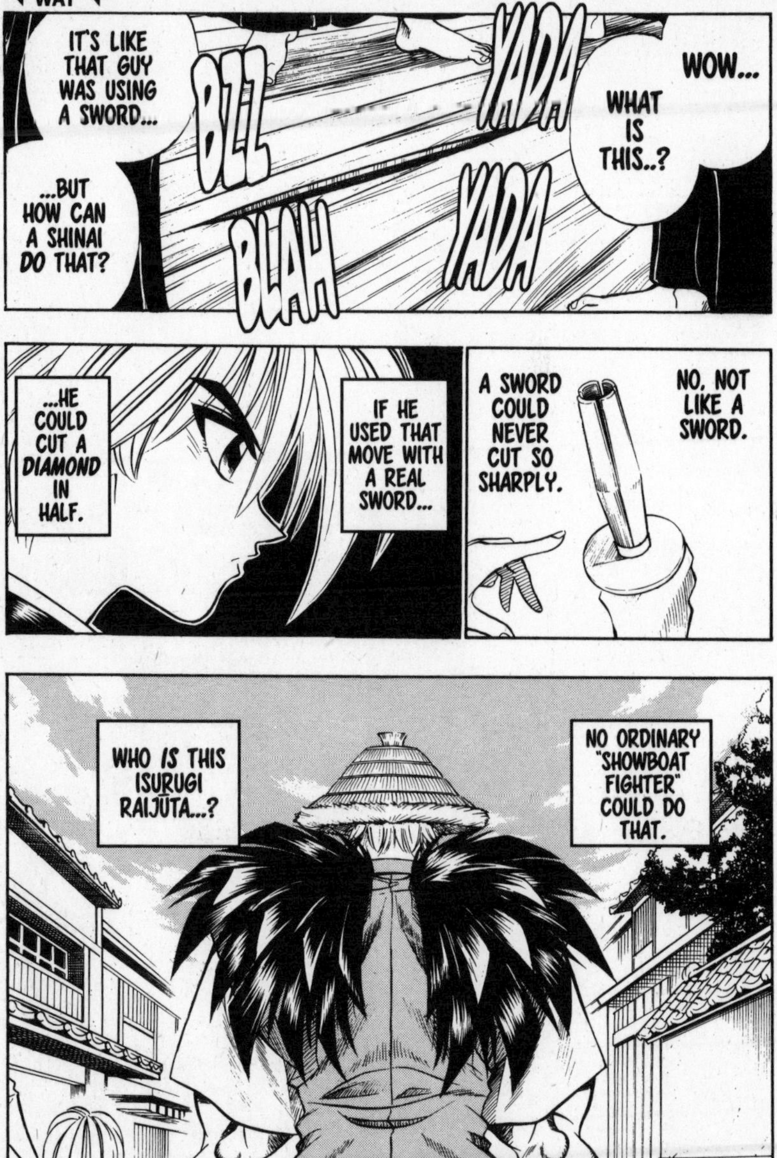
WOW...
WHAT IS THIS..?
YADA
YADA
BZZ
BLAH
IT'S LIKE THAT GUY WAS USING A SWORD...
...BUT HOW CAN A SHINAI DO THAT?
NO, NOT LIKE A SWORD.
A SWORD COULD NEVER CUT SO SHARPLY.
IF HE USED THAT MOVE WITH A REAL SWORD...
...HE COULD CUT A DIAMOND IN HALF.
NO ORDINARY "SHOWBOAT FIGHTER" COULD DO THAT.
WHO IS THIS ISURUGI RAIJŪTA...?

Rurouni Kenshin

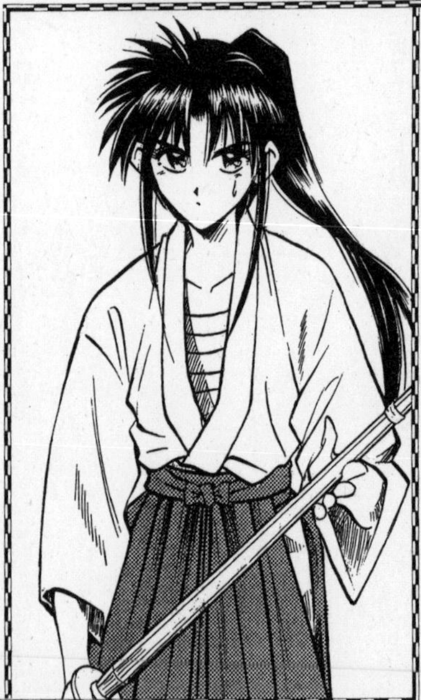

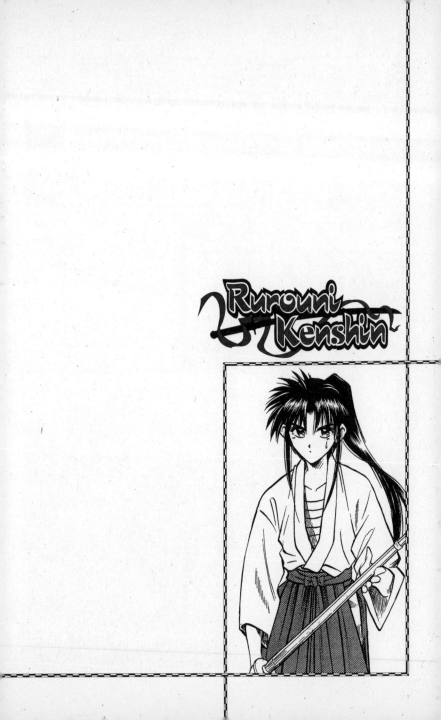

READ THIS WAY

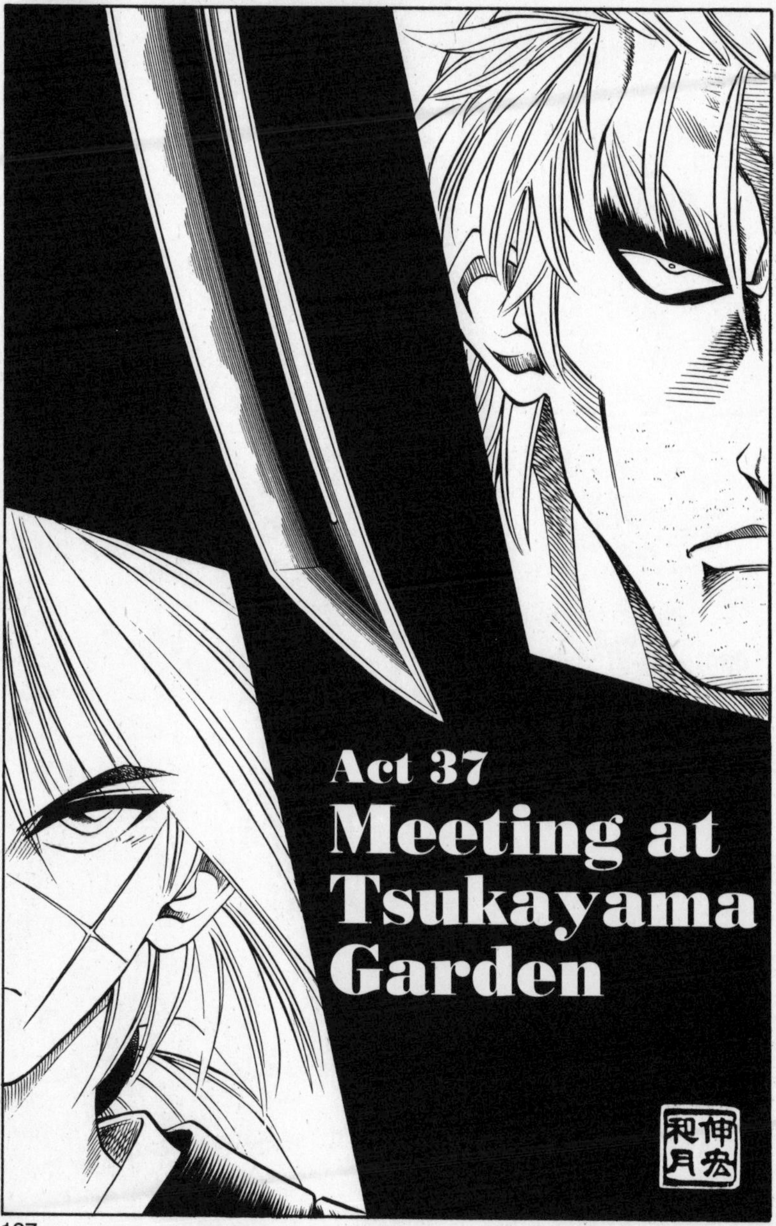
Act 37
Meeting at Tsukayama Garden

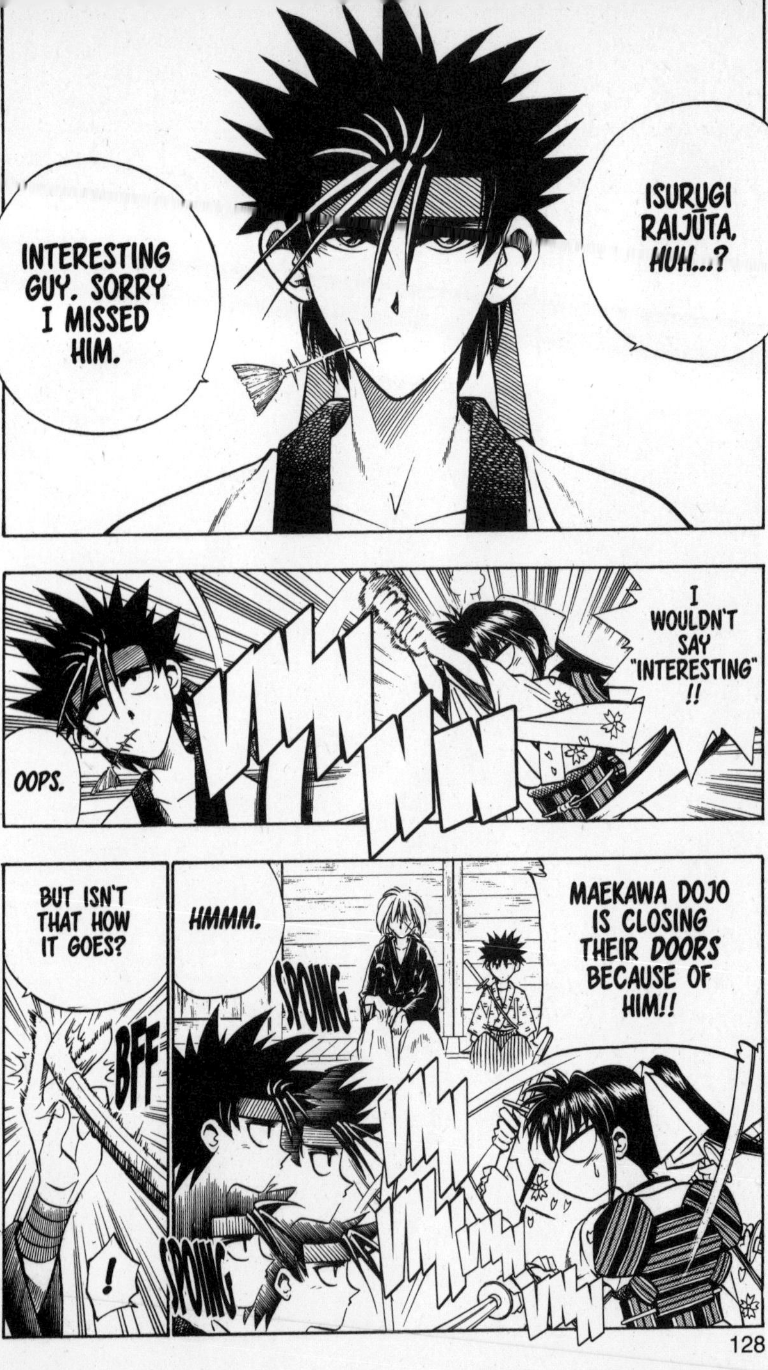
ISURUGI RAIJŪTA, HUH...?
INTERESTING GUY. SORRY I MISSED HIM.
I WOULDN'T SAY "INTERESTING"!!
VMMNNN
OOPS.
MAEKAWA DOJO IS CLOSING THEIR DOORS BECAUSE OF HIM!!
HMMM.
SPOING
VMM VMM VMM VMM
BUT ISN'T THAT HOW IT GOES?
BFF
!
SPOING

READ THIS WAY

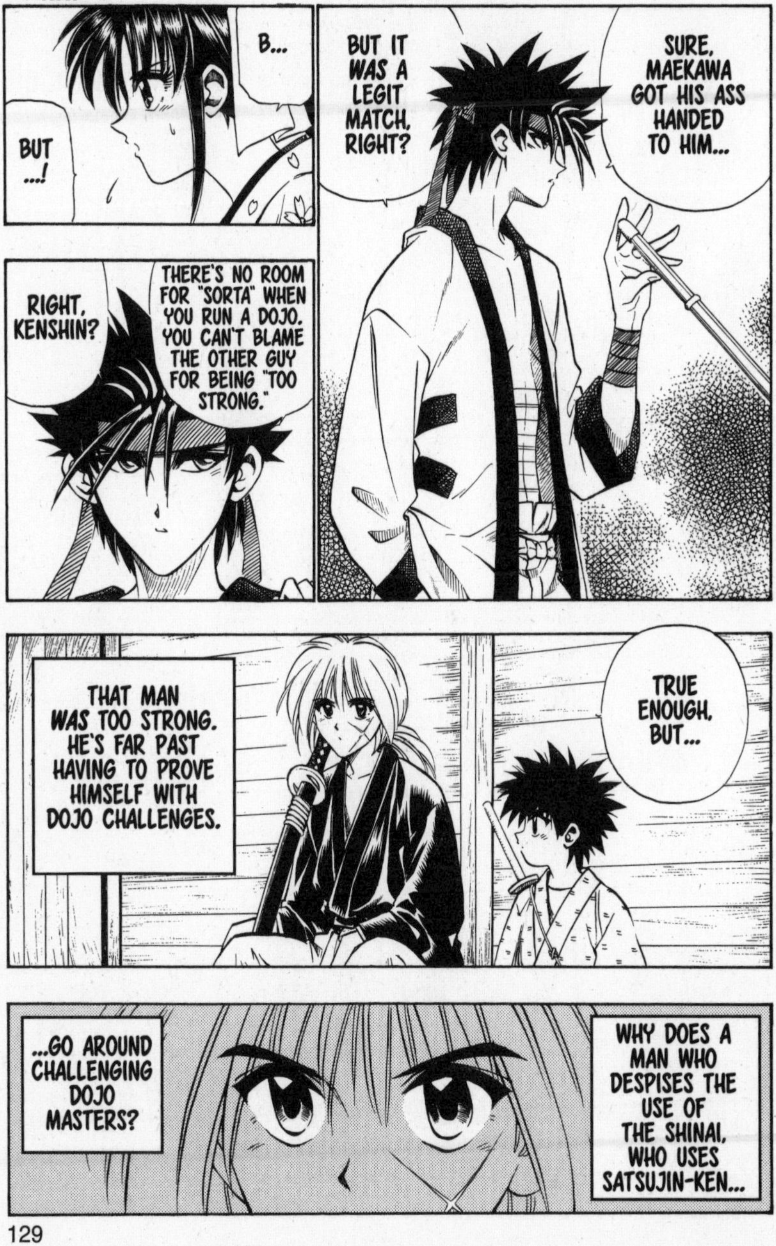
SURE, MAEKAWA GOT HIS ASS HANDED TO HIM...
BUT IT WAS A LEGIT MATCH, RIGHT?
B...
BUT ...!
THERE'S NO ROOM FOR "SORTA" WHEN YOU RUN A DOJO. YOU CAN'T BLAME THE OTHER GUY FOR BEING "TOO STRONG."
RIGHT, KENSHIN?
TRUE ENOUGH, BUT...
THAT MAN WAS TOO STRONG. HE'S FAR PAST HAVING TO PROVE HIMSELF WITH DOJO CHALLENGES.
WHY DOES A MAN WHO DESPISES THE USE OF THE SHINAI, WHO USES SATSUJIN-KEN...
...GO AROUND CHALLENGING DOJO MASTERS?

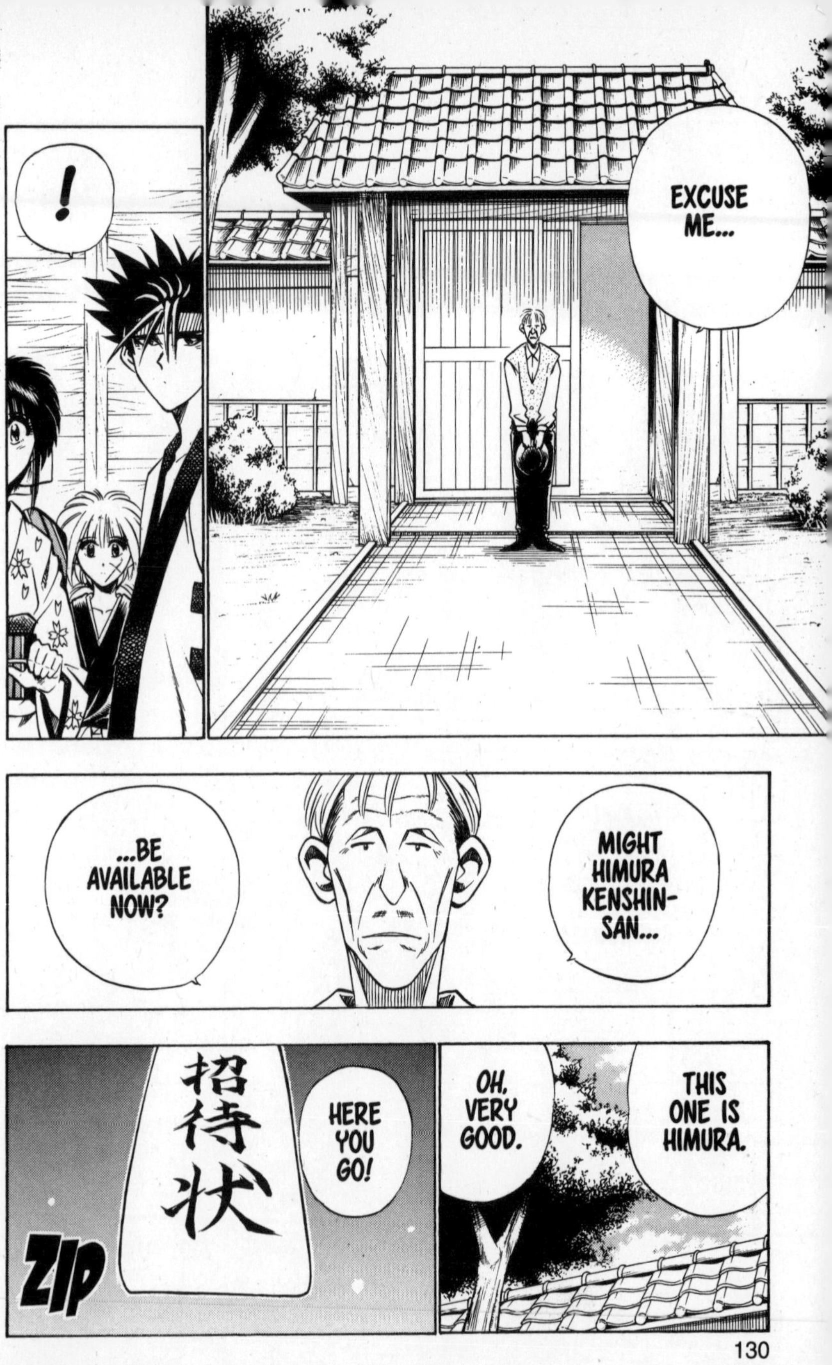
EXCUSE ME...
!
MIGHT HIMURA KENSHIN-SAN...
...BE AVAILABLE NOW?
THIS ONE IS HIMURA.
OH, VERY GOOD.
HERE YOU GO!
招待状
ZIP

READ THIS WAY

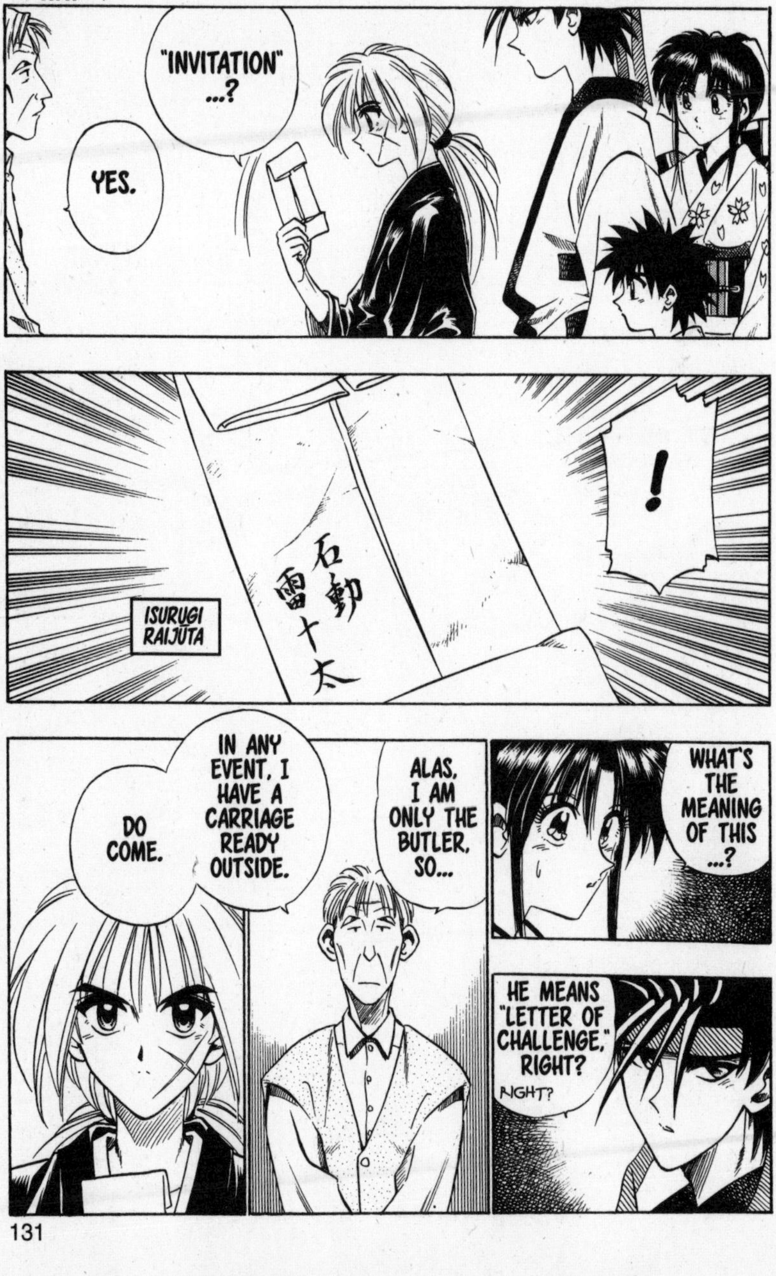
"INVITATION" ...?
YES.
!
石動雷十太
ISURUGI RAIJŪTA
WHAT'S THE MEANING OF THIS ...?
HE MEANS "LETTER OF CHALLENGE," RIGHT?
RIGHT?
ALAS, I AM ONLY THE BUTLER, SO...
IN ANY EVENT, I HAVE A CARRIAGE READY OUTSIDE.
DO COME.

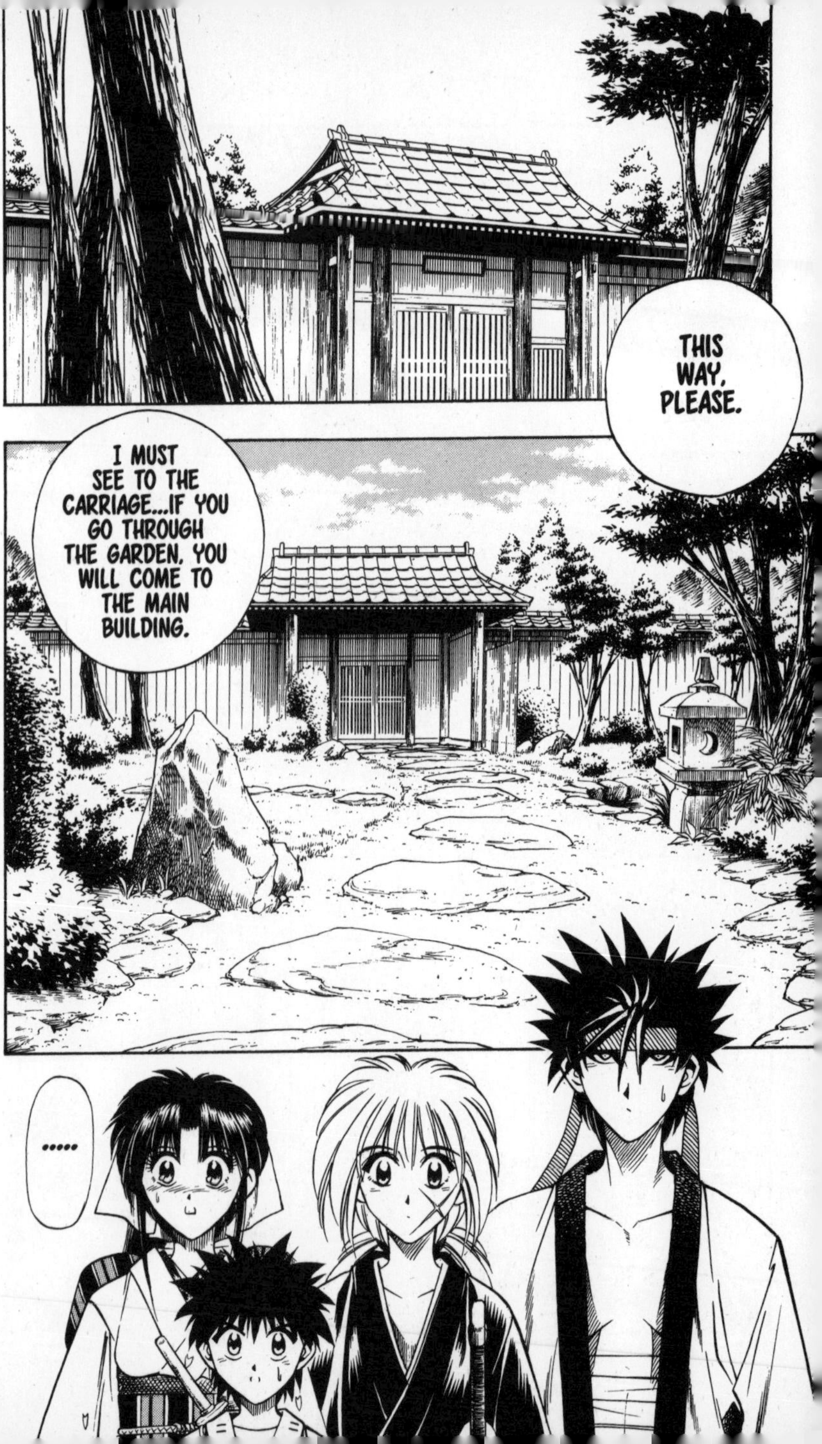
THIS WAY, PLEASE.
I MUST SEE TO THE CARRIAGE...IF YOU GO THROUGH THE GARDEN, YOU WILL COME TO THE MAIN BUILDING.
.....

READ THIS WAY

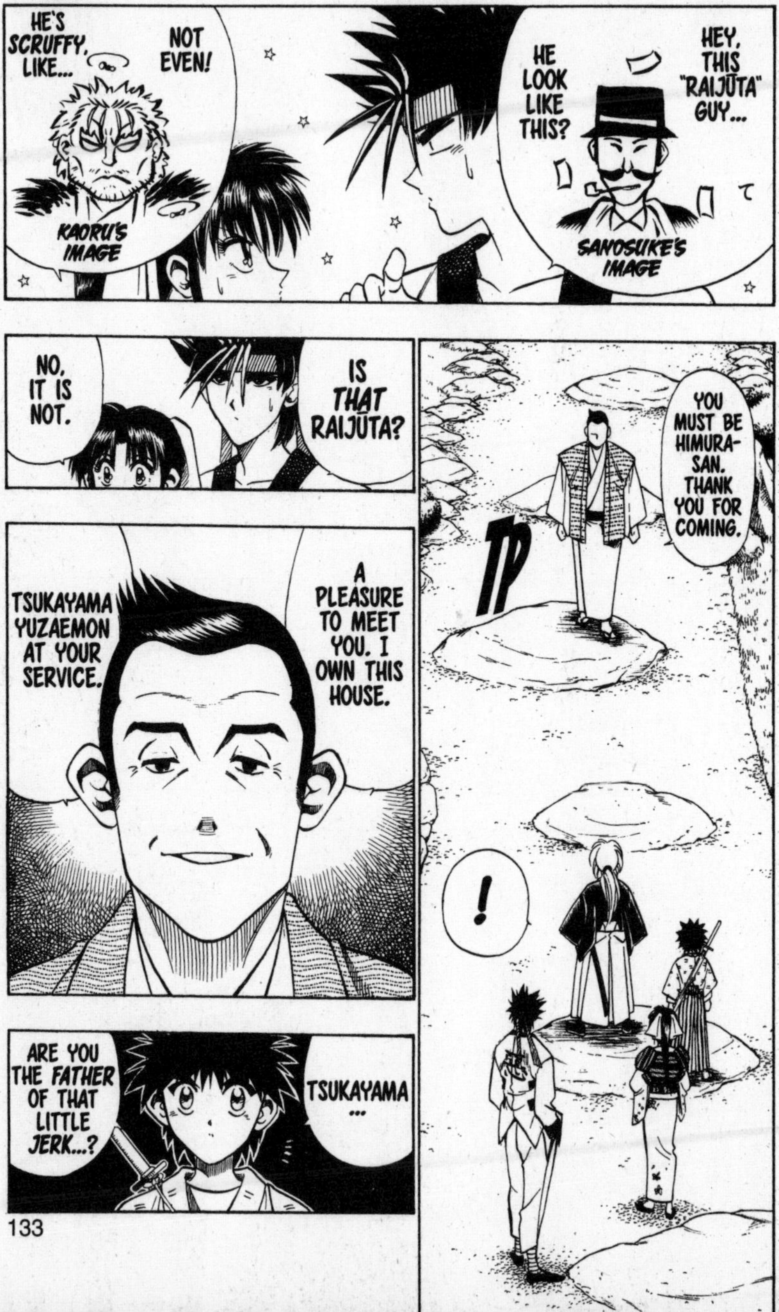

HEY, THIS "RAIJŪTA" GUY...
HE LOOK LIKE THIS?
SANOSUKE'S IMAGE
NOT EVEN!
HE'S SCRUFFY, LIKE...
KAORU'S IMAGE
YOU MUST BE HIMURA-SAN. THANK YOU FOR COMING.
TP
!
IS THAT RAIJŪTA?
NO, IT IS NOT.
A PLEASURE TO MEET YOU. I OWN THIS HOUSE.
TSUKAYAMA YUZAEMON AT YOUR SERVICE.
TSUKAYAMA...
ARE YOU THE FATHER OF THAT LITTLE JERK...?

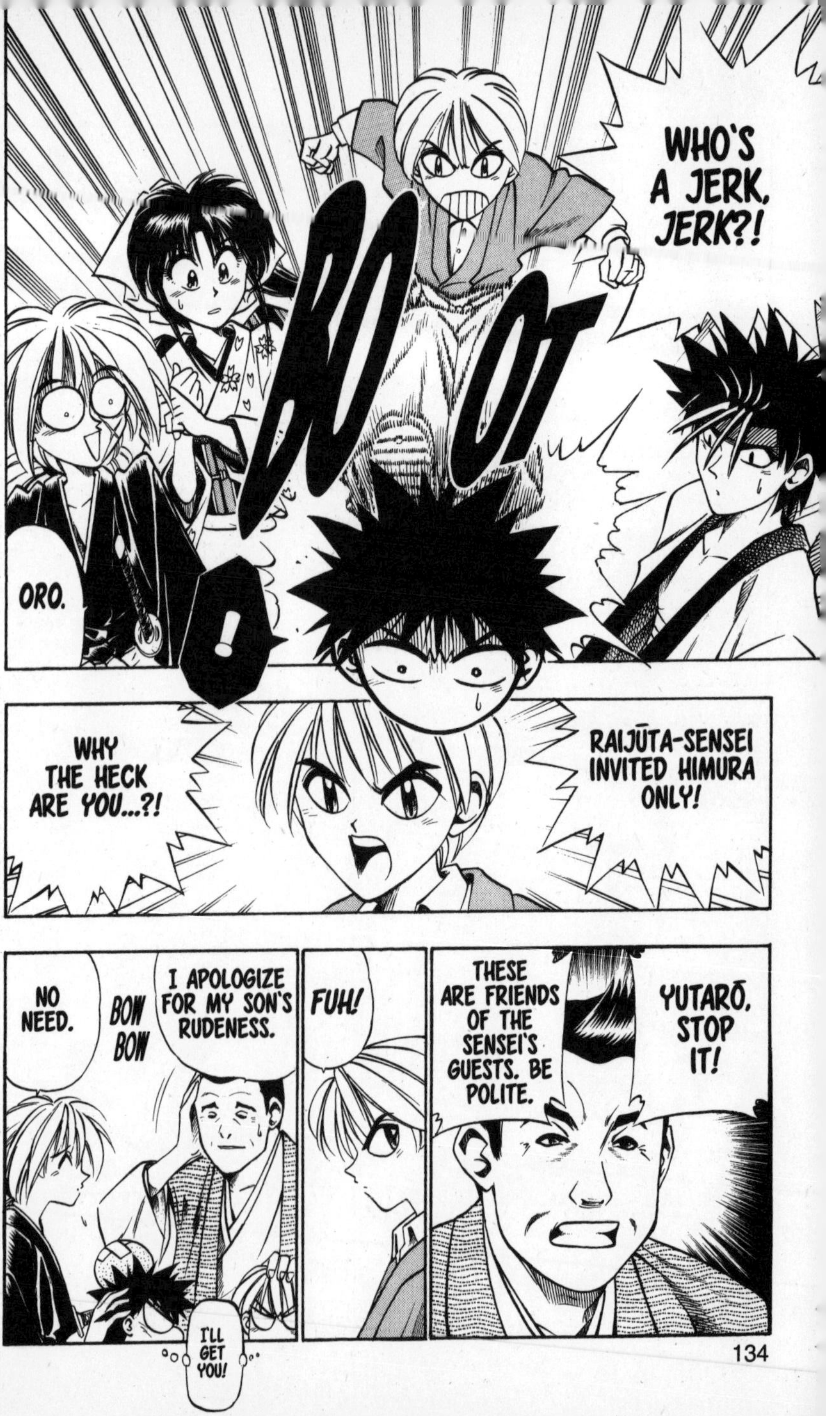
WHO'S A JERK, JERK?!
BOOT
ORO.
!
RAIJŪTA-SENSEI INVITED HIMURA ONLY!
WHY THE HECK ARE YOU...?!
YUTARŌ, STOP IT!
THESE ARE FRIENDS OF THE SENSEI'S GUESTS. BE POLITE.
FUH!
I APOLOGIZE FOR MY SON'S RUDENESS.
BOW BOW
NO NEED.
I'LL GET YOU!

READ THIS WAY

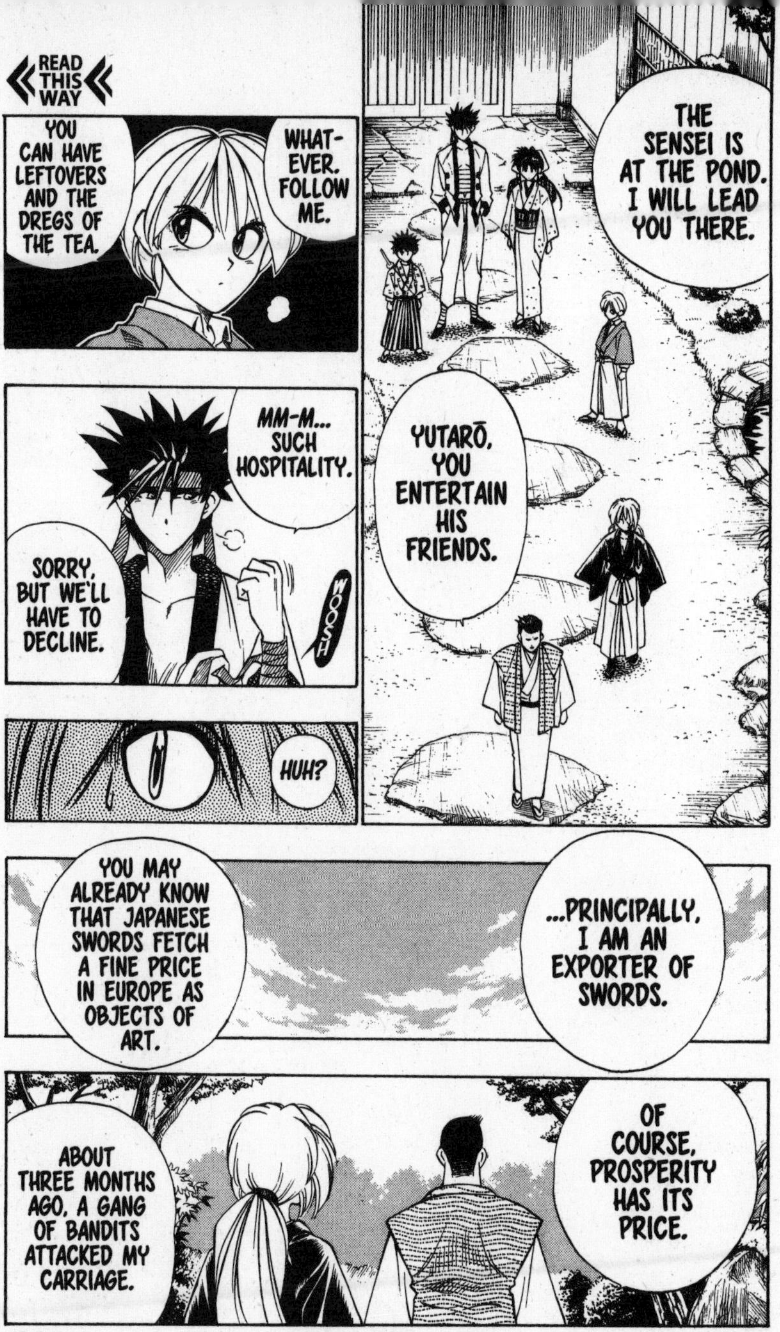
THE SENSEI IS AT THE POND. I WILL LEAD YOU THERE.
YUTARŌ, YOU ENTERTAIN HIS FRIENDS.
WHAT-EVER. FOLLOW ME.
YOU CAN HAVE LEFTOVERS AND THE DREGS OF THE TEA.
MM-M... SUCH HOSPITALITY.
SORRY, BUT WE'LL HAVE TO DECLINE.
WOOSH
HUH?
...PRINCIPALLY, I AM AN EXPORTER OF SWORDS.
YOU MAY ALREADY KNOW THAT JAPANESE SWORDS FETCH A FINE PRICE IN EUROPE AS OBJECTS OF ART.
OF COURSE, PROSPERITY HAS ITS PRICE.
ABOUT THREE MONTHS AGO, A GANG OF BANDITS ATTACKED MY CARRIAGE.

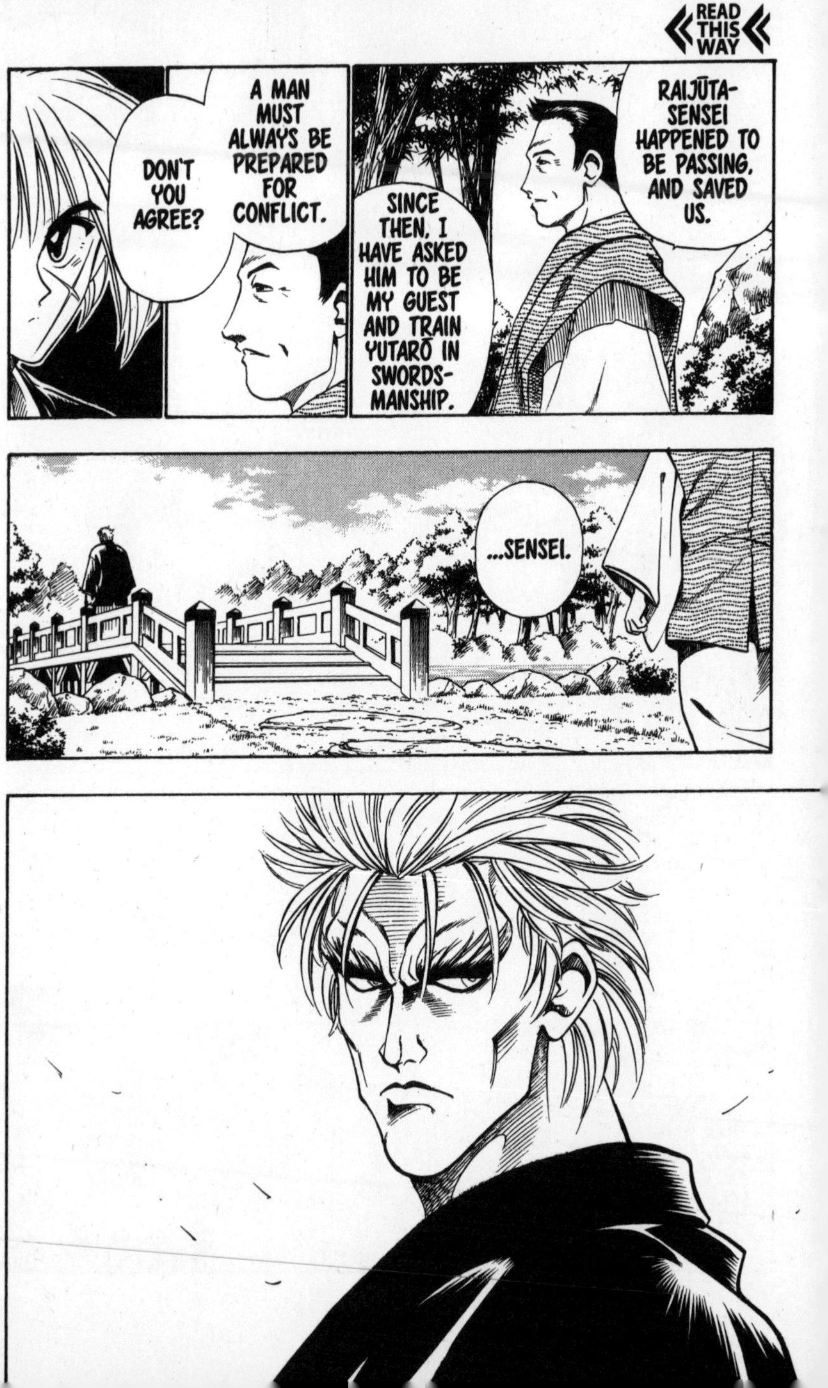
READ THIS WAY
RAIJŪTA-SENSEI HAPPENED TO BE PASSING, AND SAVED US.
SINCE THEN, I HAVE ASKED HIM TO BE MY GUEST AND TRAIN YUTARŌ IN SWORDSMANSHIP.
A MAN MUST ALWAYS BE PREPARED FOR CONFLICT.
DON'T YOU AGREE?
...SENSEI.

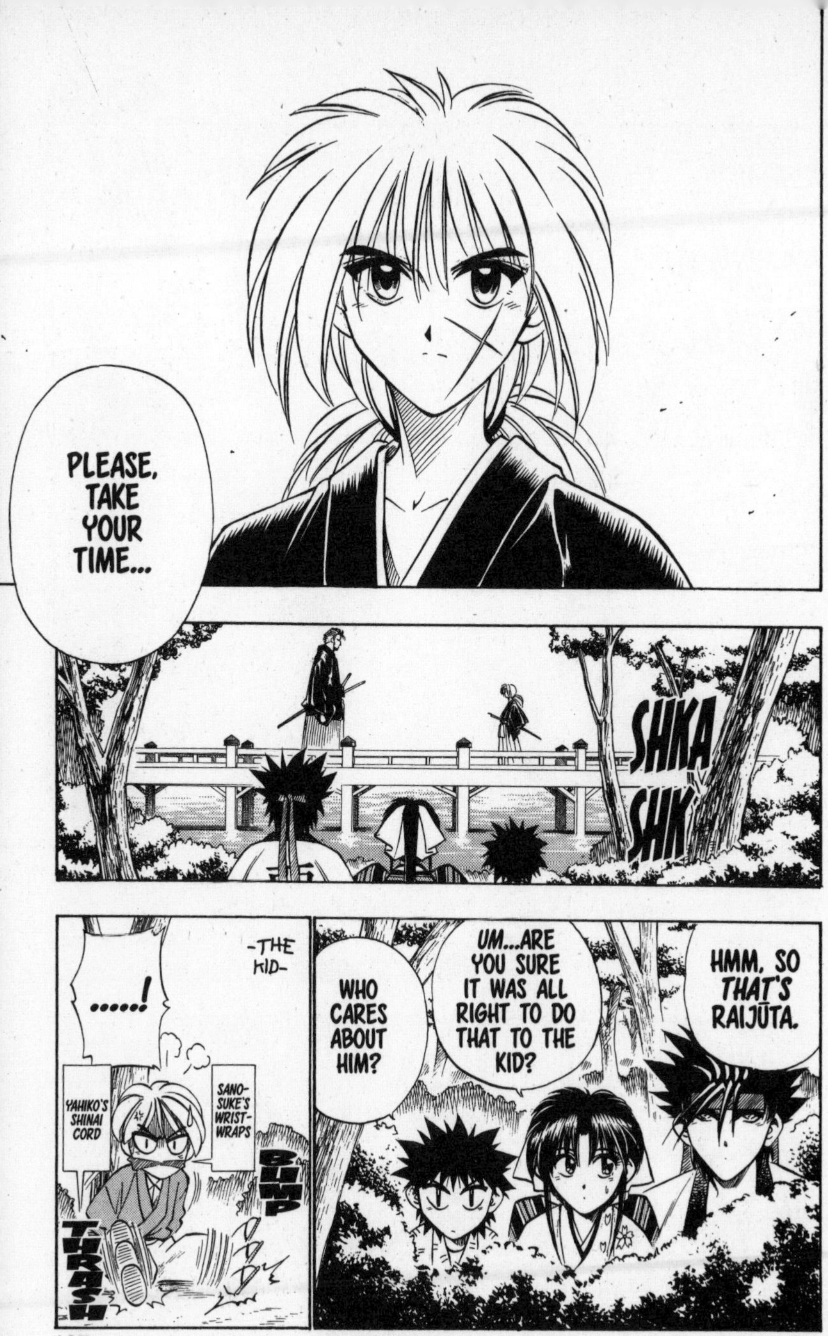
PLEASE, TAKE YOUR TIME...
SHKA SHK
HMM, SO THAT'S RAIJŪTA.
UM...ARE YOU SURE IT WAS ALL RIGHT TO DO THAT TO THE KID?
WHO CARES ABOUT HIM?
-THE KID-
......!
SANO-SUKE'S WRIST-WRAPS
YAHIKO'S SHINAI CORD
BUMP
THRASH

READ THIS WAY

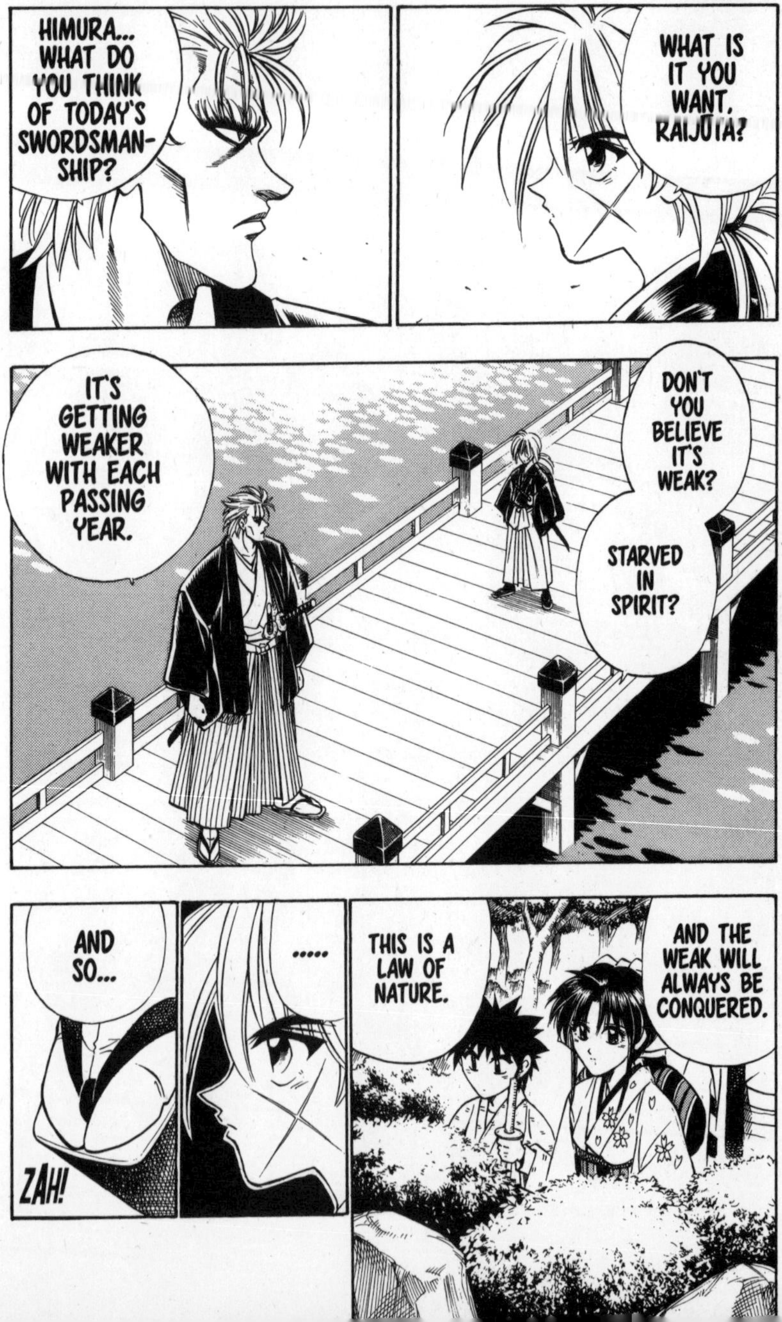
WHAT IS IT YOU WANT, RAIJUTA?
HIMURA... WHAT DO YOU THINK OF TODAY'S SWORDSMAN-SHIP?
IT'S GETTING WEAKER WITH EACH PASSING YEAR.
DON'T YOU BELIEVE IT'S WEAK?
STARVED IN SPIRIT?
AND THE WEAK WILL ALWAYS BE CONQUERED.
THIS IS A LAW OF NATURE.
.....
AND SO...
ZAH!

READ THIS WAY

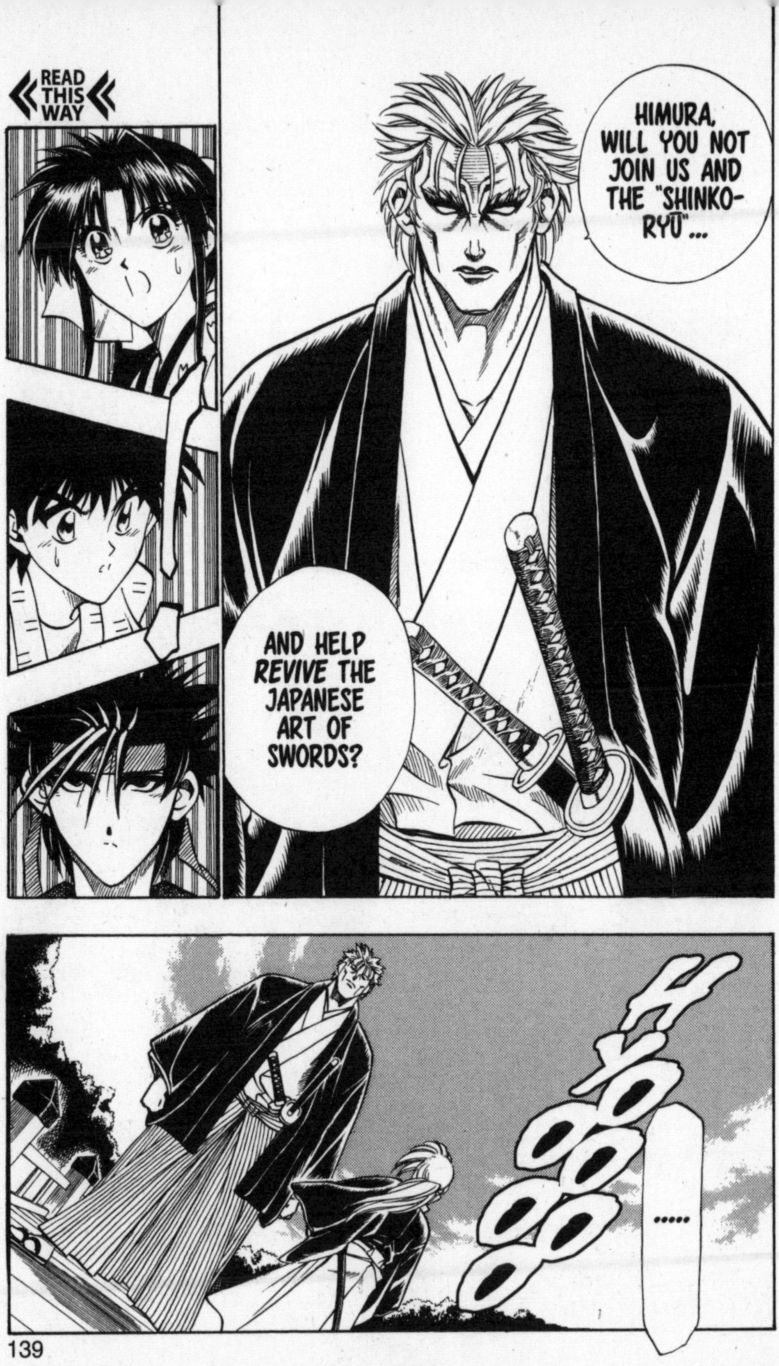
HIMURA, WILL YOU NOT JOIN US AND THE "SHINKO-RYŪ"...
AND HELP *REVIVE* THE JAPANESE ART OF SWORDS?
HYOOOOOO
.....

READ THIS WAY

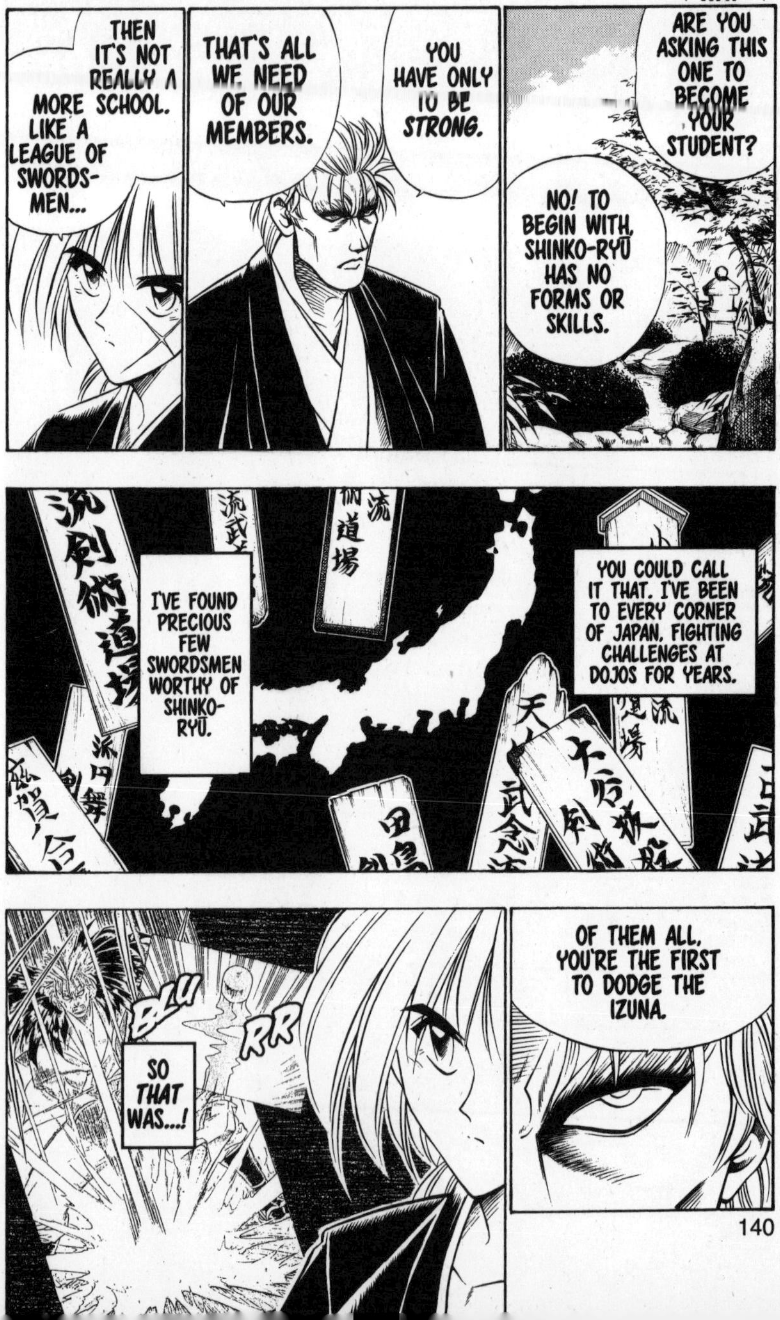
ARE YOU ASKING THIS ONE TO BECOME YOUR STUDENT?
NO! TO BEGIN WITH, SHINKO-RYŪ HAS NO FORMS OR SKILLS.
YOU HAVE ONLY TO BE STRONG.
THAT'S ALL WE NEED OF OUR MEMBERS.
THEN IT'S NOT REALLY A SCHOOL. MORE LIKE A LEAGUE OF SWORDSMEN...
YOU COULD CALL IT THAT. I'VE BEEN TO EVERY CORNER OF JAPAN, FIGHTING CHALLENGES AT DOJOS FOR YEARS.
I'VE FOUND PRECIOUS FEW SWORDSMEN WORTHY OF SHINKO-RYŪ.
OF THEM ALL, YOU'RE THE FIRST TO DODGE THE IZUNA.
BLURR
SO THAT WAS...!

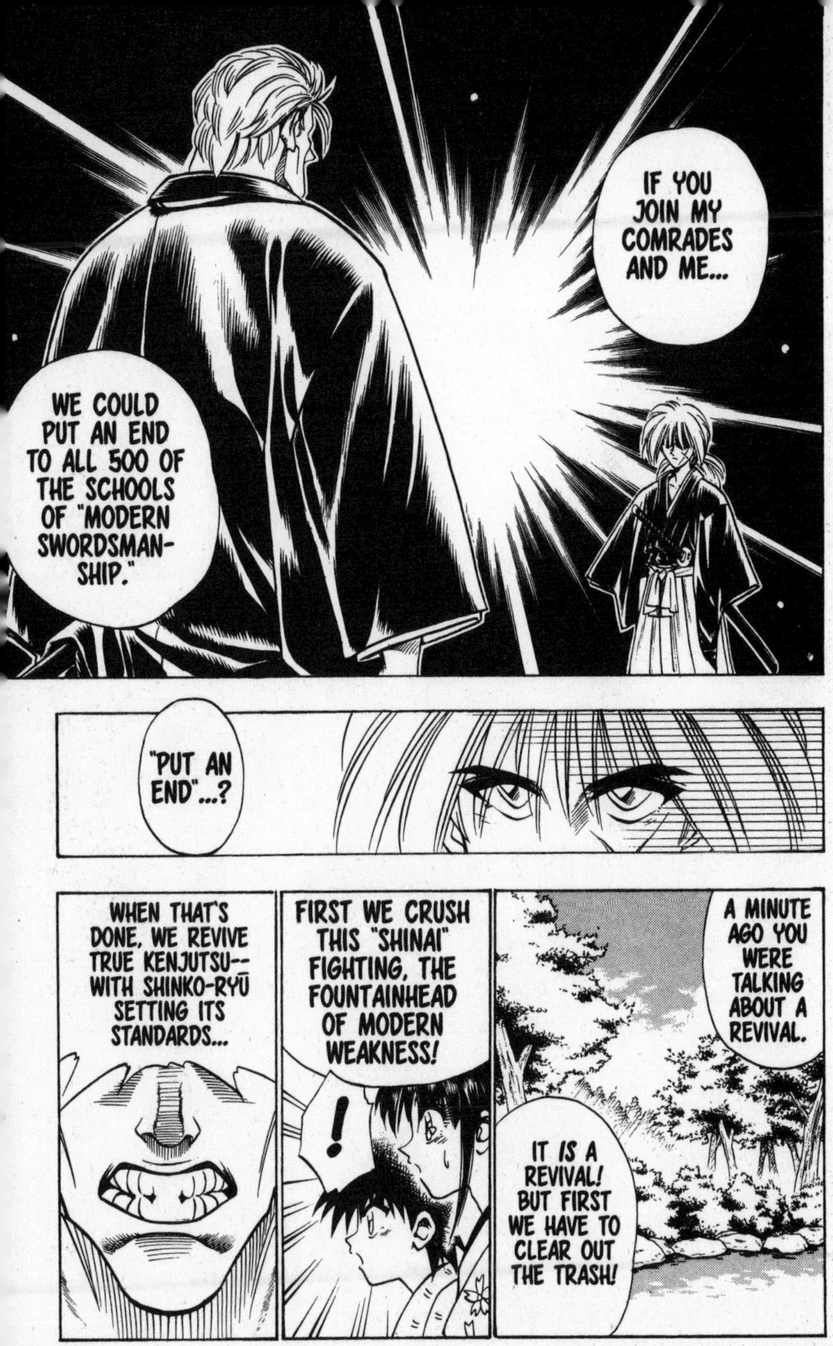
IF YOU JOIN MY COMRADES AND ME...
WE COULD PUT AN END TO ALL 500 OF THE SCHOOLS OF "MODERN SWORDSMANSHIP."
"PUT AN END"...?
A MINUTE AGO YOU WERE TALKING ABOUT A REVIVAL.
IT IS A REVIVAL! BUT FIRST WE HAVE TO CLEAR OUT THE TRASH!
FIRST WE CRUSH THIS "SHINAI" FIGHTING, THE FOUNTAINHEAD OF MODERN WEAKNESS!
!
WHEN THAT'S DONE, WE REVIVE TRUE KENJUTSU-- WITH SHINKO-RYŪ SETTING ITS STANDARDS...

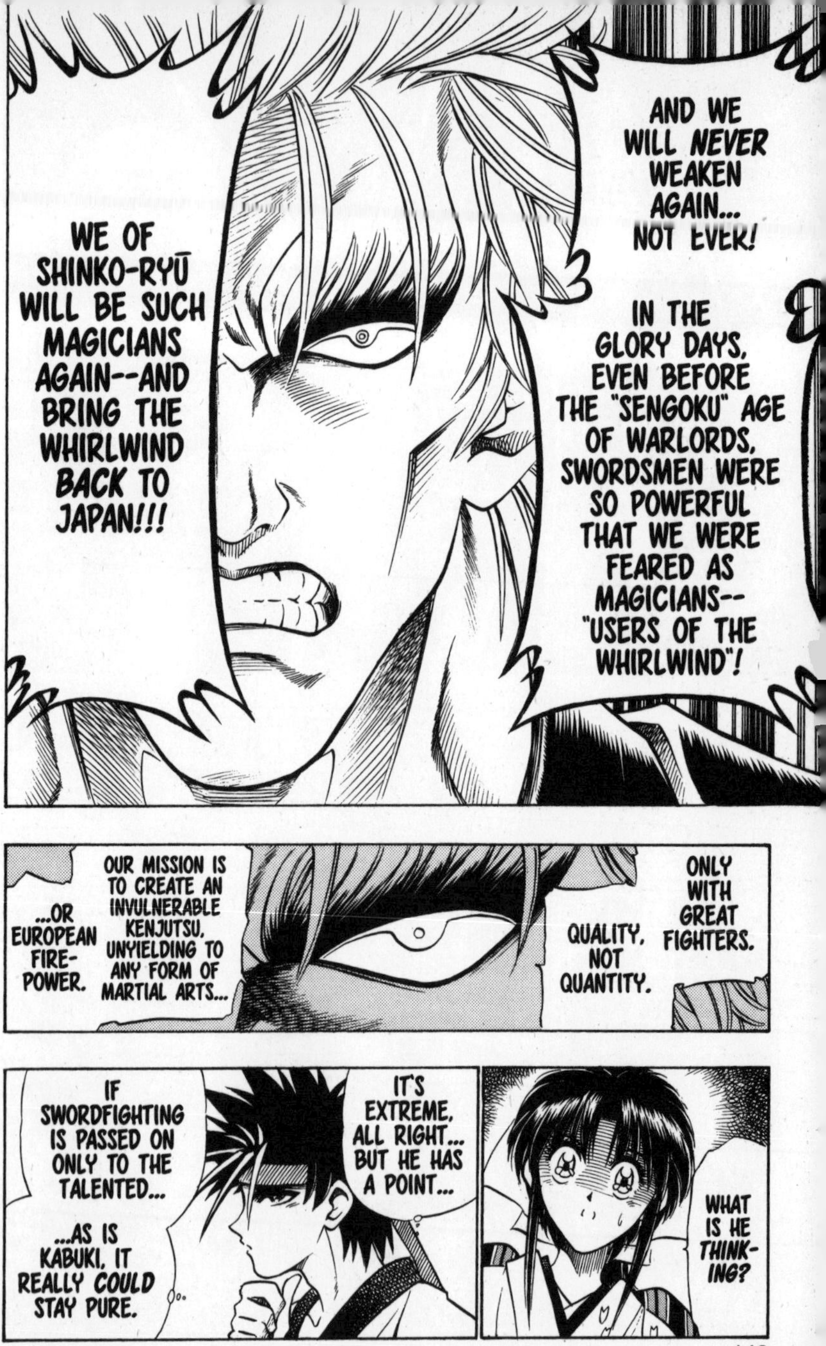
AND WE WILL NEVER WEAKEN AGAIN... NOT EVER!
IN THE GLORY DAYS, EVEN BEFORE THE "SENGOKU" AGE OF WARLORDS, SWORDSMEN WERE SO POWERFUL THAT WE WERE FEARED AS MAGICIANS-- "USERS OF THE WHIRLWIND"!
WE OF SHINKO-RYŪ WILL BE SUCH MAGICIANS AGAIN--AND BRING THE WHIRLWIND BACK TO JAPAN!!!
ONLY WITH GREAT FIGHTERS.
QUALITY, NOT QUANTITY.
OUR MISSION IS TO CREATE AN INVULNERABLE KENJUTSU, UNYIELDING TO ANY FORM OF MARTIAL ARTS...
...OR EUROPEAN FIRE-POWER.
WHAT IS HE THINKING?
IT'S EXTREME, ALL RIGHT... BUT HE HAS A POINT...
IF SWORDFIGHTING IS PASSED ON ONLY TO THE TALENTED...
...AS IS KABUKI, IT REALLY COULD STAY PURE.

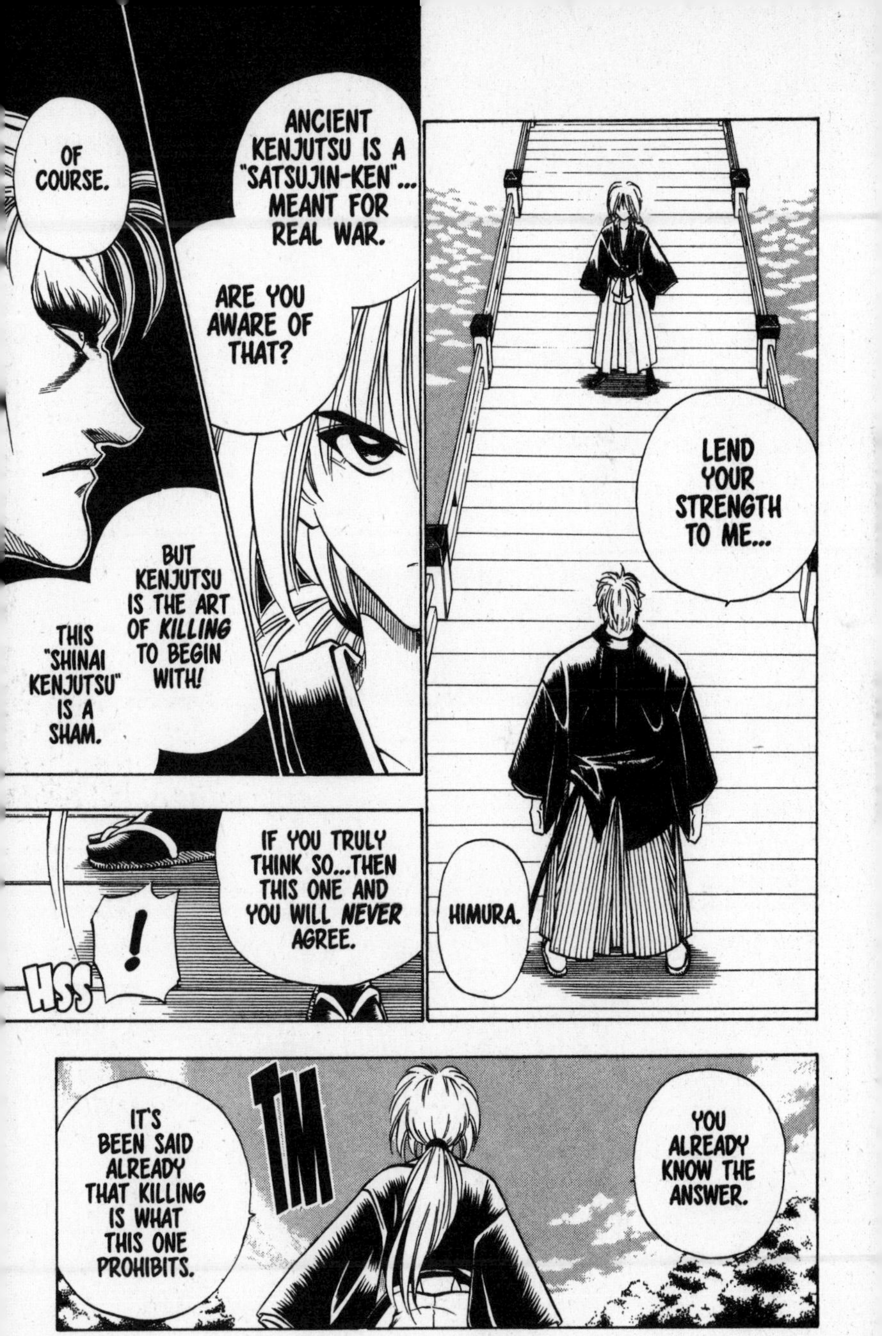
LEND YOUR STRENGTH TO ME...
HIMURA.
ANCIENT KENJUTSU IS A "SATSUJIN-KEN"... MEANT FOR REAL WAR.
ARE YOU AWARE OF THAT?
OF COURSE.
BUT KENJUTSU IS THE ART OF *KILLING* TO BEGIN WITH!
THIS "SHINAI KENJUTSU" IS A SHAM.
IF YOU TRULY THINK SO...THEN THIS ONE AND YOU WILL *NEVER* AGREE.
!
HSS
YOU ALREADY KNOW THE ANSWER.
TM
IT'S BEEN SAID ALREADY THAT KILLING IS WHAT THIS ONE PROHIBITS.

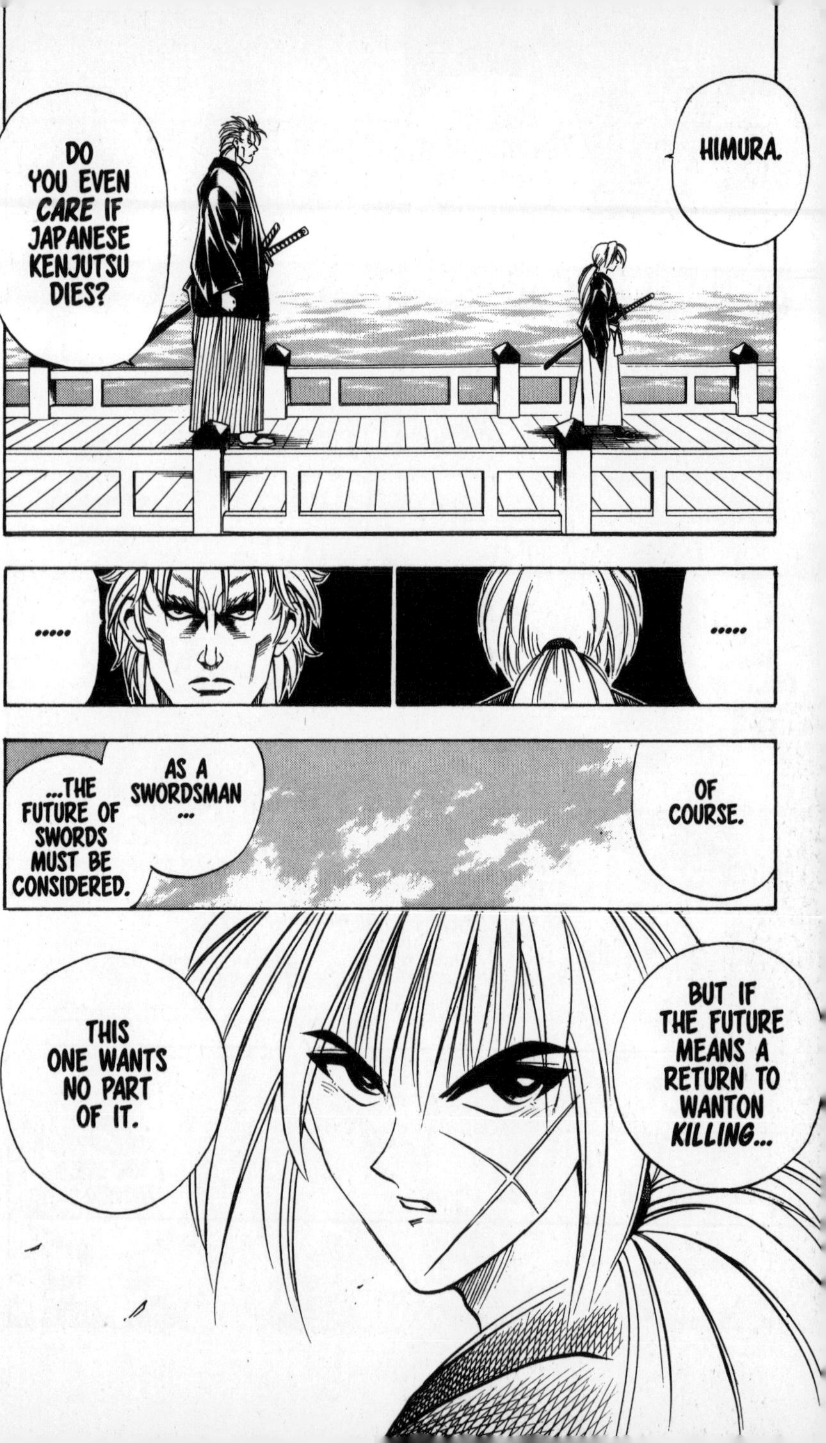
HIMURA.
DO YOU EVEN CARE IF JAPANESE KENJUTSU DIES?
.....
.....
OF COURSE.
AS A SWORDSMAN ...
...THE FUTURE OF SWORDS MUST BE CONSIDERED.
BUT IF THE FUTURE MEANS A RETURN TO WANTON KILLING...
THIS ONE WANTS NO PART OF IT.

READ THIS WAY

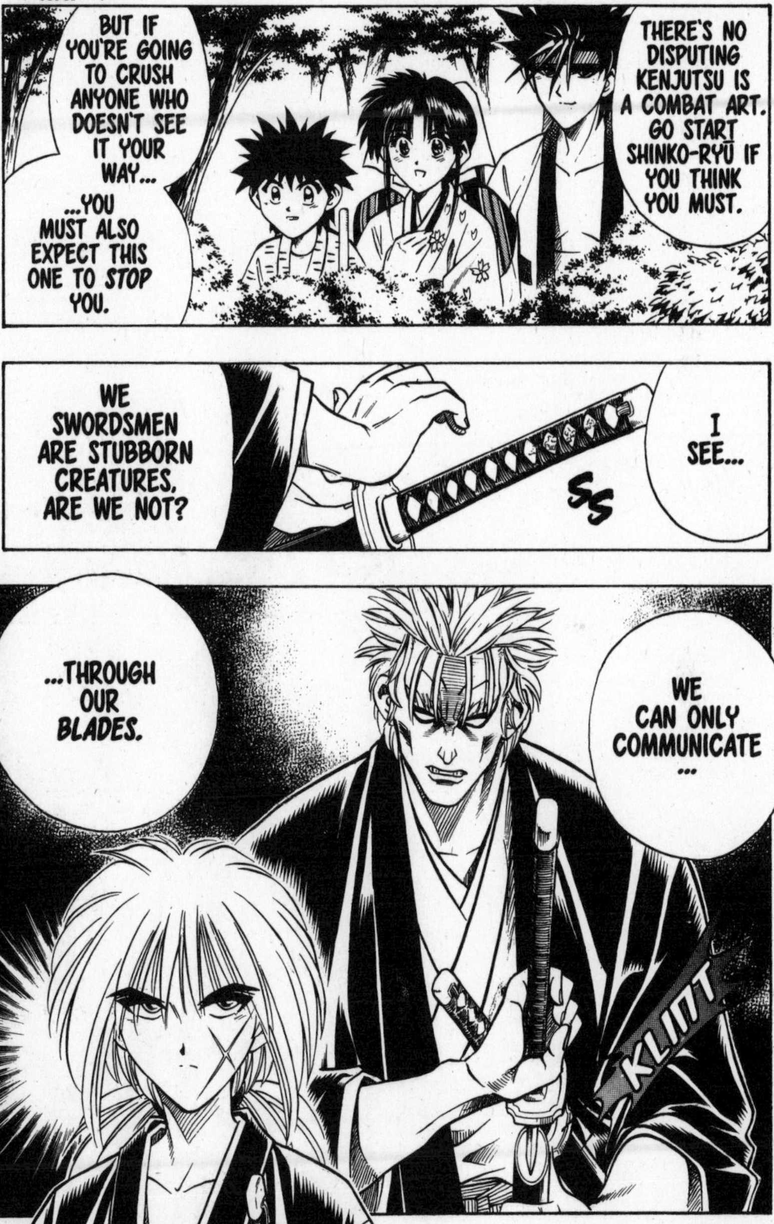
THERE'S NO DISPUTING KENJUTSU IS A COMBAT ART. GO START SHINKO-RYŪ IF YOU THINK YOU MUST.
BUT IF YOU'RE GOING TO CRUSH ANYONE WHO DOESN'T SEE IT YOUR WAY...
...YOU MUST ALSO EXPECT THIS ONE TO *STOP* YOU.
I SEE...
SS
WE SWORDSMEN ARE STUBBORN CREATURES, ARE WE NOT?
WE CAN ONLY COMMUNICATE ...
...THROUGH OUR *BLADES.*
KLINT

Rurouni Kenshin

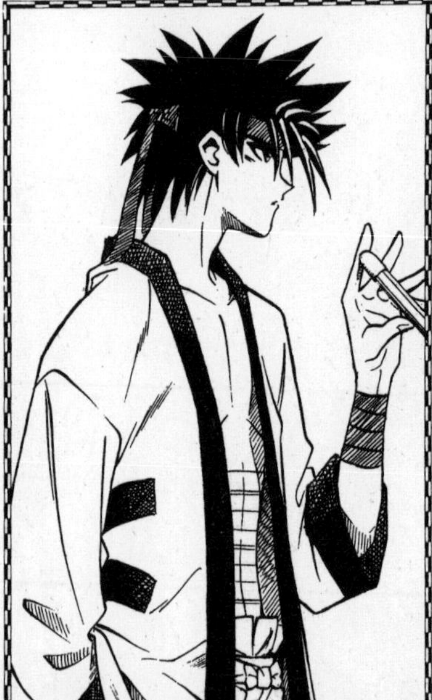

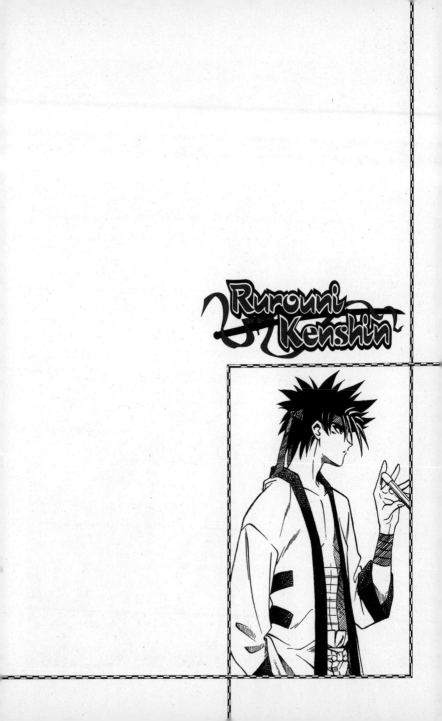

READ THIS WAY

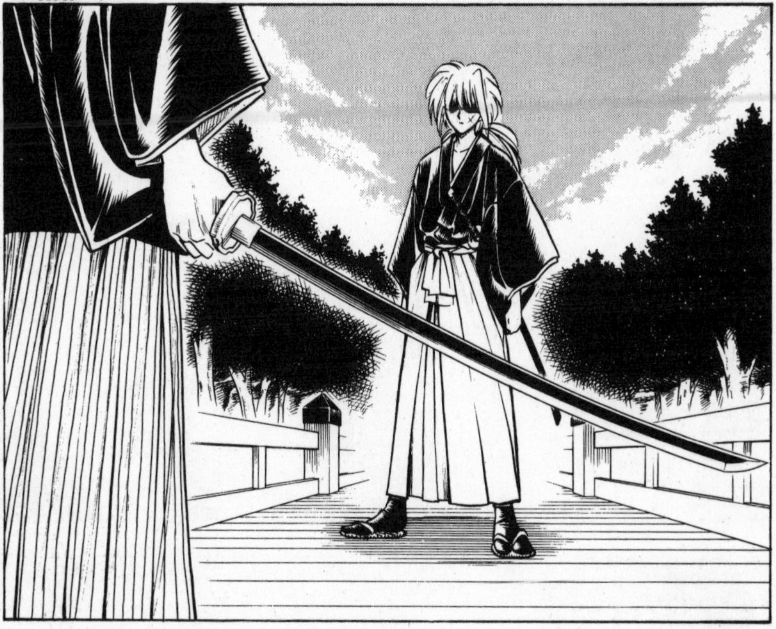

# Act 38
# Yutarō's Skill

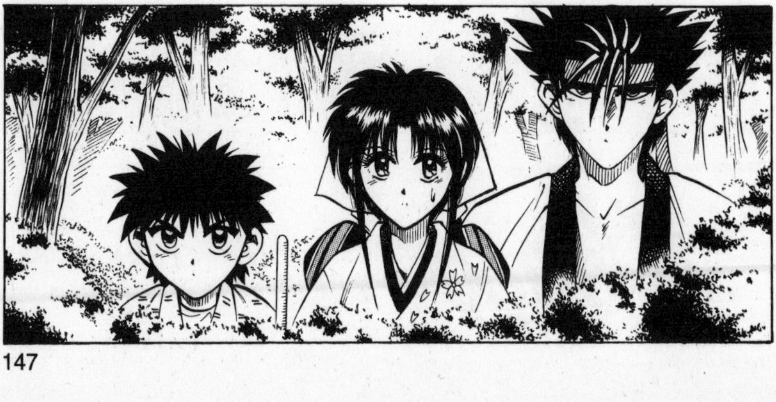

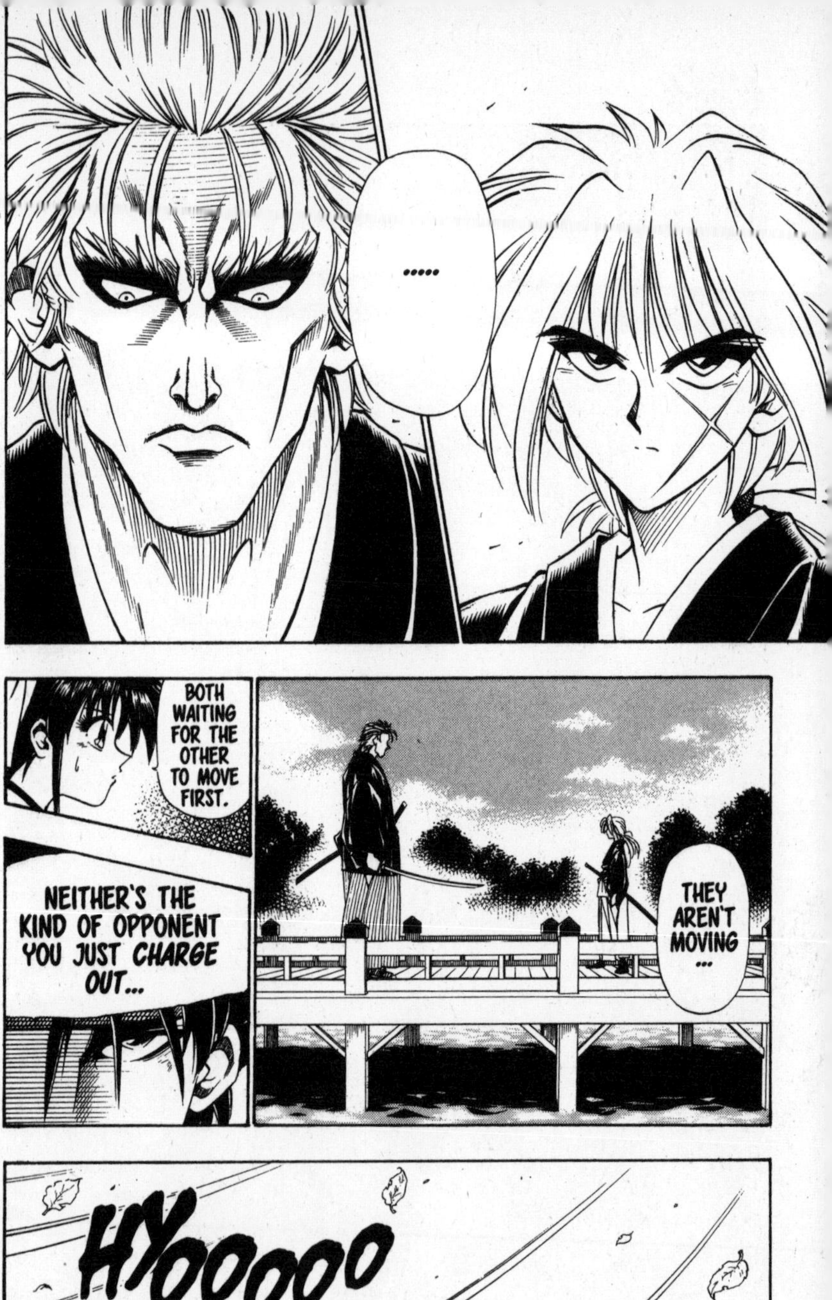
......
THEY AREN'T MOVING ...
BOTH WAITING FOR THE OTHER TO MOVE FIRST.
NEITHER'S THE KIND OF OPPONENT YOU JUST *CHARGE* OUT...
HYOOOOO

READ THIS WAY

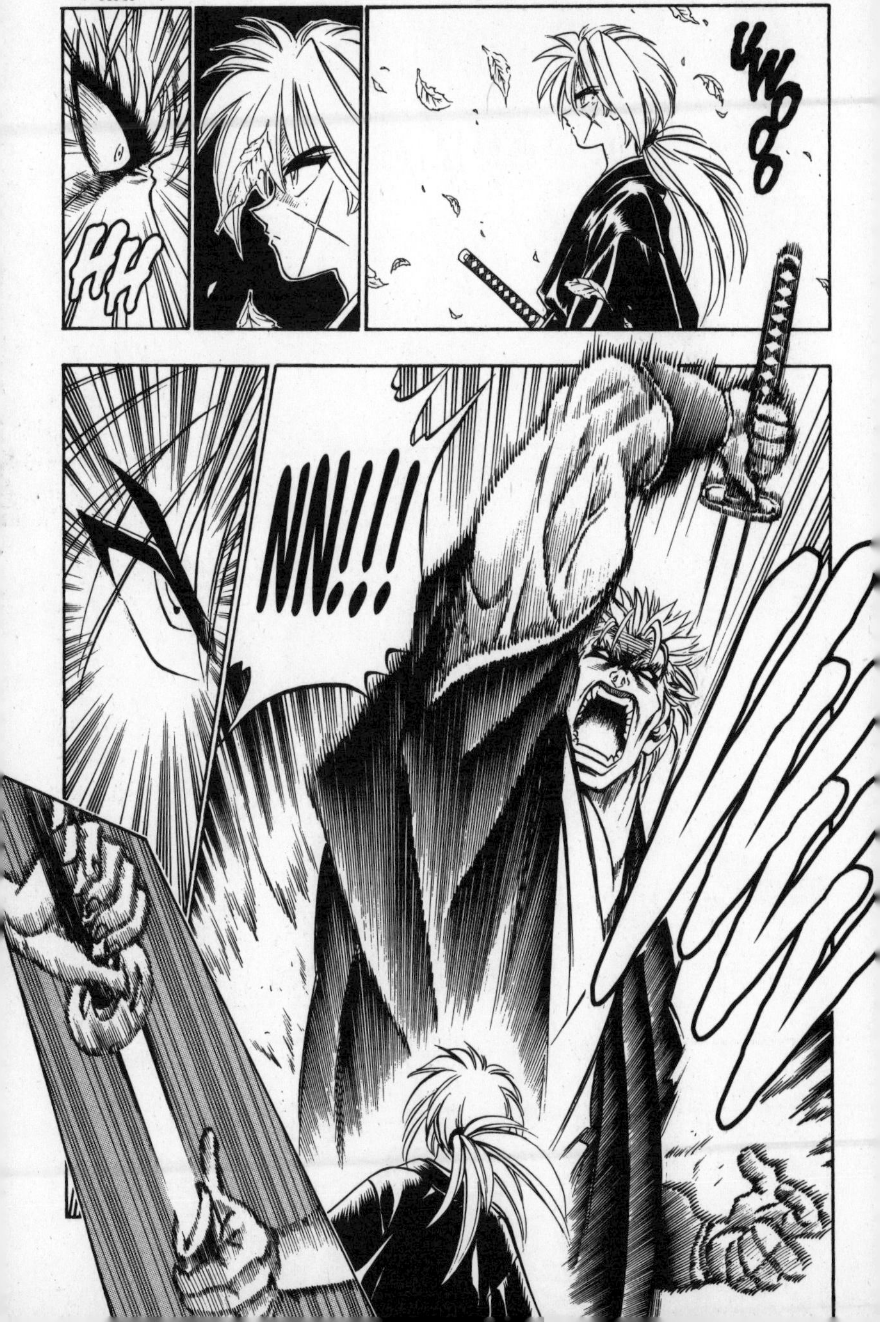
UWOO
HH
NN!!!

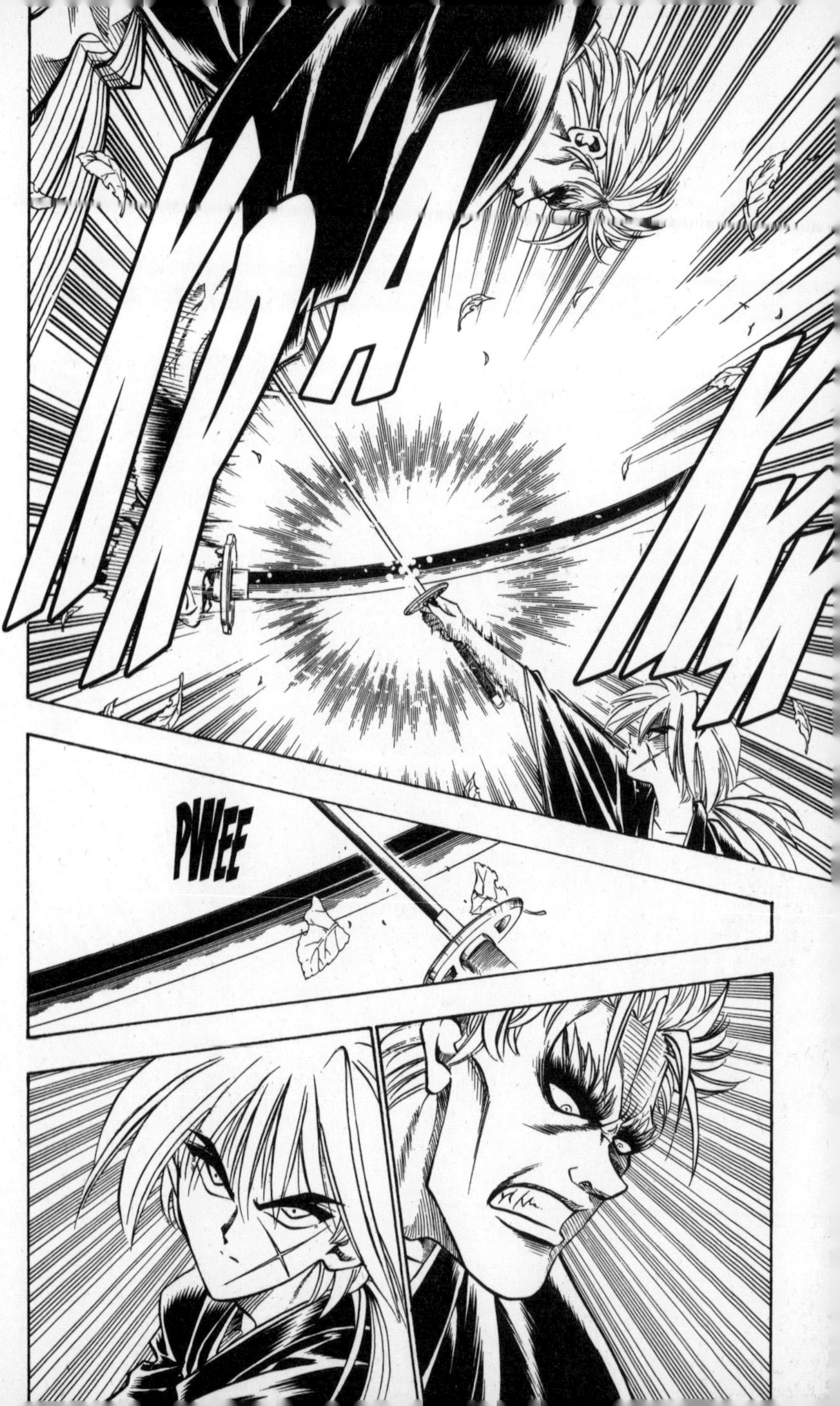
PWEE

READ THIS WAY

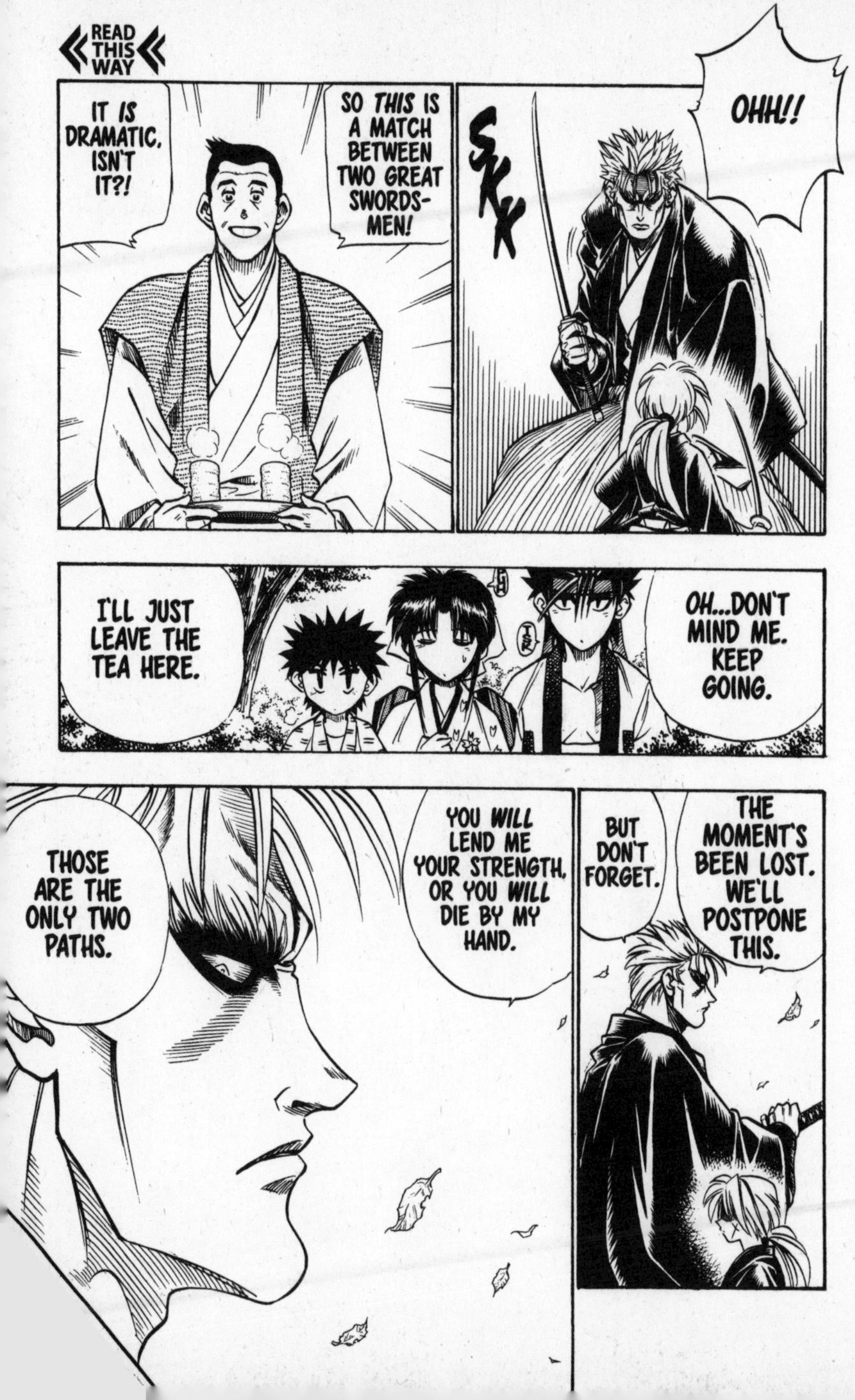
SKK
OHH!!
SO *THIS* IS A MATCH BETWEEN TWO GREAT SWORDS-MEN!
IT *IS* DRAMATIC, ISN'T IT?!
OH...DON'T MIND ME. KEEP GOING.
I'LL JUST LEAVE THE TEA HERE.
THE MOMENT'S BEEN LOST. WE'LL POSTPONE THIS.
BUT DON'T FORGET.
YOU *WILL* LEND ME YOUR STRENGTH, OR YOU *WILL* DIE BY MY HAND.
THOSE ARE THE ONLY TWO PATHS.

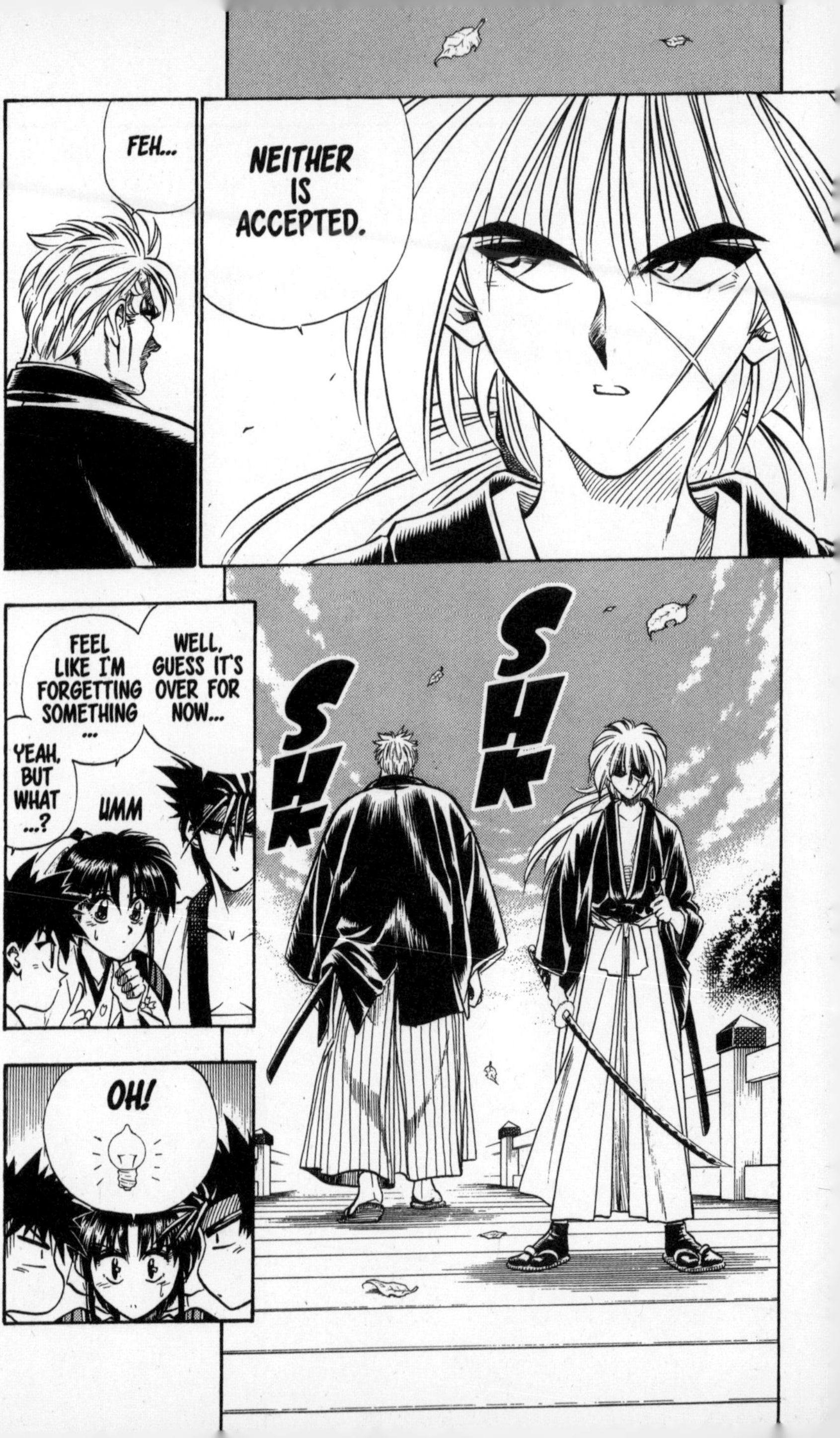
NEITHER IS ACCEPTED.
FEH...
SHK
SHK
WELL, GUESS IT'S OVER FOR NOW...
FEEL LIKE I'M FORGETTING SOMETHING...
YEAH, BUT WHAT...?
UMM
OH!

READ THIS WAY

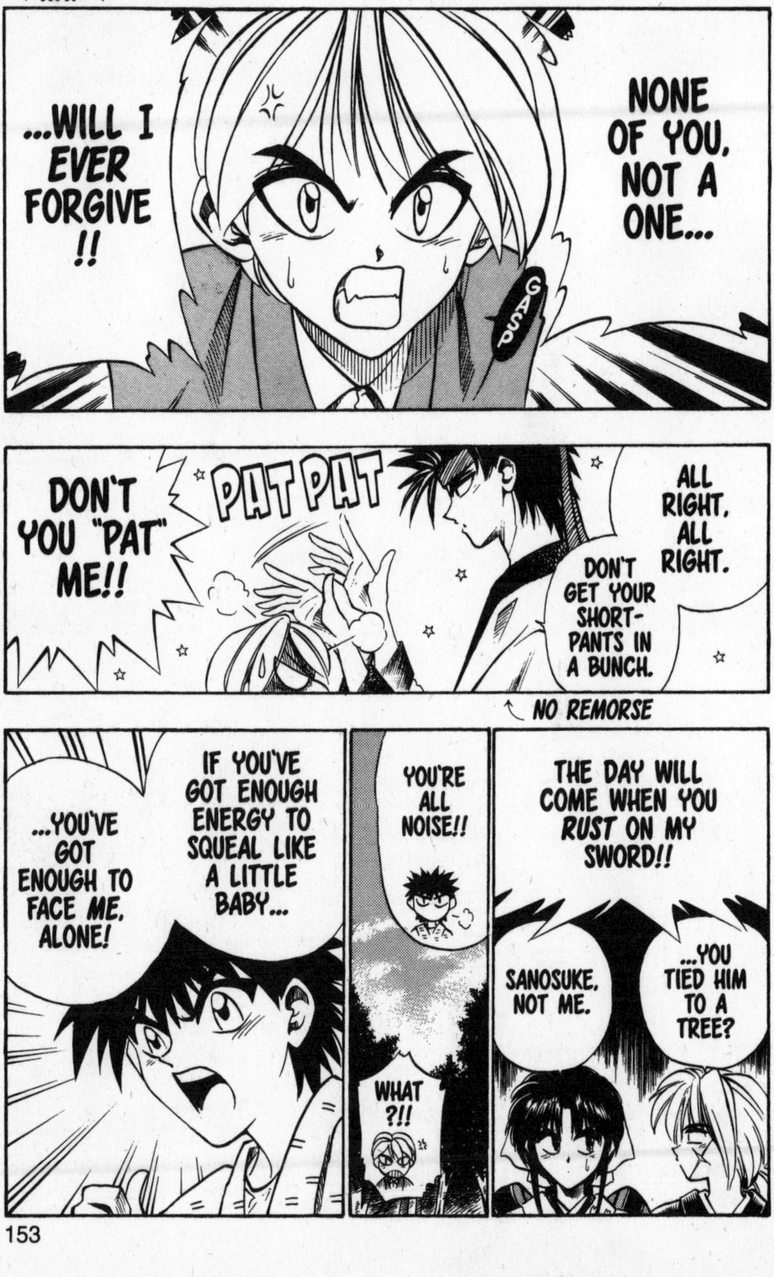

NONE OF YOU, NOT A ONE...
...WILL I *EVER* FORGIVE!!
GASP
ALL RIGHT, ALL RIGHT.
DON'T GET YOUR SHORT-PANTS IN A BUNCH.
PAT PAT
DON'T YOU "PAT" ME!!
NO REMORSE
THE DAY WILL COME WHEN YOU *RUST* ON MY SWORD!!
...YOU TIED HIM TO A TREE?
SANOSUKE, NOT ME.
YOU'RE ALL NOISE!!
WHAT?!!
IF YOU'VE GOT ENOUGH ENERGY TO SQUEAL LIKE A LITTLE BABY...
...YOU'VE GOT ENOUGH TO FACE *ME*, ALONE!

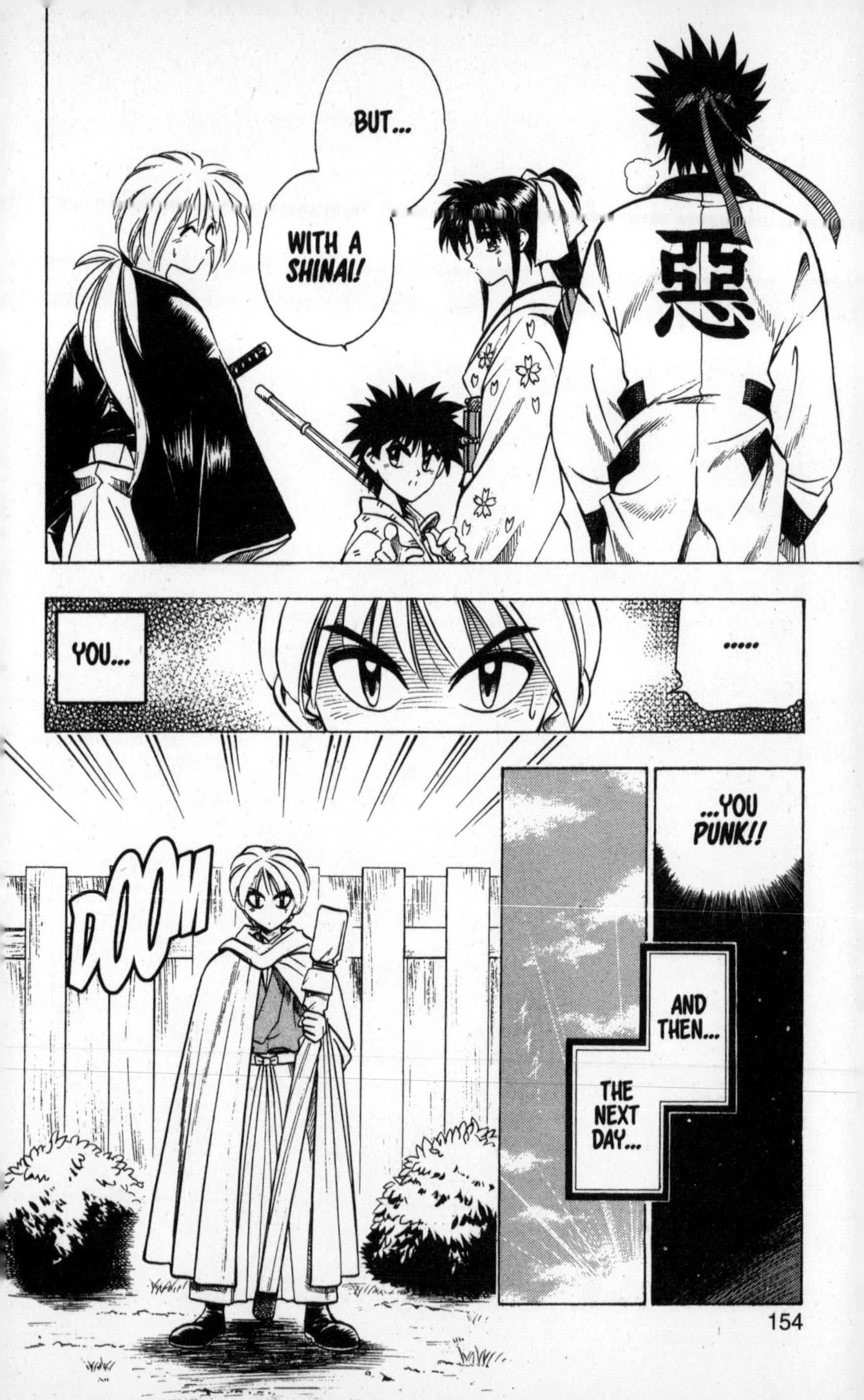
悪
BUT...
WITH A SHINAI!
.....
YOU...
...YOU PUNK!!
AND THEN...
THE NEXT DAY...
DOOM

READ THIS WAY

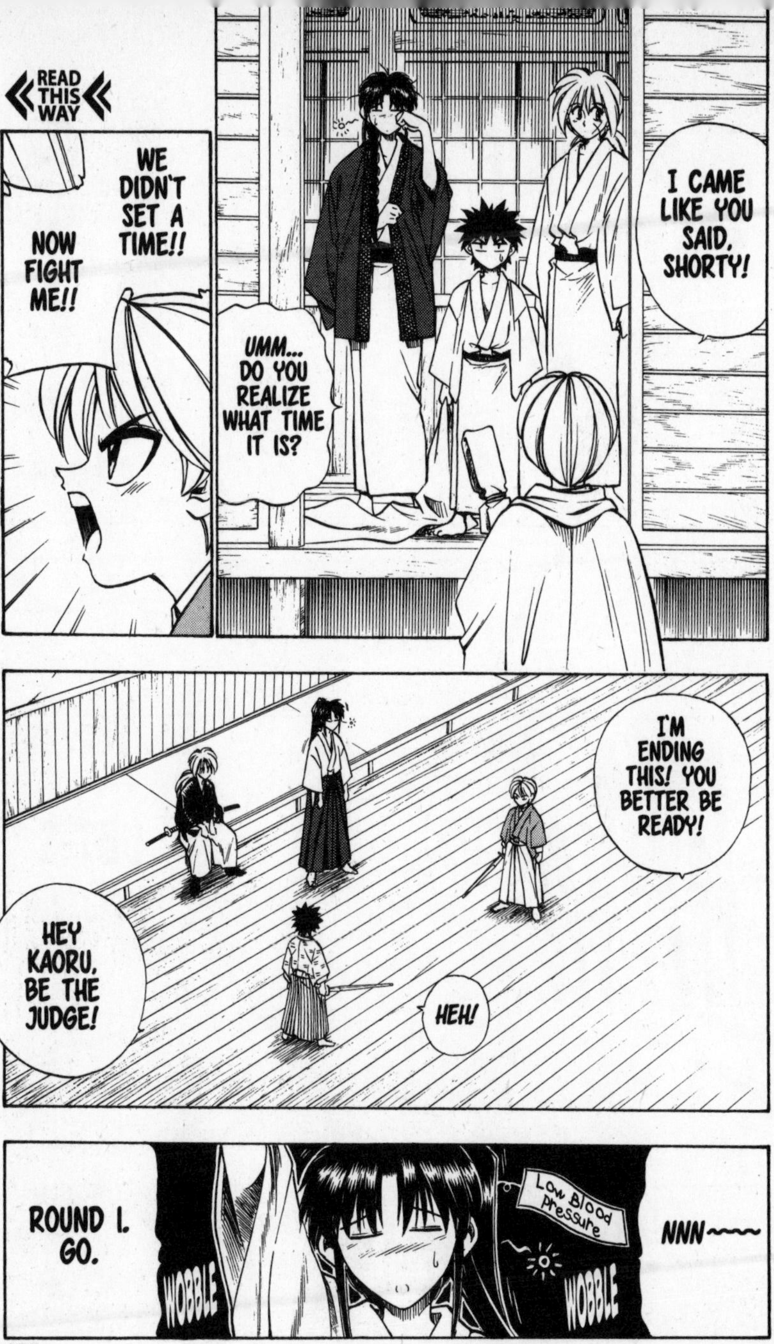
I CAME LIKE YOU SAID, SHORTY!
UMM... DO YOU REALIZE WHAT TIME IT IS?
WE DIDN'T SET A TIME!!
NOW FIGHT ME!!
I'M ENDING THIS! YOU BETTER BE READY!
HEH!
HEY KAORU, BE THE JUDGE!
NNN~~~
Low Blood Pressure
WOBBLE
WOBBLE
ROUND 1. GO.

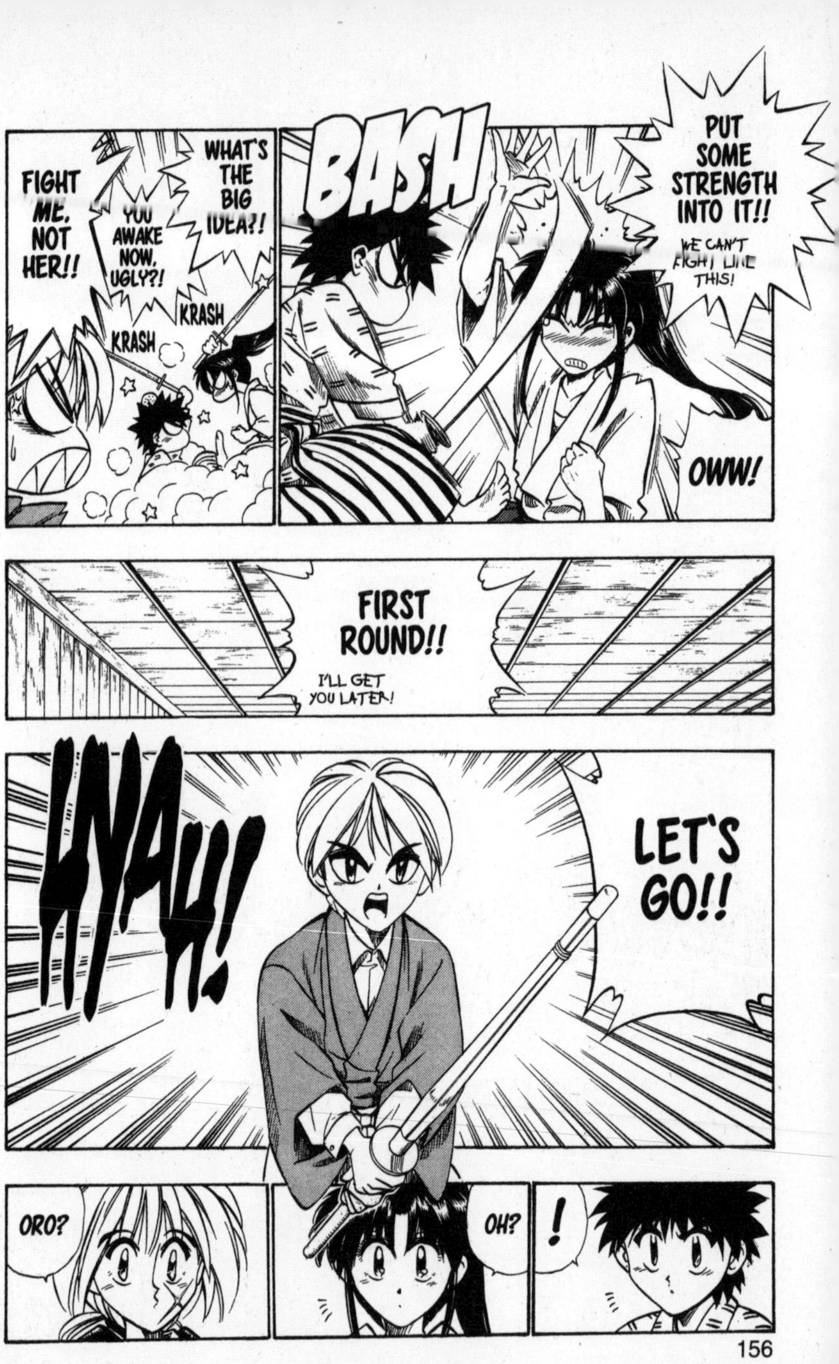
BASH
PUT SOME STRENGTH INTO IT!!
WE CAN'T FIGHT LIKE THIS!
OWW!
WHAT'S THE BIG IDEA?!
YOU AWAKE NOW, UGLY?!
FIGHT ME, NOT HER!!
KRASH
KRASH
FIRST ROUND!!
I'LL GET YOU LATER!
LET'S GO!!
HYAH!
!
OH?
ORO?

READ THIS WAY

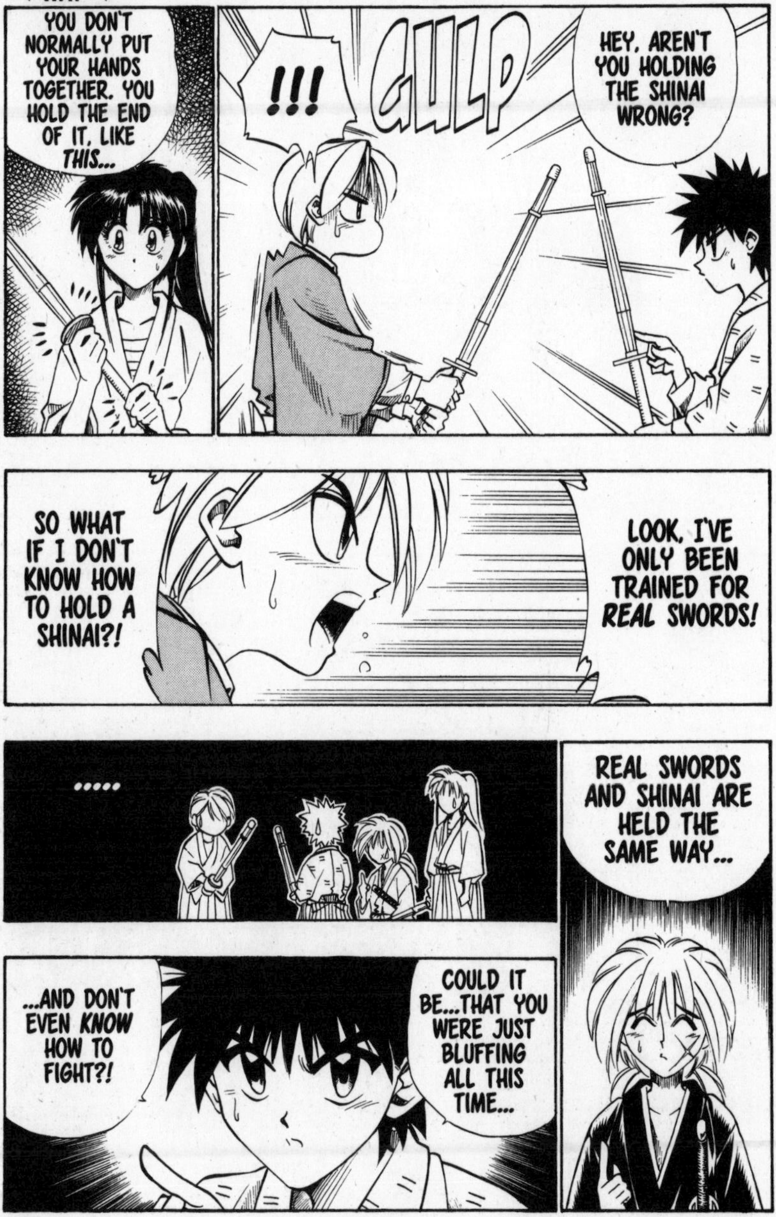
HEY, AREN'T YOU HOLDING THE SHINAI WRONG?
GULP
!!!
YOU DON'T NORMALLY PUT YOUR HANDS TOGETHER. YOU HOLD THE END OF IT, LIKE *THIS*...
LOOK, I'VE ONLY BEEN TRAINED FOR *REAL* SWORDS!
SO WHAT IF I DON'T KNOW HOW TO HOLD A SHINAI?!
REAL SWORDS AND SHINAI ARE HELD THE SAME WAY...
.....
COULD IT BE...THAT YOU WERE JUST BLUFFING ALL THIS TIME...
...AND DON'T EVEN *KNOW* HOW TO FIGHT?!

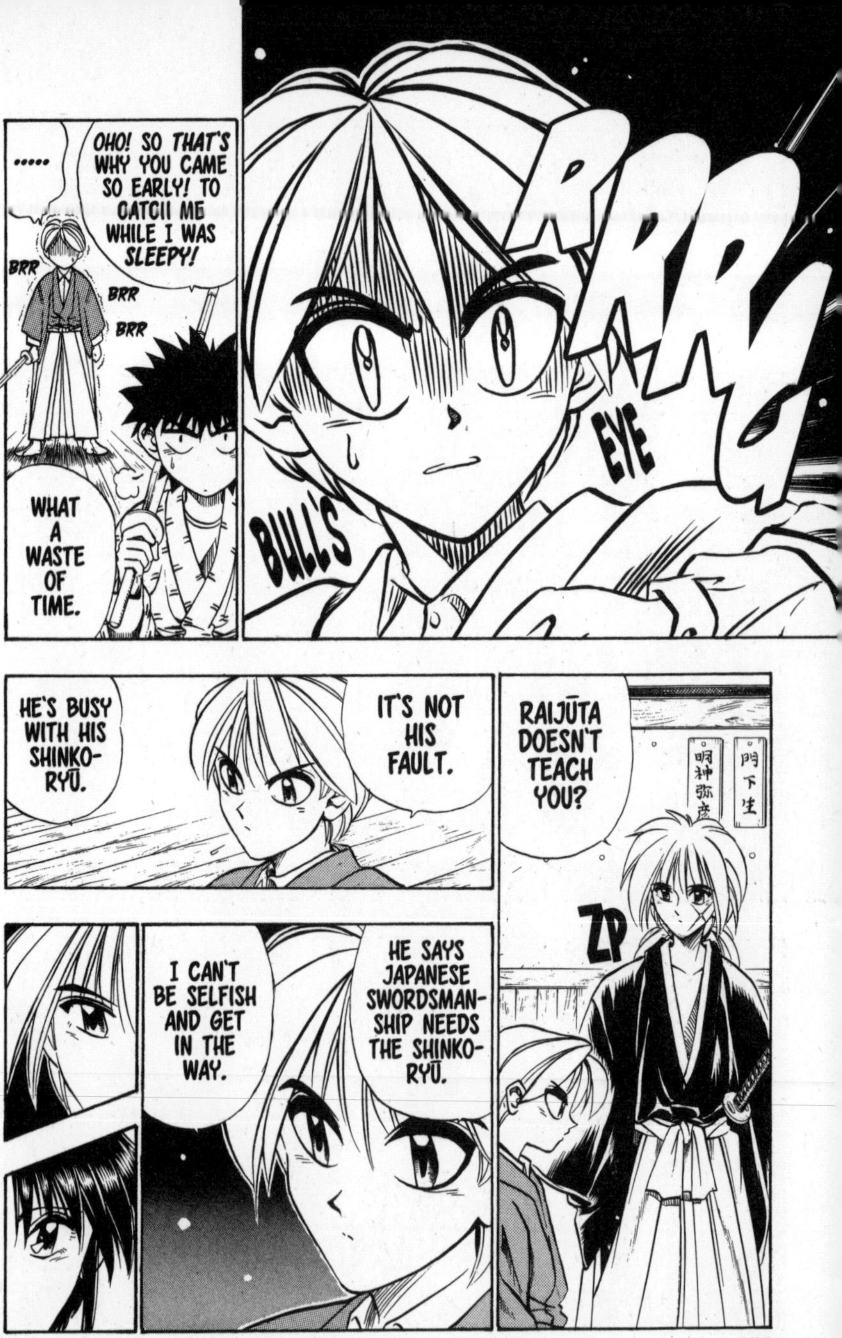
RRRG
BULL'S EYE
OHO! SO THAT'S WHY YOU CAME SO EARLY! TO CATCH ME WHILE I WAS SLEEPY!
.....
BRR
BRR
BRR
WHAT A WASTE OF TIME.
RAIJŪTA DOESN'T TEACH YOU?
門下生
明神弥彦
ZP
IT'S NOT HIS FAULT.
HE'S BUSY WITH HIS SHINKO-RYŪ.
HE SAYS JAPANESE SWORDSMANSHIP NEEDS THE SHINKO-RYŪ.
I CAN'T BE SELFISH AND GET IN THE WAY.

READ THIS WAY

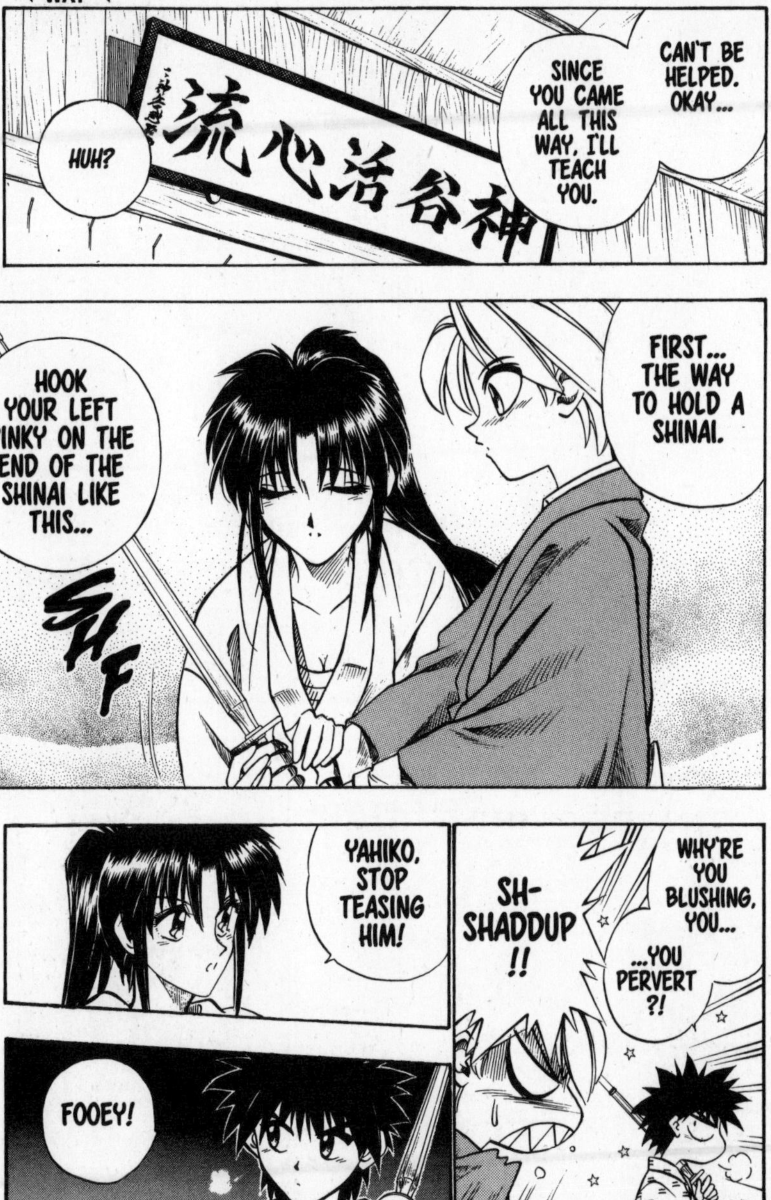
CAN'T BE HELPED. OKAY...
SINCE YOU CAME ALL THIS WAY, I'LL TEACH YOU.
神谷活心流
HUH?
FIRST... THE WAY TO HOLD A SHINAI.
HOOK YOUR LEFT PINKY ON THE END OF THE SHINAI LIKE THIS...
SHF
WHY'RE YOU BLUSHING, YOU...
...YOU PERVERT?!
SH-SHADDUP!!
YAHIKO, STOP TEASING HIM!
FOOEY!

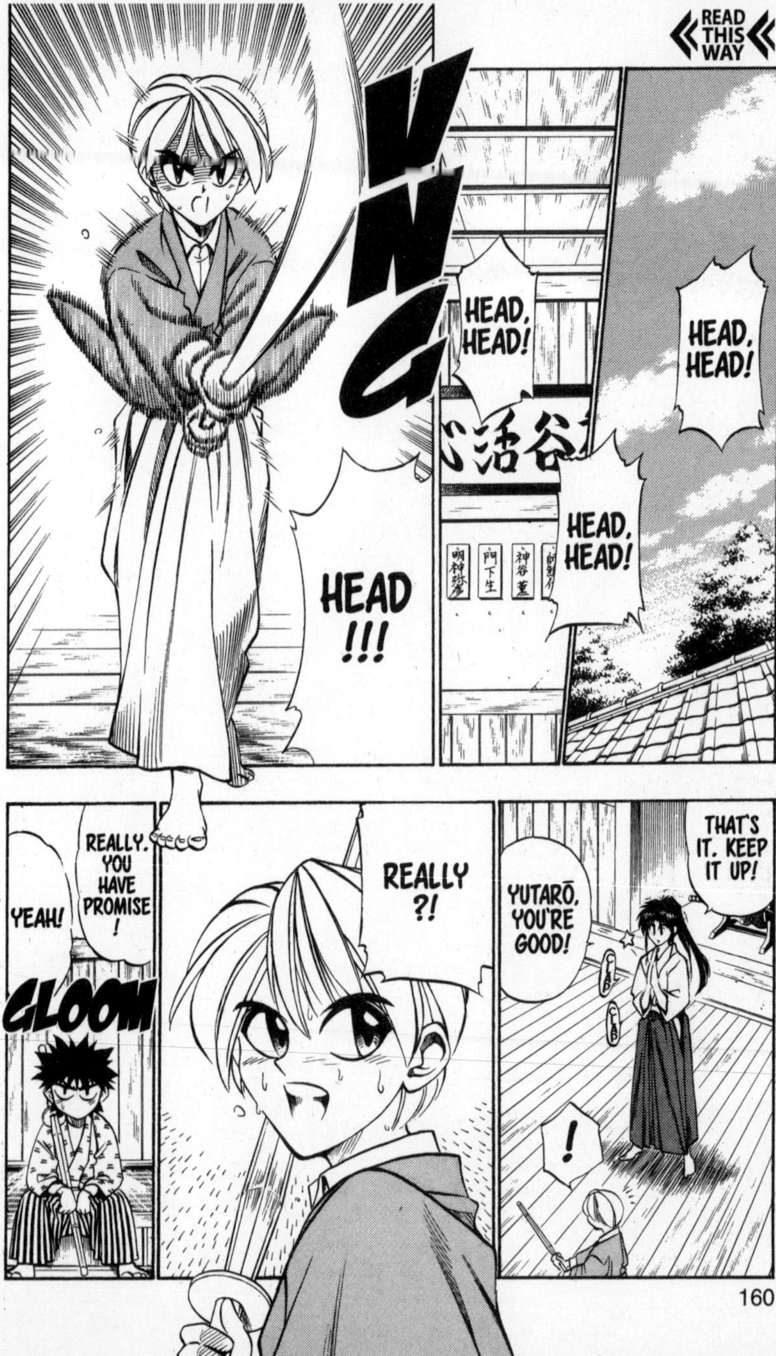
READ THIS WAY
HEAD, HEAD!
HEAD, HEAD!
HEAD, HEAD!
心活谷
明神弥彦
門下生
神谷薫
WNG
HEAD !!!
THAT'S IT. KEEP IT UP!
YUTARŌ, YOU'RE GOOD!
CLAP
CLAP
!
REALLY ?!
REALLY. YOU HAVE PROMISE !
YEAH!
GLOOM

READ THIS WAY

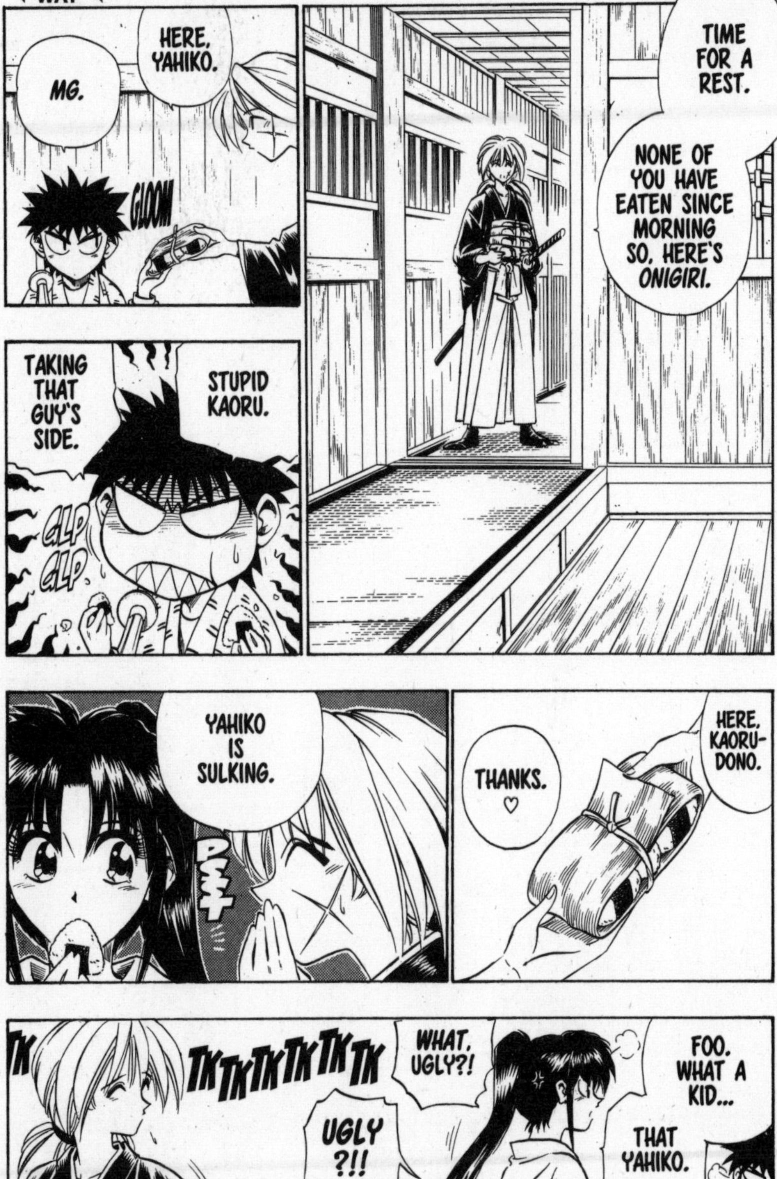
TIME FOR A REST.
NONE OF YOU HAVE EATEN SINCE MORNING SO, HERE'S ONIGIRI.
HERE, YAHIKO.
MG.
GLOOM
STUPID KAORU.
TAKING THAT GUY'S SIDE.
GLP GLP
HERE, KAORU-DONO.
THANKS. ♡
YAHIKO IS SULKING.
PSST
FOO. WHAT A KID...
THAT YAHIKO.
WHAT, UGLY?!
UGLY ?!!
TKTKTKTKTKTK
TK

READ THIS WAY

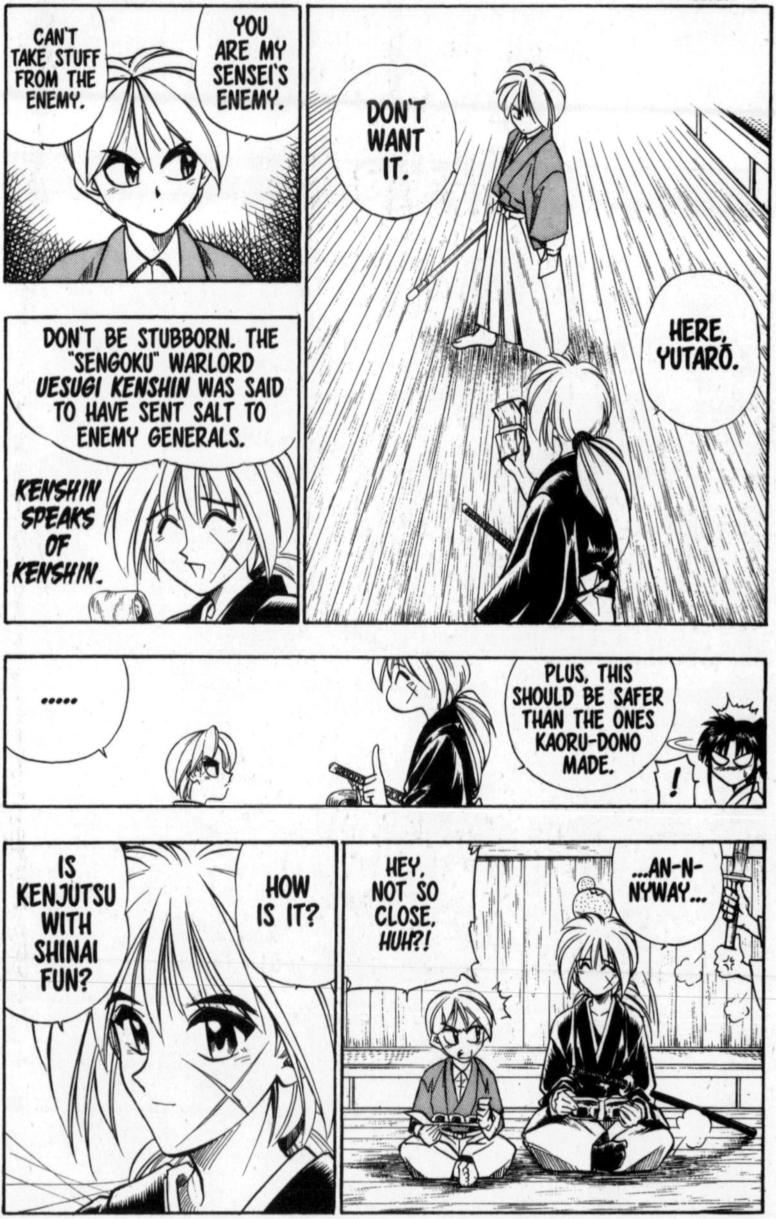
HERE, YUTARŌ.
DON'T WANT IT.
YOU ARE MY SENSEI'S ENEMY.
CAN'T TAKE STUFF FROM THE ENEMY.
DON'T BE STUBBORN. THE "SENGOKU" WARLORD *UESUGI KENSHIN* WAS SAID TO HAVE SENT SALT TO ENEMY GENERALS.
KENSHIN SPEAKS OF KENSHIN.
PLUS, THIS SHOULD BE SAFER THAN THE ONES KAORU-DONO MADE.
!
.....
...AN-N-NYWAY...
HEY, NOT SO CLOSE, HUH?!
HOW IS IT?
IS KENJUTSU WITH SHINAI FUN?

READ THIS WAY

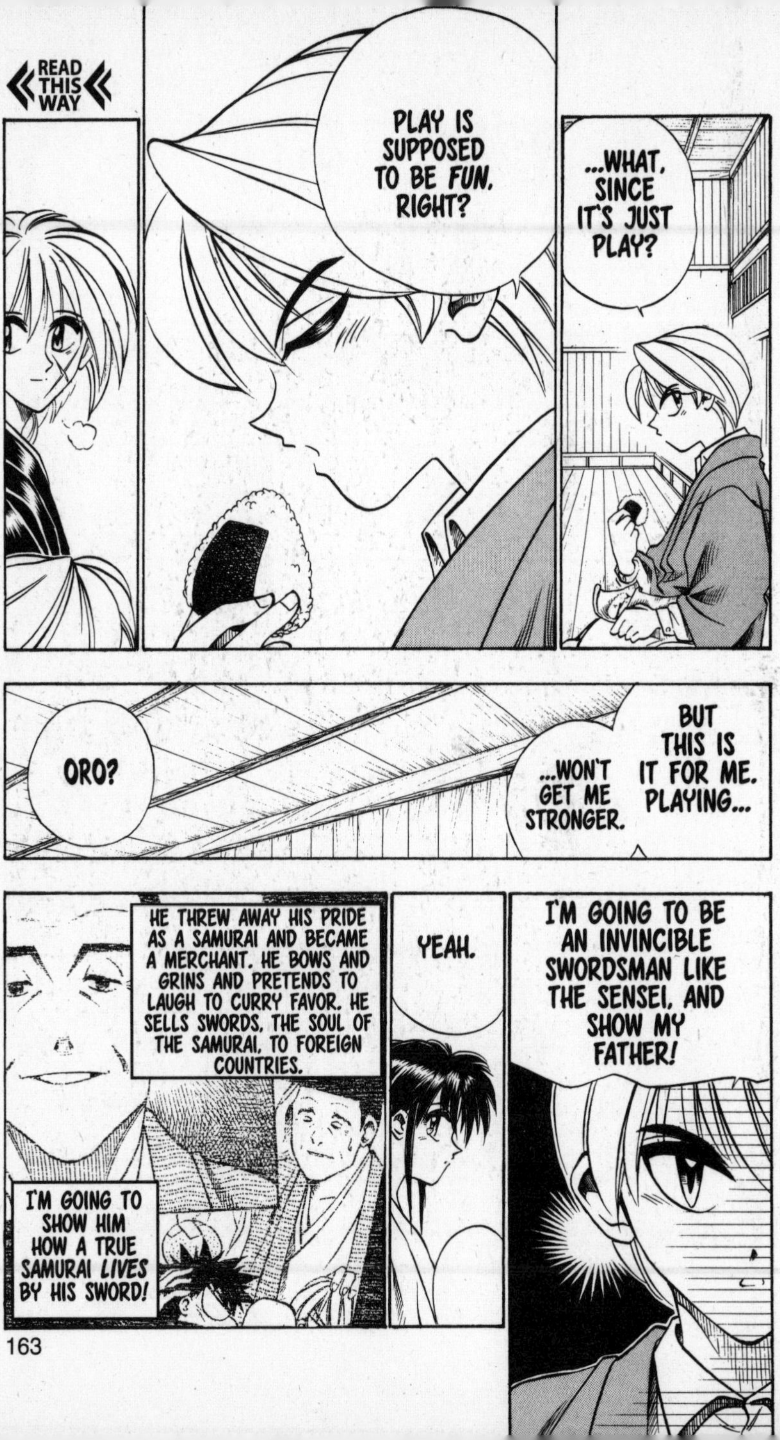

...WHAT, SINCE IT'S JUST PLAY?
PLAY IS SUPPOSED TO BE *FUN*, RIGHT?
BUT THIS IS IT FOR ME. PLAYING...
...WON'T GET ME STRONGER.
ORO?
I'M GOING TO BE AN INVINCIBLE SWORDSMAN LIKE THE SENSEI, AND SHOW MY FATHER!
YEAH.
HE THREW AWAY HIS PRIDE AS A SAMURAI AND BECAME A MERCHANT. HE BOWS AND GRINS AND PRETENDS TO LAUGH TO CURRY FAVOR. HE SELLS SWORDS, THE SOUL OF THE SAMURAI, TO FOREIGN COUNTRIES.
I'M GOING TO SHOW HIM HOW A TRUE SAMURAI *LIVES* BY HIS SWORD!

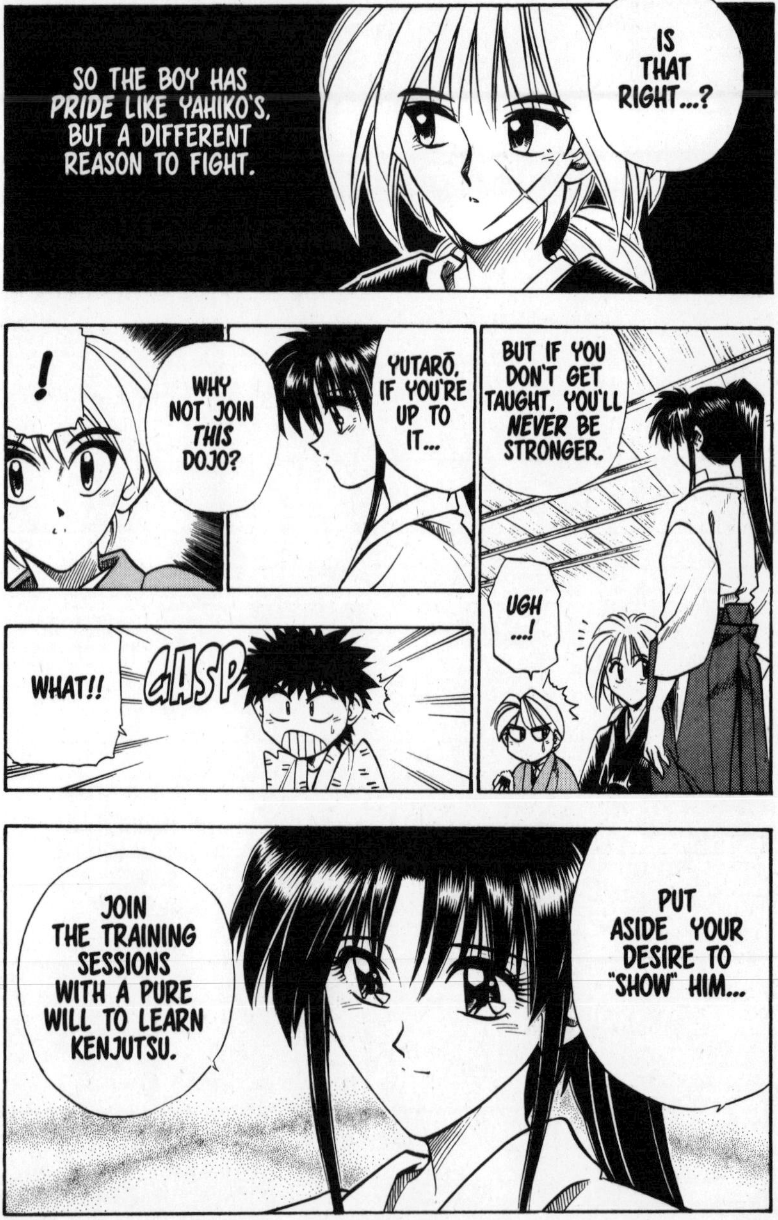
IS THAT RIGHT...?
SO THE BOY HAS PRIDE LIKE YAHIKO'S, BUT A DIFFERENT REASON TO FIGHT.
BUT IF YOU DON'T GET TAUGHT, YOU'LL NEVER BE STRONGER.
UGH ...!
YUTARŌ, IF YOU'RE UP TO IT...
WHY NOT JOIN THIS DOJO?
!
GASP
WHAT!!
PUT ASIDE YOUR DESIRE TO "SHOW" HIM...
JOIN THE TRAINING SESSIONS WITH A PURE WILL TO LEARN KENJUTSU.

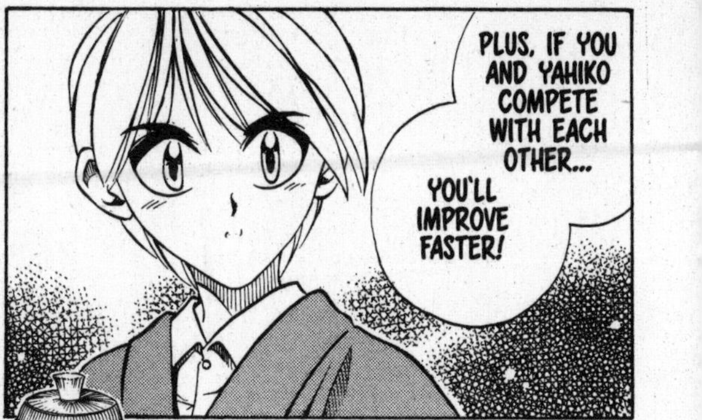
PLUS, IF YOU AND YAHIKO COMPETE WITH EACH OTHER...
YOU'LL IMPROVE FASTER!
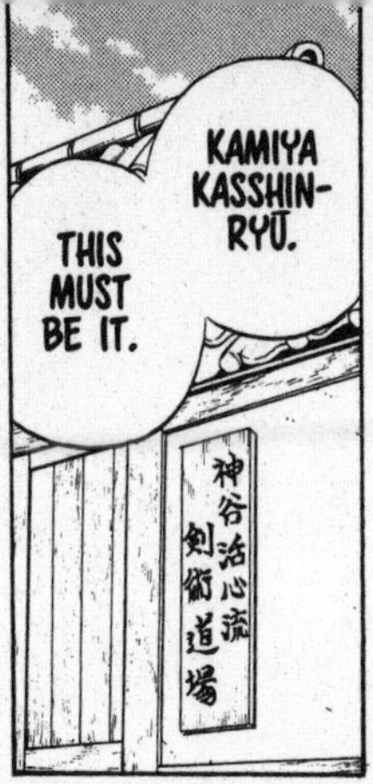
KAMIYA KASSHIN-RYŪ.
THIS MUST BE IT.
神谷活心流
剣術道場
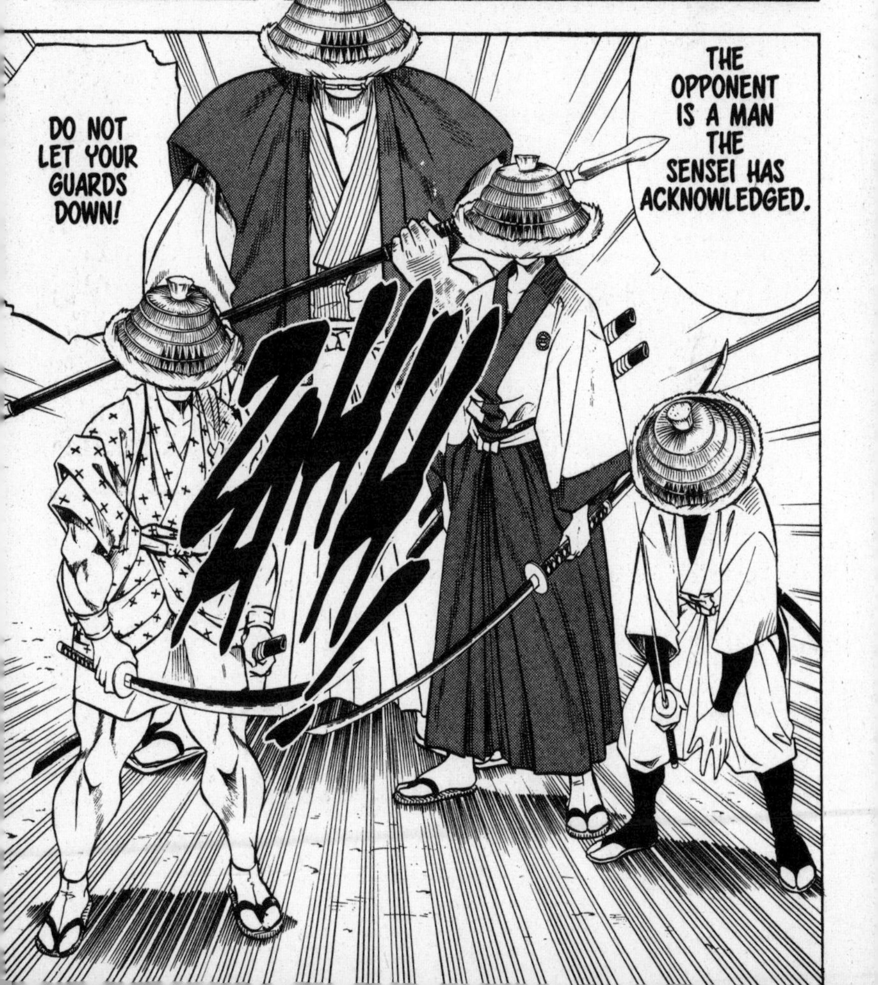
THE OPPONENT IS A MAN THE SENSEI HAS ACKNOWLEDGED.
DO NOT LET YOUR GUARDS DOWN!

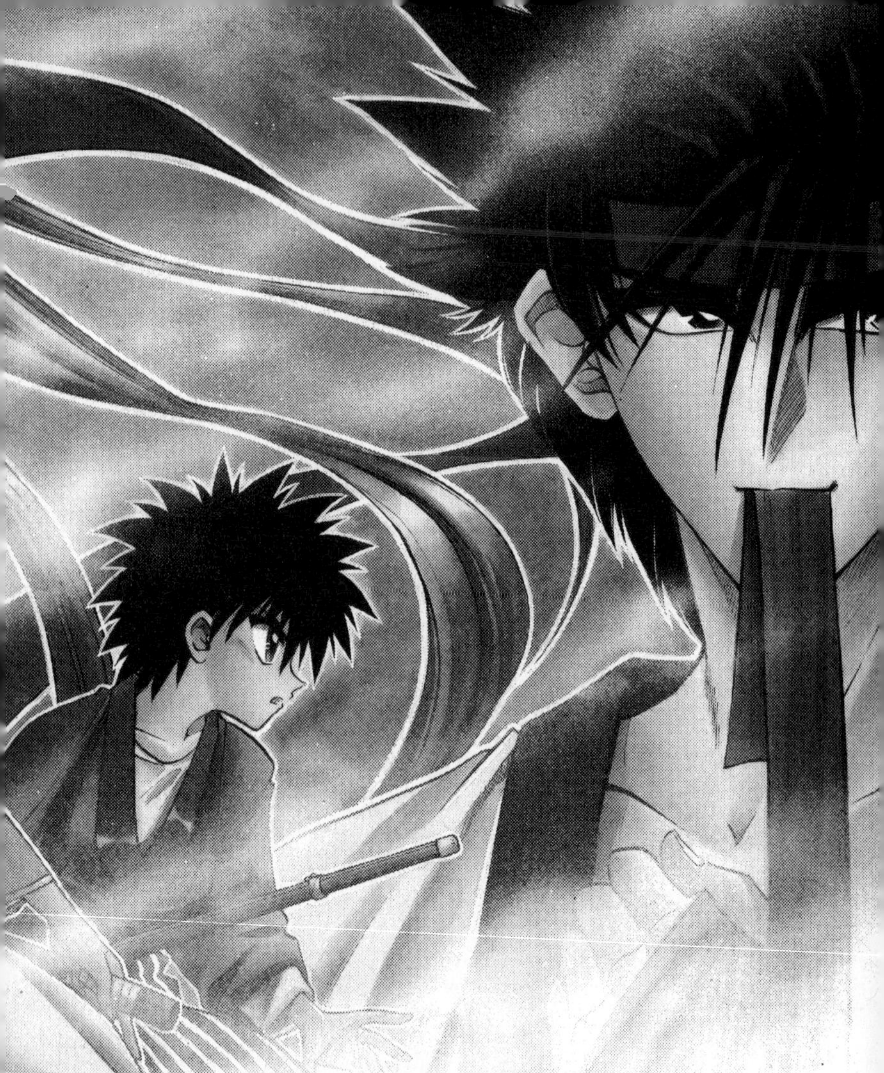

# Act 39
# Clash

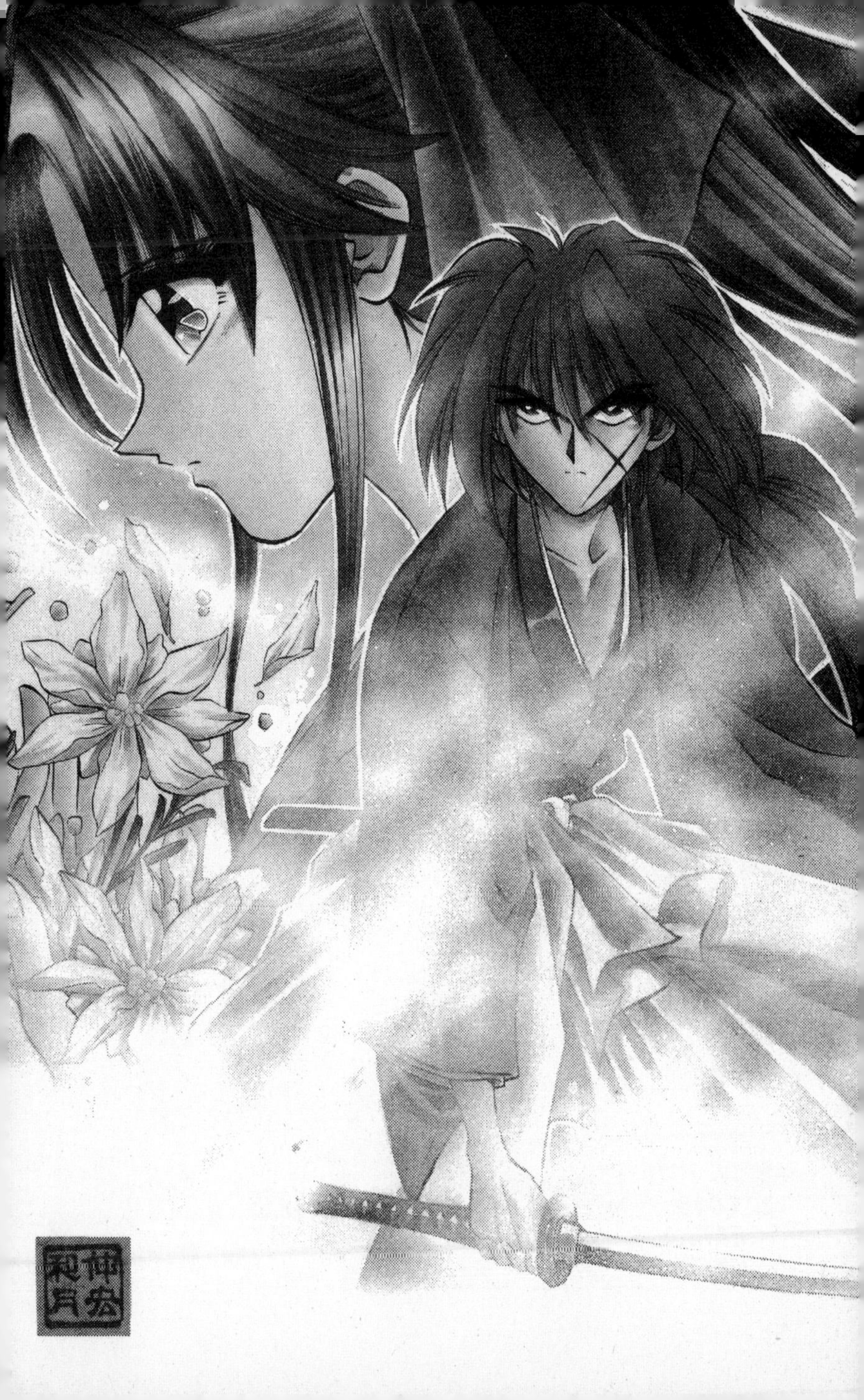
和月伸宏

READ THIS WAY

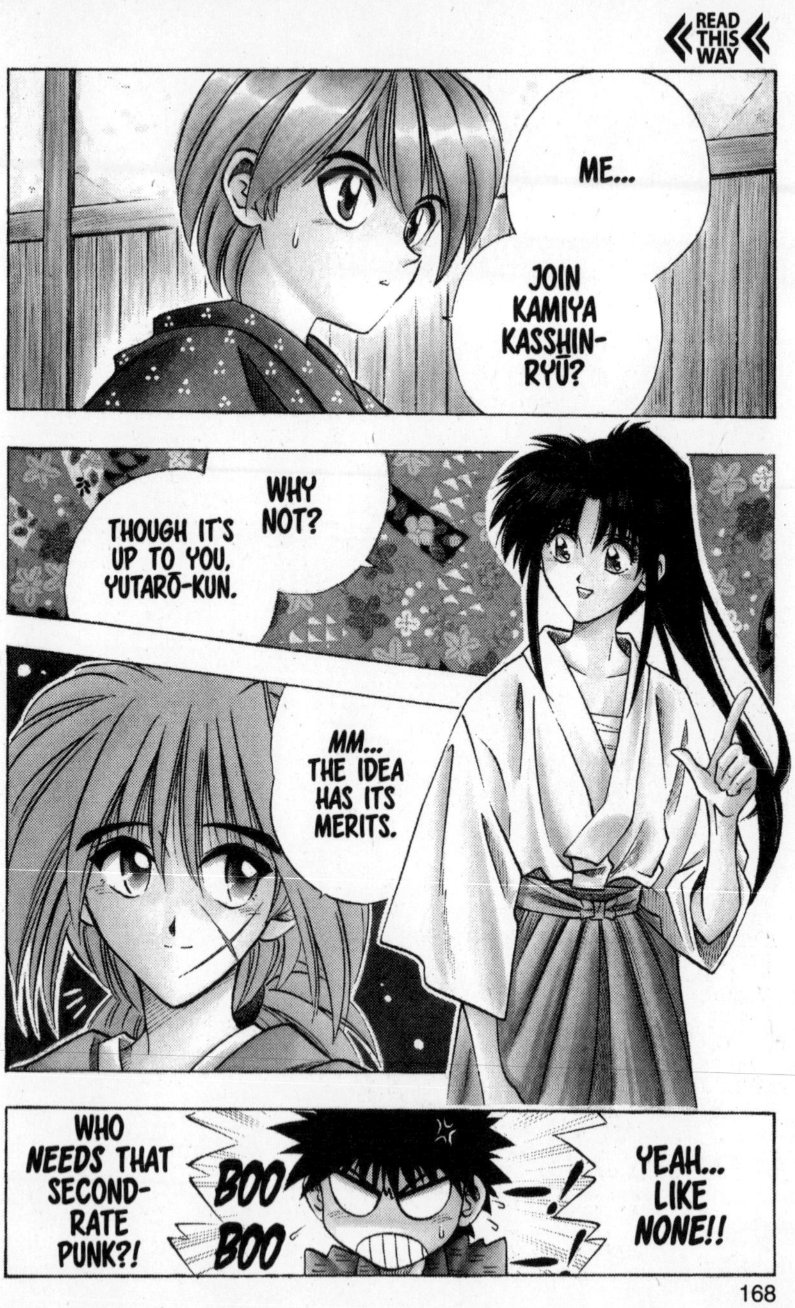

ME...
JOIN KAMIYA KASSHIN-RYŪ?
WHY NOT?
THOUGH IT'S UP TO YOU, YUTARŌ-KUN.
MM... THE IDEA HAS ITS MERITS.
YEAH... LIKE NONE!!
BOO BOO
WHO NEEDS THAT SECOND-RATE PUNK?!

READ THIS WAY

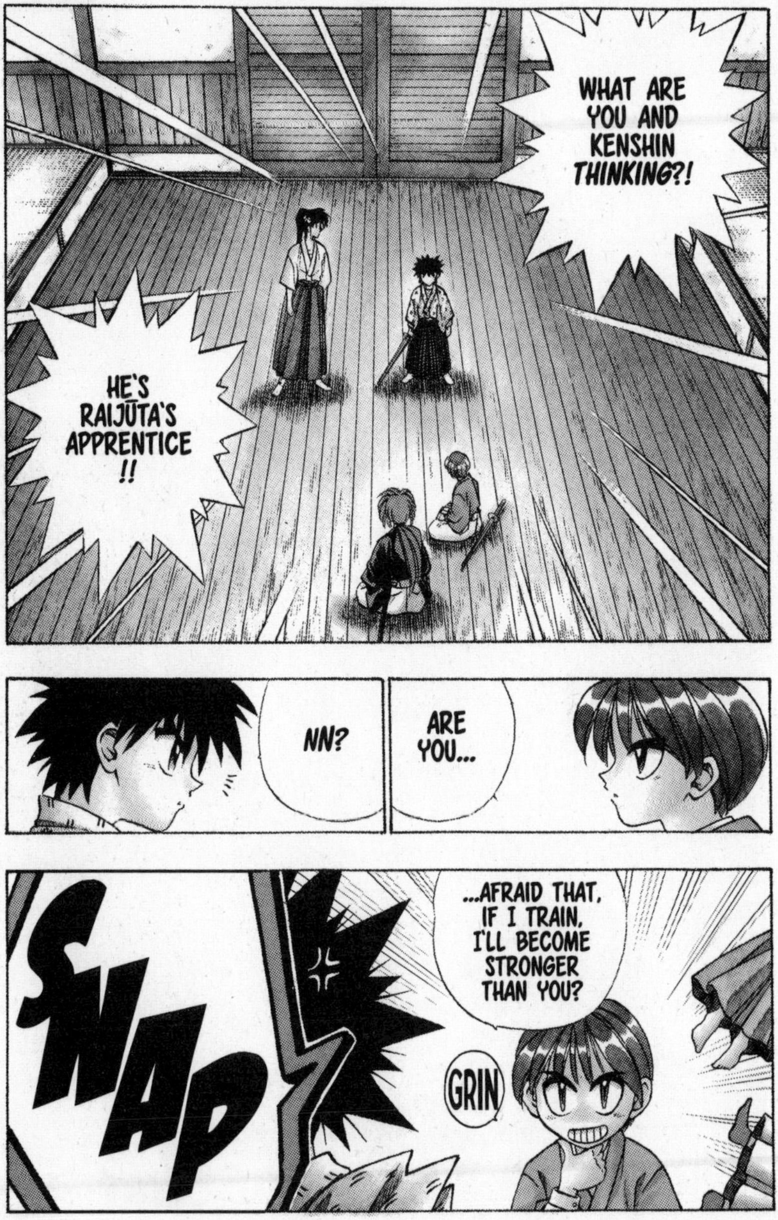
WHAT ARE YOU AND KENSHIN THINKING?!
HE'S RAIJŪTA'S APPRENTICE!!
ARE YOU...
NN?
...AFRAID THAT, IF I TRAIN, I'LL BECOME STRONGER THAN YOU?
GRIN
SNAP

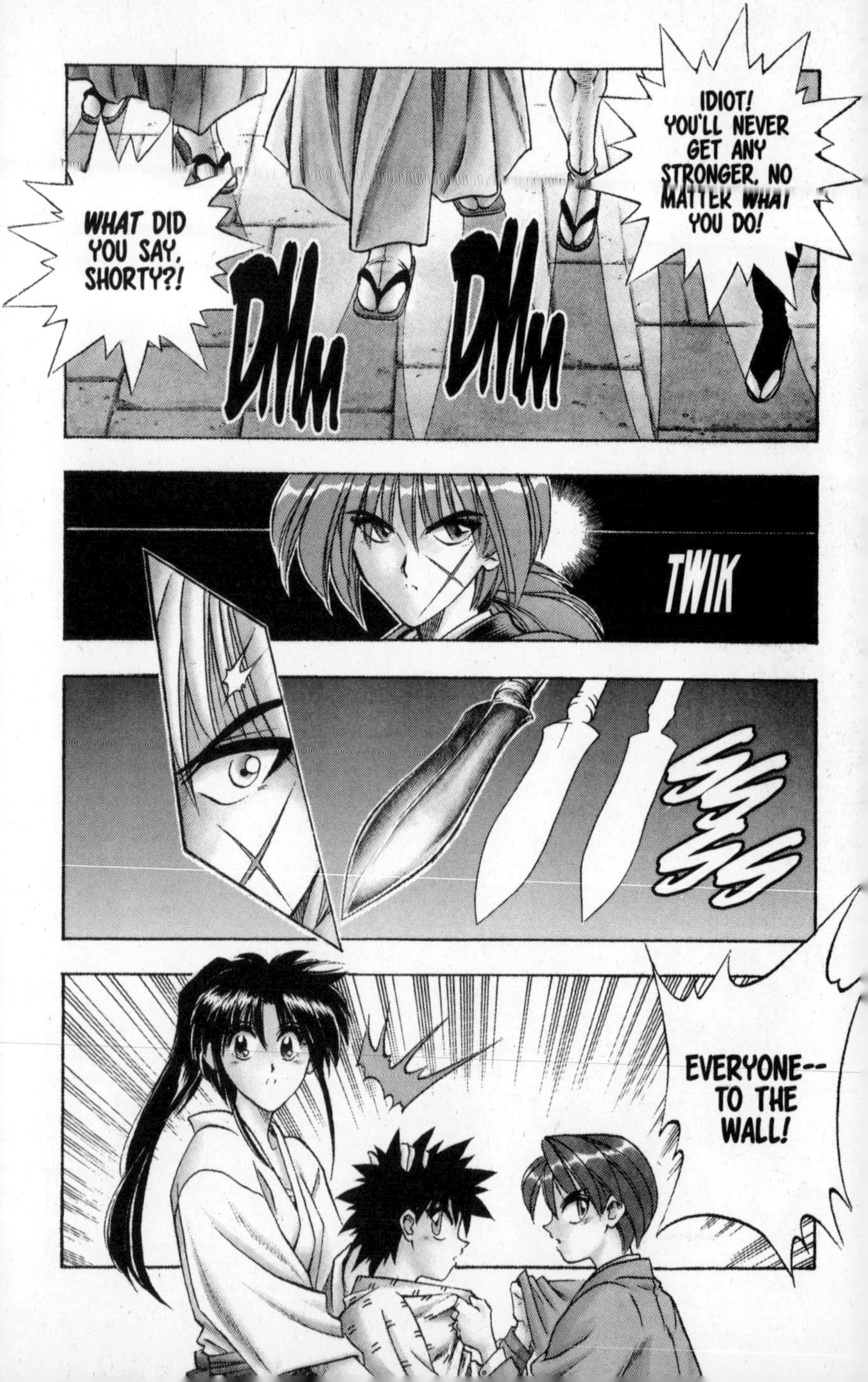
IDIOT! YOU'LL NEVER GET ANY STRONGER, NO MATTER WHAT YOU DO!
DMM
DMM
WHAT DID YOU SAY, SHORTY?!
TWIK
SSSS
EVERYONE-- TO THE WALL!

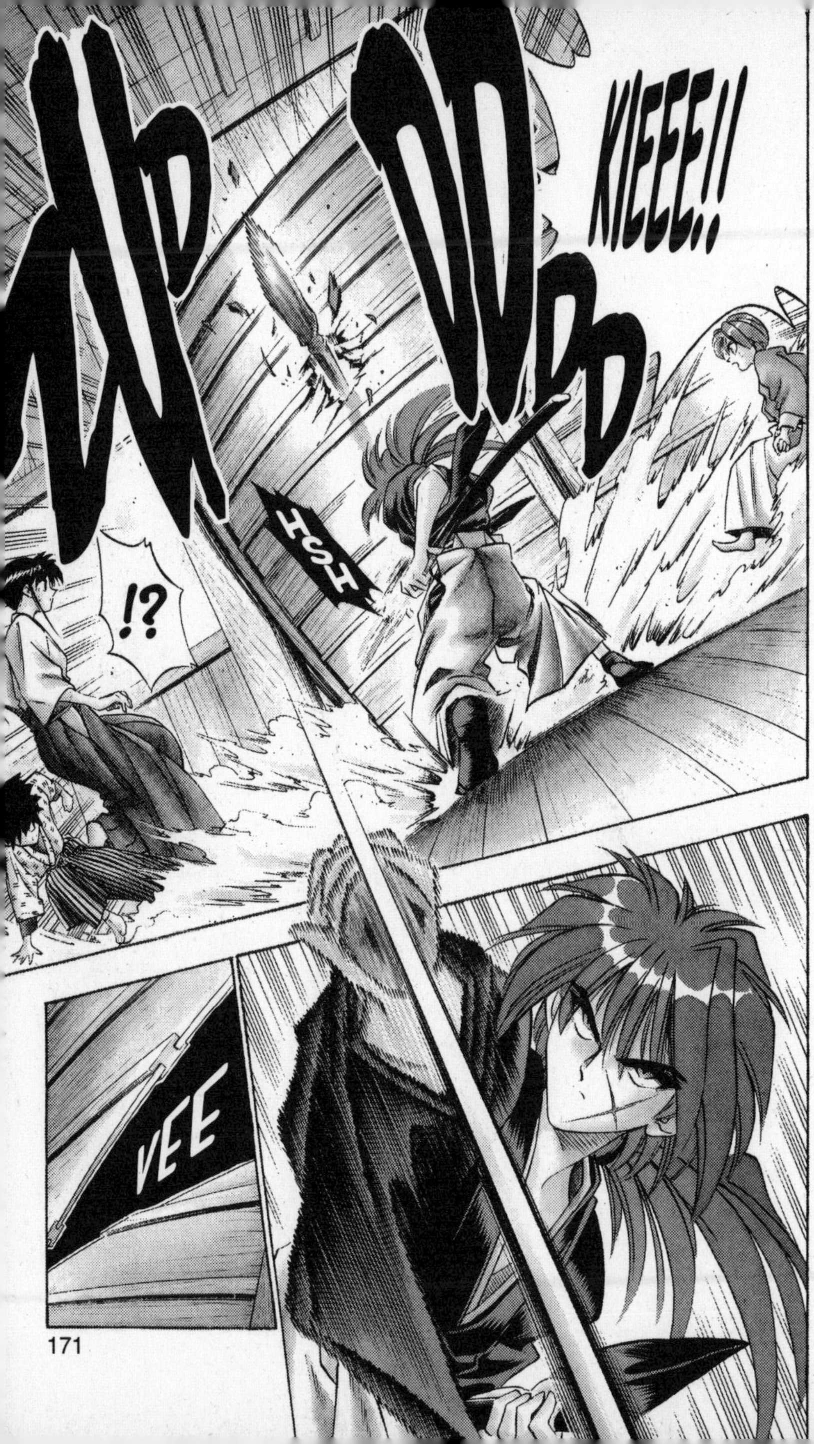
KIEEE!!
HSH
!?
VEE

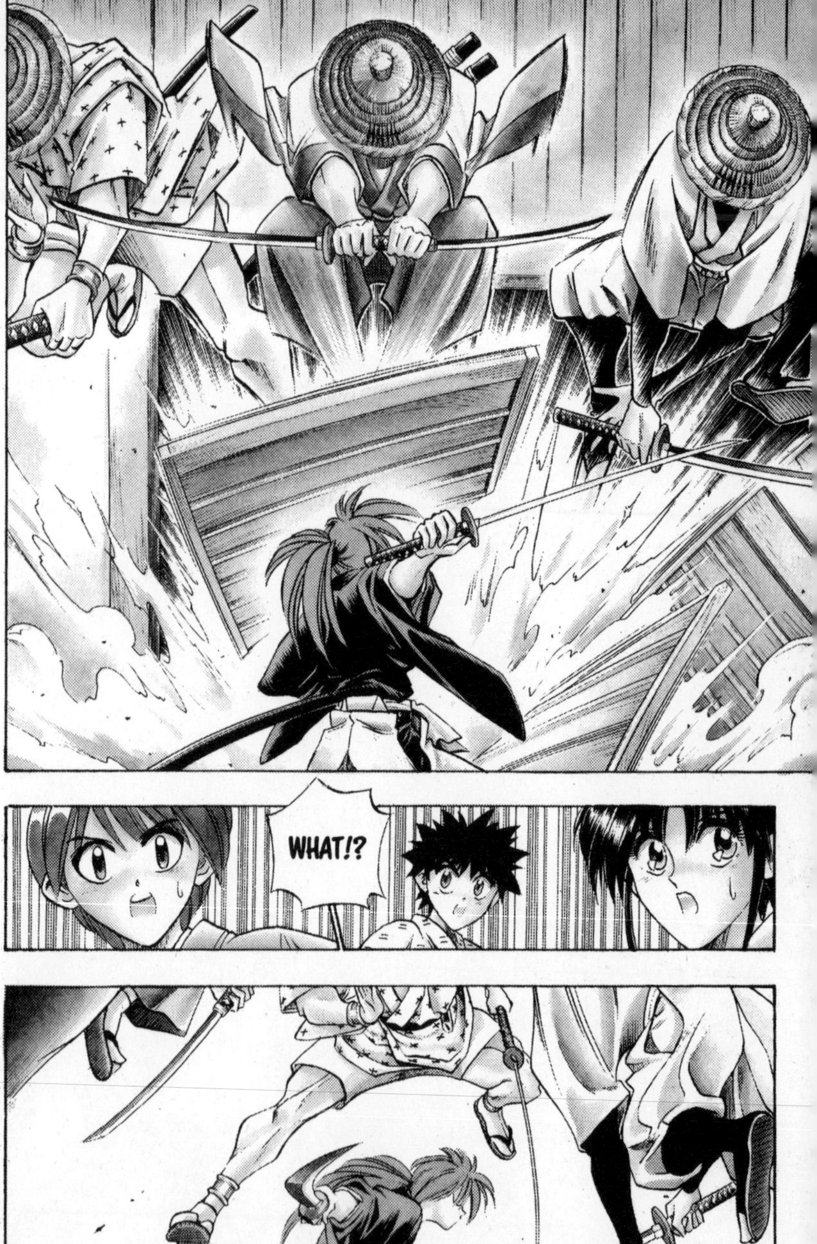
WHAT!?

READ THIS WAY

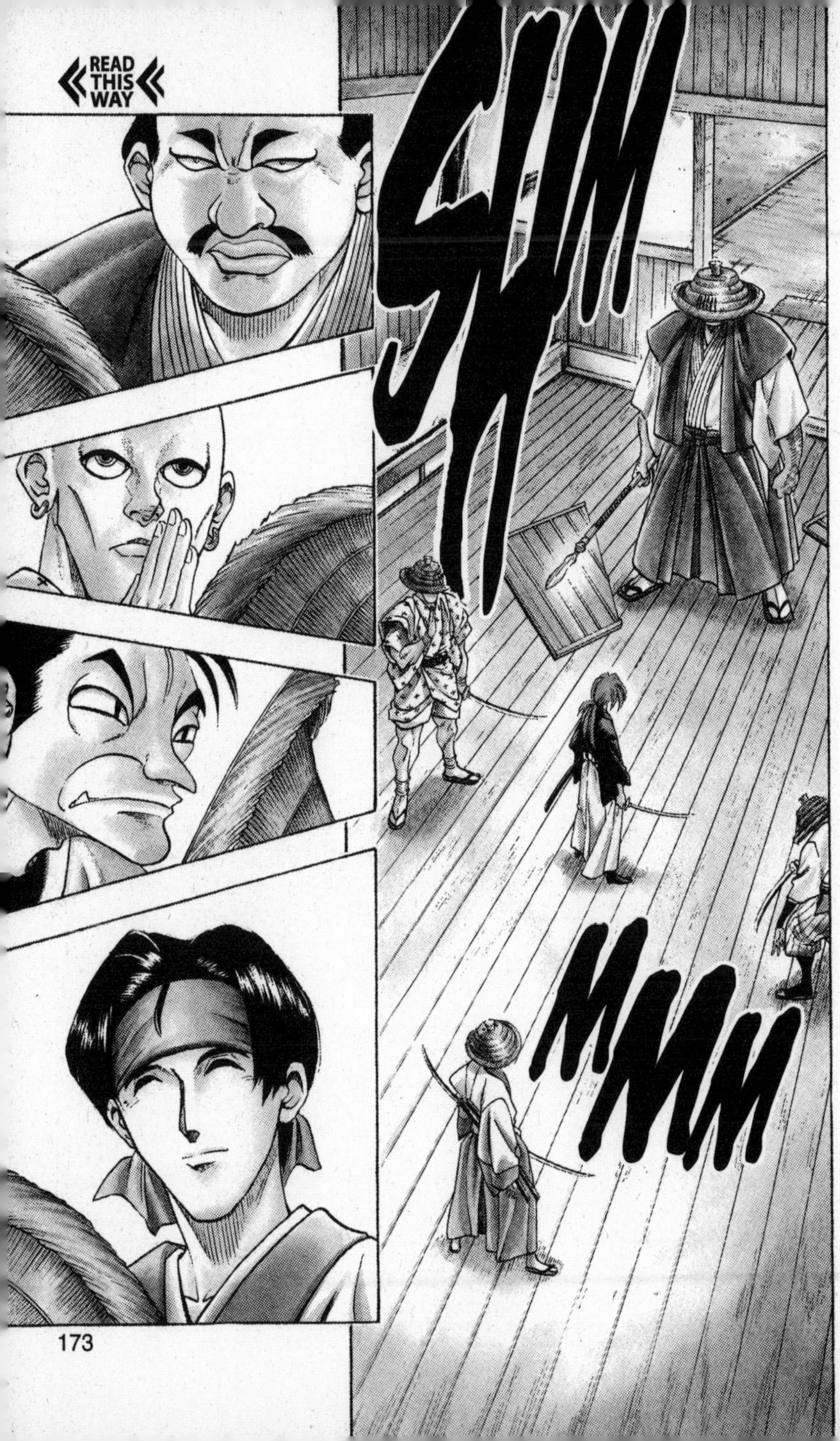

READ THIS WAY

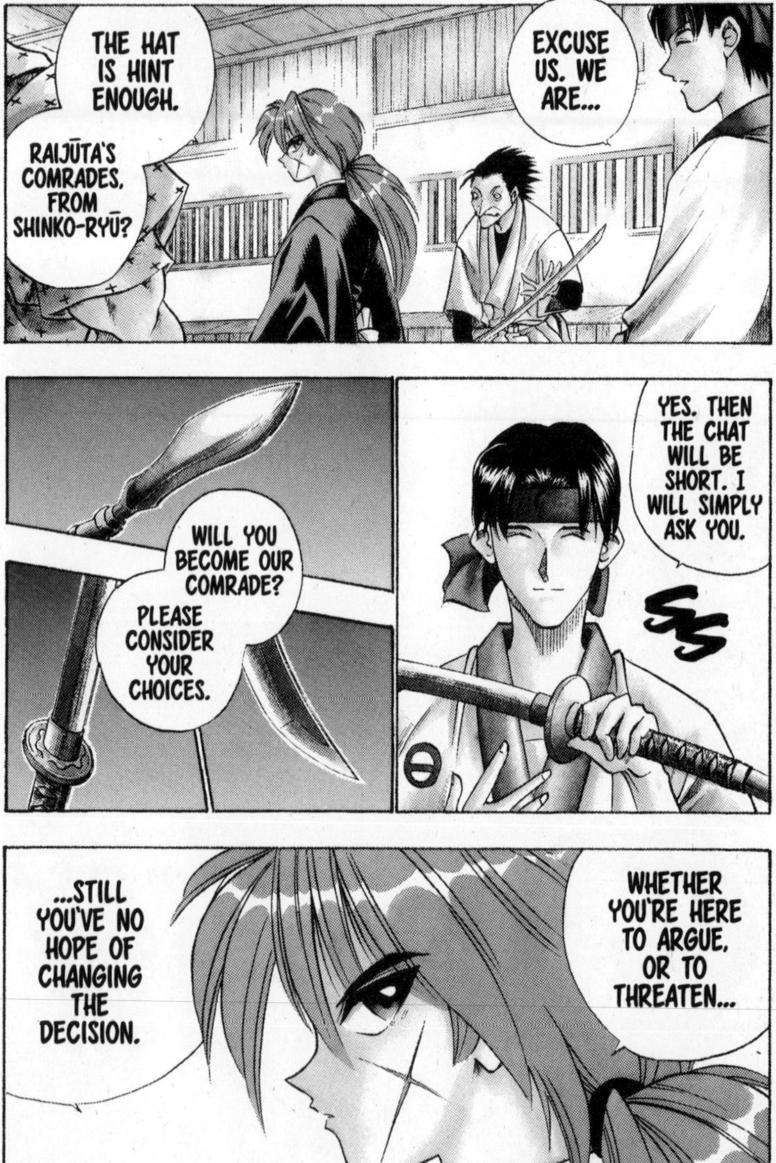

EXCUSE US. WE ARE...
THE HAT IS HINT ENOUGH.
RAIJŪTA'S COMRADES, FROM SHINKO-RYŪ?
YES. THEN THE CHAT WILL BE SHORT. I WILL SIMPLY ASK YOU.
WILL YOU BECOME OUR COMRADE?
PLEASE CONSIDER YOUR CHOICES.
WHETHER YOU'RE HERE TO ARGUE, OR TO THREATEN...
...STILL YOU'VE NO HOPE OF CHANGING THE DECISION.

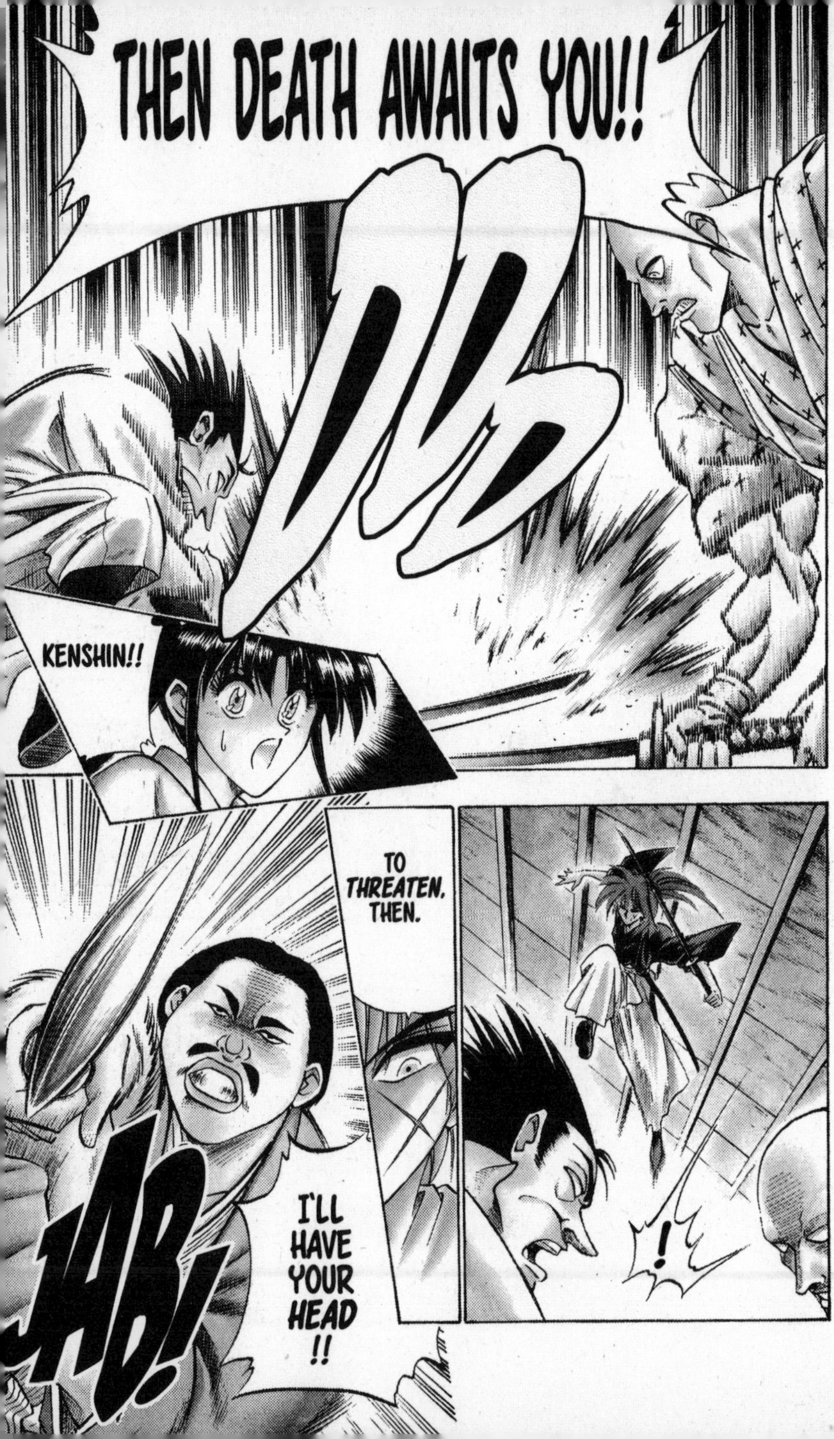
THEN DEATH AWAITS YOU!!
KENSHIN!!
!
TO THREATEN, THEN.
I'LL HAVE YOUR HEAD!!
HAB!

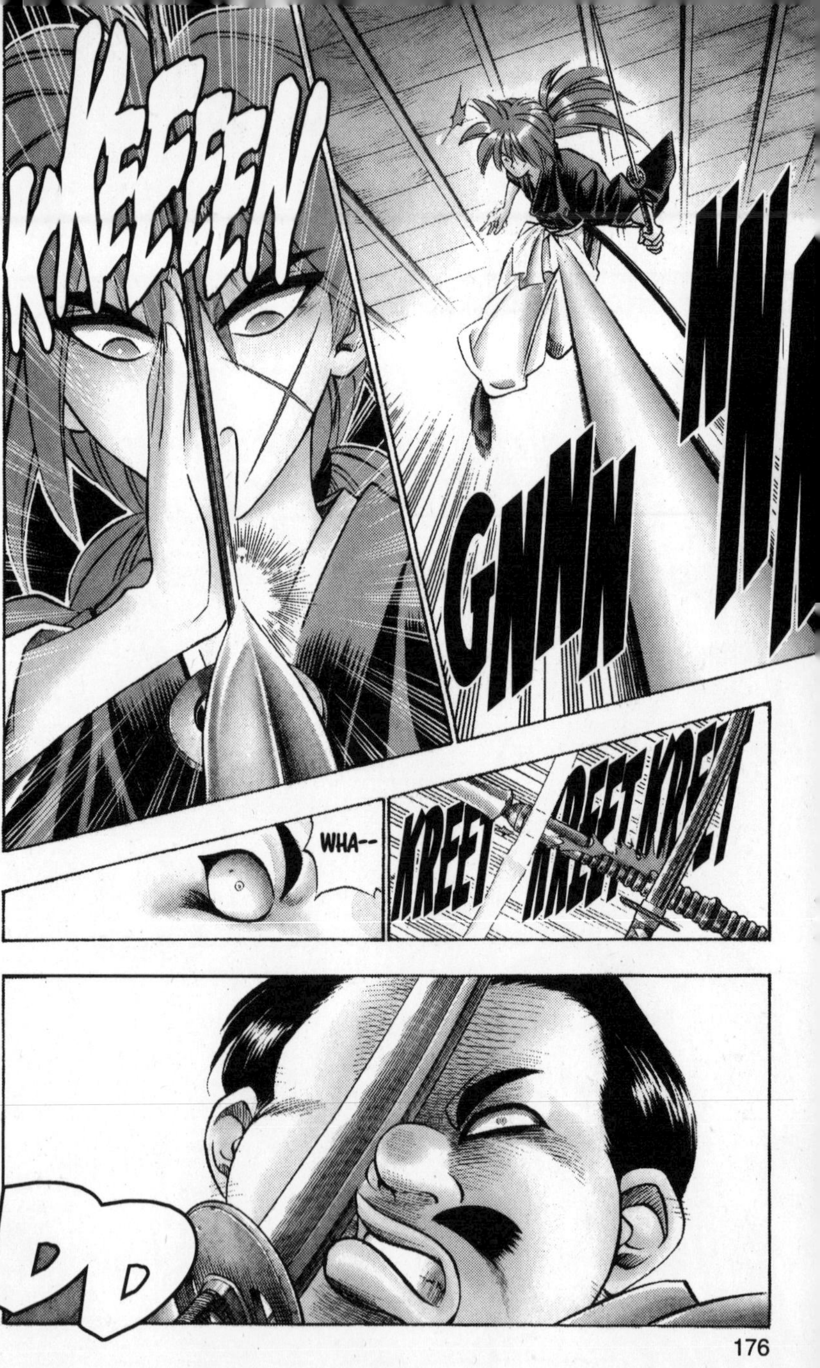
KREET KREET KREET
WHA--

READ THIS WAY

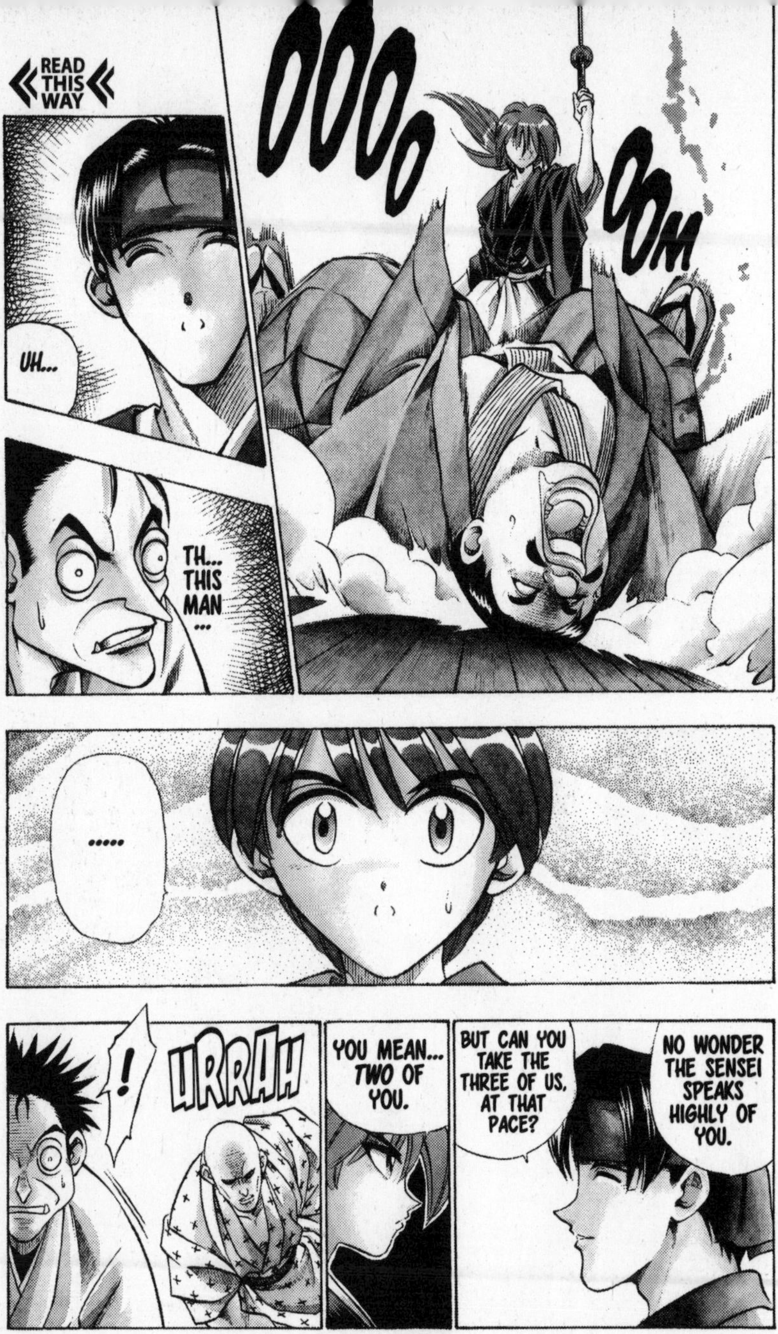
OOOOOOOOM
UH...
TH... THIS MAN...
......
NO WONDER THE SENSEI SPEAKS HIGHLY OF YOU.
BUT CAN YOU TAKE THE THREE OF US, AT THAT PACE?
YOU MEAN... TWO OF YOU.
URRAH
!

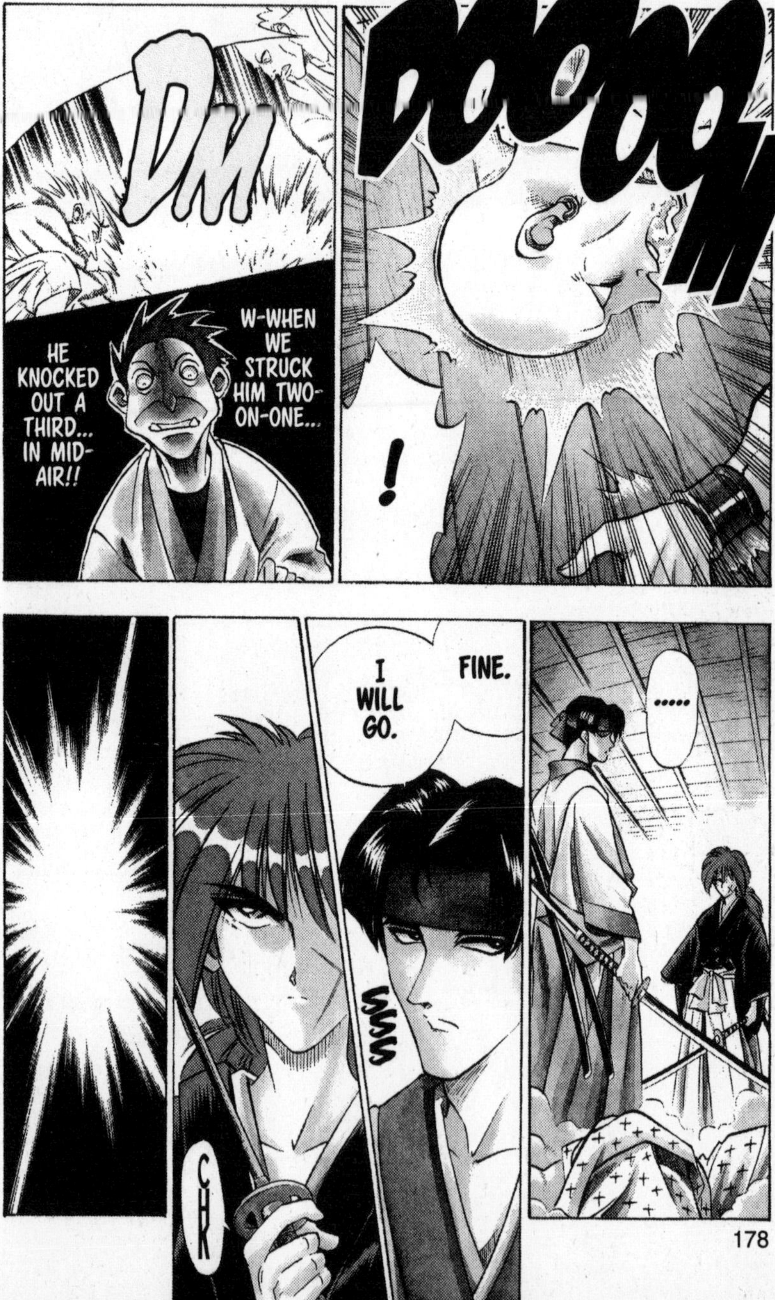
DOOOOM
!
DM
W-WHEN WE STRUCK HIM TWO-ON-ONE...
HE KNOCKED OUT A THIRD... IN MID-AIR!!
......
FINE.
I WILL GO.
SSS
CHK

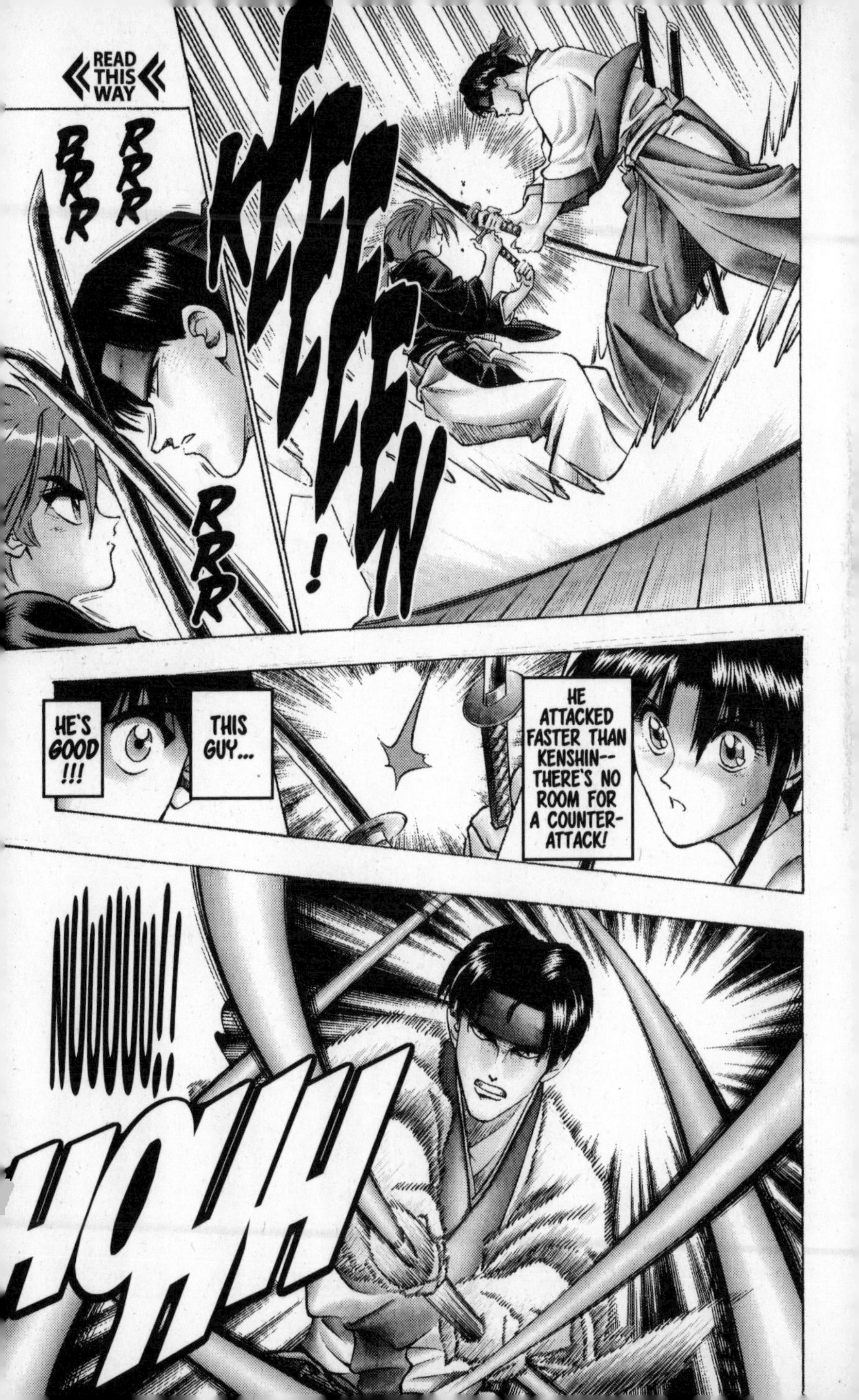

READ THIS WAY
RRR
RRR
RRR
HE ATTACKED FASTER THAN KENSHIN-- THERE'S NO ROOM FOR A COUNTER-ATTACK!
THIS GUY...
HE'S GOOD!!!

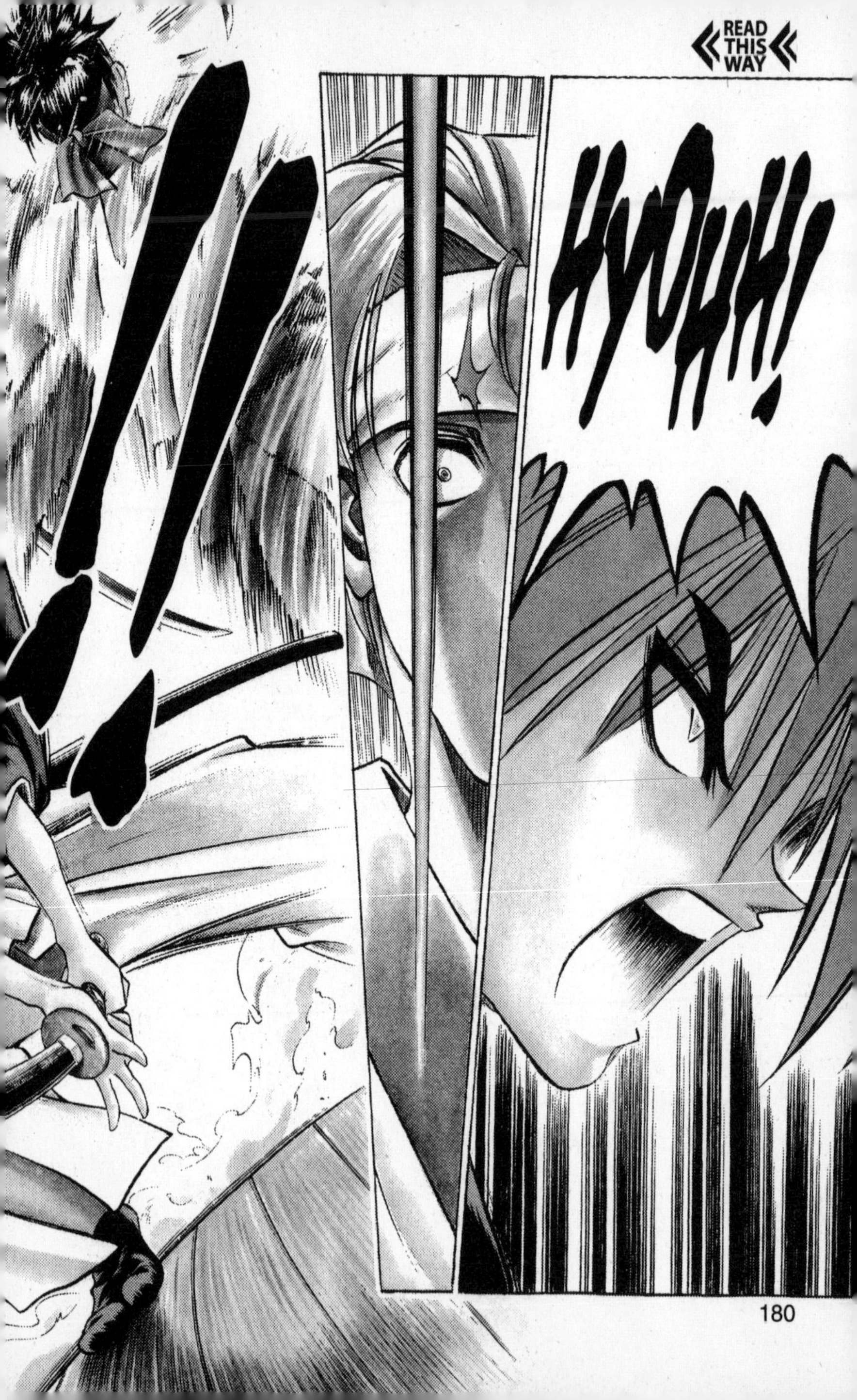
HYOAH!
!!

READ THIS WAY

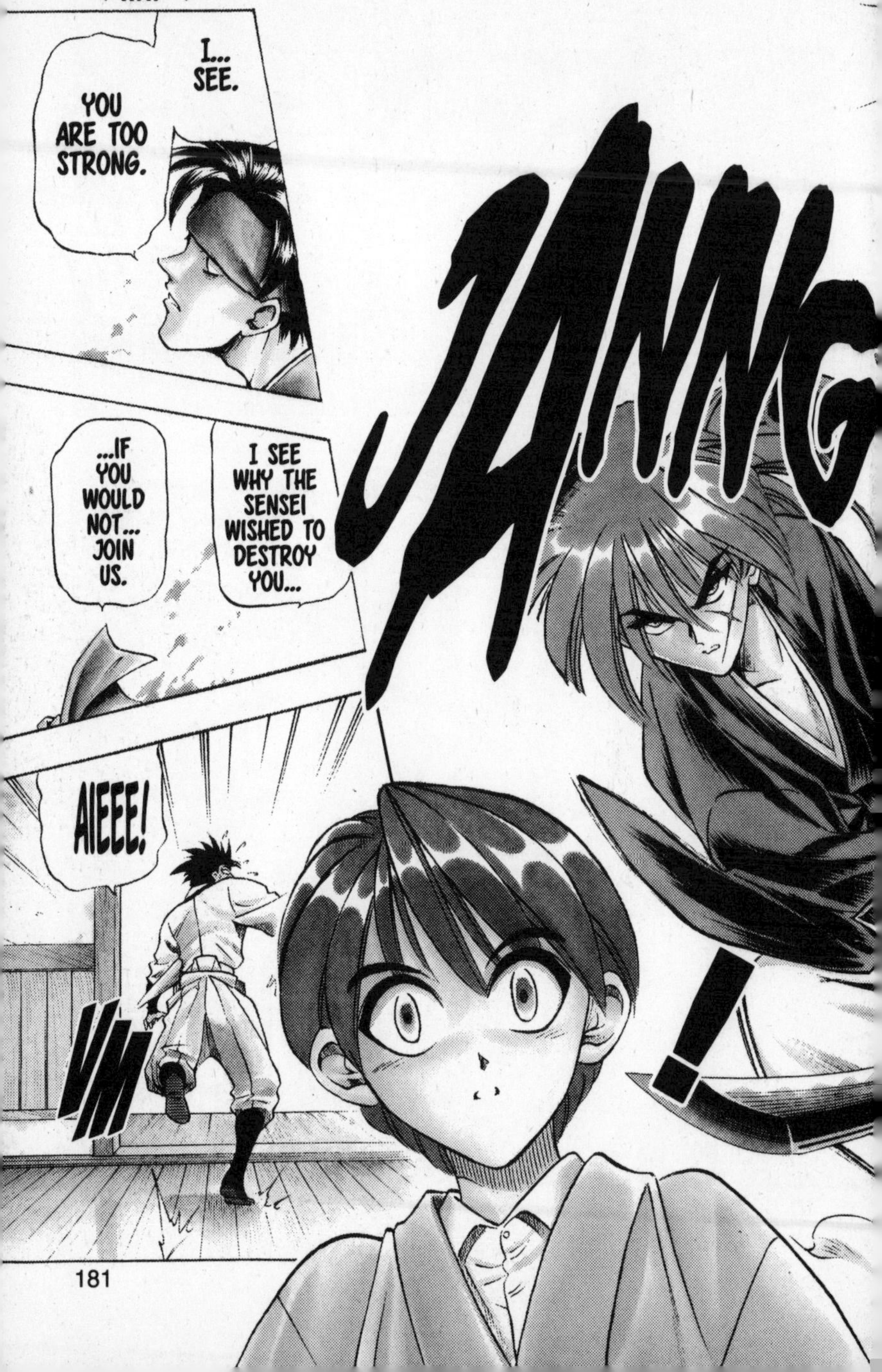

I... SEE.
YOU ARE TOO STRONG.
I SEE WHY THE SENSEI WISHED TO DESTROY YOU...
...IF YOU WOULD NOT... JOIN US.
AIEEE!
VM
ZANNG!

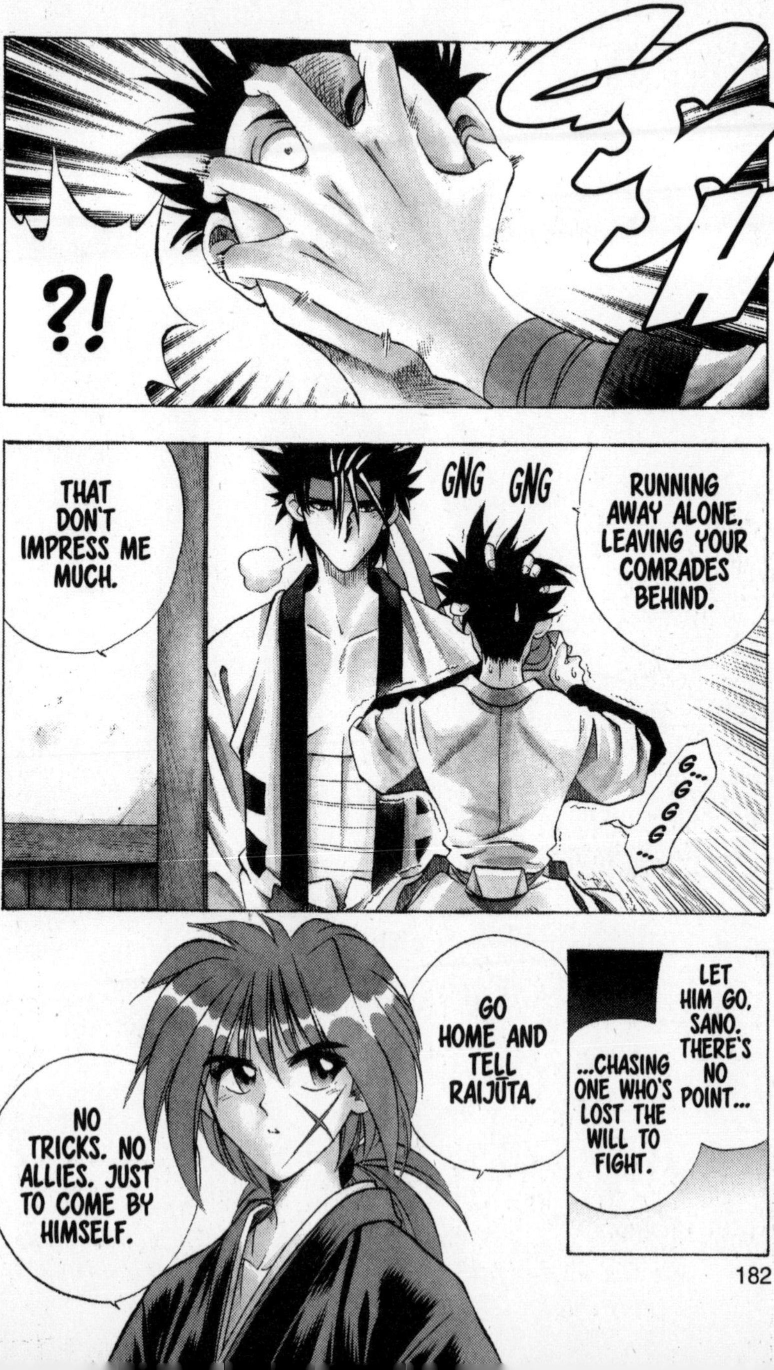
?!
RUNNING AWAY ALONE, LEAVING YOUR COMRADES BEHIND.
GNG GNG
G... GGGG...
THAT DON'T IMPRESS ME MUCH.
LET HIM GO, SANO. THERE'S NO POINT...
...CHASING ONE WHO'S LOST THE WILL TO FIGHT.
GO HOME AND TELL RAIJŪTA.
NO TRICKS. NO ALLIES. JUST TO COME BY HIMSELF.

READ THIS WAY

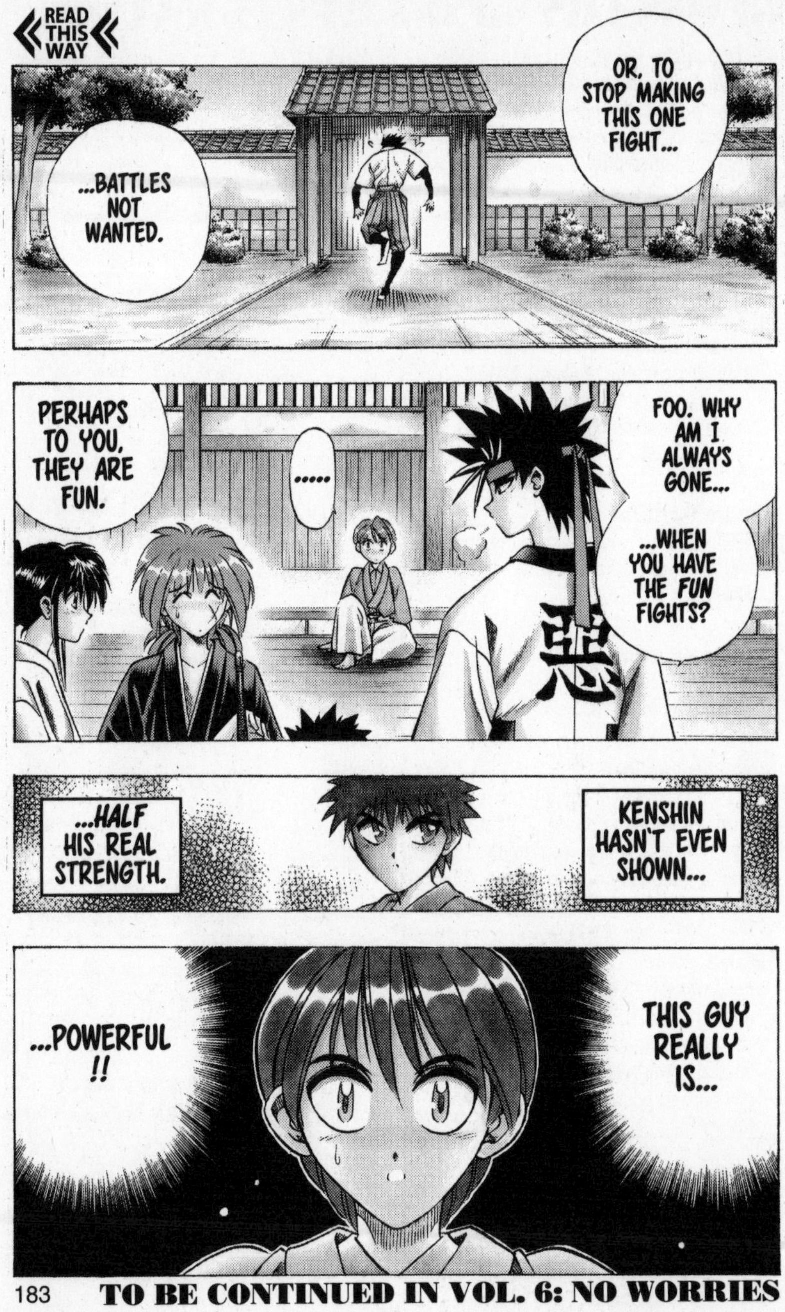
OR, TO STOP MAKING THIS ONE FIGHT...
...BATTLES NOT WANTED.
FOO. WHY AM I ALWAYS GONE...
...WHEN YOU HAVE THE *FUN* FIGHTS?
.....
PERHAPS TO YOU, THEY ARE FUN.
KENSHIN HASN'T EVEN SHOWN...
...*HALF* HIS REAL STRENGTH.
THIS GUY REALLY IS...
...POWERFUL !!



**TO BE CONTINUED IN VOL. 6: NO WORRIES**

# GLOSSARY of the RESTORATION

*A brief guide to select Japanese terms used in **Rurouni Kenshin**. Note that, both here and within the story itself, all names are Japanese style—i.e., last or "family" name first, with personal or "given" name following. This is both because **Kenshin** is a "period" story, as well as to decrease confusion—were we to take the example of Kenshin's sakabatô and "reverse" the format of the historically established assassin-name "Hitokiri Battôsai," for example, it would make little sense to then call him "Battôsai Himura."*

### "goldfish turd"
Translated from the Japanese. A "*kingyô no fun*" is someone of little worth, a hanger-on, who profits from the skills/exploits of others by merely "trailing behind." In this story, it's the worst thing Yahiko can think of to call Yutarô, Raijûta's ostensible apprentice

### Himura Battôsai
Swordsman of legendary skills and former assassin (*hitokiri*) of the **Ishin Shishi**

### Himura Kenshin
Kenshin's "real" name, revealed to Kaoru only at her urging

### Hiten Mitsurugi-ryû
Kenshin's sword technique, used more for defense than offense. An "ancient style that pits one against many," it requires exceptional speed and agility to master

### hitokiri
An assassin. Famous swordsmen of the period were sometimes thus known to adopt "professional" names—**Kawakami Gensai**, for example, was also known as "Hitokiri Gensai"

### Ishin Shishi
Loyalist or pro-Imperialist **patriots** who fought to restore the Emperor to his ancient seat of power

### Bakumatsu
Final, chaotic days of the Tokugawa regime

### -chan
Honorific. Can be used either as a diminutive (e.g., with a small child— "Little Hanako or Kentarô"), or with those who are grown, to indicate affection ("My dear...")

### Chûetsu-ryû
Sword-style founded by Maekawa Miyauchi, *Sensei* or "Master" of the Maekawa Dojo, where Kaoru sometimes visits as "guest instructor"

### dojo
Martial arts training hall

### -dono
Honorific. Even more respectful than **–san**; the effect in modern-day Japanese conversation would be along the lines of "Milord So-and-So." As used by Kenshin, it indicates both respect and humility

### Edo
Capital city of the **Tokugawa Bakufu**, renamed **Tokyo** ("Eastern Capital") after the Meiji Restoration

inferior" form, intended as a way to emphasize a difference in status or rank, as well as to indicate familiarity or affection

**loyalists**
Those who supported the return of the Emperor to power; *Ishin Shishi*

**Meiji Restoration**
1853-1868; culminated in the collapse of the *Tokugawa Bakufu* and the restoration of imperial rule. So called after Emperor Meiji, whose chosen name was written with the characters for "culture and enlightenment"

**onigiri**
Usually filled with bits of fish or vegetable in the center, seaweed-wrapped "rice balls" have long been a (highly portable and convenient) staple of the Japanese diet

**patriots**
Another term for *Ishin Shishi*...and when used by Sano, not a flattering one

**rurouni**
Wanderer, vagabond

**sakabatô**
Reversed-edge sword (the dull edge on the side the sharp should be, and vice-versa); carried by Kenshin as a symbol of his resolution never to kill again

**-san**
Honorific. Carries the meaning of "Mr.," "Ms.," "Miss," etc., but used more extensively in Japanese than its English equivalent (note that even an enemy may be addressed as "*-san*")

**Izuna**
Described by its wielder, Raijûta, as a "secret sword," the *Izuna* will later be explained by Kenshin as a "wave of vacuum, a moving gap in the air"

**Kamiya Kasshin-ryû**
Sword-arts or *kenjutsu* school established by Kaoru's father, who rejected the ethics of *Satsujin-ken* for *Katsujin-ken*

**katana**
Traditional Japanese longsword (curved, single-edge, worn cutting-edge up) of the samurai. Used primarily for slashing; can be wielded either one- or two-handed

**Katsujin-ken**
"Swords that give life"; the sword-arts style developed over ten years by Kaoru's father and founding principle of *Kamiya Kasshin-ryû*

**Kawakami Gensai**
Real-life, historical inspiration for the character of *Himura Kenshin*

**kenjutsu**
The art of fencing; sword arts; kendô

**Kôgen Ittô-ryû**
An actual historical swordsmanship style, *Kôgen Ittô-ryû* is said to be especially "spare" and is characterized by its economy of movement, with little extraneous content. Used in this story by the bullying thief, Nagaoka Mikio

**-kun**
Honorific. Used in the modern day among male students, or those who grew up together, but another usage—the one you're more likely to find in *Rurouni Kenshin*—is the "superior-to-

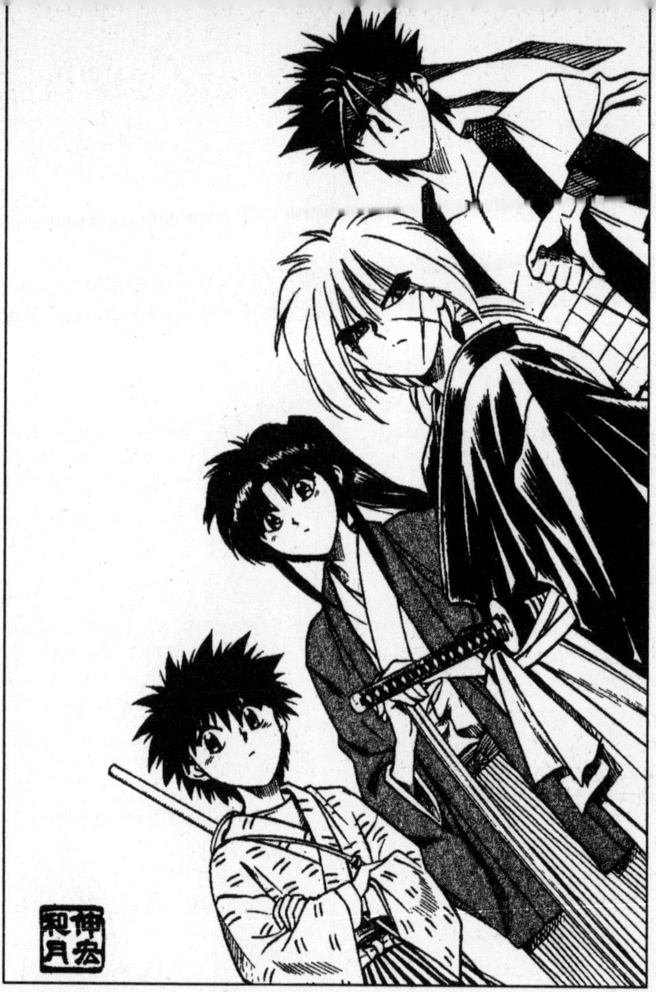

# IN THE NEXT VOLUME...

Kenshin's duel with the fearsome Raijûta, a battle to decide the fate of Meiji Era swordsmanship, is coming to a head. One fact quickly becomes apparent: that Raijûta will stop at nothing to ensure the supremacy of his school of sword fighting. Sanosuke runs into some serious trouble of his own when he is reunited with a member of the Sekihô Army, the doomed civilian-run unit that they both served in. Old alliances are challenged when Sano's friend shares his plan to topple the current government. Plus, a bonus installment containing the first story Nobuhiro Watsuki ever published!

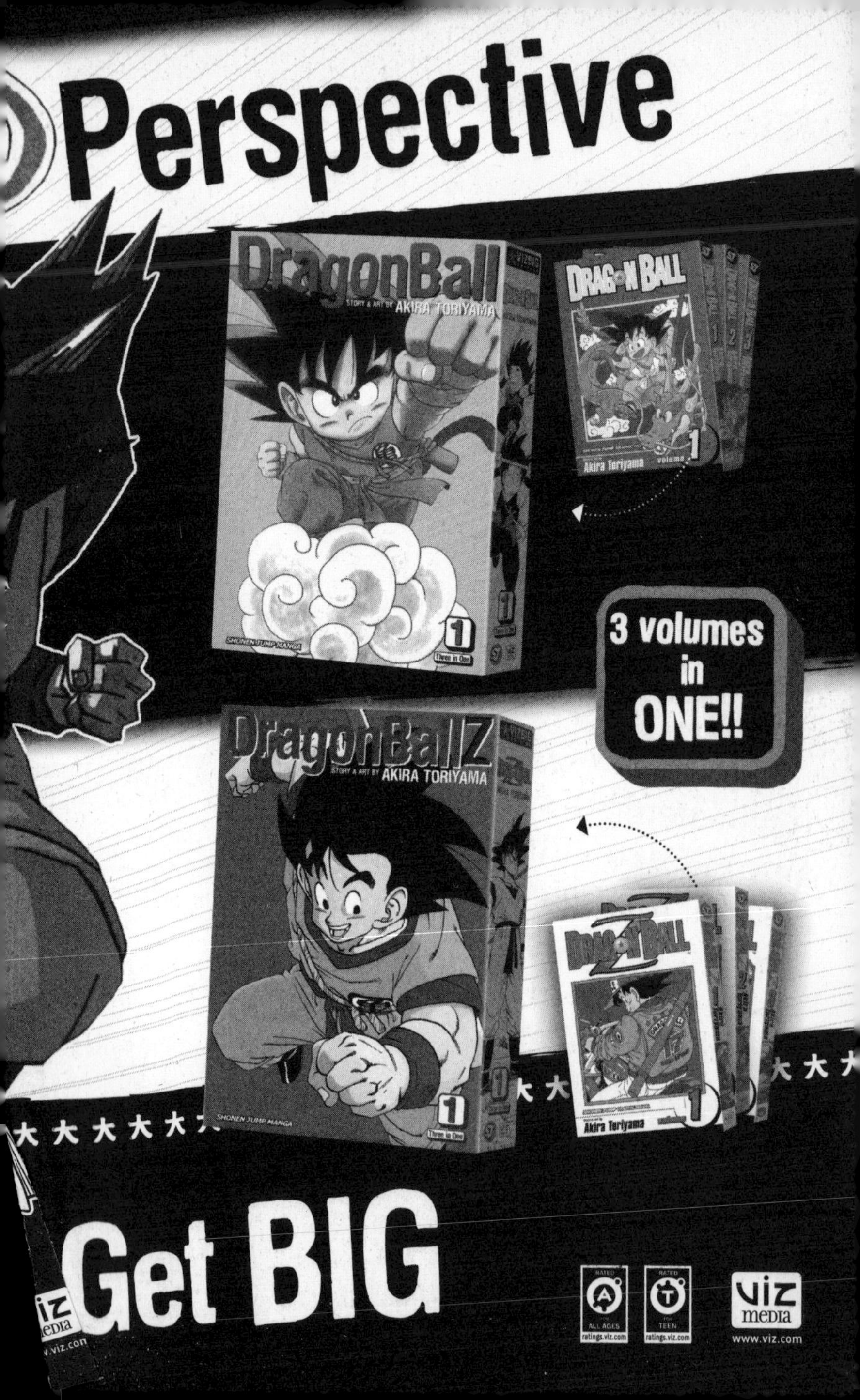
Perspective
DragonBall
STORY & ART BY AKIRA TORIYAMA
1
Three in One
SHONEN JUMP MANGA
DRAGON BALL
Akira Toriyama
volume 1
3 volumes in ONE!!
DragonBallZ
STORY & ART BY AKIRA TORIYAMA
1
Three in One
SHONEN JUMP MANGA
DRAGON BALL Z
Akira Toriyama
1
Get BIG
RATED A FOR ALL AGES ratings.viz.com
RATED T FOR TEEN ratings.viz.com
viz media
www.viz.com

# Tell us what you think about SHONEN JUMP manga!

Our survey is now available online.
Go to: www.SHONENJUMP.com/mangasurvey

## Help us make our product offering better!